THE POCKET BIBLE DICTIONARY

with Comprehensive Bible Helps

Instructive and useful information on many
subjects of interest in the Bible including
a concise history of the Bible; many scripture proper names,
with their pronunciation and meaning;
the coins, weights and measures of the Bible.

Revised and edited by
Philip Schaff, D.d., LL.D.,
Professor of church history in
The Union Theological Seminary, New York;
Author of "Church History," "Creeds of Christendom,"
"Bible Dictionary;" and Editor of
"International Illustrated Commentary,"
"Schaff-Herzog Religious Encyclopedia."

and further condensed by:
Jubilee Publishers, Inc.
Lebanon, TN 37088

A

A and O, or **Al'pha** and **O'mega,** or **Omeg'a,** first and last letters of Greek alphabet, used of Jehovah, Isa. 41:4; 44:6, and of Christ, Rev. 1:8, 11; 21:6; 22:13, to denote the idea of the beginning and the end, or of eternity. Often used in connection with the cross as the symbol of Christ.

Aaron, ar'on (enlightened), the first high-priest of the Israelites, was born B.C. about 1570. He was the elder brother and the spokesman of Moses, and aided him in the deliverance of the Israelites from bondage in Egypt. As high-priest he was an eminent type or emblem of christ. He was about 120 years old when he died on Mount Hor, now called the "Mountain of Aaron."

Aar'on's Rod. The staff of Aaron which was preserved in the ark as a symbol of priesthood, ever blossoming and yielding fruit. Heb. 9:4.

Abad'don (destroyer) is a Hebrew word having the same meaning as the Greek APOLL'YON. It is applied to the angel of the bottomless pit. Rev. 9:11.

Ab'ba (father), a Chaldee word corresponding to the Hebrew ab, father; applied to God. Mark 14:36; Rom. 8:15; Gal. 4:6.

Ab'di (servant of Jehovah). [1] A descendant of Merari, the son of Levi. 1 Chron. 6:44; 2 Chron. 29:12. [2] A descendant of one of the two Elams. Ezra 10:26.

Abdiel, ab'di-el. an ancestor of one of the families of Gad. 1 Chron. 5:15.

Abed'nego (servant of Nego), a name given by the prince of the king of Babylon's eunuchs to Azariah, one of the young Jewish princes who were carried to Babylon by Nebuchadnezzar. Dan. 1:7; 2:49; 3:12, 20.

A'bel (transitoriness, or, when applied to a town, grassy place or meadow). [1] The second son of Adam. He was a shepherd; offered to God a sacrifice from his flocks, and was killed by his brother Cain because Abel's sacrifice was received, and not Cain's. Gen. 4. Abel was the first martyr of faith, who, "being dead, yet speaketh." Matt. 23:35; Heb. 11:4. [2] The name of a place in the north-west part of Judah, where the ark rested when it was sent back by the Philistines. 1 Sam. 6:18. [3] The name of a place near Beth-maachah, sometimes called Abel of Beth-maachah, and sometimes Abel. 2 Sam. 20:14, 15, 18. [4] Abel is also the beginning of the names of several towns.

Abel-maim, a'bel-ma'im (meadow of the water), a town in

the northern part of the territory of Manasseh, east of the Jordan, 2 Chron. 16:4, supposed to be the same with Abel'Beth-maachah and with Abel.

A'bez (whiteness), a city of Issachar. Josh. 19:20.

A'bi (Jehovah is father), the wife of Ahaz and mother of Hezekiah, kings of Judah. 2 Kings 18:2. She is called ABIJAH in 2 Chron. 29:1.

Abi-albon, a'bi-al'bon (father of strength), one of David's mighty men from Arabah. 2 Sam. 23:31. He is called ABIEL in 1 Chron. 11:32.

A'bib (sprouting), the first month of the Hebrew sacred year and the seventh month of the civil year. It was so called because grain, especially barley, was then in ear. After the Babylonian captivity it was called Nisan. It corresponded nearly with our April.

Ab'idan (father of judgment), the captain of the tribe of Benjamin, who was appointed with Moses and a chief man from every tribe to number the people. Num. 1:11; 2:22.

Abi'el (father of might). [1] An Israelite of the tribe of Benjamin, who was the grandfather of Saul, the first king of Israel. 1 Sam. 9:1; 14:51. [2] One of David's valiant men. 1 Chron. 11:32. He is called ABI-ALBON in 2 Sam. 23:31.

Abiezer, ab-i-e'zar (father of help). [1] Head of a family descended from Manasseh, probably same as Jeezer, the son of Gilead (Num. 26:30). Josh. 17:2; 1 Chron. 7:18. [2] A district in Manasseh inhabited by the Abiezrites. Judg. 6:34; 8:2. [3] One of David's valiant men, an inhabitant of Anathoth, in the tribe of Benjamin. 2 Sam. 23:27; 1 Chron. 11:28.

Ab'igail (cause of delight). [1] The wife of Nabal of Carmel, and afterward of David. [2] A sister or a niece of Zeruiah and mother of Amasa.

Abihail, ab-i-ha'il (father of might). [1] A Levite of the family of Merari, who was the father of Zuriel, the chief of the Merarites in the time of Moses. Num. 3:35. [2] The wife of Abishur, a descendant of Hezron, of the tribe of Judah. 1 Chron. 2:29. [3] Head of a family in the tribe of Gad. 1 Chron. 5:14. [4] A daughter of Eliab, David's brother, who became wife of Rehoboam, the son of Solomon. 2 Chron. 11:18. [5] The father of Esther the Jewess, whom Ahasuerus, king of Persia, made queen instead of Vashti. Esth. 2:15; 9:29.

Abi'jah (my father is Jehovah). [1] A son of Jeroboam who died young. 1 Kings 14:1. [2] A priest in the time of David who was at the head of eighth course in the temple service. 1 Chron. 24;10. [3] A Levite appointed in the time of David over the treasures of the sanctuary. 1 Chron. 26:20. [4] One of the sons of Rehoboam, the son of Solomon, by Maachah, the daughter of Absalom. [5] The mother of Hezekiah, king of Judah. 2 Chron. 29:1. [6] A priest that sealed the covenant made by Nehemiah and the people to serve the LORD. Neh. 10:7. [7] A priest that went up from Babylon with Zerubbabel. Neh. 12:4, 17.

Abimelech, a-bim'e-lek (father of the king). [1] A king of Gerar of the Philistines who made a league with Abraham. [2] Another king of Gerar contemporary with Isaac. He made a league with Isaac at Beersheba. Gen. 26. [3] A son of Gideon by a concubine in Shechem. He made himself king after the death of his father and slew his father's seventy sons, leaving only Jotham, the youngest. Abimelech was disgracefully killed in attacking Thebez. [4] Abimelech, the son of Abiathar, who was high-priest in David's time. 1 Chron. 18:16. [5] The name given in one place apparently to Achish, the king of Gath to whom David fled (1 Sam. 21:10). Ps. 34, title.

Abishai, a-bish'a-i (source of wealth), one of the bravest of David's "mighty men," was the eldest son of David's sister Zeruiah. He was generally a personal attendant of David, and was victorious in many battles.

Ab'ner (father of light), 1 Sam. 14:50, the son of Ner, was either uncle or cousin of Saul, the first king of Israel, and became his general. He supported King Ishbosheth seven years after Saul's death, and endeavored afterward to unite the whole kingdom under David, then king of Judah, but was treacherously slain by Joab.

Abomina'tion, in Scripture, means an object of abhorrence. Idols and the worship of them were so called. Deut. 7:25, 26; 12:31. the same term was applied to The Hebrews in Egypt. Exod. 8:26; Gen. 46:34.

A'braham (father of a multitude), Gen. 17:4,5, formerly ABRAM, a Hebrew patriarch, was called the "Father of the faithful." He was born at Ur in Chaldea. The year of his birth is doubtful, and is given by Ussher as B.C. 1996, and by Hales as B.C. 2153. According to Bunsen he lived B.C. about 2850. At the call of God, Gen. 12:1, Abram (afterward called Abraham) left his idolatrous kindred and migrated to Canaan. He lived a wandering life in tents, and was greatly distinguished for his piety and wisdom. In the Bible he is repeatedly called "the friend of God." He was chiefly remarkable for his simple and unwavering faith, and died at the age of 175 years. See Genesis, chapters 11-25; Acts 7; Rom. 4:1-6, 9-22; Heb. 11:8-17.

3

A'braham's Bosom, in Luke 16:22, means the bliss that Lazarus was enjoying in paradise, or paradise itself, Luke 16:23. Leaning on one's bosom, John 13:23, refers to the Oriental manner of reclining at table.

Ab'salom (father of peace), the third son of King David, born B.C. about 1033. His mother was a Syrian princess named Maacah. Absalom was remarkable for beauty of person. After gaining the favor of the people he rebelled against his father and raised a large army, which was defeated by that of David. While he was retreating from battle Absalom was killed by Joab, although David had ordered that his life should be spared. 2 Sam. chapters 13-19.

Accept'ed, in Luke 4:24; Eph. 1:6, means received with favor.

Accusa'tion, a written statement of the crime for which a person was executed.

Accu'ser. [1] An enemy or adversary, particularly in a court of law. Matt. 5:25. [2] In Job 1:6; Zech. 3:1; Rev. 12:10, Satan is the public accuser of the people of God.

Aceldama, a-sel'da-mah (field of blood), Acts 1:19, a small field south of Jerusalem, purchased by the chief priests with the thirty pieces of silver which Judas received as the price of our Saviour's blood. Aceldama was the "potter's field," and was used for the burial-place of strangers. In Acts 1:18 Judas is said to have purchased the field, because it was bought with his money.

Achan, a'kan (trouble), son of Carmi of the tribe of Judah, disobeyed the command of the Lord by taking some of the spoils of Jericho which were to be destroyed. This action brought a curse and defeat upon the people. He was discovered by lot, and stoned to death with all his family in the valley of Achor. Josh. 6:18; 7:18. He is called ACHAR in 1 Chron. 2:7.

Achim, a'kim (woes), an ancestor of Joseph, husband of Mary, mother of Jesus. Matt. 1:14.

Achor, a'kor (trouble), a valley leading up from Ai to Jericho, and thence to Jerusalem. In this valley Achan was stoned to death and buried with his property. This valley was regarded as the key of the land. Josh. 7:24, 26; Isa. 65:10.

Achsah, ak'sah. or **Achsa** (serpent-charmer), daughter of Caleb, was given with a large dowry in marriage to Othniel for taking the city of Debir, formerly called Kirjath-sepher. Josh. 15:16, 17; Judg. 1: 12, 13; 1 Chron. 2:49.

A'cra, one of the hills on which Jerusalem is built.

A'cre. The Jews had no such system as our "square measure," which enables us to name an area by its size. In the original the word signifies a yoke, and the meaning intended was apparently the extent of ground that could be ploughed by a yoke of oxen in a day. Isa. 5:10. In 1 Sam. 14:14 the Hebrew expression used means literally half a furrow of a yoke.

Acts of the Apos'tles, the fifth book of the New Testament. It was written by Luke, probably about A.D. 63 or 64, and forms the sequel to his Gospel. It contains the history of the progress of Christianity from Jerusalem, the capital of Judaism, to Rome, the capital of heathenism. It embraces the period from 30-63. Although this part of the Scriptures is called the Acts of the Apostles, it mentions only the acts of Peter, Paul, and James. Only Paul's acts are given fully and connectedly in this book. It gives an account of those great events in the history of the apostles which would naturally most interest the Christian Church. Prominent among them are the ascension of our Lord, the outpouring of the Holy Spirit at Pentecost, the martyrdom of Stephen, the conversion of Paul (then called Saul), and his principal missionary journeys and labors till his arrival and first imprisonment in Rome, which lasted two years (61-63). The Acts is an inspiring book of spiritual conquests. It illustrates the EPISTLES, as these illustrate and confirm the ACTS.

Ad'am (red, or earth-born). [1] The first man. He was created, according to Hebrew chronology, B.C. 4004, and, according to the Septuagint or Greek chronology, B.C. 5411. Adam was made in "the likeness of God." Gen. 5:1. He was the last and greatest work of the creation, and received dominion over all the earth. He was made pure and holy, yet liable to fall by the abuse of free will, and placed in EDEN on probation. He broke the express command of God, and brought a curse upon himself and his descendants. He was banished from Eden, and died at the age of 930 years. It is generally believed that he is the first among the saved as he was the first among sinners. [2] The REDEEMER is called "the last Adam," 1 Cor. 15:45, who is the author of righteousness and life, as the first Adam was the author of sin and death. Rom. 5:12-21. [3] A town on the east of the Jordan, some distance above the place where the Israelites, under Joshua, crossed it. Josh. 3:16. [4] The word is found in the original in many passages, where it is translated MAN.

Ad'amant (that cannot be subdued or broken), an ancient name used figuratively in Ezek. 3:9 for the diamond; also indicates any substance of extreme hardness. It is an old English name for diamond, the hardest of minerals. The diamond seems to have been unknown to the ancients as a precious stone. In the Bible it means the corundum known to us in a ground state as emery-powder. Adamant is once (Ex. 28:18) translated "diamond," and was used for engraving upon stone.

A'dar (fire-god), the sixth month in the civil year of the Jews. It included part of February and March. The celebrated feast of Purim occurred on the fourteenth and fifteenth of this month. Adar was the twelfth month of the sacred year of the Jews. It was doubled every second year to make the lunar year agree with the solar year. Ezra 6:15; Esth. 3:7.

Adbeel, ad'be-el (languishing for God), son of Ishmael and grandson of Abraham. Gen. 25:13; 1 Chron. 1:29.

Ad'der, a common name given to the viper, is a species of serpent. Adder is used in the Bible as a translation of four Hebrew words. In the Authorized Version it signifies four different serpents—namely, the cobra, Ps. 58:4; 91:13 (see ASP); the horned snake or cerastes, Gen. 49:17; the viper, Ps. 140:3; and in Prov. 23:32 a snake elsewhere called the "cockatrice," and may represent indefinitely different species of vipers. The horned snake or cerastes, Gen. 49:17, is about a foot long, and has black spots and two horns. It lies hidden in the sand, which is like it in color, and darts upon the unsuspecting traveller. It has a very deadly bite, and is often found in the wilderness of Judea.

Adjure, Josh. 6:28, to bind under a curse or put under oath.

Admira'tion, in Rev. 17:6, means wonder; astonishment.

Adonijah, ad-o-ni'jah (Jehovah is my lord). [1] Fourth son of David. He was put to death by Solomon for aspiring to the throne. [2] One of the Levites sent by Jehoshaphat to teach the law. 2 Chron. 17:8. [3] A chief of the people that with Nehemiah sealed the covenant. Neh. 10:16.

Adon'ikam (my lord is risen). [1] An Israelite whose descendants returned from Babylon after the exile. Ezra 2:13; Neh. 7:18. [2] An Israelite, some of whose posterity returned from Babylon with Ezra. Ezra 8:13. Probably the same as No. 1.

Adop'tion (placing as a son) is used for many kinds of admission to a more intimate relation, and is nearly equivalent to reception. [1] The taking and treating of another as one's own child. Mordecai adopted Esther as a daughter. Esth. 2:7. The daughter of Pharaoh adopted Moses, and he became her son. Exod. 2:10. [2] In the New Testament adoption means the act of God's free grace by which, being justified through faith in Christ, we are received into God's family and made heirs of the inheritance of heaven. Gal. 4:4, 5; Rom. 8:14-17.

Ahi'lud (a brother born), father of Jehoshaphat the recorder. 2 Sam. 8:16; 1 Chron. 18:15.

Ahimelech, a-him'e-lek (brother of the king). [1] The son of Ahitub and brother of Ahiah. He succeeded the latter as high-priest, and received David at the tabernacle in Nob when fleeing from Saul, and gave him the show-bread and Goliath's sword. Saul caused Ahimelech to be put to death for this act. [2] A Hittite, an officer of David's army when pursued by Saul. 1 Sam. 26:6.

Ahithophel, a-hith'o-fel (foolish brother), one of David's intimate friends and counsellors. He afterward joined Absalom in his rebellion and became a bitter enemy of David. Foreseeing the result of the rebellion, he hanged himself.

Ahi'tub (a good brother). [1] A grandson of Eli and son of Phinehas. He succeeded Eli as high-priest, Phinehas having been killed in battle. 1 Sam. 14:3; 22:11. [2] Father of Zadok, who was high-priest in David's time. Sometimes supposed to be the same as No. 1. [3] Another priest, who lived in seventh generation after No. 2. 1 Chron. 6:11, 12. [4] Perhaps same as No. 3. He was a priest and the ruler of God's house in Nehemiah's time. 1 Chron. 9:11; Neh. 11:11.

Ahlai (Jehovah is staying.) [1] A daughter of Shehan. 1Chron.2:31. [2] Father of one of David's valiant men. 1 Chron.11:41.

Aho'hite. [1] A descendant of Ahoah. 2 Sam. 23:28; 1 Chron. 11:12. [2] This word is in the English version of 2 Sam. 23:9, but in the original it means the son of Ahohi, and seems to be a proper name. 1 Chron. 11:12, 29.

Aho'lah (her own tent) and **Ahol'ibah** (my tent in her) are symbolical names used by Ezekiel to represent the kingdoms of Samaria and Judah. They are spoken of as sisters of Egyptian descent in an allegory which is a history of the Jewish church.

Aho'liab (a father's tent), a skilled worker employed in the construction of the Tabernacle. Exod. 31:6; 35:34.

A'i (the heap). [1] **Aiath,** a-i'ath, **Ai'ja,** a-i'jah, or **Ha'i,** a royal city of the Canaanites, east of Bethel. Abraham built an altar near it. Ai is noted for Joshua's defeat on account of the sin of Achan and for his later victory. It is called HAI in Gen. 12:8, AIJA in Neh. 11:31, and AIATH in Isa. 10:28. [2] A city of the Ammonites, near Heshbon. Jer. 49:3.

A'in (a fountain) is spelled "En" in compound words like En-rogel, in the English Bible. [1] Ain is the name of a city of Judah. It was subsequently assigned to Simeon. Josh. 15:32. This city was given to the priests, and is called ASHAN in 1

Chron. 6:59. [2] A place west of Riblah, in the northern part of Canaan. Num. 34:11.

Air. In the Bible the air or atmosphere which surrounds the earth is often indicated by the word "heaven." "The fowls of heaven" means the birds of the air. To "beat the air" and to "speak in the air" means to speak or act without judgment. In Eph. 2:2 "the powers of the air": probably means demons. Many Jews and heathens thought that the lower part of the air was occupied by spirits, especially evil spirits.

Al'abaster, from Alabastron in Egypt, a name given to two kinds of white mineral substances different in composition, but similar in appearance. The true alabaster is a fine-grained kind of gypsum. The other variety is a crystalline carbonate of lime, harder than the first. Alabaster was commonly used for boxes or bottles to contain perfumes. Matt. 26:7; Mark 14:3; Luke 7:37.

Aleph (A). The first letter of the Hebrew alphabet. Both the Hebrews and Greeks used their letters as numerals. The 119th Psalm is divided into twenty-two parts, the number of letters in the Hebrew alphabet. One of these letters is used as a heading for each of these parts, Aleph being used for the first part, and so on.

Alexan'der (helper of men). [1] Alexander the Great, king of Macedon, born B.C. 356. He was the son of King Philip, and succeeded his father as king, B.C. 336. He was generalissimo of the army of Greece, B.C. 334, conquered most of the then known world, and died at Babylon in his thirty-third year, B.C. 323. He is not mentioned by name in the canonical books, but in the apocryphal book of Maccabees, 1:1-9; 6:2, and in the prophecies of Daniel, where he is represented by the belly of brass in Nebuchadnezzar's dream of the colossal statue, Dan. 2:39, and in Daniel's vision. Dan. 7:6; 8:5-7; 11:3, 4. [2] Son of Simon the Cyrenian, who was compelled to carry the cross of Jesus. Mark 15:21. [3] A leading man in Jerusalem when Peter and John were apprehended. Acts 4:6. [4] A Jewish convert who was with Paul when a tumult was raised by the Ephesians. Acts 19:33. Perhaps the same as No. 2. [5] A convert who afterward apostatized. 1 Tim. 1:20. [6] A man who hindered the work of Paul. 2 Tim. 4:14. Perhaps the same as No. 5.

Alexan'dria, Acts 6:9, a famous city of Egypt, was situated between the Mediterranean Sea and Lake Mareotis, twelve miles from the western mouth of the Nile. It was founded B.C. 332 by Alexander the Great, and named after him. It was the birthplace of Apollos. Acts 18:24. It became the capital of the Grecian kings reigning in Egypt, and was one of the largest and grandest cities in the world. It contained the greatest library of ancient times and the famous museum. In its best days it is supposed to have had six hundred thousand inhabitants, mostly Greeks and Jews. The modern city is near the site of the ancient one, and has a population of over two hundred thousand.

Alien, ayl'yen, a foreign-born resident of a country. Many references are made in the Bible to aliens.

Alleging, al-lej'ing, in Acts 17:3, means showing; proving.

Al'legory, a story in which the literal or direct meaning is not the principal one, but sets forth some important truth. In Gal. 4:24 "which things are an allegory" signifies that the events referred to concerning the life of Isaac and Ishmael have been applied allegorically.

Allelu'ia (Praise ye the Lord).

Alli'ance. God's peculiar people were strictly forbidden to ally themselves with the heathen by family or by political ties, and especially as to the ancient Canaanites. Deut. 7:3-6. Hebrews sometimes married converts from heathenism, as in case of Ruth.

Almond-tree, ah'mund-tree, is like a peach tree, but is larger. Its blossoms are pinkish-white and come out before the leaves; hence its Hebrew name, which signifies to watch and hasten. Aaron's rod was from an almond tree. Num. 17:8. In Palestine the almond blossoms in January and bears fruit in March. Eccl. 12:5; Jer. 1:11.

Alms, in Acts 3:3; 10:2, means a charitable gift. The word is not found in the Old Testament, but is frequently used in the New. The Jews were required by the law of Moses to provide for the poor. Lev. 19:9, 10; Deut. 15:11, etc.

Al'oes. [1] A perfume spoken of in connection with "myrrh, cassia, and cinnamon," or a spice for embalming the dead, John 19:39, in which case it was the gum of the eagle-tree of Cochin-China and North India. This perfume is not the aloes of modern apothecaries. [2] Lign-aloes, used by Balaam, Num. 24:6, with the cedars as an illustration of the noble situation of Israel planted in a choice land. It has nothing in common with our bitter aloes.

Aloof', in Ps. 38:11, means afar off.

Alpha, al'fah, the first letter of the Greek alphabet, of which Omega, o'me-gah, or o-meg'ah, is the last. They signify the first and the last, and are used in Rev.1:8 as a title of the Lord Jesus Christ.

A

Altar, awl'ter, a table or elevated place on which sacrifices and incense were offered to some god. Altars were originally made of turf, and afteward of stone, wood or horn, and were of various forms. Sacrifices were offered by Cain and Abel, but the first mention of altars in history is in Gen. 8:20, which states that Noah "builded an altar unto the Lord." Moses built an altar of earth. Ex.20:24. The altars in the Jewish Tabernacle and in the Temple were [1] THE ALTAR OF BURNT-OFFERINGS, which in the Tabernacle was a hollow box of shittim-wood about seven and a half feet square and four and a half feet high, covered with "brass" plates. At the corners were elevations called horns. It was movable, and had rings and staves for carrying it. The fire was a perpetual one, miraculously kindled and carefully kept. Lev. 6:12, 13; 9:24. On this altar the lamb of the daily morning and evening sacrifice was offered; also other sacrifices. At this altar certain fugitives were allowed to find protection. In Solomon's Temple the altar of burnt-offerings was much larger, being at least thirty-feet square and fifteen feet high. It is often called the "brazen altar." [2] THE ALTAR OF INCENSE, OR GOLDEN ALTAR, which in the Tabernacle was a small table of shittim-wood covered with plates of gold. Exod. 39:38. It was eighteen inches square and three feet high. At the corners were elevations called horns and around its top was a border or crown. There were two rings in each side, in which staves were inserted to carry it. It stood in the Holy Place, before the Holy of Holies and between the golden candlestick and the table of show-bread. The priests burned incense on it morning and evening. [3] THE TABLE OF SHEW-BREAD. An altar at Athens was ascribed "to the unknown God." Acts 17:23. The name "altar" is applied to a part of the furniture of Christian churches.

Am'alek (warlike). [1] One of the princes of Edom; was the son of Eliphaz, and a grandson of Esau. Gen. 36:12, 16; 1 Chron. 1:36. The name Amalekites was not derived from him, as they existed long before his time. Gen. 14:7. [2] The name is also given to the people descended from him.

Amalekites, am'a-lek-ites, a wandering and warlike people, living at the time of the Exodus, in the wilderness between Egypt and Palestine. They opposed the march of the Israelites and were defeated at Rephidim, and were destroyed by David hundreds of years afterward.

Amasa, am'a-sah (burden-bearer). [1] David's nephew, the son of David's sister, Abigail, and Jether, an Ismaelite. He was general of Absalom's army, and was defeated by Joab, by whom he was subsequently treacherously murdered. 2 Sam. 20: 4-10; 1 Chron. 2:17. [2] A chief of Ephraim. 2 Chron. 28:12.

Ambassador, am-bas'sa-dor. [1] An interpreter. 2 Chron. 32:31. [2] A messenger. Ambassadors were sent by the Jews only as occasion required, in peace or war. Ministers are Christ's ambassadors. 2 Cor.5:20

A-men (steadfast, faithful, true), meaning "so be it;" "so let it be;" "verily." In Rev.3:14 our Lord is called "the Amen, the faithfull and true witness." When used at the beginning of a sentence, it is transelated "verily". In the Gospel of John it is often used thus double - "verily," "verily." In oaths, after the priest had repeated the words of the covenant or imprecation, all who said "amen" bound themselves by the oath.

Am'e-thyst, a precious stone, so named from its reputed virtue of preventing intoxication, is transparent quartz of a violet blue near to purple. Exod. 39:12; Rev. 21:20. The Oriental is more valuable than the common amethyst.

A'mi, a servant of Solomon whose descendants went up from Babylon with Zerubabel after the captivity. Ezra 2:57. He is called AMON in Neh. 7:59.

Am'mah (an aqueduct), a hill near Gibeon of Benjamin, where Abner was defeated. 2 Sam. 2:24.

Am'mon-ites, the descendants of AMMON (which see). They lived on the east side of the Jordan, and often made war on the Israelites, but were conquered by Jephthah, and later by David and Judas Maccabaeus.

Am'non (tutelage). [1] The eldest son of David by Ahinoam of Jezreel. 2 Sam. 3:2. Absalom caused him to be assassinated. 2 Sam. 13. [2] The son of Shimon. 1 Chron. 4:20.

A'mon or A'men (the hidden), the name of an Egyptian god. Nah. 3:8, in the marginal notes.

A'mon (workman). [1] Govenor of Samaria in the time of Ahab. 1Kings 22:26; 2 Chron. 18:25 [2] A son of Manassah, king of Judah, who succeeded his father. [3] One of the servants of Solomon whose decendants went up with Zerubbabel after the captivity. Neh.7.59. It is given AMI in Exra 2:57

Am'o-rites (mountaineer), a warlike and powerful nation which in the time of Moses occupied the country on both sides of the Jordan and resisted the Israelites on their way to the Promised Land. Moses defeated their kings, Sihon and Og. The Amorites were subsequently conquered by Joshua, but he was unable to destroy them. The term AMORITE is often used in the Bible for CANAANITE in general.

A'mos (burden-bearer). [1] One of the minor prophets who lived B.C. about 780, in the time of Isaiah. He was a herdsman, and also gathered sycamore fruit in Tekoa, near Jerusalem. He prophesied in the time of Uzziah and Jeroboam to the ten tribes, and vigorously and eloquently denounced the prevailing idolatry, taking his illustrations from rural and pastoral life. He described the coming punishment of Israel and the advent of the Messiah. His prophecies seem to have been given in a single year, and to have brought against him a charge of conspiracy against the government because he alienated the people by his plain speaking. The authorship and genuiness of the book of Amos are not disputed. [2] One of the ancestors of Joseph, the husband of Mary. Luke 3:25.

Am'u-lets, small objects, of a variety of forms, worn as charms. They were supposed to protect the wearer against real and imaginary evils, and were common in ancient times in the form of earrings and necklaces. Precious stones were often thus used.

Anammelech, a-nam'me-lek (the king's rock), an idol worshipped by the people of Sepharvaim whom Shalmaneser placed in the cities of Israel after he had carried away the inhabitants. 2 Kings 17:31.

Ananias, an-a-ni'as (Jehovah is gracious). [1] The husband of Sapphira. He was a Jew of Jerusalem who joined the Christians and pretended to give them the full price of his lands. Being convicted of falsehood by Peter. Acts 5: 1-10, he died instantly. [2] A Christian of Damascus who restored the sight of Saul (Paul) after his vision of Christ. Acts 9:10; 22:12. [3] A high-priest of the Jews. A.D. 48. Before him and the Sanhedrin Paul was summoned. Acts 23:2; 24:1. **Ananias** is the Greek form of HANANIAH.

Anathema, a-nath'e-mah, word usually translated "a curse" or "accursed," but in one passage left untranslated. "Anathema Maranatha." 1 Cor. 16:22. Ecclesiastically, anathema means excommunicated, or cut off from the church. (It occurs in the Greek. Rom. 9:3; Gal. 1:8, 9.

Ancient, ayn'shent (aged), when used as a name of any person, as in Isaiah 3:14 and in Job 12:12, means an elder.

An'cient of Days, the name given by Daniel to the supreme Judge he saw in vision. Dan. 7:9, 22.

An'drew (manly), John 1:40, one of the twelve apostles, was from Bethsaida and was a brother of Simon Peter. Both of them were fishermen. Andrew was a native of Bethsaida in Galilee and a disciple of John the Baptist. Matt. 4:18; 10:2; Mark 1:16, 29, etc. According to tradition, he preached the gospel in

Greece and Scythia and suffered martyrdom at Patrae in Achaia, on a cross formed thus (X), commonly called "St. Andrew's cross."

An-dro-ni'cus (conqueror), a Jewish Christian living at Rome, was a fellow prisoner and relative of Paul. Rom. 16:7.

An'gel (messenger), the name or title given to those beings whom the Lord employs as his messengers. The Jews believed there were several orders of angels. Angels that rebelled against God are angels of Satan, or the devil. The word angel is often used to denote an ordinary messenger to individuals, as in Job 1:14, etc.; to prophets, Isa. 42:19; to priests, Eccl. 5:6; and sometimes to objects without life, as in 2 Cor. 12:7. In a general sense it is applied to Christ as the Angel or Messenger of the covenant; also to the ministers of his gospel.

An'gel of the Lord, or the Angel Jehovah, is considered by some as one of the common titles of Christ in the Old Testament. Gen. 16:7-13.

An'ger, a strong emotion of indignation, usually called in the Bible a great sin, though sometimes it may be just. Anger is frequently ascribed to God because he punishes the wicked with the justice of a ruler provoked to anger.

An'i-mals were known to the Hebrews as either "clean" or "unclean," the use of the latter being forbidden. See the eleventh chapter of Leviticus for a list of them.

An'ise, a common herb of little value, resembling caraway, but more fragrant. It is the dill, which is found in Palestine and was tithed by the scribes and Pharisees. Matt. 23:23.

An'na (grace), Luke 2:36-38, a prophetess, daughter of Phanuel, of the tribe of Asher, became a widow while still young, and devoted herself to God's service, being constant in attendance at the temple. At the age of eighty-four she saw the infant Saviour, heard the prophetic blessing of Simeon, and joined earnestly in it.

An'nas (grace of Jehovah), a Jewish high-priest along with Caiaphas, his son-in-law. Annas was appointed high-priest A.D. 7, but was removed from that office, which, after many changes, was given, A.D. 23, to Caiaphas, his son-in-law. Annas, having much influence and power, could properly be called high-priest along with Caiaphas. Christ, on the night of his seizure, was first taken before Annas. Annas also assisted in presiding over the Sanhedrin when Peter and John were brought before it. Luke 3:2; John 18:13, 24; Acts 4:6.

A-noint'ed (consecrated by anointing). [1] Applied to a priest or a king. [2] Indicating the Redeemer.

A-noint'ing, a common act among the Hebrews and other Eastern nations. It was done by pouring or by rubbing olive oil or some precious ointment upon the hair, head, beard, or sometimes on the whole body. The omission of anointing was a sign of mourning. It was a common mark of respect to guests and a sign of prosperity. Dead bodies were often wrapped in spices and ointments to preserve them. Kings, high-priests, and sometimes prophjets, were anointed when put into office; also the sacred vessels of the Temple. The anointing of sacred persons and objects indicated that they were set apart and consecrated to the service of God. The costly mixture then used was prohibited for all other uses.

A-non', in Matt. 13:20, means quickly.

Ant, a small insect remarkable for its industry, economy, social habits, and skill as a builder. It is referred to by Solomon in Prov. 6:6 and 30:24, 25.

An'ti-christ (opposed to Christ), is found in the Bible only in the epistles of John, 1 John 2:18, 22; 4:3; 2 John 7, and signifies false Christians and heretical teachers, who denied the incarnation of Christ. There were many such in the days of John. The term was afterward used for an individual who was expected to precede the second advent.

An'ti-och. [1] A city of Syria, on the river Orontes. It was founded B.C. about 300 by Seleucus Nicator and named by him after his father Antiochus. It was the most splendid city of Syria, and had a population of at least 400,000. It was a great resort for Jews, and afterward for Christians. The name of Christians was here first given to the followers of Christ. Acts 11:26. It is famous as the place of Paul's first regular labors in the gospel and as the city from which he started on his missionary tours. It is now a small town called Antakia. [2] A city called "Antioch of Pisidia," so named because it was attached to the province of Pisidia in Asia Minor. Paul established a church in this city, which is now called Yalobatch. There were not less than six other Oriental towns called Antioch.

Ape, an animal somewhat resembling man. Solomon imported apes from Ophir. They were worshipped in Egypt. None are found now in Palestine. 1 Kings 10:22.

A-poc'a-lypse, the Greek word for Revelation, used in reference to the Revelation of John.

A-poc'ry-pha (hidden). Under this title are comprised a number of books: two of Esdras, Tobit, Judith, some chapters of the book of Esther, the Wisdom of Solomon, Ecclesiasticus,

14

or the Wisdom of Jesus the son of Sirach, Baruch, the Song of the Three Holy Children, the History of Susanna, the Destruction of Bel and the Dragon, the Prayer of Manasses, and the two Maccabees. They are not in the Hebrew Bible, but in the Septuagint, so called, or Greek translation of the Old Testament, dating from the third century B.C. From internal and external evidences it appears that they were not written by the men with whose names they are inscribed, but belong to a much later date, and probably originated in Alexandria. They are consequently without divine authority, but they are by no means without interest, forming a transition, in many respects very instructive, from the Old to the New Testament. The Jews seem to have looked upon them in the same light, and so did most of the Christian Fathers. Jerome, A.D. 340-420, one of the most learned of the early Fathers, says: "The other books (the Apocrypha) the Church reads for example of life and instruction of manner, but it does not apply them to establish any doctrine;" and this verdict has been recognized by the Thirty-Nine Articles of the Church of England and the reformed churches generally. Nevertheless, from the Septuagint they were transferred to the Vulgate, the authorized Latin translation of the Bible, dating from the fourth century A.D., and from thence to other translations. Since the Council of Trent, A.D. 1545-63, recognized them as canonical, with the exception of the two books of Esdras and the Prayer of Manasses, they are found in all Roman Catholic Bibles, and for a long time they were also printed in Protestant Bibles. In 1826 the British and Foreign Bible Society decided to omit them, and the American Bible Society followed the example.

The New Testament may be said to have no Apocrypha, as the various apocryphal Gospels, Acts, and Revelation are generally of an altogether inferior character, but they confirm the canonical Gospels in the same way that counterfeit coins presuppose genuine ones.

A-pol'los (a destroyer), a learned and eloquent Jew of Alexandria who became a Christian. He preached in Achaia and Corinth with great success, especially among the Jews. He was with Paul at Ephesus. Apollos is said to have been Bishop of Corinth.

A-pos'tle (one who is sent). This name is applied in Heb. 3:1 to Jesus Christ, but is commonly given to "the twelve," Matt. 10:2, and to Paul. Gal. 1:1, 12, 16; 2:9. It is the name translated "messenger" in 2 Cor. 8:23, where it means delegate on a charitable mission. It is also applied, in Rom. 16:7, to men of note among the apostles.

15

A-pos'tles' Creed. This is the most universal creed of the Christian Church. According to a tradition of the fourth century, it was composed by the apostles, but this statement is now generally discredited. It is called also the Creed, or Confession of Faith, and is as follows: "I believe in God, the Father Almighty, Maker of heaven and earth. And in Jesus Christ, His only Son, our Lord; who was conceived by the Holy Ghost, born of the Virgin Mary; suffered under Pontius Pilate, was crucified, dead, and buried; he descended into hell [or hades]; the thrid day he rose from the dead; he ascended into heaven, and sitteth on the right hand of God the Father Almighty; from thence He shall come to judge the quick and the dead. I believe in the Holy Ghost; the Holy Catholic Church; the communion of Saints; the forgiveness of sins; the resurrection of the body; and the life everlasting. Amen." The clause "He descended into hell: (that is, the place of departed spirits) first appeared in the Creed of Aquileia, A.D. 390, and then passed into the Roman Creed. The word "Catholic," in this creed, means "Universal."

A-pos-tol'ic Fa'thers, the disciples and fellow-laborers of the apostles, particularly those who left writings, namely, Clement, Barnabas, Polycarp, Ignatius, and Hermas.

A-poth'e-ca-ry, Exod. 30:25, one who prepared and sold anointing oil, sweet spices, etc.

Ap-peal'. The Mosaic law, Deut. 17:8, 9, allowed appeals. They were also granted in the time of the Judges and the Kings. Paul, who was a Roman citizen, appealed for trial before the emperor. Acts 25:1-12.

Ap'ple. The apple mentioned in Scripture is commonly supposed to have been different from the fruit now known by that name. The apple of the Bible was probably the apricot, which is common in Palestine; some say the citron is referred to, and some the quince. The apple is used in Prov. 25:11 as an illustration of "a word fitly spoken." Apple trees are several times mentioned in the Bible, and as there described are very much like the apricot.

Ap'ple of the Eve. Deut. 32:10. This phrase means, literally, "the little man," or "pupil" of the eye.

A'prons, mentioned in Gen. 3:7, were made of fig-leaves by Adam and Eve after they had sinned, and in Acts 19:12 aprons of another kind are referred to.

A-ra'bi-a (wilderness), the south-west part of Asia. It is situated south and east of Palestine. It extends about 1600 miles north and south and 1400 miles east and west, and is divided into three parts—ARABIA DESERTA (the desert), ARABIA

PETRAEA (the rocky), and ARABIA FELIX (the happy).
Arabia Petraea is south of Palestine. Its capital was Petra. It was inhabited by the southern Edomites, the Amalekites, etc. Their successors are now called Arabs. It contained the peninsula of Mount Sinai, the land of Midian, etc. Here the Hebrews spent forty years of wandering on the way to the Promised Land. The queen of Sheba was probably from part of Arabia Felix, which was very rich and abounded with spices. It now contains the famous cities of Mecca and Medina. Southern Arabia contains descendants of Ham, Shem, Ishmael, of Abraham by Keturah, Gen. 25:2, also of Esau and Lot.

A'ram (high). [1] A son of Shem. Gen. 10:22,23; 1 Chron. 1:17. [2] A descendant of Nahor, the brother of Abraham. Gen. 22:21. [3] Son of Shamer of Asher. 1 Chron. 7:34. [4] The son of Esrom, Matt. 1:3,4; Luke 3:33, elsewhere called RAM. [5] The elevated country north-east of Palestine, toward the river Euphrates. Num. 23:7; 1 Chron. 2:23. It was nearly the same as SYRIA.

Ar'a-rat (holy land). [1] A region of Armenia, between the river Araxes and the lakes Van and Urumiah. The name Ararat was sometimes applied to a larger portion of Armenia. 2 Kings 19:37; Jer. 51:27. [2] A grand volcanic mountain on the boundary between Persia, Turkey, and Russia; has two principal peaks. Greater Ararat is about seventeen thousand feet above the sea, and is covered with perpetual snow. Lesser Ararat is twelve thousand eight hundred and forty feet high. Ararat is called by the Persians the "Mountain of Noah." Noah's ark rested "upon the mountains of Ararat." Gen. 8:4.

Arch'an-gel (a chief angel). 1 Thess. 4:16; Jude 9.

Archelaus, ar-ke-la'us (people's chief), a son of Herod the Great by his fourth wife, Malthace, was destined by his father to become his successor, but Augustus refused to make him a king. He ruled, however, for several years as ethnarch over Judea, Samaria, and Idumaea, but was cruel and tyrannical, with all his father's evil passions and none of his ability. He was deposed by Augustus in A.D. 6, and banished to Vienne in Gaul, where he died. He is mentioned in Matt. 2:22.

Archippus, ar-kip'pus (chief groom), a "fellow-soldier" of Paul. Col. 4:17; Philem. 2.

Arc-tu'rus (group), a fixed star of the first magnitude in the constellation Bootes, so called because it is near the tail of the constellation called the Great Bear. In Job 38:32 the "sons" of Arcturus are probably starts in the Great Bear.

A-re-op'a-gus (hill of Mars). [1] A rocky hill near the centre of the city of Athens. Acts 17:19. See MARS' HILL. [2] The celebrated court of justice which was held at Areopagus. It was orgainized earlier than B.C. 740. Paul addressed the Athenians there. Acts 17:19-34.

Ar'e-tas, 2 Cor. 11:32, was the king of northwestern Arabia. He made war on Herod Antipas, and afterward appointed a governor over Damascus who attempted to put Paul in prison.

Ar-is-to-bu'lus (best counsellor), a resident of Rome whose household was saluted by Paul. Rom. 16:10.

Ark, a word meaning three structures. [1] NOAH'S ARK, a vessel made at God's command, in which Noah and his family and the animals to be saved were preserved during the deluge which destroyed the rest of the human race for their sins. Gen. 6:14-16; 8:1-13. [2] MOSES' ARK, in which the infant Moses was hidden by his mother. Exod. 2:3-5. It was made of bulrushes, a kind of reed growing on the banks of the Nile. [3] THE ARK OF THE COVENANT or TESTIMONY. Exod. 37:1-8. It was a covered chest of shittim-wood, overlaid within and without with gold. In it were the stone tables on which the law or "covenant" made by God with the Hebrews was inscribed; also the pot of manna, Aaron's rod, and the books of the Law. The mercy-seat with the cherubim was on its lid. It was kept in the most holy place (the "Holy of Holies") of the sanctuary. No object was more sacred among the Jews than the "ark of God." In their journeys in the wilderness it was borne by the priests before the hosts of Israel. Before it the Jordan was divided and the walls of Jericho fell. It was brought to the Temple by Solomon, 2 Chron. 5:2, where it remained till the time of the later idolatrous kings. Its ultimate fate is unknown.

Arm, the symbol of power. Job 38:15.

Ar-ma-ged'don (mountain of Megiddo). Rev. 16:16. Megiddo is a city at the foot of Mount Carmel, and had been the scene of great slaughter. Hence the above reference to it in Revelation as the place in which God will collect his enemies for destruction.

Ar-me'ni-a, a large portion of Asia, between Media on the east, Cappadocia on the west, Colchis and Iberia on the north, Mesopotamia on the south, and the Euphrates and Syria on the south-west. It is between the Caucasus and Taurus ranges, contains Mount Ararat near its centre, and is the source of the Euphrates, Tigris, and Araxes Rivers. 2 Kings 19:37; Isa. 37:38.

Ar'mor and **Arms.** The armor used by the Hebrews consisted of helmets for the head, cuirasses for the body (called also coat of mail, habergeon, and breastplate), the shield, target or buckler, and greaves used to protect the legs. Armor was made of leather and metallic scales or plates. Their offensive arms were the bow and arrow, the battle-axe, the spear, dart, and javelin or short spear, the sling, and the sword. The sword was straight, short, and two-edged.

Ar'mor-bear'er, an attendant who bore the heavy arms, such as spear and shield, of a warrior of rank. Judg. 9:54; 1 Sam. 14:7. He was also employed to carry orders, and was expected to stand by his chief in time of danger.

Ar-tax-erx'es (great king). [1] A king of Persia, Ezra 4:7-24, in whose time the governor of Samaria obtained an order to stop the rebuilding of Jerusalem by Zerubbabel. He is supposed to have been Smerdis the Magian. [2] A king of Persia, in the seventh year of whose reign Ezra went up from Babylon to Jerusalem with some of his countrymen; fourteen years afterward Nehemiah was allowed by Artaxerxes to return and rebuild Jerusalem. Ezra 7:7; Neh. 2:1. He is supposed to be the same as Artaxerxes Longimanus, son of Xerxes, who reigned B.C. 464-425.

Ar-tif'i-cers, workmen especially skilful in working in metals, carving wood and plating it with gold, setting precious stones, and designing embroideries. King Solomon procured many artificers from Hiram, king of Tyre. Gen. 4:22; 2 Chron. 34:11.

Ar-til'ler-y, in the Bible, means bows, arrows, javelins, darts, etc.; in 1 Sam. 20:40 it means bow and arrows.

Arts, in Acts 19:19, means pretended skill in astrology, magic, etc.

A'sa (physician). [1] Son and successor of Abijah as king of Judah. He reigned forty-one years, beginning B.C. 955, and fought a great battle with Zerah, an Ethiopian king, whom he defeated at Maresha. See 2 Chron. 14:8-15. Asa is said to have done "that which was good and right in the eyes of the LORD his God." 2 Chron. 14:2. [2] A Levite, the head of a family that dwelt near Jerusalem. 1 Chron. 9:16.

A'saph (gatherer). [1] A Levite, a chief leader of the choir of the Temple and a poet. 1 Chron. 6:39. Twelve Psalms are attributed to him—Ps. 50 and Ps. 73 to 83. In connection with David he is referred to as a "seer." 2 Chron. 29:30; Neh. 12:46. [2] Hezekiah's recorder. 2 Kings 18:18. [3] An officer appointed by the king of Persia to keep the forests in Judea. Neh. 2:8. [4] A Levite, an ancestor of Mattaniah. Neh. 11:17. Perhaps same as No. 1. [5] A Levite whose descendants dwelt in Jerusalem after the captivity. 1 Chron. 9:15. [6] A descendant of Kohath. 1 Chron. 26:1.

Ash, a tree mentioned in Isa. 44:14, is supposed to be a variety of the pine. The true ash is not a native of Palestine.

Ash'dod (fortress) or **A-zo'tus** was a stronghold of the Philistines, who defeated the people of Israel in Samuel's time and captured the ark of the covenant, which they took to the temple of Dagon in Ashdod. The place is called AZOTUS in the New Testament, and is now a small village called Esdud.

Ash'er (happy). [1] The eighth son of Jacob. [2] One of the twelve tribes. [3] A territory about sixty miles long, extending from Carmel to Lebanon, and from ten to twelve miles wide. The Phoenicians retained the plain by the sea, and Asher occupied the mountains. Josh. 19:24-31; Judg. 1:31, 32. [4] A town on the border of Ephraim and Manasseh. Josh. 17:7.

Ash'es. Ps. 102:9. This word is often used in the Bible in connection with SACKCLOTH (which see), and signifies penitence and grief. The ashes of a red heifer were used in ceremonial purification. Num. 19:17, 18; Heb. 9:13.

Ash'ke-lon or **As'ke-lon,** one of the five principal Philistine cities, was a seaport on the Mediterranean, about ten miles north of Gaza. It was captured by Judah, Judg. 1:18, and visited by Samson. Judg. 14:19. It was the birthplace of Herod the Great and the seat of worship of the goddess Astarte. It was ruined in A.D. 1270 by Sultan Bibars, who filled its harbor with stones. Ruins abound there, and near them is the village of Jurah.

Ash'pe-naz, the master of the eunuchs of Nebuchadnezzar. He was very kind to Daniel and his three companions. Dan. 1:3.

Ash'ur (black), father of Tekoa; that is to say, the founder of that city. 1 Chron. 2:24; 4:5.

Ash'ur-ites, a tribe occupying the whole country west of the Jordan, above Jezreel. They were descendants of Ashur. Ezek. 27:6.

A'sia, the largest of the continents, comprises nearly one-third of the land of the globe. The word Asia in the Bible refers to only a small part of the continent of Asia; in some instances to the whole of what is now known as Asia Minor, which lies between the Black Sea and the Mediterranean, but usually to only the western part of that country, namely, the region of which Ephesus was the chief city. The word Asia is used only in the New Testament.

Asp, a serpent whose poison is deadly and very sudden in its operation. It is identified by modern naturalists with a species

of hooded viper found in Egypt. On the Egyptian monuments
it is a sacred and royal emblem, the sign of the protecting
divinity.

Ass, one of the most common animals mentioned in the
Bible, is found wild in Mesopotamia, and was introduced into
Palestine by Abraham. Asses were an important part of the
wealth of ancient times. The ass and the ox were the principal
beast of burden among the Hebrews. Kings, judges, and
prophets rode on the large Babylonian ass, an animal of a higher
breed and very spirited. Judg. 12:14. The white variety was
most prized. Judg. 5:10. Christ rode into Jerusalem on an ass.
Zech. 9:9; Matt. 21:5. The wild ass is found in droves in
desolate places in Asia, and is very shy and swift. Job 39:5; Jer.
2:24. It is seldom found now in Palestine.

As-syr'ia, the second of the four great Asiatic monarchies,
was founded by Asshur, Gen. 10:10, 11, and peopled from
Babylon. The mother-country, Assyria proper, corresponds
nearly to the present Kurdistan, stretching west from the
frontier of Persia to the Euphrates. But at the height of its power
it comprised the whole of western Asia and parts of north-
eastern Africa. The first Assyrian king mentioned in the Bible
is Pul, who invaded Israel under the reign of Menakem and
levied a heavy tribute. 2 Kings 15:19. The next is Tiglath-
pileser, who aided Judah in its war against Israel and Syria. 2
Kings 16:7-9. The third is Shalmaneser, who under the reign of
Hoshea took Samaria, B.C. 721, carried the Israelites away into
captivity, and repeopled the country with Assyrian colonists. It
is, however, first after that time that Assyria became a great
empire. Under Sennacherib, B.C. 704-682, Egypt, Philistia,
Armenia, Media, and Edom were conquered. But immediately
after his defeat before Jerusalem, 2 Kings 19:35-37, the downfall seems to have begun, and in B.C. 625 the empire was
overthrown by the Medes and Babylonians, and Nineveh, its
capital, was destroyed. The Assyrians were of Shemitic origin,
and during the last forty years excavations about Nineveh have
shown that they were possessed of a civilization which in many
respects surpassed even that of Egypt. Their language they had
derived from Chaldea, and they put it into writing by means of
some peculiar arrow-headed, wedge-shaped, cuneiform characters. Thousands and thousands of clay tablets, covered with
inscriptions in those characters, have been dug up from the
mounds of Nineveh, and they confirm the truth of the Bible
narrative down to minute details.

As-trol'o-gers pretended to prophesy future events by observations on the stars, which they fancied had an influence either good or bad upon human affairs. Isa. 47:13; Dan. 2:2, 27.

As-tron'o-my treats of the motions and appearances of the heavenly bodies, and also of their constitution. It was much studied in Asia in ancient times. The Chaldeans were proficient in it. The Hebrews seem to have had little knowledge of astronomy. Several heavenly bodies are mentioned in the Bible; for instance, in Isa. 14:12; Rev. 2:28; Job 9:9; 38:31.

A'tad (thorn-bush), a Canaanite who had a threshing-floor near the cave of Machpelah, where those who came from Egypt with the body of Jacob seemed to have halted, and which was called by the inhabitants ABEL_MIZRAIM (which see). Gen. 50:10, 11.

Ath-a-li'ah (Jehovah is strong). [1] Daughter of Jezebel. She became the wife of Jehoram, king of Judah, and ruled in Judah after the death of her son Ahaziah. 2 Kings 8:26; 11:3. [2] Son of Jeroham, a Benjamite. 1 Chron. 8:26. [3] Father of Jeshaiah. Ezra 8:7.

Ath'ens, capital of Attica, was the most celebrated city of ancient Greece. It was founded B.C. 1566, and was subsequently named from the goddess Minerva or Athene that was worshipped there. Athens is on the Saronic Gulf, forty-six miles east of Corinth, and was the perfection of ancient civilization, but given to idolatry. The apostle Paul preached there. Acts 17:22. It contained the AREOPAGUS (which see). Athens began to decline toward the end of the sixth century of the Christian era. In A.D. 1834 it became the capital of the new kingdom of Greece. It has a good harbor (now Drako), the ancient Piraeius, and a population of over eighty thousand. Acts 17: 15, 16, 22; 18:1; 1 Thess. 3:1.

A-tone'ment, the expiation of sin made by the obedience and sufferings of Christ.

A-tone'ment, Day of, Lev. 16; 23:27-32, the annual day of humiliation,and the only Jewish fast-day by the Mosaic law, was kept five days before the Feast of Tabernacles, or on the tenth day of Tisri, which was early in October.

Au-gus'tus (venerable), title of Octavius, who became emperor of rome after the death of Julius Caesar. Luke 2:1. In Acts 25:21-25 Nero is meant.

A-ven'ger of Blood, a person who pursued a murderer or a manslayer, by virtue of the ancient Jewish law, to avenge the blood of one who had been murdered or slain. Deut. 19:6; Josh. 20:3.

B

Ba'al or **Ba'al-im** (master), the chief male deity of the Phoenicians and Canaanites, as Ashtoreth was their principal female deity. [1] An idol of the Phoenicians and Tyrians. The worship of Baal, together with that of Astarte, was common among the Hebrews. The Babylonians worshipped Baal under the name of BEL. Human sacrifices were offered to Baal by the Jews. See Jer. 19:5.[2] A city of Simeon. 1 Chron. 4:33. [3] A descendant of Reuben. 1 Chron. 5:5. [4] A descendant of Benjamin 1 Chron. 8:30; 9:36. In connection with other words, Baal denotes local idols, or some reference to them.

Baalbec or Baalbek, bahl-bek' an ancient and magnificent city of Syria, was about forty miles north-west of Damascus. Nothing is known of its origin and early history. Its ruins are stupendous and wonderful. They include the remains of three beautiful temples, including the great temple of the sun. It was called by the Greeks HELIOPOLIS (city of the sun).

Ba'bel (confusion), a city in the plain of Shinar, which formed part of the dominions of Nimrod. Gen. 10:10; 11:9.

Ba'bel, the Tow'er of, Gen. 11:4,5 was destroyed, according to old Jewish tradition. Nevertheless, the captive Jews at Babylon thought that they recognized it in the famous temple of Belus, the present Birs Nimrud, a huge mound about two hundred and fifty feet high and twenty-three hundred feet in circumference, situated west of Hillah, on the Euphrates. In this mound, consisting of bricks twelve inches square by four inches thick, it is easy to trace the outlines of a pyramidal or tower-like construction rising in terraces.

Bab'y-lon (confusion), the Greek form of the Hebrew word BABEL, is the name of an ancient kingdom and of its capital. The kingdom of Babylon comprised originally only an area of about thirty thousand square miles, situated in the lowlands around and between the Euphrates and the Tigris, and between Chaldea on the south and Assyria on the north. It was inhabited by a mixed population, half Chaldean and half Assyrian in its origin, and noted for its subtle wisdom, its commercial eagerness, its luxury, and its military valor. Babylonian civilization was very old, dating back more than two thousand years before our era. But the splendor of the Babylonian Empire was very short-lived, beginning with the fall of Nineveh, B.C. 625, reaching its greatest power under Nebuchadnezzar, and becoming a province of Persia in B.C. 538. Of the four great monarchies of Asia, it occupies the third place, preceded by

Chaldea and Assyria and succeeded by Persia. During this period the empire comprised, besides Babylonia proper, the provinces of Susiana, with the great city of Susa, Syria, Palestine, Phoenicia, Idumaea, and Lower Egypt. The principal cities of Babylonia proper were Babylon, Sippara or Sepharvaim, Isa. 36:19, Cuthah, 2 Kings 17:24, etc.

Bab'y-lon, the City of, was the capital both of the Chaldean and of the Babylonian empires. It was built on both sides of the Euphrates River, about two hundred miles above its junction with the Tigris and three hundred miles from the Persian Gulf. According to the description of the Greek historian Herodotus, who had seen it himself, it was one of the largest and most magnificent cities which ever existed, fifty-six miles in circumference and covering an area of about two hundred square miles. (London covers only one hundred and twenty-two square miles). Among its wonders were Nebuchadnezzar's palace, the temple of Belus, the hanging gardens, etc. It was founded by Nimrod, Gen. 10:10, taken by Cyrus, and again by Alexander the Great, and gradually fell into ruins so utterly that only "the wild beasts of the desert" came to lie down there. It is mentioned over two hundred and fifty times in the Bible, often with wonder and admiration, and often, too, as the doomed city. During the captivity it was the residence of the richest and most distinguished prisoners among the Jews, Dan. 1: 1-4, and for a long time after the captivity it was one of the principal centres of Jewish learning and rabbinical lore. Its ruins are very extensive. The inscriptions upon its brick confirm in many ways the statements of the Bible concerning it. The modern town of Hillah, occupies part of the site of ancient Babylon.

Bab'ylon, mentioned in Rev. 14:8; 16:19, etc., is a symbolical name for heathen Rome. Reference is also made to Babylon in 1 Pet. 5:13. Various opinions are held concerning the place referred to.

Bab-y-lo'ni-ans (sons of Babel), inhabitants of Babylonia. Ezra 4:9; Ezek. 23:23.

Baca, ba'kah (weeping), a valley near Jerusalem. Its exact location is very uncertain. Ps. 84:6, the allusion here being to the joy of the worshippers going up to Jerusalem.

Ba'rab'bas (father's son), a noted robber and murderer who was in prison when Christ was condemned, and whom the Jews, at the instigation of the priests, preferred to Jesus when Pilate would have released him. Mark 15:7, 11, 15; John 18:40.

Bar-ba'ri-an, Bar'bar-ous, uncivilized, a title given to other nations by the Greeks. Acts 28: 2,4; Rom. 1:14.

24

Barb'ed, in Job 41:7, means fringed or bearded with projecting points.

Bar-je'sus (son of Joshua), a false prophet, also called ELYMAS, who withstood Barnabas and Saul at Paphos. Acts 13:6.

Bar-jo'na (son of Johanan), a name applied by Christ to Simon Peter the apostle. Matt. 16:17.

Bar'na-bas (son of consolation), also called JOSES, a Levite and the companion of Paul in several journeys. Acts 4:36; Gal. 2:9. He is regarded by some as the author of the Epistle to the Hebrews.

Barns, in Palestine, were often caves in the rocks, the entrance being carefully concealed to prevent robbery. They were used for grain and other produce, rather than for hay. Caves are still used for this purpose on the hill of Jezreel. Domestic animals often occupy the ground floor of the owner's house in some parts of the East, and the family live in the rooms above. Job 39:12; Prov. 3:10.

Bar'rel, the word in Hebrew generally translated PITCHER. 1 Kings 17:12; 18:33.

Bar'ren-ness was peculiarly lamented in the East, especially among the Jewish women, who hoped for the honor of being the mother of the promised Messiah. Gen. 3:15.

Bar'sa-bas (son of Saba). [1] Joseph Barsabas, disciple of the Lord, who was nominated along with Matthias to succeed Judas Iscariot. Acts 1:23. Some consider him as the same person as BARNABAS. [2] Judas Barsabas, a disciple sent with Silas to Antioch. Acts 15:22.

Bar-thol'o-mew (son of Tolmai), one of the apostles. Matt. 10:3; Acts 1:13. Some suppose him to have been the same as Nathanael in John 1:45-51, and mentioned among the other apostles in John 21:2.

Baruch, ba'rook (blessed). [1] A Jew who rebuilt part of the wall of Jerusalem. Neh. 3:20; 10:6. [2] A descendant of Pharez. Neh. 11:5. [3] A Jew whom Jeremiah the prophet employed as amanuensis when he was in prison. Jer. 32:12; 43:6,7.

Base, in 1 Cor. 1:28, means lowly; humble.

Ba'sins or **Ba'sons** of various kinds are mentioned in the Bible; namely a hand-basin, for washing of hands; a covered basin, used in the Sanctuary; the "omer," a common domestic vessel of Egypt, holding half a peck, for cooking; and the foot-basin, in which Christ washed the disciples' feet; probably same as wash-pot in the Psalms. Exod. 24:6; John 13:5.

Bas'kets of various forms, sizes, strength, and structure were used by the Jews, and were generally made of wickerwork, though sometimes of network or of ropework. 2 Kings 10:7; Jer. 24:1; Deut. 26:2; Amos 8:1; Gen. 40:16; 2 Cor. 11:33.

Bat, a very common animal in Palestine, especially in the vaults under the Temple and in the caves of Galilee. It is included among the unclean fowls in Lev. 11:19, and among birds in Deut. 14:18.

Bath, the standard Hebrew measure for liquids, contained about seven gallons. 1 Kings 7:26; Isa. 5:10.

Bat'ter-ing-Ram, an engine of war used to batter down walls in ancient times. It consisted of a long, solid wooden beam, armed at one end with a mass of metal in the shape of a ram's head, and suspended by the middle. The beam was swung repeatedly and with great violence against the wall of a city or fort until a breach was made. This beam was sometimes placed in the base of a wooden tower which was on wheels. About a hundred men were employed in working it. The top of the tower was filled with archers and slingers. 2 Sam. 20:15; Ezek. 4:2.

Bat'tle-axe, a powerful weapon of war. We have no knowledge of it form and manner of use in very ancient times. Jer. 51:20.

Be'a-loth (ladies), the plural feminine form of Baal, is a town of Judah. Josh. 15:24. Probably same as BAALATH-BEER, 19:8, the modern Kurnub.

Beans are grown in Palestine, and are still used for food as vegetables, and in flour. 2 Sam. 17:28; Ezek. 4:9.

Bears were common in Palestine, and resembled the common brown bear. They are still found in Galilee, Lebanon, and Mount Hermon. 1 Sam. 17:34; Prov. 17:12.

Beard. The Jews gave much attention to the beard, and regarded it, when long and full, as the noblest ornament of man. Ps. 133:2. To neglect, tear out, or cut off the beard were signs of deep mourning. Ezra 9:3. The Egyptians left a small tuft of beard on the chin. The Jews were forbidden in Lev. 19:27 to imitate this fashion. To be deprived of the beard was a mark of servility and infamy.

Beast. [1] This word is improperly given (in the Authorized Version) as the translation of the term used to designate the "living beings" that were round about the throne in heaven. Rev. 4:6; 6:1. [2] Another word, meaning wild beast, is given in Revelation to the antichristian power (probably heathen Rome). Rev. 11:7; 13:11.

Beat'en work, in Exod. 25:18, means not cast in a mold, but wrought or hammered.

Beauty, bu'ty, the name given by the prophet Zechariah to one of the two staves by which he symbolized the Lord's covenant with the house of Jacob, and the brotherhood of Israel and Judah. Zech. 11:7, 10.

Bed, when used in the Bible, refers usually to a mattress like a thick quilt. It was rolled up during the day and spread only at night, often in the open air. The poorer people used skins for beds. Other kinds of beds, often like a low sofa, were used by wealthy people in the East. In Deut. 3:11 the iron bedstead of Og, king of Bashan, is mentioned. Beds are noticed in Exod. 8:3; John 5:11.

Bees, well-known insects common in Palestine; not only domesticated, but wild. Deut. 1:44; Matt. 3:4.

Beelzebub, be-el'ze-bub (lord of the fly), an evil spirit whom the Pharisees called the prince of the devils. Matt. 10:25; Mark 3:22; Luke 11:15.

Be'er-she'ba (well of the oath), a name which Abraham gave to a well in the southern extremity of Palestine, dug when he and Abimelech swore friendship to each other. Gen. 21:31; Judg. 20:1. The town that was afterward situated here became quite noted. In Judges 20:1 "from Dan even to Beersheba" means the whole length of Palestine. Beersheba was a city of Judah, and afterward of Simeon. It was again occupied by the Jews after the captivity, and continued an important place many centuries after Christ. Neh. 11:27, 30. It is now in ruins, and is called Bir-es-seba.

Bee'tle, in Lev. 11:22, means a species of locust.

Be'he-moth, a large beast, Job 40:15, is generally supposed to refer to the hippopotamus.

Bell. Small bells are still much used in the East. Bells of gold were fastened to the bottom of the robe of the high-priest, Exod. 28:33, and were attached to horses. Zech. 14:20.

Be-lov'ed, a title of Christ. Eph. 1:6.

Bel-shaz'zar (Bel's prince), son of Nebuchadnezzar and the last king of the Chaldeans. Dan. chap. 5. He made an impious feast in Babylon.

Ben (son), a Levite in the service of song. 1 Chron. 15:18. The word is a part of many Hebrew names.

Ben-e-fac;tor, a title of honor given to kings. Luke 22:25.

Ben'ja-min (son of the right hand). [1] The twelfth and youngest son of Jacob and the second son of Rachel. He was born near Bethlehem B.C. about 1729. His mother, who died soon after his birth, named him Benoni (son of my sorrow), but his father gave him the name of Benjamin. He was greatly

27

beloved by his father, who could hardly allow him to go to Egypt with his brethren. Gen. chapters 42 and 43. [2] The tribe of Benjamin had their part of the Promised Land adjoining Judah, and when the ten tribes revolted it became part of the kingdom of Judah. [3] A grandson of Jediael. 1 Chron. 7:10. [4] A descendant of Harim who took a foreign wife. Ezra 10:32. [5] A Jew who repaired part of the wall of Jerusalem. Neh. 3:23. [6] A Jew who took part in the ceremonial of purifying the wall of Jerusalem. Neh. 12:34. [7] A gate of Jerusalem. Jer. 20:2; Zech. 14:10.

Ben'jam-ite, a person of the tribe of Benjamin. Judg. 19:16; 1 Sam. 9:1. King Saul and Saul of Tarsus were Benjamites.

Berachah, ber'a-kah (blessing). [1] An Israelite who aided David at Ziklag. 1 Chron. 12:3. [2] A valley of Judah. 2 Chron. 20:26.

Be-ri'ah (unfortunate). [1] A son of Asher. Gen. 46:17; 1 Chron. 7:30. [2] A son of Ephraim. 1 Chron. 7:23. [3] Son of Elpaal. 1 Chron. 8:13, 16. [4] A Levite descendant of Gershom. 1 Chron. 23:10, 11.

Be-ri'ites, a family of Israelites descended from BERIAH, son of Asher. Num. 26:44.

Be'rith (a covenant), a word often used to designate the covenant which God made with his people, is found in Judges 9:46 as the name of an idol (otherwise called BAALBERITH) worshipped at Shechem.

Bernice, ber-ni'se, or **Berenice,** ber-e-ni'se, daughter of Herod Agrippa. Acts 25:13, 23; 26:30.

Ber'yl, a precious stone used in the high-priest's breastplate. It is supposed to resemble the emerald. Exod. 28:20; Rev. 21:20.

Be-stead', in Isa. 8:21, means circumstanced; situated.

Be-stow', in 2 Kings 5:24 and Luke 12:17, means to lay away safely.

Beth'a-ny (house of dates or figs), a village on the Mount of Olives, about two miles east of Jerusalem, on the road to Jericho. It was the residence of Lazarus and his sisters Martha and Mary. Christ often visited it, and it was the scene of some of the most interesting events of his life. Matt. 21:17; 26:6; Mark 11:11, 12; 14:3; Luke 19:29; 24:50; John 11:1, 18; 12:1. Its modern name is el Aziriyeh (place of Lazarus). [2] Some manuscripts read BETHANY for BETHABARA in John 1:28.

Beth-a'ven (house of idols), a town of Benjamin, near Bethel. Josh. 7:2; 18:12; 1 Sam. 13:5; 14:23. Used as a name for BETHEL (house of God); changed to BETHAVEN (house of

28

idols). Hos.4:15; 5:8.

Beth-da'gon (house of Dagon). [1] A town of Judah. Josh. 15:41. [2] A town of Asher. Josh. 19:27.

Beth'el (house of God). [1] A town about twelve miles north of Jerusalem. It was visited by Abraham. Gen. 12:8; 13:3. Was the scene of Jacob's vision of the ladder from earth to heaven. Gen. 28:11-19. He named the place Bethel. Gen. 28:19. It was first called LUZ, Judg. 1:22, 23, was the dwelling-place of Jacob, Gen. 35:1-8, the home of prophets, 2 Kings 2:2, 3 and was called BETH-AVEN (house of idols). Hos.10:5,8. It is now called Beitin. [2] A town in the south of Judah. Josh.12:16. It is called also CHESIL, BETHUL, and BETHUEL. [3] Mount Bethel, a hilly region near Bethel. Josh. 16:1; 1 Sam. 13:2.

Bethesda, be'thez'dah (house of mercy), a pool or cistern in Jerusalem, near the sheep-market gate. Its location is doubtful. It was a great resort for the sick. See John 5:2-9.

Beth'le-hem (house of bread). [1] A village of Judah, originally called EPHRATH, Gen. 35:19, and which is more fully named BETHLEHEM JUDAH or BETHLEHEM EPHRA-TAH. It is about six miles south of Jerusalem, and was the birthplace of David. 1 Sam. 17:12, and of Christ. Matt. 2:1. Rachel was buried near it, and it was the home of Boaz, Naomi, and Ruth. It was visited by the shepherds, Luke 2:15-17, and by the wise men. Matt.2. It has been a town for more than four thousand years, but was a small village till after the time of Christ. It is now called Beit-Lahm, and has five thousand inhabitants. [2] A town of Zebulun, six miles west of Nazareth. Josh. 19:15. [3] A descendant of Caleb. 1 Chron. 2:51, 54; 4:4.

Beth-sa'i-da (place of nets), a city on the west side and near the north end of the Sea of Galilee. Matt. 11:21; Luke 10:13; John 1:44. [2] It seems possible that there was another city of the same name on the east bank of the Jordan, near the Sea of Galilee. See Mark 8:22; Luke 9:10.

Be-thu'el (dweller in God). [1] A son of Nahor. Gen. 22:22; 25:20. [2] A town of Simeon. 1 Chron. 4:30.

Betrothing or **espousing**, ez-powz'-ing. In ancient times the Jews often betrothed their daughters without their consent and while they were quite young. A written contract was sometimes made, in which the bridegroom agreed to give a certain sum to the bride. The betrothal could not be dissolved, except by divorce or death. Deut. 20:7; Exod. 21:9.

Beu'lah (married), a term used by Isaiah to denote the intimate relation of the Jewish Church to God. Isa. 62:4.

Bi'ble. The word bible is of Greek origin, and means simply "the book" or "the books." In the sense which it now has throughout the world, it was first used in the fourth century by the Greek Father, Chrysostom, but it was so natural to the Christians to designate the volume which contains the standard of their faith and duty and the foundation of their hope as "The Book," that the word was bodily transferred from Greek into Latin, and thence into all modern languages. Before that time the Christians generally designated the collection of their religious books by terms corresponding to our "Scriptures," "Holy Writ," "Sacred Writings," etc.

The Bible consists of the OLD and the NEW TESTAMENT. The word testament is of Latin origin, and a translation of the Greek word diatheke, used by Paul, 2 Cor. 3: 14, meaning "covenant;" so that the terms OLD TESTAMENT AND NEW TESTAMENT actually mean the books of the OLD and of the NEW COVENANT. A peculiar place, so to speak, between the Old and the New Testament, is occupied by the apocryphal books. What should be said about them is given under the special heading APOCRYPHA (which see).

I. THE OLD TESTAMENT consists of thirty-nine books arranged so as to correspond to the twenty-two letters of the Hebrew alphabet, the twelve minor prophets counting as one, Ruth being coupled with Judges, Ezra with Nehemiah, Lamentations with Jeremiah, and the two books of Samuel, Kings, and Chronicles counting as one each; and further, so that the five double books, Samuel, Kings, Chronicles, Ezra and Jeremiah, correspond to the five double letters of the alphabet. The dates when these thirty-nine books were written, in whole or in part, vary from the age of Moses to the time of Ezra. The collection of them was consequently gradual. Moses ordered that the books of the Law should be put in the ark of the covenant, Deut. 31:26; Joshua and other annals, the Proverbs and Prophecies were added, Zech. 7:12; Isa. 29:18; 34:16; and finally the collection was closed, according to Jewish tradition, in the time of Ezra and Nehemiah by the men of the Great Synagogue. At all events, the Hebrew Canon in its present shape existed at the time of Christ.

The existence of the APOCRYPHA, as well as the circumstance that several books unknown to us are mentioned both in the Old and New Testaments, proves that the Old Testament collection did not embrace the whole sacred literature of the Jews, but only their Canon; that is those books which were received among them as written by divine authority. The Greek word canon meant first a straight staff, then a measuring rod, and finally, since the fourth century, the word has been used to denote the rule according to which the genuineness of the writings of the Old and the New Testament was defined, or those writingss themselves. The Old Testament Canon is mentioned in the prologue to the Greek translation of Ecclesiasticus (B.C. 131), by Philo Judaeus (B.C. 20-A.D. 40), by Josephus (A.D. 38-100), who, in speaking of the books of the Old Testament, adds that since the death of Artaxerxes (B.C. 424) no one had dared to add anything to them, to take anything from them, or to make any change in them. From the Synagogue the Canon passed into the Christian Church. The Jews generally arranged the books of their Canon into three classes; the Law, comprising the five books of Moses; the Prophets, divided into two groups:the former prophets, or the historical books of Joshua, Judges, Samuel, and Kings; and the later prophets, or the prophets proper (though with the exception of the book of Daniel, which they placed in the last class); and the Hagiographa (or Holy Writings), embracing the Psalms, Proverbs, Job, Canticles, Ruth, Lamentations, Ecclesiastes, Esther, Daniel, Ezra, Nehemiah, and Chronicles—an arrangement very similar to the common modern division namely [1] The PENTATEUCH (or five books of Moses); [2] THE HISTORICAL BOOKS (from Joshua to the end of Esther); [3] THE POETICAL or DEVOTIONAL BOOKS (from Job to the Song of Solomon); [4] THE PROPHETICAL BOOKS (from Isaiah to Malachi).

All the writings of the Old Testament Canon are in Hebrew, with the exception of a few minor portions, which are in Chaldee. Hebrew belongs to the Shemitic group of languages, and is very different from any language belonging to the Aryan group. It is somewhat lacking in that precision and flexibility which fit a language for philosophical and dialectial reasoning, but its great imaginative power and its depth of feeling have made it a wonderful vehicle for the expression of religious devotion. The books of the Old Testament are the only works extant in pure Hebrew. Each of these—namely, GENESIS, EXODUS, LEVITICUS, NUMBERS, DEUTERONOMY, JOSHUA, JUDGES, RUTH, I SAMUEL, II SAMUEL, I KINGS, II KINGS, I CHRONICLES, II CHRONICLES, EZRA, NEHEMIAH, ESTHER, JOB, PSALMS, PROVERBS, ECCLESIATES, SONG OF SOLOMON, ISAIAH, JEREMIAH, LAMENTATIONS, EZEKIEL, DANIEL, HOSEA, JOEL, AMOS, OBADIAH, JONAH, MICAH, NAHUM, HABAKKUK, ZEPHANIAH, HAGGAI, ZECHARIAH, and MALACHI—

will be treated separately under its own heading.

II. THE NEW TESTAMENT consists of four Gospels, the Acts of the Apostles, twenty-one Epistles, and the Revelation. All of these books were written within the first century after Christ, but between two and three more centuries passed before the Canon was finally settled. This was done by the councils of Laodicea (A.D. 369), Hippo Regius (A.D. 393), and Carthage (A.D. 397). All the Christian churches agree on this important point and have the same New Testament, though in different versions.

The books of the New Testament are written in Hellenistic Greek as commonly spoken and generally understood, not only in Asia Minor, but also in Syria, Palestine, Egypt, and even in Rome. It is not classical Greek; it shows influences of the Hebrew, beside which it was used. But it was best adapted for the expression of the truths of the Christian religion and for the Christians of the apostolic age. It admits of easy translation into other languages without losing its force and beauty.

III. MANUSCRIPTS AND EDITIONS OF THE BIBLE— Before the invention of the art of printing, in the middle of the fifteenth century, books were reproduced by rewriting, and existed only as manuscripts. These manuscripts were generally made on finely prepared skin (parchment), or later on paper made from the leaves of the papyrus-plant or otherwise, and were generally in the form of rolls—just as we often have maps rolled on sticks—or later in the form of books consisting of leaves tied together with strings.

Ancient Hebrew Books or Rolls.—The "book" kept in the sacred place of the Israelites was not such a book as the reader now holds in his hand, of paper, with leaves and a cover, and opening by a flexible back; nor were the words and verses and chapters arranged like ours. In those days, and down to a period long after the time of Christ, the "book" was a parchment roll made of skins fastened together in a long strip; the text was written upon it in narrow columns from top to bottom, without any break between words, sentences, verses, or chapters; and the direction of its writing and reading was from right to left, exactly the reverse of ours. The same order is still used in the Hebrew language, as any one may see who will examine a Hebrew book as now printed. To make this clear we will give the first three verses of Genesis in the English words and letters, but arranged as in the ancient Hebrew roll:

gfotiripsehtdnapee   rcdoggninnigebehtnI

afehtnopudevomdo	htdnanevaehehtdetae
dnasreta wehfoec	htraeehtdnantraee
eberehtteldiasdog	dnamroftuohtiwsaw
awerehtdnathgil	awssenkraddnadiov
thgils	dehtfoecafehtnopus

The above example must be read from right to left, beginning with the capital letter "I" in the first line of the right hand column. The two columns contain the following verses:

1. In the beginning God created the heaven and the earth.

2. And the earth was without form, and void; and darkness was upon the face of the deep. And the Spirit of God moved upon the face of the waters.

3. And God said, Let there be light: and there was light.

Each ancient letter was probably an eighth, or even a quarter of an inch high and wide; the columns were a foot long and four inches wide, or even considerably more. We copy from Horne the description of a parchment roll now in the British Museum, containing the Pentateuch alone: "It is a large double roll, containing the Hebrew Pentateuch, written with very great care on forty brown African skins. These skins are of different breadths, some containing more columns than others. The columns are one hundred and fifty-three in number, each of which contains about sixty three lines, is about twenty-two inches deep, and generally more than five inches broad." With the prescribed margins above and below, and the spaces between the columns, this "roll," therefore, if unrolled and laid on the ground, would occupy a space seventy-six feet long and two feet two inches wide. It is thus evident that the rolls of those ancient times were extremely cumbrous and inconvenient compared with the books of the present day. The skins of parchment in such a roll were tied together with strings made of the skin of some clean animal, and the whole was rolled upon a round stick at each end, while a disk above and below the parchment on each stick, like the heads of a spool, served to guide the parchment in rolling up and to protect the edges of the skins. It was, of course, unavoidable, with this manner of reproduction, that errors, either from misunderstanding or from carelessness, should creep into the text, but no book from ancient times has come down to us better preserved than the Bible. Of small variations there are many, but few of them materially affect the sense and most of them can be corrected by collation of manuscripts.

The sacred original manuscripts of the Old Testament were

lost when Nebuchadnezzar took Jerusalem (B.C. 588), and the original manuscripts of the collection and the manuscript arrangement by Ezra and Nehemiah were lost in the destruction of Jerusalem by Titus (A.D. 70). The text was, nevertheless, preserved with the most scrupulous care, both for service in the synagogues and for private use, and was regarded with extreme reverence.

Specially noteworthy in this connection are the Masoretes, from masora, "tradition," a body of scholars who lived at Tiberias and at Sora in the Euphrates Valley between the fifth and twelfth centuries. To them we owe the addition of the vowel-points in the writing down of the text; and the text, such as we now have it, is generally called the Masoretic, after them. The oldest manuscript extant dates from the tenth century. The Hebrew Bible was first printed in parts, the Pentateuch in 1482, the older Prophets in 1485, the later Prophets in 1486, the Hagiographa, or Sacred Writings, in 1487. The whole Old Testament in Hebrew appeared first in 1488 (Sorino: Abraham ben Chayin de' Tintori), in double columns, folio.

The manuscripts of the New Testament are both older and more numerous than those of the Old Testament. They are in two distinct groups: uncials, written in capitals throughout, and without any division of sentences or words; and cursives, written in running hand, as we now write. The former are the oldest, ranging from the fourth to the tenth century. The oldest two manuscripts extant, dating from the age of Constantine the Great, are [1] Codex Vaticanus, so called because it belongs to the Vatican library. A facsimile edition of the New Testament (one hundred copies) was published in Rome, 1889. [2] The Codex Sinaiticus, which was discovered by a German scholar, Tischendorf (A.D. 1859), in the monastery of Mount Sinai. It is now in St. Petersburg, and a quasi-facsimile was published in 1862, in four volumes. The original manuscripts of the apostles and evangelists were written on perishable Egyptian paper, and had therefore disappeared in the second century. But there are more copies of them than of any other ancient writings, and the materials for the restoration of the original text are abundant—about two thousand manuscripts of all kinds, ancient versions, and patristic quotations. An immense amount of labor and skill has been spent, during the last and present centuries, upon the critical examination and collation of these sources. We have now a pure and reliable text of the Greek Testament, which has been utilized by the Committees of British and American Revisers of 1881 for the benefit of the

English-reading community.

The division into chapters and verses was introduced very early in the Old Testament for liturgical purposes; first in the Law, then in the Prophets; first simply in fifty-four sections, to correspond to the Sabbaths in the Jewish intercalary year; then more elaborately in minor sections. As for the New Testament, the division was first applied to the Gospels by Ammonius of Alexandria (A.D. 220), in order to facilitate the comparison of corresponding portions of the several Gospels. The general application of it to all the books is of much later date, and due to Cardinal Hugo of St. Cher (died A.D. 1263), whose Concordance to the Vulgate has also a division into verses. The present system of verse-divisions was introduced by Robert Stephens in his edition of the Greek Testament (A.D. 1551).

The first published edition of the Greek text of the New Testament is that by Erasmus, Basel (A.D. 1516). The first printed edition of the original text of the whole Bible is that in the Complutensian Polyglot (A.D. 1514-20), six volumes folio, thus called from Complutum, the Latin name of the place where it was printed (Alcala in Spain), and the Greek word polyglot, "many-tongued," because the original Hebrew and Greek text was printed in parallel columns between the Greek and Latin translations.

IV.—VERSIONS OF THE BIBLE, or at least of parts of it, are now found in almost every language spoken on the globe. The Esquimaux of Greenland, the Indians of North America, the Negroes and Kaffirs of Africa, the remnants of the old native races in the East Indies, the numerous tribes in the Malayan Archipelago, the Chinese, the Japanese, etc., all have access to the Bible. We mention below only those among the oldest versions which are important for the right understanding of the original text and the English versions.

OLD VERSIONS OF THE BIBLE.—The Targums are not exactly a translation, but rather a paraphrase of the Old Testament's Hebrew text into Chaldee, made after the return from the captivity, when the Jews had lost the ready command of their native tongue and had adopted the Aramaic dialect, a mixture of Hebrew and Chaldee. The word targum means "interpretation."

The Septuagint, or the LXX., a Greek translation of the Old Testament, made by seventy (a round number for seventy-two) Jewish scholars, whence its name, in Alexandria, under the patronage of Ptolemy Philadelphus, B.C. 285.

The Peshito, a translation of the Bible into Syriac, done by Christians, and from the original text, Hebrew and Greek, probably in the beginning of the third or perhaps toward the close of the second century, and in general use throughout Syria during the fourth century. The word peshito means "simple."

Itala, the oldest latin translation, but known to us only from fragments in the early Latin Fathers (Tertullian, Cyprian, etc.).

The Vulgate, the authorized Latin translation of the whole Bible, was made by Jerome (A.D. 385-405) from the original text, on the basis of an older Latin version called the Itala. It was generally adopted by the Western Church. The Council of Trent (A.D. 1563) ascribed to it the same authority as to the original text, and calls it "The old and commonly accepted version," whence its name, Vulgate.

ENGLISH VERSIONS OF THE BIBLE.— Translations of the Psalms and other parts of the Bible were made as early as the thirteenth century, and even in the Saxon period.

A. D. 1381.—Wyclif's Translation was made by John Wyclif (about 1324-84) and Nicholas Hereford from the Latin Vulgate. The New Testament was printed in 1581; the whole work, in an authentic revision, not until 1850. But in manuscript it seems to have had a very wide circulation. It was the first translation of the whole Bible into the English language.

A.D. 1525.—Tyndale's Translation of the New Testament was made by William Tyndale (born 1484; burnt at the stake 1536) from the original text as published by Erasmus. The New Testament was printed at Worms in 1525. Of the Old Testament he only translated the books of Moses, republished by Mombert (New York, 1884).

A.D. 1535.--Miles Coverdale's Translation of the whole Bile was made from Tyndale, The Latin Vulgate and the German. It was the first version of the whole Bible published in modern english (Wyclif's translation being in medieval English).

A.D. 1537.—Thomas Matthew's Bible was made (under this assumed name) from the translations of Tyndale and Coverdale by John Rogers, the first martyr under Queen Mary (1555). It was published under the king's license, and was the first "Authorized Version."

A.D. 1539.—Taverner's was a purified edition of Thomas Matthew's Bible, edited by Taverner.

A.D. 1539.—The Great Bible, or Cranmer's Bible, was a new edition of Thomas Matthew's Bible, published in England under the authority of the English reformer, Thomas Cranmer, who was burned at the stake in 1556. It was the first edition in which the words not found in the original were printed in different type.

A.D. 1560.—The Geneva Version, made in Geneva by refugees from the persecutions of Queen Mary, appeared 1560. It was the favorite version of the Puritans, and many copies were brought to America by the early settlers of New England.

A.D.1568.—Bishops' Bible, a folio version based on Cranmer's. amd executed by fifteen theologians, eight of whom were bishops, in opposition to the Geneva Bible. It was issued in three parts in 1568-72. It was large, costly, and short-lived.

A.D. 1582.—The Douai Bible, or the Rheims Version, was made from the Latin Vulgate by English Roman Catholic divines who were at first connected with the college at Rheims, and later with that at Douai, a town of France. The New Testament was published in 1582; the Old Testament, in 1609-10.

A.D.1611.—King James's Version, or the Authorized Version, was proposed at the Hampton Court Conference, January, 1604, and begun in the same year by forty-seven Biblical scholars, who, at the invitation of King James I. of Great Britain, though not at his expense, assembled, formed themselves into six companies, and immediately went to work. It appeared in 1611, and has ever since been one of the mainstays of the religious life of the English-speaking race, "a sacred thing, which doubt has never dimmed and controversy never soiled." The Bible, or parts of it, is now printed in about two hundred and thirty different languages or dialects.

A.D. 1881; 1885.—The Revised Version is a revision of King James's Version, and was made by an English and an American committee of Biblical scholars, of all the evangelical denominations, working together, 1870-85, for the purpose of bringing the Authorized Version into perfect harmony with the present state of the English language and the results of the latest Biblical researches in textual criticism, philology, archaeology, and history. The New Testament was published by the University Presses of Oxford and Cambridge in 1881; the Old Testament, in 1885. The sacred text is arranged in paragraphs instead of chapters and verses. The chapters and verses of the Authorized Version are indicated in the Revised Version by figures on the margin. The poetical books of the Old Testament, and such quotations from them in the New Testament as extend to two or more lines, are arranged so as to agree with the metrical divisions of the Hebrew original. The hymns in the first two chapters of Luke are arranged in the same way.

Bier, a frame on which a dead body is carried to the grave by men. Luke 7:14.

Bil'dad (lord Adad), one of Job's three friends that visited him in his affliction. Job 2:11; 42:9.

Bind, in Job 26:8 and Acts 9:14, means imprison or confine closely.

Birth'right, special privileges enjoyed among the Hebrews by the firstborn son.

Bish'op, an official title used interchangeable with"elder" and in Acts 20:28 translated OVERSEER. Phil. 1:1; 1 Pet. 2:25.

Black, a sign of affliction and mourning. Job 30:30; Jer. 14:2.

Blas'phe-my, reproachful, irreverent, or insulting language concerning God.

Blem'ish-es, deformities or imperfections which made men unfit for priests, and animals not acceptable for sacrifice. Lev. 21: 18-20; 22: 20-24.

Bles'sed, the word used by the high-priest in asking Jesus if he was the son of God. Mark 14:61. It is used also as an adjective.

Blood. Blood often signifies the guilt of murder. 2 Sam. 3: 28; Matt. 27:25. Also, relationship.

Boar, the original stock of the common hog. In a wild state it is a furious and formidable animal. It is found on Mount Carmel and near the Sea of Galilee. Ps. 80:13.

Bo'az (fleetness, strength). [1] A Bethlehemite of Judah. He was the husband of Ruth the Moabitess, and was an ancestor of David, B.C. 1312. See Ruth chaps. 2,3,4; 1 Chron. 2:11. Matt. 1:5; Luke 3:32. Boaz is called Booz in the New Testament. [2] The name which Solomon gave to a brazen pillar he erected in the porch of the Temple. 1 Kings 7:21; 2 Chron. 3:17. Its companion was JACHIN.

Bra'zen Ser'pent, an image prepared by Moses and set up in the camp of the Israelites in the desert. It resembled the fiery serpents so destructive to Israel. See Num. 21: 6-9. It was long preserved, but being worshipped, it was broken in pieces by Hezekiah. It was a type of Christ. John 3: 14, 15.

Bread, in the Bible, is often used for food in general. Gen. 3:19. Manna is called bread from heaven. Exod. 16:4. Bread, in the literal sense, usually means in the Bible cakes of wheaten flour. Gen. 14:18. Barley was used chiefly for the poor and for horses. The Hebrews did not cut their bread, but broke it.

Breast'plate. [1] A piece of embroidery about ten inches square worn by the high-priest; it was set with twelve precious stones, on each of which was engraved the name of one of the twelve tribes of Israel. Exod. 28: 15-30. [2] A piece of ancient armor worn by warriors to protect the breast. The word is figuratively used in Eph. 6:14; Isa. 59:17.

C

Cab, the smallest definite measure for dry things that is mentioned in the Old Testament. It contained about three pints. 2 Kings 6:25.

Caesar, se'zer, in the New Testament, always means the Roman emperor. It is often improperly spelled CESAR. The Jews paid tribute to him, and those who were Roman citizens had the right of appeal to him. Paul availed himself of this right. Acts 25:11.

Caesarea, ses-a-re'a, a city of Palestine on the Mediterranean, forty-four miles south of Acre and forty-seven miles north-west of Jerusalem, was built by Herod the Great B.C. 10, and was the principal centre of Roman influence among the Jews. There Felix and Festus resided, Herod Agrippa I. died, Acts 12:19-23, and Vespasian was proclaimed emperor. Paul was kept in bonds at Caesarea two years. Acts 24:27. The evangelist Philip lived there. Acts 8:40; 21:8. It is now a small village called Kaisarieh.

Caesarea Philippi, ses-a-re'a phil-ip'pi, a city of Palestine, probably the BAAL-GAD of Old Testament history, certainly the Paneas of the Greek, thus called in honor of the god Pan, was rebuilt and much enlarged by Philip the tetrarch, and by him called Caesarea Philippi to distinguish it from Caesarea on the Mediterranean. It stood at the foot of Mount Hermon, about twenty miles north of the Sea of Galilee, and was the northern limit of our Lord's journeys. Matt. 16:13; Mark 8:27. It is called Banias by the Arabs, and is now a small village among great ruins.

Caiaphas, ka'ya-fas (depression), the high-priest of the Jews. At a council of the chief priests and Pharisees he advised that Jesus should be put to death, John 11:49-52; 18:14, and presided at his trial. Matt. 26:57. Peter and John were brought before Caiaphas for trial. Acts 4:6.

Cain (possession); the first son of Adam. Gen. 4:1; 1 John 3:12. He slew his brother Abel.

Cain (lance), a town in the south of Judah. Josh. 15:57

Ca'leb (capable). [1] A son of Hezron. 1 Chron. 2:18, 42. Called also CHELUBAI in 1 Chron. 2:9. He was the father of Hur. [2] The son of Jephunneh, Num. 13:6, one of the twelve chiefs, one from each tribe, sent by Moses to spy out the land of Canaan. He and Joshua were the only spies that brought back a favorable report, and they were the only adults born in Egypt who entered Canaan as conquerors. Caleb was one of the princes that divided the land. Num. 34:19. He received as his share the city of KIRJATH-ARBA, with the adjacent hill country. This city was the stronghold of the giants, but Caleb drove them out and took possession of it. It was afterward called HEBRON. [3] Caleb, the son of Hur, is mentioned in 1 Chron. 2:50. He may be CALEB the spy.

Cal'va-ry (skull), an elevation in the shape of a skull. The word used in the original means a skull, and was properly rendered by the Latin translators Calvarium. The translators of the English Version retained the Latin word, giving it an English termination. Luke 23:33. Calvary, or GOLGOTHA, Matt. 27:33; Mark 15:22; John 19:17, the latter being the Hebrew term, is the place where Christ was crucified, near Jerusalem, John 19:20, but outside of its walls. Heb. 13:12. There is no sanction for the expression "Mount Calvary." It is not found in the Bible. The exact location of Calvary is unknown.

Cam'el (carrier), an unclean animal among the Jews. It is very docile, is ussually six or seven feet high, and is exceedingly strong and patient of labor. The feet of the camel have tough, elastic soles, which prevent them from sinking in the sand. Its stomach will contain a supply of water sufficient for many days. Its food is coarse, such as leaves, twigs, and thistles, and the animal is specially adapted to crossing the deserts. In the East the camel is called the land-ship or ship of the desert. The Arabian species commonly referred to in the Bible has only one hump. The dromedary is a lighter and swifter variety. It has been much used in the East from very early times, Gen. 12:16; Exod. 9:3; Gen. 37:25, for riding, drawing chariots, carrying burdens and messengers, and in war. Camels were formerly, and still are, in the East, among the chief possessions of the rich.

Ca'na, a village of Galilee a few miles north of Nazareth, noted as the scene of Christ's first miracle, John 2:1-11, and of a later one. John 4:46. It was the home of NATHANAEL. John 21:2.

Canaan, ka'nan or ka'na-an (low). [1] The name of the fourth son of Ham, Gen. 10:6; 1 Chron. 1:8, the father of the Canaanites who, before the arrival of the children of Israel, inhabited Canaan. [2] The land stretching from Lebanon on the north to the wilderness of Arabia on the south, and from the Dead Sea on the east to the frontiers of Phoenicia and Philistia on the west, with but little access to the Mediterranean or Great Sea. Abraham dwelt in the land, and it was promised to his descendants. But Jacob left it on account of famine, and went with his sons to Egypt. When the twelve tribes of Israel came out of Egypt under Moses, they found Canaan occupied by the HITTITES, JEBUSITES, AMORITES, and other tribes originally comprised under the common title CANAANITES, and after a terrible war they succeeded, under Joshua, in conquering it.

Canaanite, ka'nan-ite or ka'na-an-ite, a name used in reference to one of the apostles, who is otherwise called ZELOTES, "the zealous." Matt. 10:4; Mark 3:18.

Canaanites, ka'nan-ites or ka'na-an-ites, the national name of the descendants of Canaan, afterward confined to the inhabitants of the land of Canaan.

Candace, kan'da-se, a queen of Ethio-pia, or, according to some, a general title. Acts 8:27.

Can'dle, a word often used in the Bible, Job 18:6; Prov. 31:18; Luke 15:8, for LAMP (which see). (Candles were not known in the East.) The word candle is often used figuratively in the Bible to denote light generally.

Can'dle-stick. The golden "candlestick," or rather lampstand, of the Tabernacle was on the left hand of one entering the Holy Place and opposite the table of shew-bread. It was made of fine gold, and consisted of a stem, supposed to have been five feet high, with six braches. The braches came out a three points, two at each point of the stem, and the width of the whole across the top was about three feet and a half. It was richly ornamented. At the extremity of each branch and at the top of the stem there was a socket for the lamp, making seven in all. The lamps were supplied with pure olive-oil and lighted every evening. In Solomon's Temple there were ten golden "candlesticks" or lampstands. There was but one in the second Temple. It was carried to Rome when Jerusalem was destroyed, and is copied on the triumphal arch of Titus at Rome.

Can'ker-worm, in the Authorized Version of the Bible, is used where the Hebrew word means a kind of locust, perhaps in the larva state. Joel 1:4; Nah. 3:15, 16.

Ca-per'na-um (village of Nahum) is not mentioned in the Old Testament, but frequently in the four Gospels as the home of Jesus after he left Nazareth, and as the scene of many of his miracles and discourses. Matt. 8:5-14; 9:2; 17:24; John 6:17-59; 4:46, etc. It was a city of Galilee, on the shore of the Sea of Galilee, and had a custom-house and a noted synagogue. The site is either at Khan Minyeh or, more probably, at Tell Hum, where there are extensive ruins, including a synagogue.

Cap'tain. [1] The Jewish army had captains of different grades. The captain of the host was the commander of the whole army. Deut. 1:15, etc. [2] The commander of a thousand Roman soldiers. Mark 6:21; Acts 21:31. [3] A leader of Roman soldiers. Luke 22:4. A captain of a hundred soldiers was called a CENTURION. [4] The captain of the Temple, Acts 4:1, was the chief of the priests and Levites who guarded the Temple and its vicinity. In this sense it is applied to Christ in Heb. 2:10.

Where "Captivity" is used in these "Helps," it refers to the Babylonian Captivity.

Car'bun-cle, a precious stone. The term represents two different Hebrew words. The one in Exod. 28:17; 39:10, and in Ezel. 28:13 is generally supposed to mean the emerald or the beryl. The other, in Isa. 54:12, may mean a kind of ruby.

Car'mel (fruitful, place), [1] The name of that mountain-ridge, twelve miles long, which from the western highlands of Palestine juts out into the Mediterranean Sea. It is noted as the scene of the most remarkable events in the history of ELIJAH and ELISHA, and is kept sacred not only by the Jews and Christians, but also by the Mohammedans The Carmelite monks had their first monastery there, and took their name from it. [2] A town where Saul, set up a monument, 1 Sam. 15:12; 25:2, 5, 7, 40, and Uzziah had his vineyards. 2 Chron. 26:10. It was situated in the mountains of Judah, ten miles south-east of HEBRON. It is now called KURMUL.

Car'nal (fleshly), the opposite of spiritual and holy. Rom. 7:14; 1 Cor. 3:3.

Car'pen-ter. The original word signifies artisan or mechanic. When used alone it generally denotes one who works in wood. The trade of a carpenter or worker in wood was followed by Joseph, Matt. 13:55, the reputed father of Jesus, and by Jesus himself. Mark 6:3. Carpenters are often mentioned in the Bible.

Cast'a-way (worthless). 1 Cor. 9:27. Infants in heathen countries are frequently exposed in the fields and allowed to perish. Ezek. 16:5

Cas'tle, in Acts 21: 34, 37; 22:24; 23:10, 16, 32, means the tower of Antonia, which was a fortress at the north-west corner of the Temple in Jerusalem.

Cat'er-pil-lar, an insect of the locust kind in an immature state. They are extremely destructive to vegetation, and were often employed to execute God's judgments. Ps. 78:46; 105:34.

Cath'o-lic (universal), a name originally given to the Christian Church in general, but now claimed by the Roman Catholic Church. The "Catholic epistles"—namely, JAMES, PETER I

AND II. JOHN I and JUDE— are so called because they were addressed to the church in general.

Cause'way, in 1 Chron. 26:16, 18, is supposed to mean the ascent from Zion to the west side of the Temple area.

Ce'dar is used in the Bible in reference to the whole pine tree family, and specially to the cedar of Lebanon, which is a noble evergreen tree, greatly celebrated in the Scriptures. Ps. 92:12; Exek. 31:3-6, etc. Everything about this tree has a strong odor of balsam, and is very pleasant. The wood is exceedingly durable, and was used in the noblest and most costly edifices, including Solomon's Temple.

Cedron, se'dron, a brook in the valley between Jerusalem and the Mount of Olives. John 18:1.

Cen'sus. The Old Testament mentions twelve censuses of the Jews. The first was taken in the third or fourth month after the exodus, and showed that there were 603,550 men. Exod. 38:26. The order for the second numbering was made directly after the Hebrews entered Canaan. Num. 26. King David made the fourth census. 2 Sam. 24:9; 1 Chron. 21:1. The last general census was made at the time of the return. Ezra 2:64; 8: 1-14. The census of Cyrenius (or Quirinius) is mentioned in Luke 2:2.

Cen-tu'ri-on, an officer among the Romans commanding a hundred soliders. Matt. 8:5; Acts 22:25.

Ce'phas (rock), a Syriac surname which Jesus gave to SIMON. John 1:42.

Chaff was separated from the grain in ancient times, by throwing both together against the wind with the winnowing shovel. The wind blew away the chaff and the grain fell to the ground. Notice the figurative use of the word chaff in Ps. 1:4; 35:5.

Chaldea, kal-de'a, a country comprising an area of about 23,000 square miles, occupied the southernmost part of the Mesopotamian plain along the Euphrates, down to the Persian Gulf. Abraham was born there, Gen. 11:31, but its native inhabitants were of Cushite descent. Their principal city was UR; their great hero Nimrod, the son of Cush. The Chaldeans formed very early a great empire, the first of the four grand monarchies of Asia, extending north to the sources of the Euphrates. But B.C. about 1300 this empire was overthrown by the Assyrians, and from that time Chaldea became only a part or province, first of Assyria, afterward of Babylonia; the Chaldeans lost their Cushite nationality and became by amalgamation Shemites. After the establishment of the Babylonian Empire under Nabopalazzar, B.C. 625, CHALDEANS or

CHALDEES became the generally accepted names for the subjects of the empire, Jer. 21:4; Hab. 1:6; Ezek. 23:14, and in the book of Daniel, 1:4; 2:2, etc. the name is evidently applied to only a peculiar portion of the Babylonian people—the learned class.

Cham'ber-lain, 2 Kings 23:11, an officer who has charge of the royal chambers, or the king's lodgings, wardrobes, etc. In Eastern courts eunuchs were commonly thus employed. Esth. 1:10, 12, 15. In Rom. 16:23 the treasurer of the city is probably referred to.

Chameleon, ke'meel'yun, a lizard-like reptile whose color changes with that of objects about it or when its temper is disturbed. It feeds on insects which it catches by darting out its long, sticky tongue. It is mentioned in Lev. 11:30, among the unclean creeping things.

Cham'pion, in ancient warfare, was one who challenged a foe to single combat in the presence of contending armies. The issue of the battle was sometimes staked on such an encounter.

Char'i-ots, mentioned in the Bible, were of two kinds, both of which were two-wheeled and drawn by horses. One kind was used for princes and generals to ride in, Gen. 41:43; 46:29; 2 Kings 5:9; Acts 8:28, or dedicated to idols. 2 Kings 23:11. Another kind was used in war: "chariots of iron," not made of iron, but armed with iron scythes or hooks extending from the ends of the axletrees. An archer or a spearman usually stood by the side of the charioteer as he drove furiously into the battle. Many chariots were used by the army of Pharaoh which pursued the Israelites at the time of the exodus. Exod. 14:28. In Solomon's Song 3:9 "chariot" seems to mean a kind of palanquin.

Char'i-ty (love). The Greek word means love, and is generally so translated.

Charm'ers, people who claim to be able to tame and control serpents even the most venomous kinds. Ps. 58:5; Jer. 8:17.

Cheese is several times mentioned in the Bible, and is now an important article of food in the East. It is generally white, very salt, soft when new, but soon becomes hard and dry. Job. 10:10; 1 Sam.17:18.

Cherith, ke'rith (gorge), a brook or torent which emptied into Jordan from the east, near Jericho. Elijah was commanded to hide himself near it from Ahab, and was there fed by ravens. 1 Kings 17: 3-5.

Cher'ub plural **Cher'u-bim,** beings of unknown nature, but not angels. The word "cherubim" occurs first in Gen. 3:24, where it is applied to the guard placed over Eden after Adam was driven out. Cherubim are the witnesses of God's presence, and representations of them were used in the Tabernacle and Temple. Two golden cherubim stood in the Holy of Holies, upon the mercy-seat in the Tabernacle. Exod. 37:8. Precise directions are given in Exod. 25:18, etc. concerning their material attitude, and position, and they are described in 2 Chron. 3: 10-13, but nothing is said about their shape except that they had wings.

Chittim, kit'tim, or **Kit-tim.** Num. 24:24; Isa. 23:1, 12; Jer. 2:10; Ezek. 27:6; Dan. 11:30. the "isles," "ships," "products," and "people" of Chittim are here mentioned or alluded to, and therefore the name has been supposed to mean the island of CYPRUS. Some think it applies to the islands and coasts west of Palestine.

Christ (anointed), the official name of the long-promised and long-expected Saviour. It is the Greek equivalent to the Jewish MESSIAH. Jesus was his personal name among men during his life on earth, and he is generally so called in the Gospels, while the CHRIST of JESUS CHRIST is generally used in the Epistles.

NAMES, TITLES, AND OFFICES OF CHRIST.

Adam, The Second. 1 Cor. 15:45, 47.
Advocate. 1 John 2:1.
Alpha and Omega. Rev. 1:8
Amen. Rev. 3:14.
Author and Finisher of our faith. Heb. 12:2.
Author of eternal salvation. Heb. 5:9.
Beginning of the creation of God. Rev. 3:14.
Blessed and only Potentate. 1 Tim. 6:15.
Branch. Zech. 3:8.
Bread of God. John 6:33.
Bread of Life. John 6:35.
Captain of Salvation. Heb. 2:10.
Child, Little. Isa. 11:6.
Christ, the. Matt. 16:16.
Corner-stone. Eph. 2:20.
Counsellor. Isa. 9:6.
David. Jer. 30:9; Hos. 3:5.
Day-spring. Luke 1:78.
Deliverer. Rom. 11:26.
Desire of all nations. Hag. 2:7.
Emmanuel. Isa. 7:14; Matt. 1:23.
Everlasting Father. Isa. 9:6.

45

Faithful Witness. Rev. 1:5.
First and Last. Rev. 1:17.
First-begotten of the dead. Rev. 1:5.
God. Isa. 40:9.
God blessed for ever. Rom. 9:5.
Good Shepherd. John 10:11.
Governor. Matt. 2:6.
Great High-Priest. Heb. 4:14.
High-Priest. Heb. 5:10
Holy child Jesus. Acts 4:27.
Holy, the most. Dan. 9:24.
Holy One. Luke 4:34.
Holy Thing. Luke 1:35.
Horn of Salvation. Luke 1:69.
I AM. Exod. 3:14, with John 8:58.
Image of God. 2 Cor. 4:4.
Jehovah. Isa. 26:4.
Jesus. Matt. 1:21.
Just One. Acts 7:52.
King everlasting. Luke 1:33.
King of Israel. John 1:49.
King of the Jews. Matt. 2:2.
King of kings. 1 Tim. 6:15.
Lamb of God. John 1:29.
Lawgiver. Isa. 33:22.
Light of the world. John 8:12.
Light, True. John 1:9.
Lion of the tribe of Judah. Rev. 5:5.
Living stone. 1 Pet. 2:4.
Lord. Matt. 3:3.
Lord God Almighty. Rev. 15:3.
Lord of all. Acts 10:36.
Lord of Glory. 1 Cor. 2:8.
Lord of lords. Rev. 17:14.
Lord our Righteousness. Jer. 23:6.
Maker and Preserver of all things. John 1:3.
Mediator. 1 Tim. 2:5.
Mediator of the new covenant. Heb. 12:24.
Messiah. Dan. 9:25.
Mighty God. Isa. 9:6.
Mighty One of Jacob. Isa. 60:16.
Morning Star. Rev. 22:16.
Nazarene. Matt. 2:23.
Our Passover. 1 Cor. 5:7.

Priest for ever. Heb. 5:6.
Prince. Acts 5:31.
Prince of Life. Acts 3:15.
Prince of Peace. Isa. 9:6.
Prince of the kings of the earth. Rev. 1:5.
Prophet. Deut. 18:15.
Redeemer. Job 19:25.
Righteous, the. 1 John 2:1.
Root and offspring of David. Rev. 22:16.
Root of David. Rev. 5:5.
Ruler in Israel. Mic. 5:2.
Same yesterday, to-day, and for ever. Heb. 13:8.
Saviour. Luke 2:11.
Shepherd and Bishop of souls. 1 Pet. 2:25.
Shepherd in the land. Zech. 11:16.
Shepherd of the sheep, Great. Heb. 13:20.
Shiloh. Gen. 49:10.
Son, a. Heb. 3:6.
Son, the. Ps. 2:12.
Son, My beloved. Matt. 3:17.
Son, only-begotten. John 1:18.
Son of David. Matt. 9:27.
Son of God. Matt. 8:29.
Son of man. Matt. 8:20.
Son of the Highest. Luke 1:32.
Star, bright and morning. Rev. 22:16.
Star and Sceptre. Num. 24:17.
Vine, the. John 15:5.
Vine, true. John 15:1.
Way, Truth, and Life. John 14:6.
Witness, faithful and true. Rev. 3:14.
Wonderful. Isa. 9:6.
Word. John 1:1.
Word of God. Rev. 19:13.

Chris'tians, the name given to the followers of Christ. It was first used, Acts 11:26, at Antioch in Syria, about A.D. 42.

Chron'i-cles, the First and Second Books of, are the thirteenth and fourteenth books of the Old Testament Canon. They give an account of the history of the Jewish people from their origin to their return from the captivity, embracing a period of nearly 3500 years. They were drawn from the same sources as FIRST and SECOND BOOKS OF KINGS, namely, the national diaries and journals and the living popular tradition, but were written from a specific sacerdotal point of view. They date from the time of Ezra or later. They were accepted in the Canon on account of the many additions to the BOOKS OF KINGS which they contain, but as they were of so recent date they were placed among the HAGIOGRAPHA (the holy writings of the Jews).

Chro-nol'o-gy, the method of ascertaining the years when past events took place, and arranging them in order according to dates. The chronology in the Authorized Version of the Bible in the first part of this book is indicated in the marginal notes on each page. The dates are given at the head of every column of notes, and in many cases at other points in it. In these notes, B.C. before a date means before Christ; cir. means about; A.D. means the year of our Lord.

Chry-sop'ra-sus, Rev. 21:20, a precious stone of a greenish color.

Church is the translation of a Greek word (ecclesia) which means an assembly, and denotes in the New Testament [1] a local congregation of Christian believers (as the church in Jerusalem, in Antioch, in Ephesus, in Corinth, in Rome, the churfches in Asia, in Achaia, etc.); [2] the whole body of believers in Christ (as Matt. 16:18; Gal. 1:13; Eph. 1:22; 5:27). In Acts 7:38 church means the congregation of Israelites at Sinai.

Cir-cum-cis'ion, a rite or ceremony of the Jewish religion.

Cis'terns, Prov. 5:15, were common in Judea. Some were merely holes dug in the ground to receive the water from a spring. When these pits were empty there was mire at the bottom. They were used for the most cruel and extreme punishments. Joseph was probably cast into such a pit. Gen. 37:24. see also Ps. 40:2; Jer. 38:6. Other cisterns were of various forms, and were sometimes hewn out of the rock. Large cisterns are found in various parts of Palestine, and were the chief dependence of the people for water; hence the force of the allusion in Jer. 2:13.

Cit'ies of Ref'uge, Num. 35:4, 5, 14, were six of the Levitical cities divinely appointed by the Jewish law as asylums, to which any one was commanded to flee, for safety and protection, who had been undersignedly accessory to the death of a human being. His offence was investigated, and if he was not within the provisions of the law, he was delivered to the avenger, and slain.

Cit'i-zen-ship, Phil. 3:20 (in the Revised Version), is CONVERSATION in the Authorized Version. Roman citizenship is referred to in the New Testament. It denoted the privileges enjoyed by certain Roman subjects in Palestine, and was secured by inheritance or by purchase, Acts 22:28, by military service, by manumission, or by favor, and included the right of appeal unto Caesar. Acts 25:11. Paul was a Roman citizen.

Cit'y of Da'vid, the name frequently given to that part of Jerusalem which was built on Mount Zion.

Clau'di-us, the fourth Roman emperor, A.D. 41-54, was an intimate friend of Herod Agrippa I. Nevertheless, on account of their insubordination and aversion to all rule and discipline, he expelled the Jews from Rome, A.D. 53, and together with them the Christians, who were as yet considered a mere Jewish sect by the Romans. Acts 11:28; 18:2.

Clau'di-us Lys'i-as, a Roman officer who was chief captain of the army in Jerusalem when Paul was laid hold on by the Jews. Acts 23:26.

Clay was used by the ancients in many ways. It was used in sealing, as wax is with us. Job 38:14. A piece of clay was often put on the lock of a storehouse and sealed. Many impressions of seals are found on Babylonian bricks.

Clean and UNCLEAN are words often used in a ceremonial sense in the Bible.

Cleave, in Gen. 2:24; Rom. 12:9. means adhere; remain faithful.

Cle'o-pas, one of the two disciples with whom Jesus conversed on the way to Emmaus, after he had risen from the dead. Luke 24:18. Some consider him same as CLEOPHAS.

Cle'o-phas, the husband of Mary, who is by some supposed to have been a sister of the mother of Jesus. John 19:25.

Cloud, Pil'lar of, the miraculous sign of the divine presence and care which guided the Israelites in the desert.

Cock'a-trice, in Isa. 11:8, etc., is an old English word meaning a kind of crested venomous serpent.

Cock'-crow-ing, Mark 13:35, the third watch of the night in the time of Christ. It was between midnight and daybreak.

Cof'fer, in 1 Sam. 6:8, 11, 15, means a movable box on the side of a cart.

Cof'fin, in Gen. 50:26, means a mummy chest cut out of stone or sycamore-wood. Such coffins were used in burying some noted persons, but not often among the Jews.

Col'o-ny, in Acts 16:12, means a foreign town whose inhabitants were granted, for distinguished services, the same rights and privileges that the citizens of Rome enjoyed.

Co-rinth'i-ans, Second Epistle to the, was written by Paul later in A.D. 57 than the first epistle, and from Macedonia. It was probably caused by the favorable reports Paul had received from Titus and Timothy concerning the effects of the previous epistle. The question of the apostolic authority of his ministry is here treated exhaustively in chapters 1-7.

Corn is the general word used in the English Bible for grain of all kinds known to the Jews. It includes peas and beans, but never means Indian corn (or maize), which was unknown to the Hebrews. Palestine produced large quantites of grain. It was usually reduced to meal by a hand-mill.

Cor-ne'li-us, a Roman centurion dwelling in Caesarea, who was the first Gentile convert to Christianity. Acts chapter 10.

Cor'ner-Stone, a title of Christ. Eph. 2:20; 1 Pet. 2:6.

Cor'net, a curved wind instrument of music. 1 Chron. 15:28; Dan. 3:5,7.

Coun'cil, in Matt. 10:17, means a judicial tribunal. It generally signifies the SANHEDRIM or SANHEDRIN (which see). In Matt. 12:14; Acts 25:12 council means the advisers of Festus, the Roman governor; in Matt. 5:22; Mark 13:9, the lesser Jewish courts.

Coun'sel'lor (judge), a name or title applied to Messiah, by the prophet Isaiah. Isa. 9:6.

Cov'e-nant (league, thing prepared), a word expressing God's gracious purpose toward his people, and also the relation into which they are thereby brought to him. The Old and New Testaments denote the old and new covenants.

Cre-a'tion, the act of God in bringing this world into existence.

Cre'a'tor, the name used in two passages in the Bible to designate God as the Maker of all things. Rom. 1:25; 1 Pet. 4:19.

Crea'ture, in Rom. 1:25; 8:19, etc. means created thing; the creation.

Crete, a large island (now called Candia) in the Mediterrranean, one hundred and forty miles long, thirty-five miles broad, on the route from Syria to Italy, nearly midway between Syria and Malta. Acts 27: 7, 12, 13, 21. Cretans were present at Jerusalem on the day of Pentecost. Acts 2:11. Paul sailed by Crete on his voyage to Rome. Acts 27:7, 13. He left Titus there to take charge of the church, either before or probably after his first Roman captivity. Tit. 1:5. The people were proverbially untruthful.

Crim'son, a deep red color tinged with blue, is a deeper dye than scarlet; hence the force of the figure in Isa. 1:18.

Crisp'ing pins in Isa. 3:22, is not correctly translated. It means a reticule or bag, probably finely decorated.

Cross, an ancient instrument used for capital punishment. After the crucifixion of Christ it became the Christian symbol of redemption. The New Testament gives no indication of the form of the cross on which Christ died. Tradtion uniformly refers to the Roman cross. Other varieties were used. Crucifixion was regarded by the Romans as the basest and most ignominious death. It was an accursed death. Deut. 21:23; Gal. 3:13. As a Christian symbol the cross is in various forms, namely the Roman or Latin cross (+), the Saint Andres's cross (X), the Greek cross (+). A double cross is used by the Pope, and a triple cross is used by the Raskolniks, a Russian sect.

Crown, an emblem of sovereignty worn on the head by kings and queens. It was customary for a king to wear as many crowns as he had kingdoms. Another kind of crown was a sort of headdress or coronet. Newly married persons of both sexes wore crowns. Song of Solomon 3:11; Ezek. 16:12.

Crys'tal, a name applied to one of the most beautiful of precious stones, perfectly transparent, and now known as rock-crystal. It is ranked with gold in value, Job 28:17, and is alluded to in Reve. 4:6; 21:11; 22:1. The same word which is translated crystal in some passages is translated frost in Gen. 31:40, etc. and ice in Job 6:16, etc.

Cu'bit, a measure of different lengths. The common cubit was about eighteen inches. Matt. 6:27; John 21:8.

Cu'cum-bers are abundant in the East, particularly in Egypt. Num. 11:5. The Egyptian cucumber is superior to those of America. The cucumber is common now in Palestine.

Cum'min, a plant much like fennel. An aromatic oil of a warn stimulating nature is produced from its seeds. Isa. 28:25, 27; Matt. 23:23. It was only inferentially included in the law concerning tithes.

Curses are of different kinds.

Cush (black?). [1] The oldest son of Ham, Gen. 10:6, 7, 8; 1 Chron. 1:8, 9, 10, brother of Mizraim, Phut, and Canaan, and, through his five sons, ancestor of the Cushites, who, moving in a south-western direction from Chaldea, through Arabia, crossed the Red Sea and formed an empire in the land south of Egypt, the present Nubia, but then called ETHIOPIA (which see). [2] The name is applied in the original to the people descended from Cush, but in the English Version it is translated ETHIOPIAN. [3] It is frequently used to denote the land where the descendants of Cush lived; in which case it is generally translated ETHIOPIA. Isa. 11:11. [4] A man of the tribe of Benjamin, who appears to have been an enemy of David. Ps. 7, title.

C

Cym'bal, a musical instrument made of two broad convex metal plates, which, when struck together produced a piercing noise. A smaller kind was used on the fingers. Ps. 150:5; 1 Cor. 13:1. Cymbals were used in the Temple and on occasions of public rejoicing.

Cy'press, an evergreen tree resembling the Lombardy poplar in form and size, and seems to have been used for making idols, Isa. 44:14, its wood being very durable. The cypress is thought to be intended in some passages where "fir-tree" occurs.

Cy'prus, a large island of the Mediterranean, one hundred and fifty miles long and fifty miles broad, has played a conspicuous part in history from the time when it was colonized by the Phoenicians, more than a thousand years before Christ, until it, in A.D. 1878, became a British possession. It had two large cities, Salamis at the east and Paphos at the west end, and seventeen towns. Barnabas was a native of Cyprus, and it often mentioned in the the Acts. Acts 4:36; 13:4; 15:39, etc.

Cy'-re'ne was the capital of Libya, that part of northern Africa which lies between Egypt and Carthage. The city was Greek, but since the time of Alexander the Great the Jews held citizenship there on equal terms with the Greeks. They had a synagogue, and many of them accepted Christianity. Matt. 27:32; Acts 2:10; 11:20; 13:1. It was destroyed in the fourth century by the Saracens.

Cy-re'ni-us is the Greek form of the Latin name Quirinius. Publius Sulpicius Quirinius was Roman governor of Syria at the time of the birth of our Lord, Luke 2:2, and probably again. A.D. 6-11, Acts 5:37. During his first term as governor the first taxing or enrollment took place which compelled Mary and Joseph to go to Bethlehem.

Cy'rus (sun), the founder of the last of the great Eastern monarchies, the Persian, allowed the Jews after the conquest of Babylon, B.C. 538, to return home to Judea, to rebuild the Temple and reorganize a national existence on a theocratical basis. He was foretold by Isaiah as the deliverer of Judah. Isa. 44:28; 45: 1-7. The prophet Daniel was highly favored at his court. Dan. 6:28. His reputed tomb is still shown near Murgab.

D

Da'gon (fish), an idol of the Philistines, having the head and hands of a man with the body and tail of a fish. The chief seat of its worship was at ASHDOD. 1 Sam. 5:1-4; 1 Chron. 10:10.

Da-mas'cus, a city of Syria, called by the Arabs the "Eye of the Desert: or the "Pearl of the East," on account of its beautiful location, stands in a fertile plain surrounded by the desert, at the foot of the Anti-Lebanon, at an elevation of twenty-two hundred and sixty feet, one hundred and thiry-three miles north-east of Jerusalem and fifty miles east of the Mediterranean. It is one of the oldest cities in the world, said to have been founded by Uz, a grandson of Shem, and well known to the patriarchs. Gen. 14:15; 15:2. David conquered it, but under Solomon it became an independent kingdom, which was overthrown by Tiglath-pileser, B.C. 732. By the conquest of Persia by Alexander the Great it became a Greek possession, B.C. 333, and by the conquest of Greece by Rome it became a Roman province, B.C. 63. In A.D. 634 it was taken by the Arabs, and as the capital of a large Mohammedan empire it was raised to great splendor. Even under Turkish rule it is still a place of considerable importance, and noted for the unquenchable hatred with which its Mohammedan inhabitants look upon their Christian townsmen, and which in A.D. 1860 caused a frightful massacre. In the New Testament it is often mentioned in the Acts and in the Epistles. The conversion of Paul (then called Saul) took place, Acts 9:1-25, on his journey from Jerusalem to Damascus, A.D. 37, and tradition still points out the spot, at the crossing of the direct road from Jerusalem with that from Banias, where the miracle occurred. Several other places are shown as the scene of that event. The traditional window in the wall through which Paul was let down in a basket, 2 Cor. 11:33, and the houses of Ananias and Judas are also shown.

Dam-na'tion and **Con-dem-na'tion.** At the time when the Authorized Version of the Bible was issued these words were equivalent terms. In Matt. 23:33; John 5:29; Rom. 13:2; 1 Cor. 11:29 the word translated "damnation" means "judgment".

Dan (judge). [1] The name (afterward given) of a place to which Abram pursued the kings who had ravaged Sodom and carried away Lot. Gen. 14:14; Judg. 18:29; 1 Chron. 21:2. It is stated in Judg. 18:29 that a colony of the tribe of Dan settled there and changed the name of the city of which they took possession from Laish to DAN, which was the principal city of the northern part of the territory of the tribe of Dan. Judg. 20:1. It is now called Tel-el-Kady. [2] The fifth son of Jacob, and the first of Bilhah, Rachel's maid. Gen. 30:6; 49:16; 1 Chron. 2:2. [3] The name of the tribe descended from Dan, or the territory they occupied in the land of Canaan. [4] DAN, Ezek. 27:19, may be same as No. 1, but is identified with Dedar by some, and by others with Aden in Arabia.

Dan'cing, among the Jews, was anciently an expression of religious joy and gratitude. It sometimes took place in honor of a conqueror. 1 Sam. 18:6, 7. It also took place on occasions of domestic joy and when the vintage was gathered.

Dan'iel (God is judge). [1] The second son of David by Abigail the Carmelitess. 1 Chron. 3:1. He is called CHILEAB in 2 Sam. 3:3. [2] A priest of the family of Ithamar, the son of Aaron, who went up from Babylon with Ezra. Ezra 8:2; Neh. 10:6. [3] The last of the greater prophets. The prophet DANIEL (called BELTESHAZZAR by the Chaldeans), who was probably born at Jerusalem, Dan. 1:3, 6; 9:24, of noble perhaps of royal descent, and was in early youth carried by Nebuchadnezzar to Babylon, B.C. 604, where, on account of his comeliness and talents, he was educated at the court and for the royal service. Dan. 1:1-4. After interpreting a dream which the king had forgotten, Dan. 2, he was made "ruler of the whole province of Babylon and chief of the governors over all the wise men of Babylon," and he kept the position during the whole reign of Nebuchadnezzar. Under his successor, Belshazzar, he had the wisdom and the courage to interpret the mysterious handwriting on the wall, Dan. 5:25, and under Darius the Median, who took Babylon from Belshazzar, he was made one of the "three presidents" of the empire. One day, however, the king forbade all prayer save unto the king for thirty days, and when Daniel refused to obey he was thrown into the den of lions. Dan. 6:16. But when God delivered him out of this danger he was taken back to the court, retained in his office, and held in still higher esteem. In the third year of the reign of Cyrus he seems to have resigned and retired, perhaps returned to Judea, but of these later years of his life nothing is known. Ezek. 14:14, 20; 28:3; and the book of Daniel.

Dan'iel, the Book of, consists of two parts: the first, comprising chapters 1-6, is historical, and gives the narrative of the life of the author, in many points strongly reminding one of that of Joseph; the second, comprising chapters 7-12, is prophetic, and records his visions. To bring the historical part of the book into harmony with such facts as have been established from other evidences is not difficult, but to interpret rightly the

54

visions of the prophetic part seems to require something of the very spirit of the author himself, and demands, at all events, a much more minute knowledge of those times than we have. It should be noticed, however, that as the deciphering of the Assyrian and Egyptian inscriptions progresses more and more light is thrown upon this, as upon many other portions of the Old Testament. The three apocryphal additions to the Book of Daniel: THE SONG OF THE THREE HOLY CHILDREN, THE HISTORY OF SUSANNA, and the HISTORY OF BEL AND THE DRAGON, which occur for the first time in the Septuagint and thence passed into the Vulgate, have never formed part of the Hebrew Canon of the Old Testament.

Da-ri'us (restrainer) is a common name among the kings of Media and Persia. Those mentioned in the Bible are: [1] Darius the Median, Dan. 5:31, was the son of Ahasuerus. He took Babylon from Belshazzar the Chaldean. Only one year of his reign is spoken of, Dan. 9:1; 11:1, during which Daniel rose to the highest dignity. [2] Darius Hystaspec, B.C. 521-486, confirmed the decree of Cyrus concerning the building of the Temple. Ezra 4:5; Hag. 1:1; Zech. 1:1; 7:1. [3] Darius Cadomannus, Neh. 12:22, the last king of the ancient Persian monarchy, was conquered by Alexander the Great, B.C. 330, and thus the prophecy in Daniel, chapter 8, was fulfilled.

Da'vid (beloved), born at Bethlehem B.C. 1085; died in Jerusalem B.C. 1015, was the youngest of Jesse's eight sons, of the tribe of Judah, and grew up as a shepherd in his father's field. Early in youth he was brought to the court of Saul to soothe the troubled spirit of the king by playing upon the harp, and he was made one of his armor-bearers. After his triumphal contest with GOLIATH (which see) he was even made a chieftain and married the king's daughter, Michal, but the brooding suspicion and open jealousy of Saul made life at the court dangerous to David, and he was at last compelled to flee for his life. He sought refuge in the cave of Adullam, 1 Sam. 22:1, and there gradually gathered a somewhat mercenary company around him, which, however, his craft and power of command enabled him to sway and by which he began a contest with Saul. After the battle of Gilboa, in which Jonathan fell and Saul slew himself, David was recognized king and took up his residence at Hebron. There he reigned for seven and a half years, but after the death of Isbosheth, a son of Saul, who exercised regal authority over the ten tribes, he became the sole king of all the Israelites, and then he moved his residence from Hebron to Jeruslaem, which he made the political and religous capital of the Jewish nation. He enlarged the city, adorned it with many new buildings, fortified it, and laid the plan for a magnificent temple to take the place of the Tabernacle. In Jerusalem he reigned thrity-three years, and his reign was a period of rapid development and great splendor. In spite of his many domestic troubles—not incidental, but the sure results of his own faults—in spite of the insurrections of his own sons Absalom and Adonijah, he succeeded in consolidating the twelve tribes of Israel into one compact nation and in subjugating the foreign tribes or peoples living in and around Palestine. Every year the whole people assembled in Jerusalem to celebrate the Passover, and when David died he was able to leave his crown and his treasures undisputed to his son Solomon. He was buried in Jerusalem, and his tomb, still pointed out on Mount Zion, became the sepulchre of the subsequent kings and one of the sacred places of the people. David was one of the grandest and most brilliant characters of all human history, notwithstanding the small corner of the earth which was the field of his activity. No deed of human intrepidity has surpassed his encounter with the Philistine giant; no story of human affection is more famous or more touching than that of the friendship of David and Jonathan; no poems have ever so powerfully appealed to the hearts and souls of men as his psalms; and his wisdom as a ruler and his energy and valor as a commander raised a small. disorderly, disorganized, and half-subdued nation to the rank of a powerful kingdom. As a king he forms the central figure in the history of the Jews; as the author of some of the PSALMS (which see) his name is the grandest in Hebrew literature; and in his kingly character, notwithstanding all his faults and shortcomings, he is the type of symbol of the MESSIAH (which see). David was the ancestor of Joseph, the husband of Mary, Christ's mother. In Ezek. 34:23, 24 and Hos. 3:5 the word David is applied to the Messiah.

Day, a word used with various meanings. The Sabbath day of the Hebrews commenced in the evening. Lev. 23:32. The time when the sun is above the horizon was generally divided by the sacred writers into twelve hours. The sixth hour always ends at noon, and the twelfth hour is the last hour before sunset. The word day is often used for an undetermined period.

Day's Journey. An ordinary day's journey, in Bible times, was what was usually travelled on camel or horseback or about twenty-five or thirty miles. A Sabbath day's journey was nearly a mile. Matt. 24:20; Acts 1:12.

Deemed, in Acts 27:27, means concluded.

Deep, in Luke 8:31; Rom.10:7, means the abyss where lost spirits await their final doom. The same word is translated bottomless pit in Rev. 9:1, 2, 11: 7; 20: 1,3.

De-gree, in 1 Tim. 3:13, means an advance in spiritual life.

De-grees', a word which occurs in the titles of several Psalms. The meaning of it is unknown. Ps. 120-134, both inclusive. Degrees of another but unknown kind are mentioned in 2 Kings 20: 9, 10, 11 in connection with dial.

Delaiah, del-a-i'ah (Jehovah is deliverer). [1] Head of the twenty-third temple-course of priests in the time of David. 1 Chron. 24:18. [2] Founder of a family who, on their return from captivity, could not prove their genealogy. Ezra 2:60; Neh. 7:62. [3] Father of Shemaiah. Neh. 6:10. [4] A prince of Judah in the time of King Jehoiakim. Jer. 36:12, 25.

De-li'lah (languishing), a woman of the Philistines, who, being beloved by Samson, betrayed him to his enemies. Judg.16:4-18

Del'uge, the, occurred B.C. 2500 and was a judgment upon the world for the wickedness of its inhabitants. For one hundred and fifty days the waters, rose, until they stood fifteen cubits (about twenty-two feet) over the highest summits, and all human beings, save Noah and his family, perished. On the injunction of God, Noah built the ark, and place therein, besides himself, his wife, and their sons with their wives, one pair of all land-animals. When the waters subsided the ark rested on Mount Ararat in Armenia, and when the dove sent out by Noah returned with an olive-leaf in its bill, all went out of the ark; the earth was dry and inhabitable again. The record of the flood in Genesis 6-8 is almost identical with that which has been deciphered from the Assyrian tablets, and very much like the records found in Chinese literature or among the Indians of Peru and Mexico.

De'mas. [1] A disciple at Rome with Paul. Col. 4:14; Philemon 24. [2] Supposed to be the same as No. 1. 2 Tim. 4:10.

De-me'tri-us. [1] A silversmith at Ephesus who opposed Paul. Acts 19: 24, 38. He was a manufacturer of silver shrines, small temples, and images of DIANA (which see). [2] A convert of whom nothing is recorded except the consistency of his character. 3 John 12.

Des'o-late, applied by Isaiah to the land of Judah while under the displeasure of the Lord on account of the rebellion of its people. Isa. 62:4.

Dev'il, Dev'ils. Devils, in the New Testament, is often used

57

for demons, or evil spirits, as in the phrases "possessed with devils" and "cast out devils."

Dev'ils, the name of certain idols worshipped by the Israelites while they were in Egypt, and also of those set up by Jeroboam. Lev. 17:7; Ps. 106:37. The original is translated satyrs in Isa. 13:21; 34:14.

Di-an'a, a heathen goddess extensively worshipped by the Greeks, had her most magnificent temple at Ephesus. It was one of the seven wonders of the world, four hundred and twenty-five feet long, two hundred and twenty feet broad, and had one hundred and twenty-seven columns sixty feet high. It was the treasury of the Pan-Ionian League, and the worship around the statue of the goddess was celebrated with great splendor. Small silver models of the temple enclosing the image of the goddess were spread all over the world, and her worship was so earnest by her devotees that the preaching of Paul in Ephesus led to a great uproar. Acts 19: 23-40.

Dis-cern'ing of Spir'its, in 1 Cor. 12:10, means a miraculous gift of the Holy Ghost, by virtue of which the spirits of men were tried to show whether they were of God.

Dis-ci'ple. [1] The title given to those who afterward became apostles, and to all others who professed to be followers of Jesus. [2] Those who were baptized by John the Baptist, and followed his teaching.

Di'ves is found in the Latin Version of the Bible, but not in the Authorized Version. It refers to the rich man in the parable. Luke 16: 19-31.

Div-i-na'tion, the pretended divining or foretelling of future events.

Di-vorce', Deut. 24:1-4, was tolerated by Moses. It was limited by Christ to the case of adultery. Matt. 5:32; 19:3-9.

Doc'tors, Luke 2:46, or teachers of the law of Moses, were highly esteemed by the Jews, and were usually, perhaps always, of the sect called Pharisees.

Dor'cas or **Tab'i-tha** (gazelle), a charitable female disciple at Joppa whom Peter miraculously restored to life. Acts 9:36-40.

Do'than (two cisterns), a place near Mount Gilboa, Gen. 37:17, where Joseph found his brethren and where Elisha lived. 2 Kings 6:13. It was five miles south-west of Jenin and in the plain of Jezreel. Many cisterns hewn in the rock are still found there, which are thought to resemble the "pit," Gen. 37:24, into which Joseph was cast. Caravans on their way from Damascus to Egypt still pass this place.

E

Ea'gle, an unclean bird, Lev. 11:13; Deut 14:12, is often referred to in the Bible.

Ear'nest, a part paid beforehand, under a contract, as a pledge and security for the whole. It is of the same kind with the thing promised. 2 Cor. 1:22; 5:5; Eph. 1:14.

Ear'rings. Earrings were worn by both sexes in bible times, Exod. 32:2, and that fashion is often followed now in the East.

Earth, a term used in Scripture to denote—[1] The earth as distinguished from the heavens. Gen. 1:1. [2] The land as distinguished from the sea. Gen. 1:10. [3] A particular country or land; and in this case it is so translated. Gen. 2:11; 12:1.

East, a word used by the Hebrews for all countries around and beyond the rivers Tigris and Euphrates. Gen. 28:14. Also the country east or south-east of Mount Ararat. Gen. 11:2.

East'er was originally the festival of Eostre, an Anglo-Saxon goddess, and in Acts 12:4 is a mistranslation for PASSOVER. Easter is now observed by many Christians in commemoration of our Saviour's resurrection, which occurred just after the PASSOVER and about the same time of the year as the heathen festival of Eostre, mentioned above.

Ec-cle-si-as'tes, Hebrew Koheleth, **the Preach'er,** is a collection of experiences, impressions, and ideas derived from the contemplation of the follies of life, and consequently sad and almost depressing in its character, but nevertheless carrying with it a moral inspiration toward goodness and godliness as the chief end of life. According to an old tradition it was written by Solomon, and if so it corresponds to his old age as the SONG OF SOLOMON does to his youth and PROVERBS to his manhood. It contains the lesson of the life of Solomon.

E'den (delight). [1] The home of Adam and Eve before their fall; probably situated either in the highlands of Armenia or in the valley of the Euphrates, but notwithstanding the definite description in Gen. 2:8-15 its exact location has not yet been identified. [2] A son of Joah. 2 Chron. 29:12. [3] One of the Levites who, in the time of Hezekiah, were appointed to distribute the gifts among their brethren. 2 Chron. 31:15. May be same as No. 2.

E'dom (red). [1] A name given to the elder son of Isaac in a few passages. Gen. 25:30; 36;1, 8, 19. [2] The word is also used to designate both the people who descended from Esau and the country in which they lived; but the latter is sometimes called IDUMEA (which see).

E'gypt is the Greek name of the land which the Hebrews called MIZR, or more frequently, using the dual form with reference to the distinction between Upper and Lower Egypt, MIZRA'IM, and which the natives themselves called CHAM or KHEM, "black," the black country. It consists of a long valley, from six to sixteen miles wide, which the Nile has excavated in the high, stony plateau occupying the north-eastern corner of Africa, and which it has covered with its black deposit, which is the source of all Egypt's fertility. Lower Egypt, or Egypt proper, extends from the Mediterranean, 31° 37" north latitude, to the first cataract of the Nile, 24° 2" north latitude. On the south side of this cataract a high sandstone ledge between Upper and Lower Egypt crosses the whole valley of the Nile. At 30° north latitude the rocky plateau recedes on both sides of the river, and here the Nile spreads out its delta, the eastern part of which forms the province of GOSHEN (which see).

Upper Egypt is the present Nubia, which includes part of ancient Ethiopia and consists of a series of elevated plains, forming terraces over which the Nile descends between low mountain-ranges. Its soil is cultivable only in the valley of the Nile, which is much narrower here than in Lower Egypt. The climate is extremely hot. Both soil and climate contribute to make Egypt one of the most productive regions on earth. For centuries this land was the granary of the Roman Empire—or of the then civilized world—and long before there was any Roman Empire the nomadic tribes of Asia, when suffering from famine, used to go to Egypt for food: for instance, the visits of Abram and the sons of Jacob. Gen. 12:10; 42:3; 43:2. Not only cereals were produced there in abundance, but also fruits and vegetables of excellent quality, and all kinds of animals for food, such as cattle, sheep, swine, poultry, game, etc. The Israelites found it difficult to forget the fleshpots of Egypt, Exod. 16:3, and its melons, cucumbers, onions, etc. Num. 11:5. This productiveness of the country, together with its protected location, surrounded, as it was, on three sides by almost impenetrable deserts and on the fourth by the sea, made it a suitable home for the young race to grow in, and, indeed, in Egypt mankind made its first and one of its grandest attempts in civilization. When Joseph settled his brethren in Goshen the Egyptians had large and magnificent cities, an elaborate social organization, with a fully developed kingship, hierarchy, military establishment, and temples and palaces, the ruins of which fill the spectator with wonder and awe.

Egyptian history has been studied with great energy and marvellous results during the last century, but the end is still far away: namely, a complete view of the structure and development of this civilization. The sources are few and precarious. They consist of half-ruined monuments with inscriptions half blotted out, incidental scraps of documents found in the temples or the sepulchres, and notices given by foreigners, Greeks and Hebrews. The first two sources, the inscriptions and the documents, were for a long time utterly inaccessible, as the language in which they were written was not understood and the method by which that language was reduced to writing, the hieroglyphics, was not known. Champolion, the French Egyptologist, 1790-1832, found the key to the latter, and thereby also to the former, and then the deciphering began. But is slow work, and the combination of the small bits of information thus gained is liable to many mistakes. Among the notices found in the Greek literature were some extracts from the historical work of Manetho. He was supreme potiff at the temple of Hieropolis, and was commissioned by Ptolemy Philadelphus, who died B.C. 247, to write the history of Egypt, based upon the archives of the temples. He wrote his work in Greek, but it is lost, and only fragments of it have come down to us through Josephus, Africanus, and Eusebius, among which are his tables of the thirty dynasties that ruled over Egypt before its conquest by Alexander the Great, B.C. 332. Formerly the notices of Egypt contained in the Bible an in Herodotus were considered by many as fables, but they have been verified by modern discoveries.

The most difficult question with respect to the relation between Biblical and Egyptian history is one of chronology. But it must not here be overlooked that not only the Egyptian chronology before the Greek conquest but also the Biblical before Solomon are still in an unsettled state and prehaps not yet rightly understood. One point, however, and that a very important one, has been satisfactorily settled. Egyptian historians speak generally of the exodus of the Israelites as the expulsion of a rebellious tribe which was under the leadership of a Heliopolitan priest, Osarsiph, who afterward assumed the name of Moses, and state that the event took place under a king whose father's name was Rameses and whose son's name was Sethos. But in the list of Manetho there is no other king who fits this description but Menephtha, belonging to the nineteenth dynasty, the son of Rameses II. and the father of Setho II. He should also be the king of the exodus and Rames II the king of the oppression, and so they are. Rameses II was by far the greatest king of the nineteenth dynasty, and, so to speak, the culminating star of Egyptian power. No wonder, then, that he is very well known to us from the monuments. In the summer of 1881 his mummy, together with a number of papyrus rolls and objects of value, was discovered in a cave near Thebes in a perfect state of preservation, resting in a mummy-case of sycamore-wood, carved to represent him as the god Osiris, wrapped in shrouds of rose-colored and yellow linen, with the arms crossed upon the breast, the right hand holding the royal whip and the left the royal hook, and with an inscription on the bands which pass across the shrouds to keep them in place stating that the body enclosed was that of Rameses II. Among the exploits of this famous king was the construction of the great canal in Goshen, by which communication between the Nile and the Red Sea was finally completed; and building at its eastern and western terminations the two cities of Pi-Rameses and Pi-tum. But, according to Exod. 1:11, it was just the task of building those two cities, whose names are spelled Pithom and Rameses in the Bible, which filled the measure of oppression to overflowing and roused the Israelites to rebellion. With respect to Menephta, the king of the ten plagues and of the frightful disaster in the Red Sea, there is something connected with his name, not only in Egyptian history, but even in the notes of Herodotus, which reads like confused reminiscences of those events, and of the history of Joseph many traits have been distinctly verified by Egyptian discovery. The relations between the Israelites and the Egyptians after the exodus are of less interest. There has, however, lately been deciphered an inscription on the walls of the great temple at Karnak recording the capture of Jerusalem and the conquest of Judea by Shishak. 1 Kings 14:26. In this inscription is found a figure painted with very prominent Jewish features and with the superscription in Egyptian characters, "The king of Judah." The predictions of the prophets concerning the downfall of the Egyptian power are very remarkable, especially those of Isaiah and Daniel.

E'hud (strong). [1] A son of Gera who slew Eglon and delivered the Israelites from the oppression of the Moabites. He was one of the judges in Israel. Judg. 3:15, 16. [2] A grandson of Jediael. 1 Chron. 7:10. [3] A descendant of Benjamin. 1 Chron. 8:6. May be same as No. 1.

El (strength), a name of God. It is very often a part of proper names, such as Bethel, Elijah, Eloi.

E'lam-ites, dwellers in Elam. Ezra 4:9; Acts 2:9.

El-beth'el (God of the house of God), the name which Jacob gave to the place where God appeared to him when he fled from Esau. Gen. 35:7.

Eld'ers. [1] Men among the Jews invested with authority (probably as counselors or judges), and so named on account of their age. Matt. 15:2; Mark 7:3; Luke 7:3. [2] An official designation of those appointed to rule and teach in the church, interchangeably with "overseer," or "bishop." Acts 11:30; 1 Tim. 5:1; Rev. 4:4; 11:16.

E'li (Jehovah is high). The high-priest and judge of Israel who immediately preceded Samuel. Consult the CONCORDANCE.

E'li, E'li, lama sabachthani? sa-bak-tha'ni, Matt. 27:46, or **Elo'i, Elo'i, lama sabachtha'ni?** Mark 15:34, the exclamation uttered by Christ on the cross, expressive of the acuteness of his sufferings and his horror at the hiding of his Father's countenance.

E-li'as, Matt. 11:14; Mark 6:15; Luke 1:17; John 1:21, the Greek form of ELIJAH (which see).

E-li-e'zer (God is help). [1] A man of Damascus who was steward of Abram's house. Gen. 15:2. [2] A son of Moses. Exod. 18:4; 1 Chron. 23:15. [3] A son of Becher. 1 Chron. 7:8. [4] A priest who assisted in bringing up the ark out of the house of Obed-edom. 1 Chron. 15:24. [5] Ruler of the tribe of Reuben in the time of David. 1 Chron. 27:16. [6] A prophet who prophesied against Jehoshophat. 2 Chron. 20:37. [7] A chief man who went with Ezra from Babylon to Jerusalem. Ezra 8:16. [8] A priest who took a foreign wife. Ezra 10:18. [9] A Levite who took a foreign wife. Ezra 10:23. [10] A Jew of the sons of Harim who took a foreign wife. Ezra 10:31. [11] An ancestor of Joseph, the husband of Mary. Luke 3:29.

E-li'jah (my God is Jehovah), Greek ELIAS. Matt. 17:3. [1] A native of Thisbeh, in the highlands of Gilead, east of the Jordan, between Bashan and Moab. Although he wrote nothing, he stands out in the history of Israel as the greatest among the prophets. By his solitary life, far away from the noise of the world but close to God, and his sudden appearance with the message from the Lord, coming and going like the lightning on the sky; by the fearful promptness with which his prophecies of the drought, the doom of Ahab, the death of Ahaziah, etc. were fulfilled; by such deeds as the destruction by fire of the idolatrous prophets on Mount Carmel, the stopping of the drought by prayer, the destruction by fire of the soldiers sent against him, etc., he made an indelible impression on his age, which is renewed whenever the story of his life and death is read again. 1 Kings chaps. 17-21; 2 Kings chaps. 1,2; 2 Chron. 21:12-15. In the New Testament he is mentioned as the prototype of John the Baptist and as present together with Moses at the transfiguration of Christ. Luke 9:28-35. [2] A Jew, apparently of the sons of the priests, who had taken a foreign wife during or after the captivity. Ezra 10:21.

E-lis'a-beth (worshipper of God), the wife of Zacharias and mother of John the Baptist. Luke 1:5, 41.

E-li'ud (God his praise), an ancestor of Joseph, the husband of Mary. Matt. 1:14, 15.

E-li'za-phan (God is protector). [1] A Levite of the sons of Kohath. Num. 3:30; 1 Chron. 15:8. [2] Prince of Zebulun in the time of Moses. Num. 34:25.

Elm. Hos.4:13 The Original is translated elsewhere as Oak.

E'lon-beth'-ha-nan. 1 Kings 4:9. These words, which mean the oak or terebinth tree of the house of Hanan, are taken to be the full name of the town called ELON in Josh. 19:43.

E'lul (the gleaning month), the sixth month of the ecclesiastical year of the Jews, beginning with the new moon of September. It is the twelfth month of their civil year. Neh. 6:15.

Em-balm'ing, or preserving from decay the bodies of the dead, was practised by the Egyptians at a very early period. The Hebrews learned the art from them, and made use of it occasionally in a less effectual way. The bodies of Jacob and Joseph were embalmed in Egypt.

Em'e-rald, a precious stone of a pure green color, to which it owes its chief value. Exod. 28:18; Rev. 4:3.

Em-man'u-el, Matt. 1:23, a name applied in the New Testament to the MESSIAH. In the Old Testament the word IMMANUEL is used with the same meaning.

Em'ma-us (hot spring), a village about seven miles from Jerusalem, where Christ appeared to two of his disciples on the day of his resurrection. Luke 24:13. Its exact location is unknown.

En'-dor (fountain of Dor), a town where the woman lived whom King Saul consulted as having a familiar spirit. 1 Sam.28:7-25. Endor was on the northern slope of Little Mount Hermon, eighteen miles south-east of Acre.

En-gra'ver, a carver in wood or stone, as well as an engraver on precious metals. Exod. 35:35; 38:23. The art of engraving in its various forms was well known to the ancient Egyptians.

E'noch or **He'noch** (teacher). [1] A son of Cain. Gen. 4:17, 18. [2] the name given by Cain to a city which he built. Gen.

4:17. [3] The son of Jared and father of Methuselah. Gen 5:18, 21. He is called in Jude 14 "the seventh from Adam," to distinguish him from Enoch the son of Cain. He is said to have "walked with God," Gen. 5:22, and was translated to heaven—"God took him." Gen. 5:24.

En-treat'ed, in Gen. 12:16; Acts 27:3, means treated. In Isa. 19:22 it means prevailed upon.

E'phah, a measure for things dry, equal in capacity to the BATH, used for things liquid. It contained about three pecks and a half. Exod. 16:36; Lev. 5:11.

E'phah (obscurity). [1] A son of Midian and grandson of Abraham. The name is apparently also applied to the district where he settled or to his posterity. Gen. 25:4; Isa. 60:6. [2] The concubine of Caleb the son of Hezron. 1 Chron. 2:46. [3] A son of Jahdai. 1 Chron. 2:47.

E-phe'sians, the E-pis'tle of Paul to the, was, like that to the Colossians, which it resembles somewhat, written from Rome when Pual was a prisoner, between A.D. 61 and 63. It was not called forth by any special event, but was apparently written simply for the purpose of generally fortifying the Christian faith and practice of the church at Ephesus. The Epistle, aside from the brief beginning and ending, is in two parts: 1. Chapters 1-3. A very feeling exposition of Christian doctrine, especially of eternal election to holiness and salvation by Christ. 2. Chapters 4-6. An exhortation to apply the doctrines of Christianity to the duties of active life. The Epistle gives the fullest exposition of Paul's sublime idea of the Church as "the body of Christ, the fulness of him that filleth all in all" (1:23). It was a circular letter intended for all the churches of Asia Minor.

Eph'e-sus, now a desolate heap of ruins, thirty-five miles south-east of Smyrna, was in Paul's time the principal commerical city of Asia Minor, wealthy, elegant, and licentious, and the capital of the Ionian Confederacy, which had its treasury in the temple of Diana. That building was one of the wonders of the world, and looked upon by the whole Ionian race as Solomon's Temple was by the Jews. Thus the city was at once a centre of wealth and a centre of idolatry. Paul visited it twice, Acts 18:19-21 and Acts 19;1, and the last time he spent three years there. Afterward the Ephesian church was in charge of Timothy. It is addressed in Rev. 2:1-7. The excavations of J.T. Wood (1863 to 1874) have brought to light remains of the temple of Diana, the theatre, the circus, and interesting Greek and Latin inscriptions. A railroad has been built from Smyrna to Ephesus by an English company.

Eph'pha-tha, a Syriac word which means "be opened." It is the word spoken by Christ when he cured one that was deaf and dumb. Mark 7:34.

E'phra-im (doubly fruitful). [1] Joseph's second son by his wife Asenath. He was born in Egypt, Gen 41:52, and although younger than Manasseh he was regarded with special favor. He was one of the Hebrew patriarchs and the founder of one of the twelve tribes of Israel. [2] As in the case of the other tribes of Israel, the word is often used to denote the tribe which sprang from Ephraim or the territory which they occupied. [3] A city belonging to Benjamin. 2 Sam. 13:23; John 11:54. Supposed to be the same as EPHRAIN. [4] The name of one of the gates of Jerusalem. 2 Kings 14:13; Neh. 12:39. [5] Ephraim, Wood of. The name of a woody and rugged district in Gad. It is supposed to have been so named from the slaughter of the Ephraimites recorded in Judg. 12, which took place near it. 2 Sam. 18:6.

Epicureans, ep-i-ku-re'ans or ep-i-ku'-re-ans, a sect of philosophers founded by Epicurus of Attica. They were essentially atheists, and made pleasure the object of life. Acts 17:18.

E-pis'tles, the inspired letters addressed by the apostles or first preachers of Christianity to churches or individuals. Thirteen were by Paul, three by John, two by Peter, one by James, one by Jude, and the one to the Hebrews, which is anonymous.

E-ras'tus. [1] A Christian, apparently of Ephesus, whom Paul sent into Macedonia. Acts 19:22; 2 Tim. 4:20. [2] The chamberlain of Corinth who was converted under Paul's preaching. Rom. 16:23.

E-sau (hairy). [1] The elder son of Rebekah, the wife of Isaac. He sold his birthright to Jacob, his twin brother for a mess of red pottage, Gen. 25:30-33, and in a few passages in the Bible is called EDOM. He was the progenitor of the Edomites. [2] The name is sometimes, but not often used to denote the people who sprang from him or the country they dwelt in. Deut. 2:5; Obad. verse 6.

Es-chew', in 1 Pet. 3:11, means avoid.

Essenes, es-seenz', **The,** formed a small party of mystical and ascetic character among the Jews in the time of our Lord. They are not mentioned in the New Testament, and disappeared after the destruction of Jerusalem. Some theologians have supposed that the heresay combated by Paul in the Epistle to the Colossians was of Essenic origin.

Es-tate', in 1 Chron. 17:17; Esth. 1:19; Luke 1:48; Rom. 12:16; Jude 6, means a settled condition in life. In Mark 6:21;

Acts 22:5 it means a special class of men.

Esther, es'ter (star), Hebrew HADASSAH (the myrtle), a young Jewess of great beauty and careful education, an orphan child of the tribe of Benjamin adopted by her cousin Mordecai, became, in B.C. 479, the wife of Ahasuerus—that is, Xerxes—the king of Persia, and was by her position enabled to deliver the whole race to which she belonged from an overwhelming danger. Haman, the favorite and intimate counsellor of the king, had obtained from him a permit to kill all the Jews in the kingdom. Through Mordecai, whom Haman had persecuted with bitter hatred, Esther became aware of what was going on, and at the risk of her life succeeded in getting permission from Ahasuerus for the Jews to defend themselves on the appointed day of slaughter and to take vengeance on all who molested them. Haman was hanged and Mordecai took his place. In memory of this event the Purim feast was instiued by the Jews and each year celebrated with great rejoicing and gayety.

Esther, es'ter, **Book of,** is the record of the wonderful incidents of her life, some of which are mentioned in the above account of her. It reads like a novel. Of its truth, however, there can be no doubt. The existence of the Purim festival as part of the religious ritual of the nation is an incontestable evidence of the truth of the narrative, and its details correspond very closely to what is known from other sources about Xerxes and the Persian court. One peculiarity of the book deserves special mention: the name of God does not occur in it. The reason for this singular omission is probably that the festival at which the book was to be read aloud was one of national rather than religious character, and, at all events, one of gayety and glee. When it is remembered how cautious the Jews were of using the name of God the omission seems quite natural. Its author is unknown.

E'than (ancient). [1] An Israelite renowned for his wisdom. 1 Kings 4:31; Ps. 89, title. [2] A son of Zerah, the son of Judah. 1 Chron. 2: 6, 8. [3] A descendant of Gershon, the son of Levi. 1 Chron. 6:42. [4] A descendant of Merari, the son of Levi. 1 Chron. 6:44; 15:19.

E-thi-o'pi-a,[1] called **Cush** by the Hebrews and often **Me'roe** by the Greeks, included Nubia, and was situated between Egypt on the north and Abyssinia on the south. Comprised also Sennaar and Kordofan. It partakes to some extent of the character of Egypt, but it is higher, reaching at the frontier of Abyssinia an elevation of eight thousand feet, and more rolling and mountainous. It was inhabited by the Cushites, a Hamitic people, not Negroes. About one thousand years before Christ they formed there a mighty empire and developed a high civilization. In the eighth century B.C. an Ethiopian dynasty ruled in Egypt, and afterward it often shared in the destinies of that empire. It was conquered by the Persians B.C. 536, by the Greeks B.C. 330, and by the Romans B.C. 22, when Augustus defeated Candace, queen of Ethiopia, and made her country tributary to Rome. In the Old Testament Ethiopia is often mentioned in connection with Egypt. Moses married an Ethiopian woman. Num.12:1. There were Ethiopians in the army of Shishak. 2 Chron. 12:3, etc. It is also mentioned in the New Testament. Acts 8: 27-38. [2] This name is sometimes used to denote the people who dwelt in Ethiopia or Cush. Ps. 68:31; Nah. 3:9.

Eunice, u-ni'se or u'nis, the mother of Paul's disciple, Timotheus. 2 Tim. 1:5.

Eunuch, u'nuk. [1] A person employed by Eastern kings to take charge of the beds and lodging-rooms and of the secluded princesses. 2 Kings 9:32. [2] An officer of a court in general. Acts 8:27.

Eu-phra'tes, The (the abounding), the largest river of Western Asia, rises on the northern side of Mount Ararat in Armenia, runs in a south-easterly direction and discharges its waters into the Persian Gulf after a course of seventeen hundred and eighty miles and after uniting near its mouth with the Tigris. It is mentioned as one of the rivers of Eden, Gen. 2:14, and often afterward in the Old Testament, and is frequently called simply "the river," sometimes "the great river." On its banks stood Babylon.

Eutychus, u'tikus, a young man of Troas whom Paul restored to life after he had fallen from a window and been taken up dead. Acts 20:9.

E-van'gel-ist, in Acts 21:8; Eph. 4:11; 2 Tim. 4:5, means one who announces good tidings. The writers of the four gospels are called "the evangelists." Evangelists were a special class of religious teachers who preached the gospel wherever they were called.

Ev-er-last'ing Fa'ther, one of the titles or names given to Messiah by the prophet Isaiah. Isa. 9:6.

Ex-com-mu-ni-ca'tion, deprivation of church privileges.

Ex'o-dus, the Book of, the second Book of the Old Testament, contains the Ten Commandments and the story of the escape of the children of Israel from their bondage. It is the second book of the PENTATEUCH (which see).

Ex'or-cists, in Acts 19:13, means those who pretended to cast out devils by adjuring.

Eye-ser'vice, in Eph. 6:6, means service done only under supervision.

E-ze'ki-el (strength of God), the third of the greater prophets and a comtemporary of Jeremiah, was a son of a priest, Buzi and was born and educated in Judea, but was in B.C. 598, eleven years before the destruction of Jerusalem, carried into captivity by Nebuchadnezzar and settled in a Jewish community on the river Chebar in Chaldea. In B.C. 595 he began his prophetic ministration and continued for twenty-two years, till B.C. 573. We know that he had a house, Ezek. 8:1, lost his wife suddenly, Ezek. 24:16-18, conversed intimately with the elders of the community, Ezek. 8:1; 11:25 etc., and tradition adds that he was murdered, and points out his tomb near Bagdad.

E-ze'ki-el, Book of, consists of two parts: the first, chapters 1-24, written before the fall of Jerusalem, and the second, chapters 25-48, written after that event. They differ with respect to their contents, but not in reference to their character. Ezekiel was the son of a priest and a priest himself. His visions and prophecies are clear and unmistakable in their general bearing, but their details are often very obsure and many of his symbols and allegories were not understood until the modern excavations at Nineveh and Babylon brought to light those winged lions and human-headed bulls. The Jews reckoned his book among those which should not be read before the age of thirty. The grandest portion of it is the vision of the new Temple, the fulfilment of the Messianic promises, the church of Christ—chapters 40-48.

E'zer (help). [1] A descendant of Judah through Caleb, the son of Hur. 1 Chron. 4:4. Supposed to be the same as Ezra, 1 Chron. 4:17, but uncertain. [2] A descendant of Ephraim. 1 Chron. 7:21. [3] One of the valiant men of Gad. 1 Chron. 12:9. [4] A Jew who repaired part of the wall of Jerusalem after the captivity. Neh. 3:19. [5] A priest who officiated in purifying the rebuilt wall of Jerusalem. Neh. 12:42.

Ez'ra (help). [1] A Jewish priest and scholar living in Babylon, who obtained from the Persian king Artazerxes Longimanus not only permission to lead a large company of Jewish exiles back to Jerusalem, B.C. 457, but substantial assistance in the undertaking. After a journey of four months he arrived at Jerusalem and then undertook those reforms, especially in the intermarriage with foreign women, and that reorganization of public worship which have made his life a new departure in the history of the Jews. Of his later life nothing is known, but Jewish tradition credits him with the establishment of the Old Testament Canon, the founding of the Great Synagogue, the introduction of Chaldee characters instead of the old Hebrew, and the authorship of the books of EZRA, NEHEMIAH, and CHRONICLES. [2] A descendant of Judah, apparently through Caleb, the son of Jephunneh. 1 Chron. 4:17.

Ezra, the Book of, is in two parts: the first, chapters 1-6, narrates the return of the fifty thousand under Zerubbabel in the reign of Cyrus, and the second, chapters 7-10, the return of the colony under Ezra. The book may be considered a continuation of CHRONICLES. Of the authorship of the BOOK OF EZRA there can be no reasonable doubt. There exist "Two Books of Esdras," the Greek name of Ezra, and they have by some been ascribed to him, but they do not exist in Hebrew, and have never been recognized as authoritative by the Jews.

F

Fa'ble. The Old Testament contains two fables of a kind intended for instruction. Judg. 9:8-15; 2 Kings 14:9. It differs from the parable by drawing its illustrations from animal and vegetable life, while the parable teaches spiritual truths through pictures of human life. No fable occurs in the New Testament, but the word is used to denote the vain traditions of the Jews and the worthless legends of the heathen. 1 Tim. 1:4; 4:7; 2 Tim. 4:4.

Fain, in Job 27:22; Luke 15:16, means gladly.

Fair, in Isa. 54:11, means beautiful.

Fair Ha'vens, a harbor on the south coast of the island of Crete (now called CANDIA), in the Mediterranean Sea. Paul wished to winter there. Acts 27:8, on his voyage to Rome. Fair Havens still retains the same name.

Fairs are mentioned in Ezek. 27: 12, 14, 16, 19, 22, 27. The word may mean the periodical meetings of buyers and sellers, or the fixed places for such meetings, and sometimes the wares sold.

Faith'less, in Mark 9:19, means unbelieving.

Fal'low Ground, in Jer. 4:3; Hos. 10: 12, means land fit for cultivation, but not sowed.

Fam'ines are often mentioned in the Bible. The seven years' famine in Egypt, while Joseph was govenor there, is the most remarkable. A spiritual famine is mentioned in Amos 8:11.

Far'thing, a Roman piece of copper money. Farthings were of two kinds: that mentioned in Matt. 10:29; Luke 12:6 was the assarion, and was worth a cent and a half; the other kind, mentioned in Matt. 5:26, was the kodrantes, worth about four mills. It was equal to two mites.

Fa'ther, the title by which God is distinguished as being the Father of the Lord Jesus Christ and of all his true disciples. In the time of the patriarchs the father was master and judge in his family. The word father is used in Gen. 45:8 to mean an adviser or counsellor. The word is also used in various other senses, as Jubal "was the father of all such as handle the harp and the organ." Gen. 4:21.

Fath'om, a measure of length equal to about six and three-fourths feet. Acts 27: 28.

Feasts are often mentioned in the Bible. They were usually given to celebrate some important or joyful event. A great feast was made by Abraham, Gen. 21:8, at the weaning of Isaac; also

71

by Laban, Gen. 29:22 at the marriage of Jacob. Feasts were held to celebrate the end of harvest, of vintage, and of sheep-shearing. The Jews had also several festivals or seasons of ceremonial worship, which were established to commemorate great events. A list of the "feasts of the Lord" is given in Lev. 23. The three great feasts of the year were the Feast of Unleavened Bread, or of the Passover; the Feast of Pentecost, or Feast of Weeks, or Feast of Harvest; and the Feast of Tabernacles. The Jews had many other feasts.

Fe'lix (happy), the governor of Judea under the Romans, before whom Paul was accused by the Jews. Acts 23:24, 26; 24:22, 24, 25, 27.

Fes'tus, the Roman governor of Judea who succeeded Felix. Acts 24:27; 25:4, 9; 26:24, 25.

Figs abounded in Judea in ancient times, Deut. 8:8, and fig trees both wild and cultivated are now found in all parts of Palestine; they grow luxuriantly, are pleasant shade-trees, and the fruit is wholesome and much used. There are several varieties of fig trees. The fruit begins to show itself before the leaves and without apparent blossoms. Hence a fig tree in full leaf but without fruit may be known as barren for the season. Matt. 21:19.

Fire is often connected in the Bible with the presence of God, as in the burning bush and in the pillar of fire.

Fir'kin, a measure of capacity. The English firkin contained about seven imperial gallons, but the Attic metretes held only about four and three-fourths imperial gallons. It is therefore very evident that the substitution of the old English measure as a translation of the Greek name has the effect of increasing the stated capacity of the vessels by about one-half. John 2:6.

Fir'ma-ment, the expanse or space surrounding the earth. Gen. 1:6, 7; Ezek. 1:22, 23.

First'born. In order to commemorate the destruction of the first-born of the Egyptians God commanded that the first-born males of the Hebrews should be consecrated to him; also the first offspring of their cattle and the first-fruits of their ground. The word is often used figuratively.

First'-fruits were offerings to God, brought in obedience to the law of Moses. Deut. 26:1-11, to the Tabernacle or to the Temple to express the thankfulness and dependence of the giver. They included every kind of produce of the earth, sometimes in a natural and sometimes in a prepared state.

First'ling, in Gen. 4:4; Neh. 10:36, means the first offspring of an animal.

Fishes of many varieties were abundant in Egypt in ancient times, and are also plentiful there now, in the river Nile and in Lake Moeris. Many kinds of fishing are represented on Egyptian monuments. Fish were abundant in the Sea of Galilee (where four of the disciples were fishermen, Matt. 4:18-21), and in the Jabbok, Jordan, and Kishon Rivers in Palestine. All fishes which had scales and fins were clean under the Mosaic law, and were commonly used as food by the Jews.

Flea, mentioned in 1 Sam.24:14; 26:20 as the most insignificant of creatures.

Flesh, a word used in Gen. 6:13, 17, 19 for everything living, except vegetables, and in Gen. 6:12 for mankind. In Col. 2:5; 1 Pet. 4:6 it denotes the body as distinguished from the soul. In the New Testament the word "flesh" often means the bodily propensities and passions.

Flood, in Josh. 24:2, 3, means the river Euphrates. In Genesis it means DELUGE (which see).

Fly, the name of a great variety of insects, some of which are extremely annoying and destructive, found abundantly in Egypt and Judea. One of the plagues sent upon the Egyptians was "swarms of flies." Exod. 8:21.

Foot'man sometimes means infantry. In other instances it refers specially to the king's guard. 1 Sam. 22:17. The word there translated footman is elsewhere rendered guard.

Fore-knowl'edge (knowing beforehand) is an attribute of God. Acts 2:23; 1 Pet. 1:2.

Fore-run'ner, in Heb. 6:20, used in reference to Christ's entrance within the veil, means not only one who goes before, but one who leads or prepares the way.

For-tu-na'tus (fortunate), a Christian, apparently of Corinth, who is named in Paul's first Epistle to the church of the Corinthians. 1 Cor. 16:17.

Foun'tains are often mentioned in the Bible. They were of special value in the dry and thirsty land of Judea. Many places were named from some fountain in their vicinity.

Fowl, a word used in Gen. 15:11; Job 28:7; Isa. 18:6 to denote birds of prey, and in Neh. 5:18; 1 Kings 4:23 for poultry. The word is also applied to birds in general, as in Luke 12:24.

Fox, a cunning and voracious animal well known generally and abundant in Palestine. The jackal is probably meant in several passages in which the word fox occurs.

Frank'in-cense, an exceedingly aromatic gum used in the sacred incense for the Temple service. It is distilled from a tree in Arabia. The substance generally used in modern times as frankincense is produced from the Norway pine.

Friend, a word often used in the Bible. Abraham is called the "Friend of God" in James 2:23, and Christ in John 15:15 calls his disciples "friends." In Matt. 11:19 he is called "a friend of publicans and sinners." The word friend is often used where no affection or friendship is intended. Matt. 22:12; 26:50.

Fringes were attached to the hem or border of the outside garment worn by the Israelites, and contained, Num. 15:38, 39, "a ribband of blue," that they might remember and keep the commandments of the LORD. They became, in the course of time, objects of superstitious regard.

Frogs were noted as the second plague of Egypt. Exod. 8:1-14. They were worshipped by the Egyptians, but were unclean to the Hebrews. In Rev. 16:13 they represent uncleanness.

Ful'ler, in Mal. 3:2; Mark 9:3, means a bleacher of cloth. Fullers also washed clothing that had been worn.

Fur'long, a measure of length. The furlong being the eighth part of a British mile, as the stadium was of the Greek and Roman mile, the name has been arbitrarily introduced into the English Version, although the length of it (six hundred and sixty feet) exceeds that of the stadium by about fifty-six feet. Luke 24:13; John 6:19; 11:18.

Fur'nace, in the Bible, is translated from several different words, and means— [1] An oven for baking. Gen. 15:17; Neh. 3:11. [2] A smelting furnace or a lime-kiln. Gen. 19:28; Exod. 9:8. [3] A refining furnace. Prov. 17:3; Isa. 48:10; Ezek. 22:18-22. [4] A crucible. Ps. 12:6. [5] The Chaldean furnace for capital punishment. Jer. 29:22; Dan. 3:19-26; Rev. 1:15; 9:2.

Fu'ry, in Jer. 10:25, is a figurative expression for afflictive judgments.

G

G, when it comes before E and I in Hebrew Old Testament words, is pronounced hard, as in give. In Greek words it is pronounced soft, like J.

Ga'bri-el (God is mighty) an angel sent by God to Daniel, Dan. 8: 16; 9:21; to Zacharias, Luke 1:19; and to Mary, Luke 1:26.

Gad (the seer). [1] The seventh son of Jacob. Gen. 30: 11 Exod.1:4. [2] The name is also used to denote the tribe which sprang from Gad and the land which they inhabited, which was east of Jordan and between Reuben and Manasseh. [3] A prophet who lived in the time of David, and was his friend. 1 Sam. 22:5; 2 Sam 24: 13, 14.

Gad'a-ra, an ancient stronghold of Palestine about eight miles south-east of the Sea of Galilee and near the river Hieromax. Its ruins are called by the Arabs Um Keis, and are very extensive. Hot baths are found near by. Its inhabitants now live in old tombs in the rocks.

Gad-a-renes', inhabitants of a district on the east side of the Sea of Galilee, and east of the Jordan below that sea. Mark 5:1; Luke 8: 26,37.

Gain-say' in Luke 21: 15, means contradict.

Gaius, ga'yus. [1] A Macedonian who accompanied Paul in some of his journeys and was with him at Ephesus. Acts 19:29. [2] A man of Derbe in Lycaonia who accompanied Paul on his return from Macedonia into Asia Minor. Acts 20:4. [3] A Corinthian whom Paul baptized. Rom. 16:23; 1 Cor. 1:14. [4] The person to whom John's third epistle is addressed. 3 John 1.

Ga-la'tians, E-pis'tle of Paul to the, was written by Paul from Ephesus, between A.D. 54 and 57. In it with fiery eloquence he vindicates the authority of his ministry and demonstrates the true relation between the Law of Moses and the Gospel of Christ. This epistle and that to the Romans were the chief authority for the doctrines of the Reformation of the sixteenth century, and form the Magna Charta of evangelical Protestantism. Considered simply as a piece of literature, the Epistle to the Galatians is one of the grandest and most perfect that exists. The "subscription" at the end of this epistle says it was written from Rome; but this "subscription" was added by some later hand and is without authority.

Gal-i-le'ans, the inhabitants of the district called Galilee. Mark 14:70; Luke 13:1,2; 22:59; 23:6; John 4:45; Acts 2:7.

Gal'i-lee (a circle) is in the Old Testament the name of a small mountainous district of Naphtali including the twenty towns which Solomon gave to Hiram, king of Tyre, 1 Kings 9:11; 2 Kings 15:29; but having been re-peopled by strangers during the period of the captivity, it became in the time of our Lord the name of the northernmost and most populous province of Palestine. The population was very much mixed, heathen, proselytes, and Jews living together, and though the Jews probably retained the dominant influence, they were, on account of their frequent intercourse with foreigners, less strict in the observation of the law than their brethren of Judea, and consequently not very much esteemed by them. One of the most salient features of the country was the Sea of Galilee, called Chinnereth or Chinneroth in the Old Testament, Num. 34:11; Josh. 12:3, and in the New Testament the Lake of Gennesaret, Luke 5:1, the Sea of Tiberias, John 6:1, etc. (See Galilee, Sea of). Among the towns were Nazareth, Cana, Tiberias, Chorazin, Bethsaida, and Capernaum (which see). Our Lord spent most of his time in Galilee, and all the twelve apostles, except Judas, were Galileans.

Gal'i-lee, Sea of, Matt. 4:18, in Palestine, is called also Sea of Chinnereth or Chinneroth, Num. 34:11; Josh. 12:3; Lake of Gennesaret, Luke 5:1; Sea of Tiberias, John 6:1; "the sea," Isa. 9:1; Matt. 4:13, 15; 17:27; and now bahr Tubariyeh, and is about twenty seven miles east of the Mediterranean Sea. It is about fourteen miles long from north to south and from four to seven miles wide, and its greatest depth is about one hundred and sixty feet. Its surface varies from six hundred to seven hundred feet below the level of the Mediterranean. The river Jordan enters the Sea of Galilee on the north-east and flows out at the south-west. This sea abounds in excellent fish of various kinds. It is enclosed by steep hills, broken or receding occasionally, from five hundred to seventeen hundred feet high, the eastern shore being much the highest. The Sea of Galilee is still liable to sudden tempests like that mentioned in Matt. 14:22-33.

Gall, in Job 16:13; 20: 14, 25, means a bitter fluid secreted by the liver and generally called bile. In a great many other places the word gall is used for some bitter herb or plant. It was a common name for bitter substances. Gall was given to deaden the pain of persons suffering crucifixion. It was given to Christ. Matt. 27:34.

Gal'li-o, the proconsul or deputy of Achaia before whom Paul was accused by the Jews. Acts 18: 12, 14, 17.

Ga-ma'li-el (God is recompenser). [1] The captain of the tribe of Manasseh who was appointed to assist Moses in numbering the people. Num. 1:10; 2:20. [2] A celebrated rabbi among the Jews, the teacher of Paul. Acts 22:3. He was a prominent member of the Sanhedrin and a doctor of the law, and was very influential among the Jews. Acts 5:34. Gamaliel is famous for his wise counsel, Acts 5:38, 39, concerning the apostles when they were brought before the Sanhedrin.

Gar'dens are often mentioned in the Bible, and were frequently places where trees and plants were more carefully cultivated than in the open field. Gethsemane was a garden or olive grove. Gardens sometimes consisted of fruit-and shade-trees with aromatic shrubs. Song of Solomon 5:1. The Lord God planted a garden in Eden. Gen. 2:8. A garden of herbs is mentioned in 1 Kings 21:2.

Gath (wine-press), one of the cities from which Joshua did not fully cut off the Anakim. It was in the territory assigned to Dan, and was one of the five chief cities of the Philistines. It was the home of Goliath, 1 Sam. 17:14; a place to which the ark was carried, 1 Sam. 5:8; and where David sought refuge. 1 Sam. 21:10-15.

Ga'za (the strong), or **Az'zah**, as Gaza No. 1 was sometimes called. [1] A strong city situated in the south-west corner of Palestine and about three miles from the Great or Mediterranean Sea. It is one of the oldest cities in the world, was peopled by the descendants of Ham, Gen. 10:19, by the Anakim, Josh. 11:22, and was the strongest of the five royal cities of Philistines. It commanded the road to Egypt, and was the scene of many desperate struggles and the exploits of Samson. Judg. 16. It was captured by Alexander the Great after a siege of nearly five months. It is now called Ghuzzeh. [2] A city of Ephraim. Judg. 6:4; 1 Chron. 7:28.

Ge-ha'zi (valley of vision), the servant of Elisha the prophet. He was smitten with leprosy, 2 Kings 5: 20-27, on account of his covetousness and falsehood when Elisha had refused to receive a reward from Naaman the Syrian.

Ge-mal'li (camel-driver), father of the spy from Dan. Num. 13:12.

Ge-ne-al'o-gy. The lineage of a family, or list of ancestors, was preserved with extreme care by the Jews, not only because the privileges of the Jewish Church were transmitted through Abraham, but because of the predictions concerning the Messiah.

Gen-er-a'tion, in Gen. 15:16, means a single succession in natural descent, as the children of the same parents; hence an age. In Luke 9:41 it means the people of the same period, or living at the same time. Generation or generations has the following secondary meanings: [1] A genealogical register, as in Gen. 5:1. [2] A family history, Gen. 6:9; 25:12. [3] A history of the origin of things and persons; for instance the earth.

Gen'e-sis, the name of the first book of the Bible. The Hebrew name of the book is (in English) "in the beginning," according to the Hebrew custom of naming books by a title composed of their first words. The present name, "Genesis," is Greek, and means generation or creation, because the book tells the story of the Creation. It is the first book of the PENTA-TEUCH (which see).

Gen-nes'a-ret, a district adjoining the Sea of Galilee (to which it sometimes gave its name), apparently on the west side and toward the north end; but its situation and extent are uncertain. Many of Christ's miracles were wrought there. Matt. 14:34; Mark 6:53; Luke 5:1.

Gen'tiles was the name by which the Jews designated all people but themselves as idolaters. In the New Testament the name "Greeks" is sometimes used for Gentiles. Acts 16:1; Rom. 1:16.

Ger'ge-senes, the inhabitants of Gergesa. The country, of the Gergesenes was the scene of one of Christ's miracles. Matt. 8:28, in connection with the herd of swine.

Geth-sem'a-ne (oil-press), Matt. 26:36; Mark 14:32, an olive grove, called a garden, situated at the foot of the Mount of Olives, a little east of the brook Kedron and near Jerusalem. It was frequently visited by Christ and his disciples, and was the scene of his agony the last night before his crucifixion, and of his betrayal by Judas.

Ghost, gost, often used for spirit. In Gen. 25:8 "gave up the ghost" means expired; in Matt. 27:50 "yielded up the ghost" should be gave up his spirit.

Gi'ants. [1] This term is, with doubtful propriety, used in the English Version to denote a people inhabiting some part of the land east of Jordan, and in the west among the Philistines. Deut. 2:11; Josh. 12:4. (The word is sometimes left untranslated. See "Rephaim," Gen. 14:5; 15:20.) [2] It is also, in one or two instances, used as the name of a valley near Jerusalem, more frequently called the Valley of Rephaim, Josh. 15:8; Sam. 5:18; 1 Chron. 11:15; Isa. 17:5.

Gib'e-ah (a hill). [1] A town in the hill country of Judah. Josh. 15:57. [2] Gibeah of Benjamin. 1 Sam 13:2. The tribe of Benjamin was nearly destroyed by a dreadful crime of some of its people. See Judg. chapters 19-21. This town is generally considered to be the same as Gibeah of Saul. [3] Gibeah of Saul, 1 Sam. 10:26; 11:4, the home of Saul, is held by many authorities to be the same as Gibeah of Benjamin. [4] Gibeah in Kirjath-jearim; doubtless a hill in that city. 2 Sam. 6 3,4. [5] Gibeah in the field. Judg. 20:31. It was probably same as GEBA. [6] Gibeah-haaraloth, in the marginal notes, Josh. 5:3.

Gib'e-on (hill), a city of the Hivites, whose inhabitants by a stratagem made peace with Joshua. It afterward belonged to Benjamin and was made a Levitical city. It is memorable for many important events recorded in the Bible, including the battle of the Israelites under Joshua with the five kings, during which "the sun stood still upon Gibeon." Josh. 10: 12,13. The site of Gibeon is now occupied by a small village call El-Jib.

Gid'e-on (hewer), an Israelite, of Manasseh who defeated the Midianites and delivered Israel from the oppression under which they had been kept for seven years by them. He was also called JERUBBAAL (a contender against Baal), because he had thrown down the altar of Baal. He was the fifth judge of Israel, held that office forty years, and was one of her greatest rulers.

Gil-bo'a or **Gil'bo-a** (bubbling fountain), a mountainous district in Manasseh west of Jordan (or of Issachar), where Saul was defeated and slain by the Philistines. 1 Sam. 28:4; Sam. 21:12.

Gil'e-ad (rocky). [1] An extensive and mountainous district which formed the chief part of Manasseh east of Jordan and of Gad. Mount Gilead generally refers to that part of the district which lay in Manasseh, north of the river or brook Jabbok. When Gilead alone is used the whole district is commonly meant. The word sometimes means the inhabitants of GILEAD. [2] A grandson of Manasseh. Num. 26:29; Josh. 17:1. [3] The father of Jephthah, one of the judges of Israel. Judg. 11:1,2. [4] One of the chiefs of the families of Gad. 1 Chron. 5:14.

Gil'gal (rolled). [1] A place on the west side of Jordan, not far from Jericho, in Benjamin, and where the Israelites first encamped after miraculously passing over Jordan. Josh. 3:13-17. It was the resting-place of the Tabernacle for some time, and many important events recorded in the Bible took place there. [2] A place supposed to have been in the west part of Canaan, in the territory afterward possessed by the tribe of Dan; but it seems not quite certain that this Gilgal was not, as well as the other, in the east part of the land, near the Jordan. Josh. 121:23. [3] It is apparently agreed among the authorities of the present day that there was a place called Gilgal near the sea, a little to the north of Joppa, and to this reference is supposed to be made in Josh. 9:6; 10:6, 7, 9, 15, 43. Supposed to be the modern Jidjuleh, near the ancient Antipatris. [4] Some think another place bore the same name, Gilgal, about twelve miles south of Ebal and Gerizim, and that this is the place referred to in 2 Kings 2:1; 4:38. Supposed to be the modern Jiljilia.

Gir'dles of various forms were worn by the Hebrews to confine their garments, which were loose and flowing, about the waist and to serve as a pouch in which to carry small articles. A girdle, when closely bound about the loins, was thought to increase the power of endurance. Girdles of fine quality were worn by the priests.

Glass of some kind, probably semi-transparent, was made in very ancient times, and does not seem to have been used at that time for windows or mirrors, but for cups, bottles, vases, etc. It was made in Egypt as early as the exodus, and was doubtless known to the Jews. The "looking-glasses" mentioned in Exod. 38:8; Job 37:18 were made of polished metal. Many specimens of them are now in the British Museum. One of this kind is probably referred to in James 1:23 and in 1 Cor. 13:12 ("mirror" in the Revised Version).

Glory, Glo'ri-fy. The glory of God refers to the peculiar and absolute perfection of all the divine attributes. To glorify is to exalt or make glorious.

Gnash, nash, **Gnashing,** nash'ing, grinding the teeth together in anguish or despair. Ps. 112:10;; Matt. 8:12.

Gnat, nat a word not found in the Old Testament. In Matt. 23:24 "strain at a gnat" means strain out a gnat, referring to the practice of straining wine before drinking, to avoid a breach of the ceremonial law, Lev. 11, concerning unclean things. Gnats are great pests on marshy land in Egypt and Palestine.

Goad, in Judg. 3:31; Eccl. 12:11, means a pole about two or three yards long with a sharp point on one end. It was used in guiding oxen and in urging them on. In Acts 26:14 the word pricks is used for goads in the expression concerning Saul (afterward Paul), "hard for thee to kick against the pricks."

Goats in ancient times were among the chief possessions of rich people. Gen. 27:9. Their flesh and milk were used as food. They were regarded as clean for sacrifice, and on the Day of Atonement goats were used exclusively. Lev. 16:5-28. Goats' hair was used for weaving into cloth and the skins were made into bottles, etc. Several kinds of goats are kept in Palestine. The common goat of Palestine has very long hanging ears, and its horns are curved backward. Goats having long silky hair are referred to in Song of Solomon 4:1; 6:5. The wild goat is mentioned in 1 Sam. 24:2; Ps. 104:18; Job 39:l, etc. and resembles the chamois of the Alps. It is found among the high hills. The SCAPEGOAT is noticed in Lev. 16:8-26, and was used on the Day of Atonement. Two goats were set apart on that day, one of which was sacrificed to the Lord for a sin-offering; the other was the scapegoat. The high-priest laid his hands on its head, confessed "all the iniquities of the children of Israel," Lev. 16:21, and sent it away into the wilderness. The sins of the people were considered as transferred to the scapegoat, which became a type of Christ, who bore "the iniquities of us all." Isa. 53:6.

God (Good). There are four words used in the Hebrew which are translated God. [1] Adonai. [2] El. [3] Elohim. [4] Yehovah. The first and last are used exclusively with reference to the true God. The second and third are employed to designate the true God and also the false gods of the heathen. (The word "Zur" (a rock) is translated God in Isa. 44:8 and Hab. 1:12, but this is altogether exceptional.)

God'head, Col. 2:9, the nature or essential being of God. Acts 17:29; Rom. 1:20.

God'li-ness, piety and constant obedience to the commands of God. 2 Pet. 3:11. Godliness, in 1 Tim. 3:16, signifies the substance of revealed religion.

Gog (mountain). [1] A son of Shemaiah, the grandson of Joel, who is named in the genealogy of Reuben, though not enumerated with his sons. 1 Chron. 5:4. [2] The name given by the prophet Ezekiel to the chief of the land of Magog, a region whose situation is supposed to correspond with some part of Tartary or Seythia. Ezek. 38:2; 39:1. the word Gog is also found in Rev. 20:8.

Gold is first mentioned in Gen. 2:11, 12. Several places are referred to in the Bible as abounding in gold, among which are Ophir, Job 28: 16, Raamah and Sheba, Ezek. 27:22, and Parvaim, 2 Chron. 3: 6, and it was much used by the Hebrews for the Temple and in other ways. It was very plentiful in the time of David and Solomon. It was not coined until after the reign of King David, but was an article of commerce and was sold by weight.

Gol'go-tha (a skull), the Hebrew name of the place in which Christ was crucified, translated into Latim in the Vulgate: Calvaria. The site is by some supposed to be that on which now stands the church of the Holy Sepulchre. Matt. 27:33; Mark

15:22: John 19:17.

Go-li'ath (an exile), a champion of the Philistines who was slain by David "with a sling and with a stone." 1 Sam. 17:4-51; 21:9; 22:10. Another Goliath was slain by Elhanan, and is mentioned in 2 Sam. 21:19.

Go'mer (completion). [1] A son of Japheth. Gen. 10:2,3; 1 Chron. 1:5,6. [2] The people descended from him, who are supposed to have lived on the north side of the Black Sea. Ezek. 38:6. [3] The wife of the prophet Hosea. Hos. 1:3.

Go'shen. [1] The name of a district of Lower Egypt which lay apparently to the east of the Pelusiac, or eastern branch of the Nile, near to On or Heliopolis, and which Joseph assigned as the residence of his father and his brethren. Gen. 45:10; Exod. 8:22. See Egypt. [2] A district in the hill country of Judah. It appears to have been a general name for the central part of the territory of the tribe, and perhaps to have been also applied to the south part of Benjamin. Josh. 10:41; 11:16. [3] A town enumerated among the cities of Judah. Josh. 15:51.

Gos'pel, the glad tidings of salvation through Jesus Christ. The Gospels, the first four books of the New Testament, were written by the evangelists Matthew, Mark, Luke, and John. Each portrayed the life and character of Christ in the manner natural to himself. They wrote for different classes: Matthew, for the Jews; Mark, for the Romans; Luke, for the Greeks; John, for advanced Christians of all nationalities. Matthew described Christ as the Messiah and king of the Jews; John, as the incarnate Son of God and Redeemer of the world; Mark displays his official and Luke his personal history. These four books together constitute the most important and best attested history. Two (Matthew and John) were written by eye-witnesses of the facts narrated; two by disciples of the apostles (Mark, a disciple of Peter; Luke, a disciple of Paul).

Gourd, gord a rapidly growing plant with wide leaves common in the East, and used to make a shade for arbors. Jonah 4:6, 7, 9, 10. Another kind of gourd, the fruit of which is poisonous and easily mistaken for a wholesome melon, is mentioned in 2 Kings 4:39.

Grace, the free and undeserved love and favor of God toward man as a sinner.

Grass'hop-pers were sometimes used as food by the Hebrews. Lev. 11:22. They are a kind of locust, and the original is translated locust in 2 Chron. 7:13. They often came to Palestine in very great numbers, and were extremely destructive to vegetation.

Grave, a word frequently employed by the translators to denote the unseen state of the departed spirits, without any distinction of good and evil. When used in this sense, it is given as the equivalent of three words in the original, meaning --[1] Sepulchre. Job 3:22; Ps. 88:11. [2] Pit. Job 33:22. [3] Hades. Gen. 37:35; 42:38; 44:29, 31; 1 Sam. 2:6; 1 Kings 2:6; Job 7:9; 14:13; 17:13; 21:13; 24:19; Ps. 6:5; 30:3; 31:17; 49:15; 88:3; 89:48; Eccl. 9:10; Isa. 38:10, 18; Hos. 13:14.

Great Sea, in Num. 34:6; Josh. 1:4, etc., means the Mediterranean Sea.

Gre'cians. [1] The name of the inhabitants of Ionia and the Grecian Islands, whom the Hebrews accounted to be descended from Javan. Joel 3:6. [2] Jews who, dwelling in Greece or a Grecian colony, had in some degree adopted the language and customs of Greece. Acts 6:1; 9:29; 11:20.

G

Greece or **Hel'las** was in prehistoric times settled by a people of Aryan stock, the Hellenes, allied to the Celts of Western Europe, the Italians of Italy, and the Teutons of Central and Northern Europe. They occupied the mainland of Greece and the islands of the Aegean Sea, and founded flourishing colonies in Gaul, Sicily, and Southern Italy to the west, and in Asia Minor to the east. Alexander the Great made the Greek influence predominant throughout the East. He founded a great empire which reached from the Adriatic Sea in Europe to the Indus River in Asia, though that empire split into many kingdoms immediately after his death, B.C. 323. At the time of Christ the Greek language was spoken more or less throughout the whole Roman Empire. The Christian congregation of Rome used it till the end of the second century. In Jerusalem Greek was the language in which the Roman and the Jewish authorities communicated with each other. In Asia Minor and even in Syria the Greek language had so completely superseded the vernacular tongues, at least in the cities, that though Hebrew, or rather Aramaic, was the mother-tongue of Paul, since he was born a Jew, Greek was his native tongue, since he was born at Tarsus. Even the fishermen along the Sea of Galilee--John, Peter, etc.--understood and spoke Greek. The importance of this circumstance for the preaching of the gospel can hardly be overestimated. A centre of Greek incluence, particularly interesting just in the present connection, was the city of ALEXANDER (which see), founded on the Mediterranean shore of Egypt, B.C. 330, by Alexander the Great. He induced a considerable number of Jews to settle in the new city, and the prosperity of that colony as well as the general prosperity of the city soon induced more to come. At the time of Christ Alexandria was one of the greatest Jewish cities in the world, and there the Jews came into daily and most intimate contact with the Greeks. Two remarkable events resulted from this circumstance. One was the translation of the Old Testament into Greek, the SEPTUAGINT, made by seventy (a round number for seventy-two) learned Jews. It was the only medium through which the Greeks obtained or could obtain any idea of the Old Testament. The other was the development of a peculiar combination of Jewish wisdom and Greek philosophy which not only led many Jews and Greeks to accept Christianity, but also had a certain influence on the development of Christianity itself, which otherwise would have been much more difficult.

G

Grind'ers, in Ecel. 12:3, means grinding teeth, or double teeth.

Groves were used for the worship of the true God in ancient times. Gen. 21:33. It afterward became common to plant groves for the worship of idols, and, as these contained images of their gods, the words grove and idol were used interchangeably, and grove often means an image of a false god.

Guest-cham-ber, Mark 14:14; Luke 22:11, probably a large unoccupied room, usually in the upper part of the house, used for guests and social meetings.

H

Hab'ak-kuk or **Ha-bak'kuk**, (embrace), one of the twelve minor prophets, lived in the reign of Jehoiakim or of Josiah, and was a contemporary of Jeremiah, but nothing further is known of him personally, Hab. 1:1; 3:1

Hab'ak-kuk or **Ha-bak'kuk, the Book of,** consists of three chapters. The first is a prediction of the invasion by the Chaldeans; the second, a prediction of the punishment awaiting the Chaldeans themselves; and the third, a sublime psalm on the majesty of God.

Ha'dar (room). [1] A son of Ishmael, the son of Hagar, Gen. 25:15, called HADAD in 1 Chron. 1:30. [2] A king of Edom, Gen. 36:39. called HADAD in 1 Chron. 1:50, 51.

Ha'des, the under world, or realm of the dead.

Ha'gar (wandering), the Egyptian maid-servant of Sarai (afterward Sarah), the wife of Abram (afterward Abraham). Hagar became the mother of Ishmael by Abram (afterward Abraham), and is mentioned in Gal. 4: 24, 25 under the name AGAR, allegorically. Hagar's history is given in Gen. 16, 21, and 25:12.

Ha'gar-enes or **Ha'gar-ites,** a nation who dwelt apparently to the eastward of Gilead and were subdued by the tribes of Israel that settled in that land. 1 Chron. 5: 10; Ps. 83:6.

Hag'ga-i (festive), one of the twelve minor prophets, who lived at the time when the Jews returned to Jerusalem after the seventy years' captivity in Babylon. He exercised the prophetic office during the second year of the reign of Darius Hystaspes, Hag. 1:1, B.C. 520, but of his life nothing further is known.

Hag'ga-i, the Book of, has reference principally to the rebuilding of the Temple and the glory which awaited it. The construction, begun by Zerubbabel, had been interrupted by a royal decree, but the accession of a new king brought with it the cancelling of that decree, and then the Jews showed themselves lukewarm in their ardor.

Hail, in Luke 1:28, is a word used in salutation, and is the expression of a desire for the health and prosperity of the person to whom it is addressed. It was used in derision in reference to Christ in Matt. 27:29; Mark 15:18; John 19:3, and was spoken by Judas to Christ when he betrayed him. Matt. 26:49.

Hail'stones. One of the plagues of Egypt was a storm of hail. It is described in Exod. 9:23-26. A storm of hailstones was also used for the destruction of the Canaanites who fought against Joshua. Josh. 10:11.

Hair. In Egypt hair-cutting and shaving were practised, except in times of mourning. Joseph shaved himself. Gen. 41:14. The Hebrew men usually wore their hair moderately long and had full beards. The Nazarites allowed their hair to grow uncut.

Hallelujah, hal-le-lu'yah, is translated in the English Version Praise ye the Lord or Praise the Lord, and is found in many of the Psalms in this form. Ps. 106;111; l12; 113; 117; 135. In Rev. 19: 1, 3, 4, 6 the word ALLELUIA is used with a similar meaning.

Hal'low, in Exod. 29:1; 40:9, etc., means to consecrate; to make holy.

Ham (multitude), a city or country where the people called Zuzim dwelt. Its situation is very uncertain. Gen. l4:5.

Ham (hot or multitude). [1] The son of Noah and the father of Cush, Mizraim, Phut, and Canaan. Gen. 10:6. From Cush descended the Cushites who inhabited Chaldea (Nimrod was his son. Gen. 10:8), parts of Arabia, and Ethiopia. From Mizraim, which is the Hebrew name of Egypt, descended the Egyptians; from Phut, another African people not further specialized; and from Canaan, the Canaanites; that is, those tribes which inhabited Canaan when the Israelites arrived there. All these nations are called Hamitic. [2] The patronymic of the descendants of Ham.

Ha'man (celebrated), a courtier and favorite of Ahasuerus, the king of Persia, who devised persecution against the Jews. Esth. chapters 3-9. He obtained a royal decree for the extermination of the Jews in Persia, but through the influence of Esther his plan was not carried out. He was hanged on the gallows that he had prepared for Mordecai.

Hand, a symbol of skill, power, and many actions. The Hebrews in describing locations spoke as if facing the east. Hence "to the right hand" meant to the south; "to the left hand," to the north. 2 Sam. 24:5; Gen. 14:15; Job 23:9. The Hebrews at their meals picked up their food with their fingers, using no forks; hence washing the hands was specially necessary. The scribes and Pharisees made this washing a religious ceremony, in accordance with "the tradition of the elders." Matt. 15:2.

Hand-breadth, Exod. 25:25; 1 Kings 7:26, a measure of length, reckoned to have been equal to the breadth of the four fingers across the first joint-about three inches.

Hands, laying on of, a part of the ceremonial used in consecrating persons to high and holy service and in conferring spirtual gifts. Num. 27:18; Acts 8:15-17; 1 Tim. 4:14; 2 Tim. 1:6.

Hang'ing. Under Jewish law criminals were first strangled and then hanged. Num. 25:4; Deut. 21:22. It was a special mark of infamy. Deut. 21:23. In Acts 5:30; Gal. 3:13, Jesus is said to have been "hanged on a tree," which means literally "on a beam of wood," and refers to his crucifixion.

Ha'ran (a mountaineer). [1] Brother of Abraham and father of Lot. Gen. 11:26,31. [2] A son of Shimei, of the tribe of Levi. 1 Chron. 23:9.

Ha'ran (parched), a son of Caleb, the son of Jephunneh. 1 Chron. 2:46.

Ha'ran (parched, dry), the place to which Abram removed after leaving Ur, and before he went into Canaan. Gen. 11:31; 2 Kings 19:12. The city was in Mesopotamia, and more definitely in Padan-aram. Gen. 24:10; 25:20. It is called CHARRAN in Acts 7:2, 4, and is generally identified with the modern Haran.

Hare, a well-known small animal, was prohibited to the Hebrews for food. Lev. 11:6; Deut. 14:7. Several varieties of the hare are found in Palestine.

Har'lot, an abandoned woman. Prov. 29:3. Harlots are first mentioned in the case of Tamar. Gen. 38:15. Among the Hebrews harlots were often foreigners, hence their name, "strange women." The name is also applied figuratively to wicked cities, as Nineveh, Nah.3:4, and Jerusalem, Isa. 1:21; also to Israel, referring to their idolatry.

Ha'rod (trembling), a city or place in Manassah, west of Jordan, near which Gideon encamped with the army of the Israelites. Judg. 7:1.

Har'ness, in 1 Kings 20:11; 22:34; 2 Chron. 18:33, means armor.

Harps of various forms were used by the Hebrews. The harp was invented by Jubal, Gen. 4:21, and was used on joyful occasions. David was very skilful in its use and played on it before King Saul. 1 Sam. 16:23.

Har'vest usually commenced in Palestine about the beginning of April, and ended in June. In some elevated parts of the country it was later. It began with barley, and its first-fruits were taken to the Temple in Passover-week. The wheat harvest came next, and its first-fruits were offered at Pentecost. In Matt. 13:39 the end of the world is referred to as the harvest.

Hate sometimes means love in a less degree, as in Luke 14:26, which mentions father and mother, etc, as persons which must be hated if one would be a disciple of Christ.

Hats, in Dan. 3:21, are turbans in the marginal notes. Hats were unknown to the Hebrews.

Hawk, an unclean bird, Lev. 11:16, of the falcon tribe. It was sacred among the Egyptians and the Greeks. Its migrations are referred to in Job 39:26.

Ha'zel, in Gen. 30:37, is supposed to mean wild almond.

Head'bands, in Isa. 3:20, may mean little bands for the hair.

Head'stone, in Zech. 4:7, means chief stone.

Health. In Ps. 67:2 "saving health" means salvation.

Heap, in Deut. 13:16; Jer. 49:2, means ruin.

Heaps of stones were used to mark some signal providence of God. Josh. 4:4-7.

Heart, a word used in some parts of the Bible to denote the seat of the desires, affections, and motives of man, and in others to signify all his faculties and powers as an intellectual, moral, and accountable being.

Hearth, harth or herth, in Ps. 102:3, means a fagot. It usually means, in the Bible, a stone on which a fire was made for baking bread and other uses. Abraham's wife Sarah made cakes (bread) upon the hearth. Gen. 18:6.

Heathen, he'thn (nations), a word sometimes used in the Bible to denote unbelievers, Jer. 10:25, but usually with the same meaning as GENTILES (which see).

Heaven. This word has a number of meanings in the Old Testament, which may be imperfectly classed thus: [1] The atmosphere, the region of clouds. [2] The region of the sun, moon, and starts. [3] The throne of God, and the habitation of the holy angels. [4] The word is frequently used in an indefinite, figurative, or metaphorical sense. In the New Testament also it has several meanings, which are imperfectly classed thus: [1] The Natural Heavens, frequently involving a reference to the next head, No. 2. [2] The Spiritual Heavens, the throne of God, the abode of the holy angels and the spirits of just men made perfect. [3] The word is sometimes used in an indefinite, figurative, or metaphorical sense.

He'ber (alliance). [1] The grandson of Asher. Gen. 46:17; 1 Chron. 7:31. [2] A Judite, a son of Ezra. 1 Chron. 4:18. [3] The head of a family in Gad. 1 Chron. 5:13. [4] A son of Elpaal, a Benjamite. 1 Chron. 8:17. [5] A son of Shashak, a Benjamite. 1 Chron. 8:22. [6] A kenite, the husband of Fael, who killed Sisera, the captain of Jabin's army. Judge. 4:11, 17,21,22. [7] Heber, the father of Phalee. Luke3:35.

He'brew. [1] This word, which is used as a Gentile appellation for the descendents of Abraham, and applied to himself also, denotes one who comes from beyond, from the other side, or who has passed over, and is commonly regarded as having reference to Abraham's passing over the river Euphrates on his way to Canaan. [2] The language spoken by the Hebrews.

He'brews, The, were called ISRAELITES, Exod.9:7; the CHILDREN OF ISRAEL, Exod. 1:13; the SEED OF ABRAHAM, Ps. 105:6; John 8:37; or the CHILDREN OF ABRAHAM, Gal. 3:7, until after the return from the captivity, when the name JEWS was adopted. The word "Jews" was formed from the same root as JUDEA. It referred to the purity of blood and strictness of religion by which those who reoccupied Judea were distinguished from the more mixed populations of Galilee and Samaria, with their laxer ideas of religion. The name "Jews" was used during ancient and medieval times, until modern science began to feel the want of a term which, involving the ideas of purity of blood, strictness of religion, national tradition, community of language, etc., would designate the people as a race, and the name HEBREWS was chosen because it was found that in the oldest times it had steadily been used by foreigners just in that sense. Gen. 14:13; 39: 14; 41: 12; 1 Sam. 4:6.

The Hebrew race came from Chaldea, and Abraham from Ur, to which region he sent his servant to find a wife for Isaac, and Jacob went thither for the same purpose. But the home of the patriarchs was CANAAN (which see). That land was promised to them and their descendants, and Abraham bought the cave of Machpelah, near Hebron, for a burial-place. It was on account of a famine that Jacob went down to Egypt, but when he found his son Joseph there as the favorite and first counsellor of the reigning Pharaoh, he remained there, and the Hebrews were settled in one of the best provinces of Egypt. How long they stayed there cannot be stated definitely on account of the uncertainty of both Egyptian and Biblical chronology, but they stayed, at all events, long enough to become thoroughly changed themselves and to see the circumstances under which they lived as thoroughly changed. They came a mere tribe, but they left a host, a people. They came an nomadic shepherds, but they had the arts of industry and the science of commerce at least as germs among them when they left. And they were compelled to leave. The great achievements of Joseph were forgotten long ago and the Hebrews were suppressed, almost enslaved, by the Egyptinas, when Moses arose among them and led them across the Red Sea toward the Promised Land. For forty years they wandered about in the wilderness, but when they finally approached Canaan they possessed the Law, the

Tabernacle, a social organization on a religious principle, and had become a nation. Moses died in sight of the Promised Land, and Joshua led the Hebrews into Canaan, conquered the country, and divided it among the tribes. Then followed, under the administration of the judges, a period in which pitiable failings and heroic deeds alternated until, under Saul, a national kingdom was formed, and under the reigns of David and Solomon the Hebrews became conspicuous in the history of the world. Jerusalem grew into a rich and splendid city, the Temple was built, commerical connections were formed with the Phoenicians, the Egyptians, etc., and in the interior nothing but order, industry, prosperity, and progress were to be seen and a brilliant literature sprang up. Nevertheless, the very geographical position of the Hebrew kingdom was not without its peculiar dangers. There were great and ambitious empires, Egypt on one side of the Hebrews and Assyria and Babylonia on the other, and the war-path between those countries was inevitably through Palestine. Still worse, immediately after the death of Solomon the kingdom itself was divided, the ten tribes forming the kingdom of Israel, the other two (Judah and Benjamin) the kingdom of Judah. The jealousy between Israel and Judah led to wars, the wars to foreign alliances, the foreign alliances to a lowering of the national standard, and then came the doom. After the reign of nineteen rulers (in Israel), of seven different dynasties, some of them able men, all of them bad ones, Samaria was taken, B.C. 720, by Shalmaneser, the Hebrews carried away into captivity, and the land occupied by Assyrian settler. After the reign of twenty rulers (in Judah), all from the house of David and some of them both able and good men, Jerusalem was taken, B.C. 588, by Nebuchadnezzar and the Hebrew inhabitants carried to Babylon as prisoners. One would think that such calamities must be the end of Hebrew history, but they were not. Babylon was conquered by the Persians B.C. 538, and Cyrus allowed the Hebrews to return home. One colony went back under Zerubbabel, another under Ezra, etc. The Temple was rebuilt, B.C. 520; the walls of Jerusalem, B.C. 445, under Nehemiah. Under the rule of the Persian governors it seems that the Hebrews were allowed to develop their theocratic form of government with considerable freedom and success. Nor did their first contact with the Greeks cause any conflict. After the battle of Issus, B.C. 332, which meant the overthrow of the Persian monarchy, Alexander the Great visited Jerusalem, entered the Temple, had the book of Daniel with the prophecy of the downfall of Persia read to him, and treated the Hebrews with great friendliness. It should not be overlooked that he caused a considerable number of them to settle in the new city he built in Egypt, on the Mediterranean, for that event exercised a very great influence. Although Jersusalem continued to be the religious centre of the Hebrew race, there now arose two foreign centres of Hebrew intelligence: one in Babylon, among the old exiles who had remained there and lived under a strongly pronounced Oriental influence, and one in Alexandria, among the recent colonists who lived there under a still more strongly pronounced Greek influence. The first conflict, however, between Greek philosophy and Hebrew religion took place in Jerusalem. After the death of Alexander the Great, B.C. 323, and the establishment of several kingdoms on the ruins of his empire, Palestine belonged first to Egypt, but afterward to Syria, and under Antiochus Epiphanes, B.C. 175-165, a great war began. He plundered the Temple, and erected in it a statue of Jupiter to which he tried to force the Hebrews to offer sacrifices. The result was a general rebellion under the leadership of the Maccabees, and after defeating and expelling the Syrians the Hebrews again established an independent kingdom under a native dynasty. The first of the Maccabees who assumed the royal title was Aristobulus I., B.C. 107, but with Antigonus B.C. 40-37, a son of Aristobulus II., the dynasty ceased to reign and was followed by the Herodians. In the mean time Palestine had come under Roman sway, having been conquered by Pompey, B.C. 63. The Romans were as a rule not harsh masters in their conquered provinces. Especially in the East they were always willing to allow considerable religious and national liberty. But, unfortunately, the dynasty to which they confided the government of Palestine, the Herodian, was not of pure Hebrew descent: it came from Idumea. The Idumean rulers, sometimes bearing the title of king, somtimes other titles, tried to pass themselves off as Jews among the Jews, but they were in their hearts no more nor less than Greek-Roman pagans of the then prevailing type of religious indifference, and their policy was always to weaken and subdue the national feeling of the Hebrews by the introduction of Greek and Roman elements of civilization. As long as Herod the Great lived things went on with tolerable smoothness, but under his successors one insurrection followed the other, each increasing in fury and stubbornness. The Romans took a deep dislike to the Hebrews, baffled as they had been by them more than once in their undertakings, and finally their utter overthrow was decided upon. Vespasian was sent with a great army againsts them. Having been elected emperor, he left the command to his son Titus, who, with extreme cruelty, worked his way onward slowly, methodically, but irresistibly, broke down the walls around Jerusalem, burnt the Temple, and razed the city to the ground. A.D. 70.

He'brews, the E-pis'tle to the, is not addressed to any individual congregation, but generallly to all the Jewish Christians in Palestine, who were suffering severely from the persecution of their Jewish countrymen and sorely tempted to apostasy from Christ. Its purpose is to strengthen those brethren in their faith by demonstrating to them the essential unity and at the same time the specific differences between the Old and the New Testament, the Old and the New Covenant, the Laws of Moses, and the Gospel of Christ. It teaches the eternal priesthood and sacrifice of Christ. Its divine authority has never been doubted, but concerning its authorship there always has existed, and still exists, some uncertainty. It is anonymous, and has been ascribed to Paul, to Barnabas or Luke and to Apollos. It is deeply impregnated with the genius of Paul, but the style and wording belong to somebody else, probably to Barnabas. It dates from A.D. 63 and 64, soon after Paul's first captivity in Rome.

He'bron (friendship). **[1]** A city of Palestine. It stands in a narrow but exceedingly fertile valley, at an elevation of three thousand feet above the level of the sea, midway between Jerusalem and Beer-sheba, is one of the oldest cities in the world, is mentioned before Damascus, Gen. 13:18, and was built seven years before Zoan (called by the Greeks TANIS), in Egypt. Num. 13:22, Its name while it was possessed by the Canaanites was KIRJATH-ARBA (the city of Arba), Josh. 21:11; 15, 13, 14, and this name was occasionally given to it long afterward. Hebron is often mentioned in the history of the Patriarchs. Abraham pitched his tent near it, under the oaks of Mamre, and bought the cave of Machpelah for a burial-place. After it had been conquered by Josua, Josh. 10:36, 37; 12:10, it was made a Levitical city and a city of refuge. Josh. 20:7; 21:11. David resided there for seven and a half years. After the captivity it was speedily repeopled. Neh. ll:25. At present it is a city of about ten thousand inhabitants, but only about five hundred of them are Jews. There are, indeed, only few place to be found where Mohammedan fanaticism is allowed to show itself more pointedly. Over the cave of MACHPELAH (which see), where Abraham, Isaac, and Jacob are buried, stands a large and massive Mohammedan mosque, and it is so rigorously guarded that but few Christians have been allowed to enter it-the Prince of Wales in 1862, the crown prince of Prussia in 1869, etc. About two miles west of the city, on the road to Gaza, is the famous oak of Abraham. The trunk measures thirty-two feet in circumference, and at a height of nineteen feet it divides into four branches, with a crown two hundred and seventy-five feet in circumference. [2] One of the sons of Kobath, the son of Levi. Exod. 6:18; 1 Chron. 6:2. [3] The name (if it be not rather used as a patronymic) of the son of Mareshah. 1 Chron. 2:42; 15:9. [4] A city of Asher. Josh. 19:28.

Hedge, In Hos. 2:6 a way or path hedged up with thorns is mentioned. In Job 1:10 hedge is figuratively used to denote protection.

Hell, In the Old Testament the Hebrew word for hell is Sheol, which corresponds to Hades, a Greek word which means the unseen under-world or the realm of the dead. In the English Bible Sheol is variously translated by the words hell, pit and grave. 1 Sam. 2:6; Job 14:13, etc. In the New Testament the words translated "hell" are HADES and GEHENNA. In 1 Cor. 15:55 HADES is translated "grave" and in all other places "hell." HADES does not refer to the final abode of the impenitent, but to the disembodied state of man between death and the last judgment. Christ descended into hades, which was the place where he "preached" unto the spirits in prison." 1 Pet. 3:19. GEHENNA, which corresponds nearly to our word "hell," means first the valley of Hinnom, on the south of Jerusalem. It was the seat of the worship of Moloch, and was afterward used as a place in which the filth and dead animals of the city were thrown; "where their worm dieth not, and the fire is not quenched." March 9:44. Hence the word Gehenna also denotes the final state and abode of lost souls. The rebellious angels were cast into hell. 2 Pet. 2:4. The cursed are to "go away into everlasting punishment" at the great judgment day. Matt. 25:46.

Hem of his Gar'ment, the ancient fringe which Moses commanded the children of Israel to wear to remind them of the commandments of God. num. 15:38, 40. See Matt. 9:20.

Hem'lock, in Hos. 10:4; Amos 6:12, means a wild, noxious, and bitter plant which has not been identified. It is elsewhere translated "gall." Its figurative use is explained by comparing Amos 6:12 with Deut. 29:18; Amos 5:7; Heb. 12:15.

Hen, a barnyard fowl, is touchingly mentioned in our Lord's lament over Jerusalem. Matt. 23:37; Luke 13:34. hens must have been common in Palestine in New Testament times, and their eggs are probably referred to in Luke 11:12. The cock is mentioned in the account of Peter's denial of Christ. Matt. 26:34; Mark 14:30; Luke 22:60,61.

He'na (troubling) a city which a king of Assyria subdued. 2 Kings 18:34; 19:13; Isa. 37:13.

Her'ald, a person who makes formal and public announcements in the name of a king or of the rulers of the Grecian games, etc; mentioned in the Authorized Version only in Dan. 3:4.

Herbs of various kinds are found in Palestine. The variety mentioned in 2 Kings 4:39; Isa. 18:4; 26:19 is probably colewort or some kind of cabbage. The Jews were commanded, Exod. 12:8, to eat the Passover with bitter herbs. This was intended to remind them of the severe and cruel bondage in Egypt from which they had been delivered.

Her'e-tick, in Titus 3:10, means a fractious person.

Her'od was a common name in a numerous family which played a conspicuous and almost fatal part in Jewish politics in the times of our Lord and his apostles. It came from IDUMEA (which see). All its members were very zealous in professing the Mosiac law, though they did not keep it; very desirous to give no offence to Jewish prejudices, though they despised them; and very painstaking in flattering Jewish vanity when thereby they could further their own plans. But as they could never hope to realize their great ambition to establish an Idumean dynasty in Judea without the support of the Romans, many of Herod family were educated in Rome or had lived there for a long time. Thus they became a sort of middlemen between Greek-Roman civilization, Greek-Roman paganism, and Judaism, to the great injury of the Jews. [1] HEROD THE GREAT was made king of Judea by the first Roman emperor, Augustus, and reigned for thirty-seven years. Christ was born near the end of his reign. Matt. 2:1-18. Herod rebuilt the Temple at Jerusalem. He also adorned Jerusalem with other splendid buildings, but they were theatres and amphitheatres, and were intended to aid in the introduction of pagan games and festivals among the Jews. Herod was despotic and cruel, and had ten wives, one after the other. One of them, Mariamne, he murdered B.C. 29, together with her mother, brother, and grandfather; later, B.C. 7, he killed two of his sons by her, Aristobulus and Alexander; and a few days before his death a third son, by Doris, Antipater. From his house his cruelty extended to his subjects. On their arrival in Jerusalem the Wise Men had an audience with him, and when they told him that a

"King of the Jews" had been born at Bethlehem he ordered the Massacre of the Innocents. Matt. 2:16. While on his death-bed at Jericho he gathered a number of rich and distinguished people around him and gave a secret order that they should all be put to death immediately after his decease, in order that there might be mourning when he died. [2] HEROD AN'TI-PAS, a son of Herod the Great by his fourth wife, Malthace, tried to become king of Judea after the death of his father, but had to content himself with the tetrachy of Galilee, Luke 3:1, and Perea, over which he reigned B. C. 4-A. D. 39, when he was deposed by Caligula and banished to Lyons in Gaul. He married Herodias, though her legal husband, Herod Philip (not the tetrarch Philip, who married Salome), was still living. Denounced by John the Baptist for this open breach of the Mosaic law, he threw the prophet into a dungeon, and taken by surprise by Salome, the daughter of Herodias, he had John the Baptist beheaded. Mark 6:16-28. He set Christ "at naught, and mocked him." Luke 23:7-12. Herod's character is described in Mark 6:16, 22 and in Luke 13:32 where he is called "that fox." [3] ARCHELAUS, ar-ke-la'us, B.C. 4 - A.D. 6, was the son of Herod the Great by Malthace, and was the elder brother of Herod Antipas. He was ethnarch of Judea, Samaria, and Idumea; was tyrannical; was banished to Vienne in Gaul; and is mentioned in the New Testament only in Matt. 2:22. [4] PHIL'IP, B.C. 4 - A.D. 34, tetrarch of Gaulanitis, Auranitis, etc., was the son of Herod the Great, but was noted for moderation and justice. He married his niece Salome, the young woman that danced before Herod Antipas. Mark 6;22. He is mentioned in the New Testament only in Luke 3:1. [5] HEROD PHIL'IP was the son of Herod the Great and Mariamne, and was the first husband of Herodias. He seems to have lived as a private citizen, and is called PHILIP in Mark 6:17. [6] HEROD A-GRIP'PA I., king of Judea A.D. 37-44, was a grandson of Herod the Great and son of the murdered Aristobulus. He was educated in Rome and was a friend of Caligula, but observed the ceremonial of the Pharisees, persecuted the apostles, beheaded James, and tried to execute Peter. Acts 12:1-19. [7] HEROD A-GRIP'PA II., king of parts of Judea A.D. 50-100, was a son of Herod Aprippa I., and is noted in the history of Paul. Acts 26:28.

He-ro'di-ans, the court party among the Jews in the time of Herod the Great. Matt. 22:16. They willingly submitted to the government of Rome and united with the Pharisees in attempting to destroy Christ. Matt. 22:16; Mark 3:6.

H

He-ro'di-as, a granddaughter of Herod the Great, and married first to her uncle, Herod Philip, to whom she bore Salome, Matt. 14:3, and then (during her first husband's life) to Herod Antipas, another uncle.

Hez-e-ki'ah (strength of Jehovah). [1] A noted king of Judah, B.C. 726-697, the son and successor of the apostate Ahaz, but very unlike him. He was eminently godly, abolished idol-worship, tore down the "high place: dedicated to idolatry, and broke in pieces the brazen serpent of Moses, which had become an object of idolatrous worship. 2 Kings 18:4. He repaired the Temple, restored the Mosaic institutions to honor, and celebrated the Passover with a splendor and magnificence not seen since the days of David and Solomon. 2 Chron. 30:26. Under Ahaz Judah had become tributary to Assyria, but, having confidence in the promise and prophecy of Isaiah, Hezekiah claimed and asserted the independence of his kingdom, and the army of Sennacherib, by a sudden judgment of God, retired defeated from the walls of Jerusalem. 2 Kings 19:35. Sick unto death, he prayed to God to prolong his life, and Isaiah brought him the message that his prayer had been granted. 2 Kings 20:10. [2] A son of Neariah, of the house of David. 1 Chron. 3:23. [3] An Israelite who descendants returned to Jerusalem with Zerubbabel. Ezra 2:16; Neh. 7:21.

High Place. [1] The place where Saul met with Samuel. 1 Sam. 9:12, 13. [2] A name applied to Gibeon, where the Tabernacle was in the time of David. 1 Kings 3:4; 2 Chron. 1:3, 13. [3] The place "before Jerusalem" where Solomon set up idolatrous worship. 1 Kings 11:7. [4] A name applied to Bethel, where Jeroboam set up the golden calf. 2 Kings 23:15. In the plural the term is used frequently, and generally denotes places where idolatrous worship was practised.

High-Priest, the head of the priesthood of Israel. Lev. 21:10. The office was first held by AARON (whch see), and afterward by his descendants. His immediate successor was Eleazar. The high-priest originally held office for life. Solomon disregarded this rule by deposing Abiathar and appointing Zadok, because Abiathar was disloyal. 1 Kings 2:35. The consecration services of the high-priest lasted seven days, and consisted of sacrifices, etc. Exod. 29; Lev. 21:10. The high-priest's dress was much more costly than that of the inferior priest. Exod. 39:1-9. He wore a breastplate, a piece of embroidery about ten inches square, which was set with twelve precious stones, on each of which was engraved the name of one of the twelve tribes of Israel. Exod. 28:15-40. his exclusive duty was to officiate in the most holy place on the great Day of Atonement. Lev. 16. He was the overseer of the Temple, and might at any time perform the duties of an ordinary priest. At the time of Christ the high-priest presided over the Sanhedrin. Acts 5:17; John 18:13,14. Jesus is called the High-Priest. Heb. 4:14; 7: 25-28' 9:11, etc.

Hill, Hills. The words "hill" and "mountain" are used indefinitely in the Authorized Version. The "hill country," Luke 1:39, is the "mountain of Judah" in Josh. 20:7. In Luke 9:28 the same elevation is called "mountain" which in Luke 9:37 is named "hill." The original text is exact.

His is often used in the Authorized Version instead of "its." Gen. 1:11, 12; Lev. 11:22; Deut. 14:15. In Matt. 6:33 "Seek ye first the kingdom of God, and his righteousness," "his" refers to God, and not to kingdom.

Hit'tites, the descendants of Heth, the second son of Canaan. Abraham purchased Machpelah for a sepulchre from them. Gen. 23:3-13. esau married two Hittite women. Gen. 26:34,35.

Hit'tites, Land of the, the territory occupied by the Hittites. It was in the south-eastern part of Canaan, in what was afterward called the hill country of Judah, and included Kirjath-arba (Hebron) and Machpelah. Gen. 22:3.

Hivites, Land of the, the territory in Canaan occupied by the Hivites. It included part of the east coast of the Mediterranean Sea and some of the adjacent hill country on the east. The Hivites voluntarily surrendered their country to Joshua, Josh. 9:7; 11:19, and subsequently paid tribute to Solomon. 1 Kings 9:20; 2 Chron. 8:7.

Ho'ly, Ho'li-ness. Lev. 27:14; Exod. 15:11.. Holiness is an attribute of the LORD. Isa. 6:3. The word "holy" is applied to angels in Matt. 25:31. It denotes comparative freedom from sin in the case of Christians. Heb. 3:1; Col. 3:12. "Holiness to the Lord" was inscribed on the golden plate which the high-priest wore on his forehead. Exod. 28:36; 39:30.

Holy Ghost. Gift of Acts 2nd Chapters.

Ho'ly One. This expression is used, either alone or in connection with appropriate words, to designate the Supreme God, and in a few cases is applied to the MESSIAH.

Ho'mer, Lev. 27:16; Ezek. 45:11, the largest measure for dry things, used by the Israelites, contained about eight bushels.

Hor, Mount (the mountain). [1] A mountain "in the edge of the land of Edom." Num. 33:37. Edom, or Mount Seir, included the range of mountains which extends nearly from the south end of the Dead Sea to the Gulf of Akabah. About the middle of this range is its highest mountain, which is probably Mount

Hor, on which Aaron Died. Num. 20: 24-29; 33: 38, 39; Deut. 32:50. It is now called Jebel Neby Harun, "mountain of the prophet Aaron." Its summit is 4800 feet above the Mediterranean. The mountain has two peaks, on the lower of which, 4360 feet above the Mediterranean, is "Aaron's tomb" so called, a small building 28 by 33 feet, built over his supposed grave. Some suppose Jebel Madurah to be Mount Hor. [2] A mountain on the northern boundary of the Promised Land. It is mentioned only in Num. 34:7,8 is probably the extreme northern summit of the Lebanon range, has an elevation of 10,000 feet, and is the highest mountain in Syria.

Ho'reb (dry desert), a mountain or range often mentioned in the Bible. Some think that it is the name of the whole range of which Sinai is a special peak. Others consider Sinai as the range and Horeb a summit of it. In Leviticus and Numbers Sinai is exclusively used in reference to the giving of the Law. In Deuteronomy Horeb is used instead of Sinai. Sinai and Horeb are used indiscriminately in the Psalms. Sinai and its wilderness are the scene of events in the region of Horeb, and the whole of Horeb is called "the mountain of God." Exod. 3:1, 12:4:27, etc. Hence "Sinai" is sometimes mentioned alone. Exod. 19:11, 20; 24: 16, etc. But "Horeb" is often named alone, and the same events are spoken of as occuring on both "Horeb" and "Sinai." In the New Testament "Sinai" became a general name, and is so now. Acts 7:30, 38; Gal. 4: 24, 25.

Horn, in the Old Testament, is an emblem of power, honor, or glory. Deut. 33:17; Lam. 2:3. It is also the symbol of victory, and is often used in prophetic visions instead of "kings" and "kingdoms." Dan. 7: 20-24; Zech. 1:18. Horns were used to contain liquids, notably oils and perfumes, 1 Sa. 16:1, and for trumpets. Josh. 6:8, 13. They were not always actual horns, but rather horn-shaped articles.

Hor'net, a large wasp-like insect, noted for its irritability and the severity of its sting. Deut. 7:20. Hornets were used as instruments of divine judgment upon the enemies of the Israelites. Exod. 23:28; Joes. 24:12.

Horse, Gen. 49:17, a noble animal which is poetically described in Job. 39: 19-25. In very ancient times oxen and asses were generally used for labor. Horses were used chiefly in war. Exod. 14: 9,23; Esth. 6:8. They were common among the Jews in the time of Solomon.

Ho-san'na (save, we bessech!), an exclamation used by the multitudes who welcomed christ's entry into Jerusalem. Matt. 21:9-15.

Hosea, ho-ze'ah (God is help), one of the twelve minor prophets, called OSEE in Rom. 9:25, was a contemporary of Isaiah, and prophesied during the reign of Jeroboam II. in Israel and the reigns of Uzziah, Jotham, Ahaz, and Hezekiah in Judah, B.C. 790-725. Hosea is supposed to have been a native of the kingdom of Israel, as his prophecies are almost entirely addressed to that part of the Jewish nation. Nothing is known of life, but his book reveals his sad and sympathetic heart in view of the sinfulness of his people. He was nevertheless full of hope.

Hosea, the Book of, consists of threats and denunciations against the wickedness of the Israelites, mingled with predictions of the final restoration of God's people to goodness and prosperity. His prophecies are obscure and difficult, from their brief and condensed style, their sudden transitions, the indistinctness of their allusions, and the great diffculty of rightly ascertaining to what precise period or transaction many of their passages refer. But he is remarkable for intensity of passion, both in wrath and in tenderness, and for poetic beauty of imagery and style. Hosea has been called "the prophet of tragic and elegiac sorrow." He is the most patriotic of all the prophets, confining himself to his own country and people, and referring less than they to the interests of the Gentiles. His marriage, by divine command, with Gomer, "a wife of whoredoms,' Hos. 1:2-9, is best explained figuratively as a symbol of the monstrous sin of spiritual whoredom or apostasy from the true God.

Hos-pi-tal'i-ty, receiving and entertaining strangers or guests without reward, is commanded in Lev. 19:33, 34; Deut. 15:7. Many instances of it are given in the Bible, as in the histories of Abraham, Gen. 18:2-8, Lot, Gen. 19:1-3; Jethro, Exod. 2:20; Manoah, Judg. 13:15, etc. The New Testament writers enjoin hospitality upon believers. Rom. 12:13; 1 Tim. 3:2; 5:10; 1 Pet. 4:9. Hospitality was so practised by the early Christians as to win the admiration of the heathen. The abuse of it was a great crime. Ps. 41:9. To this day a fugitive, among the Arabs, is safe for the time if he gains the shelter of even an enemy's tent.

Host, a hospitable entertainer, Rom. 16:23; an inn-holder, Luke 10:35; or an army.

Hour sometimes denotes an indefinte period of time. Dan. 3:6; 4:19; Matt. 9:22. It also signifies a definte period. In the time of Christ the Jews divided the day, from sunrise to sunset, into hours, and the night into watches. The first hour began about 6 A.M.; the sixth at noon; and the twelfth about 6 P.M. There were thus twelve hours between sunrise and sunset, and they varied in length in proportion to the length of the day. "The eleventh hour" was a proverbial expression for lateness. Matt. 20:1-10. The Romans reckoned time from midnight to noon, and divided this into twelve equal parts, beginning with the first hour and ending with the twelfth.

House of God, Judg. 20:18, 26; 21:2, a name applied to BETHEL.

Hu-mil'i-ty is urged with great earnestness upon all who claim to be Christ's disciples. 1 Pet. 5:5. A perfect example of it is found in Christ. Phil. 2:5-8.

Hun'gred, preceded by "an," in Matt 12:1, means hungry.

Hunt'ing. Nimrod was "a mighty hunter," Gen. 10:9, and Esau was "a cunning hunter." Gen. 25:27. the monuments show that hunting was pursued in Egypt as a sport. We know that Isaac was fond of venison. Gen.27:3,4. Various methods of capturing animals were practised by theHebrews.

Hus'band-man, a cultivator of the ground. Cultivating the soil is one of the most ancient, useful, and honorable occupations of mankind. Gen. 9:20; Isa. 28:24-28. Christ uses the word figuratively, John 15:1, in parables and elsewhere to denote God's care for his people.

Husks, Luke 15:16, in the parable of the Prodigal Son, are doubltless the fruit of the carob tree, which is a species of locust. Husks are commonly used in Palestine by the poor as food; cattle and swine are also fattened on them. When ripe the fruit resembles a bean-pod, is four to six inches long, and filled with seeds. It is imported into England and the United States as locust beans. Also called "St. John's bread," because some suppose that John the Baptist lived upon these "locusts."

Hy-ae'na, a carnivorous animal resembling a wolf in general appearance, but of a dirty gray color, with dark transverse stripes on the sides and limbs, is common in Palestine and feeds upon carrion. "Zeboim," in 1 Sam. 13:18; Neh. 11:34, means hyaenas. "Speckled bird," in Jer. 12:9, according to some, should be translated "hyaena." Otherwise there is no reference to this animal in the Bible.

Hymns are mentioned in the New Testament with psalms and spiritual songs Eph.5:19;Col 3:16.Christ and his disciples sang a hymn after the Last Supper. Matt 26:30.

Hypocrite, hip'o-krit, one who assumes the appearance of piety and virtue while destitute of true religion.Matt. 23: 13-33.

Hys'sop, Exod. 12:22, a plant used in ceremonies of purification. Lev. 14:4, 6, 51; Ps. 51:7. It is mentioned in 1 Kings 4:33 as a small tree that "springeth out of the wall." See John 19:29.

I

I AM THAT I AM; I AM, the name by which God announced himself unto Moses in the bush of Horeb. Exod. 3:14.

Ichabod, ik'a-bod (inglorious), the name which was given by the wife of Phinehas, the son of Eli, to her son whom she bare soon after the ark of the covenant had been taken by the Philistines. 1 Sa. 4:21; 14:3.

I-co'ni-um (place of images?), an important city of the province of Lycaonia in Asia Minor. It was situated in a fertile country, on the great Roman road from Ephesus to Tarsus, Antioch, and the Euphrates, and was visited by Paul on his first and second missionary journeys. Acts 13:51; 14:1,19, 21; 16: 2; 2 Time. 3:11. Its present name is Konieh, and it has a population of about 30,000.

I'dol, I-dol'a-try. Anything which is the object of the worship due only to God is an idol. In a literal sense an idol is an image consecrated to religious worship. Deut. 29:17. In a figurative sense it is anything which withdraws the affections from God. Col. 3:5.

Idolatry consists in worshipping as the true God some created object, or in worshipping the Deity by means of symbolic representations, such as statues, and pictures. Its origin is obsure and it began in the most ancient times. It is strictly forbidden in the first and second commandments. Exod. 20:3,4,5; Deut. 5:7; 6:14, 15; 8:19,20. The first chapter of Romans, beginning at the eighteenth verse, gives the best description of the progress and accompanying immorality of idolatry. The last verse of the First Epistle of John contains the warning, "Little children, keep yourselves from idols.

Im-man'u-el (God with us), a title of the MESSIAH. Isa. 7:14; 8:8. Same as EMMANUEL. Matt. 1:23.

Im-mor'tal. In 1 Tim. 1:17 God is said to be "Immortal." The word thus translated is the same as that rendered "uncorruptible" in Rom. 1:23, and should be so translated here.

Im-mor-tal'i-ty. Belief in immortality is not specially taught in the Old Testament, but is taken for granted. The penitential and sacrificial system of the Mosaic law would be unintelligible without the doctrine of immortality. It is definitely taught in the New Testament in connection with the resurrection of Christ.

Im-po'tent, in John 5:3; Acts 4:9; 14: 8, means without strength, either on account of disease or malformation.

Im-pute', the translation of a Greek word which is rendered by many different terms in the Authorized Version, such as "reckon," Rom. 4:4; "account," Gal. 3:6; "lay to one's charge," 2 Tim. 4:16. Impute means "to put to the account of a person that of which he is or is not possessed." God imputes sin, Rom. 4:8, and the righteousness of Christ is imputed to man on condition of faith in Christ's sacrifice. Rom. 4:11-24.

In'cense, Exod. 30:8, was a mixture of frankincense and other fragrant articles. Its materials and the method of preparing it are given in Exod. 30:34-36. Its preparation for common use was forbidden. The priest burned it morning and evening on the altar of incense. No other preparation could be used as incense, nor could anyone but the priest offer it. Incense was offered as a symbol of prayer.

In-her'it-ance. The sons had priority of right, the eldest having a double portion. If there were no sons, the daughters inherited. Num. 27:8. There is no record of wills in the Old Testament; the law of Moses rendered them unnecessary. They were subsequently introduced, however. Gal. 3:15; Heb. 9:17. Believers have salvation for their inheritance, Heb. 1:14, and are "joint-heirs with Christ." Rom. 8:17.

Inn. An inn was sometimes only a station where caravans stopped for the night, near water if possible, but not necessarily having any buildings. At such an "inn" Joseph's brethren stopped, Gen. 42:27, and Moses met the LORD. Exod. 4:24. At such stations large buildings containing rooms for travellers and stalls for their animals were often erected around open square courts. No food was provided in them. In such a place our Savior was born. Luke 2:7. Another kind of an inn, in charge of a host, is mentioned in the parable of the Good Samaritan. Luke 10:35.

In-spi-ra'tion. The prophets and apostles spake "as they were moved by the Holy Ghost," 2 Pet. 1:21, but the divine Spirit influenced each author according to his individuality. Job. 32:8; 2 Tim. 3:16.

In-ter-ces'sion, prayer in behalf of others. Abraham interceded for Sodom. Gen. 18: 23-33. Paul exhorts that intercession is our Intercessor or Advocate. 1 John 2:1; John 17; Heb.9:24; Rom. 8:34. The Holy Spirit also makes intercession. Rom. 8:26.

In'ward, in Job 19:19, means familiar; confidential.

I'ra (watchful). [1] One of David's chief rulers after the rebellion of Sheba was quelled. 2 Sam. 20:26. [2,3] Two of David's valiant men. 2 Sam. 23:26, 38; 1 Chron. 11:28, 40; 27:9.

Isaac, i'zak (laughter), the second of the Hebrew patriarchs, was the son of Abraham and Sarah, and was born when his parents were very old, in fulfilment of God's promise. Gen. 17:4-17. The history of Isaac is found in Gen. 21:2-8; 22:2-13; chapter 24-28; 35:27-29. The only event of his early years which is recorded is the trial of his father's faith when, in obedience to God's command, Abraham was about to offer Isaac for a burnt offering. See Gen. 22:2-13. This is considered typical of the subsequent sacrifice of the only Son of God on Calvary. The intended sacrifice of Isaac is referred to in Heb. 11:17; Jas. 2:21. Isaac was a prosperous farmer. Gen. 26:12, 14. He died at the age of one hundred and eighty. Gen. 35:28. Isaac is used in Amos 7:9, 16 as poetic synonym for ISRAEL (the ten tribes).

Isaiah, i-za'yah (Jehovah's salvation), the greatest of the prophets, was a son of Amoz, began his prophetic ministration probably in the last years of the reign of Uzziah, Isa. 6:1, B.C. 760, and continued it under Jotham, Ahaz, and Hezekiah, B.C. 698. We know from himself that he was a married man and had two sons; that his wife was called a prophetess and his sons bore prophetical names; that he lived on intimate terms with Hezekiah, etc. A Jewish tradition preserved in the Talmud tells us that when he was ninety years old he was sawn asunder in a hollow carob tree, in the reign of Manasseh, and that the "mulberry tree of Isaiah" in the Kedron valley, near Jerusalem, indicates the traditional spot of his martyrdom. The manner of his death is not mentioned in the Bible.

Isa'iah, the Book of, which has fitly been characterized as the "Gospel of the Old Testament," consists of two parts. The first part, chapters 1-39, contains a number of separate predictions and narratives referrring to various nations--Assyria, Babylon, Moab, Ethiopia, etc. The second part, from chapter 40 to the end, refers to the close of the Babylonian captivity and the glory of the Messianic period, giving a most striking picture of the suffering Messiah, Isa. 53, as the "man of sorrows," who bore our sins and accomplished our salvation.

Ish'ma-el (whom God hears). [1] The son of Abraham by Hagar. He and his mother were expelled from the household of the patriarch at Sarah's request, Gen. 21:10, and went forth into the wilderness of Beer-sheba, where he became a hunter and married an Egyptian woman. From him descended the Ishmaelites, wild Bedouin tribes still roaming about in the same region and well known for their treachery and robberies. Ishmael, however, was present at the interment of his father's

103

remains in the cave of Machpelah. Gen. 25:9. [2] A descendant of the royal family of Judah, who murdered Gedaliah, the governor appointed by Nebuchadnezzar, in the basest manner and then was compelled by Johanan to flee to the Ammonites. Jer. 41:2 Kings 25:23, 25. [3] A son of Azel, a descendant of Benjamin. 1 Chron. 8:38; 9:44. [4] Father of Zebadiah, a ruler of the house of Judah. 2 Chron. 19:11. [5] One of the captains by whose aid Jehoiada the priest set Joash on the throne of Judah. 2 chron. 23:1. [6] A priest who had a foreign wife. Ezra 10:22.

Is'ra-el, Gen. 35:10, a name given to Jacob by the angel at Peniel, Gen. 32:28; Hos. 12:3, 4, meaning "the prince that prevails with God." The word is also used, Exod. 3:16, for all of Jacob's posterity; also for the kingdom of the ten tribes, 2 Kings 14:12; and, in a spiritual sense, for the whole body of true believers. Rom. 9:6; 11:26.

Is'ra-el, King'dom of, a name often applied to the united kingdom before the revolt of the ten tribes. 1 Sam. 13:1, 4; 15:28. It was also used to designate the territory of the ten tribes. After the death of Solomon it was usually applied to the independent kingdom of the ten tribes, so that the kings of the ten tribes were called "kings of Israel," and David's descendants, who ruled Judah and Benjamin, were called "kings of Judah." The kingdom of Israel was about as large as New Hampshire and had a population of over three millions. The capitals were Shechem, Tirzah, and Samaria. It lasted B.C. 975-721.

Issachar, is'sa-kar (God hath given me my hire). [1] The fifth son of Jacob and Leah. Gen. 30:18; Exod. 1:3. A prophetical description of him in Gen. 49:14, 15 was fulfilled, as his descendants were laborious and subject to tributes from roving tribes. [2] A porter for the Tabernacle in the time of David. 1 chron. 26:5.

Issachar, Territory of, comprised the great plain called Esdraelon or Jezreel, and extended from Mount Carmel to the Jordan and from En-gannim to Mount Tabor. It was one of the most fertile districts in Palestine and contained sixteen famous cities. Its boundaries are given in Josh. 19: 17-23.

Italian, i-tal'yan, **Band,** part of the Roman army. It was composed of Italians, Acts 10:1, and Cornelius was their centurion, or commander.

J

Ja-a'si-el (whom God has made), son Abner and chief of Benjamin. 1 Chron. 27:21.

Ja-a'zer and **Ja'zer** (Jehovah helps), a city of Gilead situated east of the Jordan. It was conquered and assigned to Gad and the Levites. Num. 21:32; 32:1; Josh. 21:39. It was subject to Moab in later times, and is denounced in Isa. 16:8, 9; Jer. 48:32.

Jab'bok (emptying), a small river which rises about twenty-five miles north-east of the north end of the Dead Sea, and, after flowing east, north, west, and south-west, empties into the Jordan about midway between the Dead Sea and the Sea of Galilee. It is now called Zerka, and abounds in small fish. Gen. 32:22; Num. 21:24; Deut. 2:37; 3:16.

Ja'cob (the supplanter). [1] The third of the Jewish patriarchs, Gen. 25:26, the son of Isaac and Rebekah and the younger twin brother of Esau. The relations between the two brothers were not good, and the fault was Jacob's Gen. 27. He bought Esau's birthright from him, Gen. 25:29-34, was compelled to flee, and went to Laban, a brother of his mother, who lived in Padanaram, and with whom he stayed for twenty years. See Gen. 28:12-22 for account of his vision at Bethel and subsequent vow. He married Laban's two daughters, Leah and Rachel, and he prospered. But he yearned after his native land, and as troubles continually arose between him and Laban they separated, though with a covenant of peace. Gen. 31:45-54. When he approached Canaan he felt anxious with respect to Esau, and then occurred that extraordinary event which made Israel, "the soldier of God," out of Jacob, "the supplanter." Gen. 32:24-32. The meeting with Esau was very friendly, and Jacob settled near Shechem, where he bought land, Gen. 33:19, and dug a well (see Jacob's Well). But new troubles overtook him and he decided to move to Hebron. On the way thither, at Bethlem, Benjamin was born and Rachel died. After staying for some time at Hebron, where he and Esau buried their father, Isaac, in the cave of Machpelah, Gen. 35:29, Jacob moved to Egypt on account of famine. There he found Joseph, and there he died, rich and honored. Gen. 49:33. His remains were carried to Hebron and buried in the cave of Machpelah, Gen. 50:13, with his ancestors. [2] The father of Joseph, the husband of Mary. Matt. 1:15,16.

Jacob's Well, at which Jesus sat and talked with the Samaritan woman, John 4:5,6, is one and a half miles south-east of Nablus, the ancient Shechem, close to the highway from Jerusalem to Galilee, in the plain of Moreh, at the eastern base of Mount Gerizim. The wall which enclosed it and the church which once was built over it are now only heaps of ruins, but the well itself, seven and a half feet in diameter, seventy feet deep, and lined throughout with heavy masonry, is still intact except so far as it has doubtless been filled up to a considerable extent with the fragments of the church and the wall. According to Jewish tradition, the well was dug by Jacob (Gen. 33:19). Christians, Jews, Samaritans, and Mohammedans all agree in keeping the place sacred. It is one of the few ancient places in Palestine that can be certainly identified.

Ja'el (mountain goat), wife of Heber the Kenite, who killed Sisera, the Canaanitish leader, when he fled from the Israelites under Deborah and Barak. Judg. 4:17, 18, 21, 22; 5: 6, 24.

Ja'ir (whom Jehovah enlightens). [1] A prominent warrior under Moses; was a descendant of the most powerful family of Judah and Manasseh. He conquered all the country of Argob east of Jordan; also villages in Gilead which he named Havothjair. Num. 32:41; Deut. 3:14; 1 Chron. 2:21-23. [2] One of the judges of Israel. Judg. 10:3-5. He judged Israel twenty-two years. [3] A Jew of the tribe of Benjamin, whose son Mordecai was cousin to Esther. Esth. 2:5. [4] Father of Elhanan, 1 Chron. 20:5, called JAARE-OREGIM in 2 Sam. 21:19.

Ja-i'rus (whom Jehovah enlightens), a ruler of the synagogue in one of the towns of Galilee near the Lake of Tiberias. Luke 8:41,42. He showed very strong faith. Christ went to his house with Peter, James, and John, and restored the daughter of Jairus to life. Mark 5:35-42.

Jambres, jam'breez, a person mentioned by Paul, 2 Tim. 3:8, as having withstood Moses. He was an Egyptian magician at the court of Pharaoh.

James, which is in Hebrew Jacob (the supplanter), is the name of two, or probably of three, persons in the New Testament. [1] James the Elder was a son of Zebedee and Salome, brother of John the Evangelist, probably a cousin of Jesus, and one of the three favorite apostles. His apostolic labors were confined to Jerusalem and Judea, and in A.D. 44 he was beheaded by order of King Herod Agrippa, thus becoming the first martyr among the apostles. Acts 12:2. [2] James the Less, or the Little, was a son of Alpheus and Mark, Mark 15:40; Matt. 10:3; Acts 1:13, and was also one of the twelve apostles. According to a tradition accepted by the Greek church, he labored in Egypt and was crucified there. [3] James, "the Brother of the Lord," Gal. 1:19; compare Matt. 13:55; Mark 6:3, or simply JAMES, Acts 12:17; 15:13, is by some identified with James the Less and regarded as a cousin of Jesus, while others distinguish between the two and take the designation 'the brother of the Lord" in the strict sense of the words. At all events, he stood at the head of the Church in Jerusalem after the dispersion of the disciples and the departure of Peter, Acts 12:17, and he presided at the Apostolical Council in Jerusalem, A.D. 50, whence he is generally styled by ecclesiastical writers "Bishop of Jerusalem." According to Josephus, the ancient Jewish historian, he was in A.D. 62 sentenced by the Sanhedrin to be stoned; according to Hegesippus, who was a Christian writer from the middle of the second century, he was thrown by the Pharisees from the pinnacle of the Temple and killed with a fuller's club while praying for his murderers.

James, the Epistle of, was written by James, "the brother of the Lord," in Jerusalem, before A.D. 62, and is addressed to "the twelve tribes scattered abroad;" that is, to all Jewish converts to Christianity. It is moral rather than doctrinal, insisting upon the necessity of true faith manifesting itself in good works.

Jang'ling, in 1 Tim. 1:6, means babbling; vain talking.

Jannes, jan'neez, and **Jambres,** jam'breez, two noted magicians of Egypt, 2 Tim. 3:8, supposed to have used their art to deceive Pharaoh. Exod. 7:9-13.

Ja'son (one who will heal), a disciple of Thessalonica whom the Jews assaulted because he received Paul and Silas into his

107

house. Acts 17:5,6,7,9.

Jas'per, the last precious stone in the high-priest's breast-plate, Exod. 28:20, and the first in the foundations of the New Jerusalem. Rev. 21:19. It is a kind of quartz of various colors and receives a high polish.

Jav'e-lin, 1 Sam. 18:10; num. 25:7, a light spear thrown from the hand.

Jeal'ous, Exod. 34:14, a name of the Lord.

Jeal'ous-y generally means suspicion of conjugal infidelity. 2 Cor. 11:2. The word is also used for anger or indignation, Ps. 79:5; 1 Cor. 10:22, or for a deep interest for the prosperity and honor of another. Zech. 1:14; 8:2. Its various meanings are generally indicated by its connection.

Je'bus (threshing-floor), an ancient name of Jerusalem. Judg. 19:10,11.

Je-bu'si, Josh. 15:8; 18:16, 28, a name for JEBUS, or JERUSALEM.

Jeb'u-sites, a tribe that lived in that part of Cannan about Jebus (afterward Jerusalem). The Israelites were commanded to destroy them. Deut. 7:1; 20:17. David conquered their stronghold. 2 Sam. 5:6, 8; 1 Chron. 11:4-6. The inhabitants of Jebus were called JEBUSITES.

Jed'u-thun (praising), a Levite, one of the chief singers in the time of David, whose descendants dwelt in Jerusalem after the captivity. 1 Chron. 9:16; 16:38, 41, 42; 25:1,3. Several of the Psalms are inscribed to him, among which are Ps. 39, 62, 77.

Je-hi'el (treasure of God?), a distinct name in Hebrew from Jehiel immediately preceding this one. [1] The father of Gibeon of Benjamin and an ancestor of Saul. 1 Chron. 9:35. [2] One of David's valiant men. 1 Chron. 11:44.

Jehoiachin, je-hoi'a-kin (whom Johovah has appointed), called JECONIAH in 1 Chron. 3:17, CONIAH in Jer 22:24, and JECHONIAS in Matt, 1:12, was son and successor of Je-hoiakim, king of Judah. 2 Kings 24:8 After a reign of three months and ten days he, with the royal family, the chief maen, and great treasures, was caried to Babylon by Nebuchadnezzar. 2 Kings 24:6-16.

Je-hoi'a-kim (whom Jehovah sets up), the name which was given by Pharaoh-necho to Eliakim, the son of Josiah, king of Judah, whom he made king in place of his father, after Pharaoh-necho had deposed and imprisoned Jehoahaz, whom the people had made king. 2 Kings 23:34; 1 Chron. 3:15.

Je-hosh'a-phat (whom Jehovah judges). [1] The royal recorder under David and Solomon. 2 Sam. 8:16; 1 Kings 4:3. [2] One of Solomon's purveyors. 1 Kings 4:17. [3] The son of Asa who succeeded his father as king of Judah. He reigned B.C. 914-890, and was pious and prosperous. 2 Chron. 17:3-6. [4] The father of King Jehu. 2 Kings 9:2, 14. [5] A priest in the time of David. 1 Chron. 15:24.

Je-hosh'a-phat, Valley of (valley of the judgment of Jehovah), a place named only in Joel 3:2, 12. It is usually identified with the valley of the brook Kedron, between Jerusalem and Mount Olivet, but is probably an ideal place in the prophet's vision of the judgment.

Je-ho'vah (he will be), a title of the Supreme Being. Exod. 6:3. Its meaning is similar to the title I AM. Exod. 3:14. In the English Bible it is generally translated "Lord" and printed in small capitals. It denotes the God of revelation and redemption.

Jeho'vah-ji'reh (The Lord will see, or provide), the name given by Abraham to the place where, when he was about to sacrifice Isaac, he was stopped by an angel of the Lord. Gen. 22:14. It is probably the same as MOUNT MORIAH in Jerusalem.

Je-ho'vah-nis'si (The LORD my banner), the name which Moses gave to the altar which he built after the Israelites had defeated the Amalekites. Exod. 17:15.

Je-ho'vah-sha'lom (The LORD send peace), the name which Gideon gave to the altar which he built when the Lord said to him, "Peace be unto thee." Judg. 6:24.

Je-ho'vah-sham'mah (The LORD is there), the name given to the city spoken of in the prophetical description of the Holy Land communicated to Ezekiel. Ezek. 48:35, marginal notes.

Jehovah-tsidkenu, je-ho'vah-sid'ke-nu (THE LORD OUR RIGHTEOUSNESS), is found in the marginal notes in Jer. 23:6. and 33:16.

109

Je'hu (Jehovah is he). [1] The son of Hanani the seer. 1 Kings 16:1, 7 12; 2 Chron. 19: 2; 20:34. [2] The son of Jehoshaphat and grandson of Nimshi. Elisha was commanded to anoint him king over Israel, and he became the instrument of God's judgments on the house of Ahab. 1 Kings 19: 16, 17; 2 Kings 9: 1-10. Jehu was tyrannical and became idolatrous. 2 Kings 10:31. He regined B.C. 884-856. [3] A descendent of Jerahmeel, the son of Hezron. 1 Chron. 2:38. [4] One of the tribe of Simeon. 1 Chron. 4:35. [5] A Benjamite who was with David at Ziklag. 1 Chron. 12:3.

Jeph'thah, jef'thah (whom God sets free), a judge of Israel who delivered them from the Ammonites. Judg. 11:1, 2, 3. Jepththah made a vow, just before the battle, that if he gained the victory he would offer up for a burnt offering whatsoever came forth from his house to welcome him on his return. This proved to be his daughter, an only child. Judge. 11: 30-40.

Jer-e-mi'ah (whom Jehovah sets up). [1] The father of Hamutal, wife of King Josiah. 2 Kings 23:31; 24: 18; Jer. 52:1. [2] Head of a family in Manasseh. 1 Chron. 5:24. [3] A valiant man who joined David in Ziklag. 1 Chron. 12:4. [4,5] Gadite warriors who joined David at Ziklag. 1 Chron. 12:10,13. [6] A priest who sealed the covenant. Neh. 10:2; 12:1, 12, 34. [7] A decendant of Janadab, the son of Rechab. Jer. 35:3. He was one of the Rechabites.

[8] JEREMIAH (whom Jehovah sets up), one of the four great prophets, was of priestly descent, consecrated to the prophetic office before his birth, and was a son of Hilkiah of Anathoth, in the land of Benjamin. He began his prophetic ministrations at an early age, in the thirteenth year of the reign of Josiah, B.C. 626, and continued it for a period of forty-two years, until after the destruction of Jerusalem and the beginning of the captivity. He denounced the vices and the idolatry of the people, proclaimed the judgment of God which awaited them, and advised submission to Nebuchadnezzar as the only means of escaping destruction. But Jerusalem swarmed with false prophets who promised the king and the people the support of God in their undertakings, and then the end came. To the exiles he wrote that their captivity would be long--that, indeed it

would last seventy years. After the murder of Gedaliah, Jeremiah was carried, against his will, to Egypt, and there he probably died.

Jeremi'ah, The Book of, contains the prophesies uttered under Josiah, B.C. 629-608, chapters 1-12; under Jehoiakim, B.C. 607-597, chapters 13, 20, 22, 23, 35, 36, 45-48, 49: 1-33; under Zedekiah, B.C. 597-588,, chapters 21, 24, 27-34, 37-39, 49:34-39; 50, 51; and under Gedaliah, chapters 40-44.

Jer'i-cho (fragrance), an ancient strongly fortifed and celebrated city of Palestine, stood in the valley of the Jordan, five miles west of that river and six miles north of the Dead Sea, in a very fertile plain watered by a large spring called the "Fountain of Elisha." 2 Kings 2:19-22. It was called the "city of palm trees." Deut. 34:3; Judge. 3: 13; 2 Chron. 28:15. The Jericho mentioned in the New Testament was about a mile and a half south-east of the ancient city. The present city, called Er-Riha, is about two miles further east than the second Jericho. Spies were sent into the ancient city and received by Rahab. Josh. 2; Heb. 11:31. It was the first city attacked by Joshua after crossing the Jordan. He was miraculously aided in capturing it, the wall "fell down flat," Josh. 6:20, and the city and its inhabitants, except Rahab and her kindred and all that she had, were destroyed. It was soon rebuilt and became properous again. It had a flourishing school of prophets which was often visited by Elijah. 2 Kings 2. After the Babylonian captivity it was immediately repeopled, Ezra 2:34; Neh. 7:36, and Herod the Great made it his winter residence, adorned it with many splendid buildings, and died there. As the Jewish pilgrims going up to Jerusalem used to assemble at Jericho, Christ passed through it several times; there he met Zacchaeus, Luke 19: 1-9, and it is mentioned often in the New Testament. Matt. 20: 24-34; Mark 10: 46-52, etc. At present it is only a miserable village. The scene of the parable of the Good Samaritaan was on the road from Jericho to Jerusalem. It is still the haunt of robbers.

Jer-o-bo'am (whose people is many) was the name of two kings of Israel. [1] JEROBOAM I., the founder of the kingdom of Israel, B.C. 975-954, came of the tribe of Ephraim, a son of

Nebat, is noted as "the man who made Israel to sin," and was by Solomon made superintendent of all the workmen furnished by his tribe. It having been foretold by the prophet Ahijah that he should become king of the ten tribes, it aroused the suspicion of Solomon and Jeroboam fled to Egypt. After the death of the king he returned, placed himself at the head of the rebellion against Rehoboam, and fixed his residence at Shechem, which he fortified. Idolatry was part of his nature and also of his policy. In order to separate the ten tribes as far as possible from the two tribes which remained faithful to the house of David, he wished to prevent his subjects from going up to Jerusalem at the great festivals, and for that purpose he erected two idols, two golden calves, one at Bethel and the other at Dan, appointed priests out of the common people, and offered sacrifices himself at the altar. [2] JERBOAM II., who reigned B.C. 825-784, was a son of Joash and great-grandson of Jehu. He was idolatrous, like Jeroboam I., 2 Kings 14:23-29, and as seen from the books of Hosea and Amos, but he was victorious over his enemies and raised the kingdom of Israel to its highest power. Not long after his death his family was cut off with the sword, 2 Kings 15:10, according to the prediction of the prophet Amos.

Je-rub'-ba-al (with whom Baal contends), Judge. 6:32.

Je-ru'sa-lem (the abode of peace), the most important city in Biblical history, was the capital of the Hebrew monarchy and of the kingdom of Judah. It is the most sacred city of the world, and is called by the Psalmist "Beautiful for situation, the joy of the whole earth," and "the perfection of beauty." Ps. 48:2,3; 50:2. Christ, in Matt. 23: 37-39, speaks mournfully of it in view of its unfaithfulness and approaching destruction.

Names.--It is call Jebusi, Josh.18:28, and JEBUS, Judg. 19:10,11, and is first mentioned as JERUSALEM in Josh. 10:1. It was also known as SALEM, CITY OF DAVID, CITY OF ZION, CITY OF JUDAH, CITY OF GOD, CITY OF THE GREAT KING, HOLY CITY, ARIEL, and prophetically, Isa. 24:10, as CITY OF CONFUSION. The word ZION sometimes denotes the whole of Jerusalem, but literally means its south-western hill. In the Latin Version Jerusalem is called HIERO-

SOLYMA, and the Roman emperor Hadrian called it AELIA CAPITOLINA. It is now known by the Mohammedans, Arabs, and Turks as el-Khuds, "the holy," and Beit-el-Makhuddis, "the holy house." Situation and Extent.-- It was built on four hills, Zion, Acra, Moriah, and Bezetha, and is latitude 31° 46" 35" north and longitude 35° 13' 30" east from Greenwich. It is near the summit of the western mountain range of Palestine; is thirty-two miles east of the Mediterranean and eighteen miles west of the Dead Sea. Its highest point is 2581 feet above the sea, and the city now covers an irregular quadrangle of about 210 acres, enclosed by a wall nearly two and one-thrid miles long. The old walls of Solomon and Zerubbabel included only about 150 acres. At the time of its greatest extent, after the third wall had been built by Herod Agrippa, the city covered about 465 acres. The ancient city included territory now outside the walls and under cultivation. Jer.26:18. Jerusalem is surrounded on all sides except the north by deep ravines which, before the invention of modern siegeguns, made it a place of great military strength. On the east is the valley of the Kedron, separating the city from the long ridge of the Mount of Olives, of which the central peak is called the Mount of the Ascension, 2665 feet high, and, still farther south, from the Mount of Offence, 2409 feet high, the seat of Solomon's idol-worship. On the west and south is the valley of Hinnom, separating the city from the Hill of Evil Counsel, 2552 feet high, where Judas is reputed to have made the bargain for the betrayal of our Lord, and where the traitor afterward hanged himself. On the side of this hill is the ACELDAMA (which see). The land on which the city itself is built comprises two parallel ridges, of which the eastern, Mount Moriah, 2440 feet high, was the site of the TEMPLE (which see), and the western, Mount Zion, 2550 feet high, the site of David's house and later of Herod's palace. These two ridges are separated by a depression called the Tyropoean Valley or the Valley of the Cheesemongers, which opens into the valley of the Kedron near the Pool of Siloam. North of Mount Zion was the Akra, or "lower city" of Josephus. The hill Bezetha was north of Mount Moriah.

History.--First of Jebusite Period, commencing B.C. 1450.-

- The first definte notice of Jerusalem is in Josh. 15:8; 18:16, 28. It was called JEBUSI, from the Jebusites who made it their stronghold, and JEBUS. Judge. 19:10. The Jebusites retained the city after the conquest of the land by Joshua. Josh. 15:63. After the death of Joshua the Israelites captured a part of the city, but the Jebusites retained the upper city for nearly four hundred years. In the eighth year of the reign of David (B.C. 1055-1015) over all Israel he orgainized an attack upon Jerusalem, the strong citadel was taken by his chief captain, Joab, and it was called "the stronghold of Zion" or "the city of David." 2 Sam. 5:7; 1 Chron. 11:7. The fame of Jerusalem commenced at this time.

Second Period: Jerusalem under the Kings.--David connected the fortress (which he used for his residence) with the city, enclosed them with a strong wall, brought up the ark of the covenant, 2 Sam. 6:2-16, and made the place the political and religious capital of the Israelites. From this time it was called JERUSALEM or ZION or the CITY OF DAVID. 2 Sam.5:7; 1 Chron. 11:7. The choice of Jerusalem as the capital of the Israelites was made by David under divine direction. Deut. 12:5-21; 1 Kings 11:36. His son Solomon, who reigned B.C. 1015-975, made it one of the most magnificent cities of the world. He extended and strengthened the walls, built the TEMPLE (which see) and several palaces, among which were the "House of the Forest of Lebanon," 1 Kings 7:2-7, and a palace for the queen, the daughter of Pharaoh, 1 Kings 7:8, and gathered within its walls immense treasures. But under his son Rehoboam, B.C. 975-957, the separation between the ten tribes and the two tribes took place, B.C. 975, and Jerusalem became merely the capital of the kingdom of Judah, exposed to the jealousy and cupidity of the kings of Israel, Egypt, and Assyria. In the fifth year of the reign of Rehoboam, the Egyptian king Shishak invaded the kingdom of Judah, instigated by Jeroboam, king of Israel, captured Jerusalem B.C. 969, and pillaged the Temple. 1 Kings 14:25,26; 2 Chron. 12:2-9. Under King Asa, thirty years later, Jerusalem again became independent after the great battle with Zerah (an Egyptian or Cushite king) at Mareshah. 2 Chron. 14:9-15. In spite of periods of idolatry and seasons of severe trouble which the city passed through, its prosperity under the reign of Hezehiah, B.C. 726-697, nearly equalled that which it enjoyed in the time of Solomon. Hezekiah made a great improvement both in the daily life of the city and in its strength in time of war. He provided it with an ample supply of water, and was eminently successful in repulsing the attacks of the Assyrians. But after that time the power of the kingdom of Judah rapidly declined, and in the frightful conflict between Pharaoh-necho of Egypt and Nebuchadnezzar of Babylon the kingdom of Judah was destroyed and Jerusalem was taken, B.C. 605, by Nebuchadnezzar. A number of its inhabitants, among whom was Daniel, were carried to Babylon as prisoners. After the revolt of Jehoiakim it was again taken by Nebuchadnezzar, B.C. 602, and ten thousand of the richest and most distinguished inhabitants, including the skilled artisans, were sent to Babylon. Finally, after the revolt of Zedekiah, the last king of Judah, the city was taken the third time by Nebuchadnezzar, B.C. 588, and this time nearly all its inhabitants (among whom was Zedekiah, whose eyes had been put out) were carried into captivity (only a few being left to be vine-dressers and husbandmen) and its Temple, palaces, houses, and walls were razed to the ground. The dreadful scenes of this siege and destruction are vivdly described by Jeremiah in Lamentations, chapters 2 and 5. For fifty years it laid deserted, a mere heap of ruins.

Third Period: Jerusalem of Ezra and the Ptolemies.--Meanwhile the Babylonian empire had been overturned by Cyrus, king of Persia, B.C. 538, and he allowed the Jews to return to their native country and rebuild their capital and their Temple. The first returned under Zerubbabel, B.C. 536, some more under Ezra, B.C. 458, and the last under Nehemiah, B.C. 445. Under the Persian governors the Temple and the walls were rebuilt and the city arose from its ashes. The overturning of the Persian empire by Alexander the Great had no evil effect on the destiny of the city. According to Josephus, he visited it B.C. 332, after the battle of Issus, had the book of Daniel and the prophecy of the downfall of Persia read to him, and showed the Jews many favors. Under the Ptolemies and Maccabees the city steadily progressed. Jerusalem was captured B.C. 63 by the Roman Pompey, who did not disturb the treasures of the Temple. Crassus plundered the Temple and city of their treasure B.C. 54, and the city was captured B.C. 40 by the Parthians under Antigonus. Herod, afterward the Great (who died soon after Christ was born), laid siege to Jerusalem the next year, supported by a Roman army, and after a siege of five months the citadel and Temple were captured by storm, the outer walls and lower city having been previously taken. Herod was afterward made king by the Romans, and at once began to improve and beautify the city, one of his principal works being the rebuilding and enlarging of the Temple, which occupied forty-six years. John 2:20. The work was begun B.C. 20, and continued long after his death. Jerusalem under the rule of Herod the Great was restored to much of its former magnificence.

Fourth Period: Jerusalem in the Time of Christ.--Very little can now be seen of the Jerusalem of the time of our Lord, the city of Zerubbabel and Herod. It lies buried twenty to eighty feet deep under ruins and rubbish. The city of David and Solomon lies still deeper, though it has been possible to trace its outlines, and even to touch the huge foundations upon which Solomon constructed the Temple. But it must be remembered that Jerusalem is more than thirty-five hundred years old, has suffered many sieges and captures, and has twice been razed to the ground and deserted. Herod was the representative of the Greek-Roman civilization, and national pride, exclusiveness, and moral indignation roused the Jews to resistance to him. With Herod began that hatred between the Jews and the Romans which ended in the second total destruction of Jerusalem, A.D. 70, by the Romans under Titus--one of the most horrible events in the history of war. The besiegers were extremely cruel and the defenders very furious and desperate. The Jews suffered terribly during the siege and, according to Josephus, over 1,000,000 of them were killed and 97,000 made captives. The rebellion was continued about three years longer, when the Jewish power was totally destroyed.

Fifth Period: Jerusalem under Roman and Christian Emperors.--Jerusalem was again in ruins for half a century. A new Jerusalem was founded by the emperor Hadrian A.D. 118-138 (which he peopled with Romans), on the site of the ancient city, and name AELIA CAPITOLINA. A temple of Jupiter was built on the ruins of the Temple of Jehovah, and the Jews were not allowed to enter the city until the country was governed by the Christian emperors. Constatine the Great, A.D. 306-337, restored the name JERUSALEM, opened the gates of the city to the Jews, etc., and his mother, Helena, built the church of the Holy Sepulchre there. Julian, commonly called the Apostate, A.D. 363, vainly endeavored to rebuild the Jewish Temple and restore Jewish worship. A fine church was founded by the emperor Justinian, A.D. 529, in honor of the Virgin. The Persians under Chosroes II. captured Jerusalem A.D. 614, killed large numbers of the monks and clergy, and destroyed the churches.

J

Sixth Period: Jerusalem of the Crusaders and Turks.--In A.D. 637 Jerusalem was conquered by the Arabs under Caliph Omar, who made it a Mohammedan city, and, though retaken by the Crusaders A.D. 1099 and held by the Christians till A.D. 1187, it is still a Mohammedan city. Since A.D. 1517 it has been in the possession of the Turkish sultan.

Modern Jerusalem is built on the ruins of the ancient Holy City, and stands on the northern parts of the hills of Zion and Moriah, the part of the old city known as Acra, and on the hill Bezetha, a part of Jerusalem which dates from Agrippa, A.D. 42. The walls do not include the southern parts of the hills of Zion and Ophel. The rubbish around the Temple walls is nearly one hundred feet deep, and on the hill of Zion about forty feet deep.

The city is divided into four parts by the main streets. The largest division is the "Mohammedan quarter," and is in the north-eastern part of the city. West of this is the "Greek and Frank or Christian quarter." The "Armenian quarter" is south of the "Christian quarter," and the "Jewish quarter" lies east of the "Armenian quarter." The garrison, the police, and the government of the city is Mohammedan. The largest and most conspicuous place in the city is the Haram enclosure on Mount

Moriah, where stands the mosque of Omar, the most magnificent building in the city, occupying the place where the Temple of Solomon once stood. It also contains the mosque El-Aksa and the mosque called the Throne of Solomon. The "Christian quarter" includes the church of the Holy Sepulchre, a Coptic convent and several others, an Abyssinian monastery, and the Muristan. The "Mohammedan quarter" has the church of Mary Magdalene, the church of St. Anne, two convents, Pilate's hall, two mosques, and the city prison. In the "Jewish quarter" are two synagogues, three hospital, and the "wailing-place," where the Jews gather every Friday evening, kiss the foundation-stones of the Temple, and bewail the downfall of their city by reading or repeating parts of the Lamentations of Jeremiah or suitable Psalms. In the "Armenian quarter" are the Towers of David and Hippicus, the church of St. James, and several convents. The wall which now encloses Jerusalem was built by the sultan Suleiman the Magnificent in A.D. 1542; it is about thirty-eight feet high, and has thirty-four towers and seven gates. The houses are generally of stone, and are two or three stories high. The roofs are usually flat; some are dome-shaped. Most of the streets are narrow, crooked, and poorly paved. The houses have few windows opening on the streets. Most of the windows open into the uncovered courts in the interior of the houses. Of the population of Jerusalem, about 13,000 are Moslems, 7000 are Christians, and 4000 are Jews. It has been very much increased lately. A new Jerusalem is being built up outside of the Jaffagate, and a railroad was in progress in 1891 to connect the city with the seaport of Jaffa (the ancient Joppa), on the Mediterranean.

Je-ru'sa-lem, New, a name used figuratively to denote the spiritual Church in its final triumph and glory. Rev. 3:12; 21:2.

Jes'se (strong), an Israelite of the tribe of Judah. He was the grandson of Ruth and the father of David. His genealogy is given in Ruth 4:18-22; 1 Chron. 2:5-12; Matt. 1:3-5; Luke 3:32-34. He had eight sons, of whom David was the youngest. Jesse is usually called "Jesse the Bethlehemite," and is announced in Isa. 11:1, 10 as the ancestor of Christ.

Je'sus (Saviour) is the Greek form for the Hebrew word

"Jehoshua," contracted to "Joshua," and is found only in the New Testament, and should be exclusively applied to CHRIST. Jesus was the personal name of CHRIST among men during his life on earth. In Acts 7:45; Col. 4:11; Heb. 4:8, "Jesus " should be "Joshua," although these two names had originally the same meaning.

Je'sus, called JUSTUS, a disciple who was a fellow-worker with Paul and who sent salutations to the Christians of Colosse. Col. 4:11.

Je'thro (his excellence), the priest of Midian who was father-in-law of Moses. He is called RAGUEL in Num. 10:29, REUEL in Exod. 2:18, and JETHER in the marginal notes in Exod. 4:18.

Jew'els, personal ornaments made of precious metals; among them were chains, bracelets, earrings, etc. They are mentioned in Gen. 24:22; Num. 31:50; Ezek. 23:26 etc. The word is figuratively used for anything peculiarly precious, as God's chosen people, Mal. 3:17, or wisdom. Prov. 20:15.

Jew'ry, Dan. 5:13, is elsewhere translated JUDAH and JUDEA.

Jews, the people of the tribes of Judah and Benjamin, as distinguished from the revolted ten tribes. 2 Kings 16:6; Ezra 4:12.

Jez'e-bel (chaste), daughter of Ethbaal, king of the Zidonians, and wife of Ahab, king of Israel. She became infamous for her idolatries and her persecution of the prophets. 1 Kings 16:31; 18:4. She introduced the worship of Baal and other idols, and was virtually the ruler of Israel.

Jez're-el (God hath planted). [1] A city of Issachar, in the valley of Jezreel, between Gilboa and Little Hermon, which Ahab chose for his residence; his "ivory house," 1 Kings 22:39, stood in the eastern part, while Jezebel lived by the city wall, near the temple and grove of Astarte. The city is now a village among ruins. [2] A town in Judah. Josh. 15:56; 1 Sam. 25:43; 29:1, 11. [3] A descendant of Judah. 1 Chron. 4:3. [4] Eldest son of Hosea the prophet. He was so named by command of God. Hos. 1:4. [5] The word is used figuratively in reference to the crimes of Ahab in Jezreel and the punishment threatened by

God on account of them. Hos. 1:4, 11.

Jez're-el, the Valley of, is an exceedingly fertile plain of central Palestine which, south of the Carmel range, intersects the western highland, between the hills of Galilee and those of Samaria, and connects the low coast-land along the Mediterranean with the Jordan valley. It was the battle-field where Gideon triumphed, Judg. chap. 7, and Deborah sung her war-song. Judg. 5:2-31. Josiah was fatally wounded near it, by the Egyptians. Saul and Jonathan fell on the mountains of Gilboa near by. 1 Sam. 31:1-6. Its Greek name Esdraelon is not in the Bible.

Jo'ash, 2 Kings 13:1, or **Je-ho'ash,** 2 Kings 12:1 (whom Jehovah bestowed). [1] The father of Gideon. Judg. 6:11, etc. [2] A son of Ahab. 1 Kings 22:26; 2 Chron. 18:25. [3] Son and successor of Ahaziah, king of Judah. He was the only son of Ahaziah that was not slain by order of Athaliah. He was hidden in the Temple six years by Jehosheba, his aunt, 2 Kings 11:2, 3, and became king of Judah when seven years old. 2 Kings 11:12. His kingdom was invaded by Hazael, but he redeemed his capital from plunder by a large sum of money and all the treasure and furniture of the Temple. 2 Kings 12:18. He reigned forty years, B.C. 878-839, and was murdered by his own servants. 2 Chron. 24:24-27. [4] Son of Jehoahaz, whom he succeeded as king of Israel. He reigned B.C. 840-825, including two years in which he was associated with his father. He was very successful in a war with Amaziah, king of Judah, and died soon afterward. 2 Kings 14:12-16. [5] A descendant of Judah. 1 Chron. 4:22. [6] One of David's heroes. 1 Chron. 12:3.

Jo'a-tham, Matt. 1:9, an ancestor of Joseph, the husband of Mary. It is the Greek form of JOTHAM.

Job (one persecuted), the patriarch, Ezek. 14:14,20; James 5:11, was of the land of Uz, Job 1:1, which was probably in eastern Edom.

Job, the Book of, is a poem on a historical foundation, or history treated poetically. The person of Job is mentioned in Ezek. 14:14, 18, 20; James 5:11. He lives also in the tradition of the Arabs. The prologue (chaps. 1 and 2) and the epilogue (chap. 42:7-17) are written in narrative prose, the rest in

Hebrew poetry. As a mere literary production it is one of the sublimest and most interesting works ever written and fully equal to the greatest productions of genius. It has been called the Shakespeare in the Bible. The person of Job is represented as a prince of the patriarchal age, who from the highest prosperity was suddenly cast down to utter poverty and misery, deprived of all his property and children, stricken with a loathsome disease, forsaken and insulted by his wife and friends, but who after the severest trial of faith and patience was restored to more than his former prosperity and happiness. He was ignorant of the Mosaic law and Jewish worship, and lived outside of Palestine on the border line, but was nevertheless a worshipper of the true God, an inspired prophet, a hero of faith, a model of patience and endurance, with the assurance of a final victory over sin and sorrow. He was a holy outsider, as it were, of the order of Melchizedek, the friend of Abraham, "without father, without mother, without genealogy" (compare Heb. 7:3). The book wrestles with the problem of all ages--to harmonize the terrible fact of sin and suffering with the government of an all-wise and merciful God. This problem is solved in the sufferings and death of Christ for the salvation of the world. The Book of Job has been called a Hebrew tragedy or Hebrew theodicy (a vindication of the justice of God in regard to the natural and moral evil that exists under his government). The authorship is unknown; some trace it to Moses or some earlier writer, others to the age of Solomon. The scenery is laid in the patriarchal age. The Book of Job has been and will continue to be a rich source of comfort to children of affliction.

Jo'el (Jehovah is his God). [1] The eldest son of the prophet Samuel, 1 Sam. 8:2; 1 Chron. 6:33; 15:17, erroneously called VASHNI (which see) in 1 Chron. 6:28. [2] A descendant of Simeon. 1 Chron. 4:35. [3] A descendant of Reuben. 1 Chron. 5:4, 8. [4] Head of a Gadite family. 1 Chron. 5:12. [5] A Levite of the family of Kohath, 1 Chron. 6:36, probably a corruption of SHAUL in 1 Chron. 7:3. [6] A descendant of ISSACHAR. 1 Chron. 7:3. [7] One of David's valiant men, 1 Chron 11:38, called IGAL in 2 Sam. 23:36. [8] A chief of the family of

Gershom. 1 Chron. 15:7, 11. [9] One of the keepers of the treasure of the house of the Lord. 1 Chron. 23:8; 26:22. [10] A prince of Manasseh. 1 Chron. 27:20. [11] A descendant of Kohath in the time of Hezekiah. 2 Chron. 29:12. [12] A Jew who had a foreign wife. Ezra 10:43. [13] An overseer of the Benjamites that dwelt in Jerusalem. Neh. 11:9. [14] JOEL, one of the minor prophets, a son of Pethuel; lived in Judah under the reign of Uzziah, but nothing further is known of his personal history. Joel 1:1.

Joel, the Book of, begins with the denunciation of the judgment of God which will strike the unrepentant people, and ends with the announcement of the blessings which will follow the coming of the Messiah. His prophecies are mentioned in Acts 2:16-21; Rom. 10:13.

John, same as **Jo-ha'-nan** (whom Jeho-vah loves). [1] A relation of Annas the high-priest. Acts 4:6. [2] The Hebrew name of the evangelist Mark. Acts 12:35; 13:5; 15:37. [3] JOHN THE BAPTIST, or, more properly, "the Baptizer," Matt. 3:1, son of Zacharias the priest and Elizabeth, a cousin of Mary, the mother of Jesus. He was born about six months before Christ. The angel Gabriel predicted his birth and work. Luke 1:5-15. His early life was spent in solitude, his raiment was of camel's hair, and his food was locusts and wild honey. When about thirty years old he began to preach in the wilderness of Judea, announcing the coming of the Messiah, calling all to repentance and reformation, pointing to Jesus as the Messiah, and baptizing with the baptism of repentance multitudes who came to him from all parts of the land and confessed their sins. Christs said of him, Matt. 11:11, "Among them that are born of women there hath not risen a greater than John the Baptist." He was the Elias (Elijah) of the New Testament, and was imprisoned and beheaded by Herod Antipas. Matt. 14: 3-10.

[4] JOHN, THE APOSTLE AND EVANGELIST, was one of the first of the apostles, he "whom Jesus loved." He was a son of Zebedee and Salome, and if Salome was a sister of Mary, John 19:25, he was also a cousin of Jesus. He was probably born at Bethsaida, Matt. 4:18, 21, on the Sea of Galilee, and pursued, like his brother, the trade of a fisherman. Both brothers were

followers of John the Baptist before they became apostles of Christ. John 1:37. After being called he seems to have been always with Christ during his whole ministry, and after the ascension he, together with Peter and James, took charge of the Christian church in Jerusalem, where he met with Paul, A.D. 50. Some years later he moved to Ephesus, and from that time till his death he was at the head of all the Christian churches in Asia Minor. He was banished to Patmos, a barren island in the Aegean Sea, by the Roman emperor, but was subsequently allowed to return to Ephesus, where he died full of days during the reign of Trajan, which began A.D. 98. Many beautiful traditions have clustered around his name.

John, the Gospel of, was written many years after the other gospels (between A.D. 80 and 90), and it is evident that John knew them when he undertook to write his own gospel. Quite naturally, therefore, though perhaps not intentionally, his gospel became a complement to the three earlier ones. He omits much which they contain, as, for instance, all the parables and most of the miracles, and concentrates his narrative on Christ's ministry in Judea, while the others are principally occupied with His ministry in Galilee. One-third of the whole book is devoted to what took place during the last twenty-four hours of Christ's life on earth. Its delineation of Christ is also an addition to what has been given by the others. It is not Christ the man or the teacher or the Messiah, but Christ the incarnate Son of God and redeemer of mankind who stood before the author, and there is in his word-painting a blending of love and awe which gives it a peculiarly sublime character.

John, the Epistles of, three in number, were all written in Ephesus and about the same time as his gospel. THE FIRST is a kind of doctrinal discourse addressed to believers in general, but more especially to the Gentiles of Asia Minor, for the purpose of confirming them in their faith and warning them against errors. THE SECOND and THIRD are very short, and addressed, it would seem, to private persons--the former to the "elect lady and her children" (The woman well known to the churches as a disciple of Christ), the latter to one Gaius or Caius.

Jo'nah (dove), the fifth of the minor prophets, was a son of Amittai, and born at Gath-hepher, in the land of Lebanon, 2 Kings 14:25, but of his life nothing further is known except what is told in his book.

Jonah, the Book of, consists of two parts: the first contains the commission given him, his refusal, and his miraculous escape from death out of the belly of "a great fish" (a whale or a shark); the second, the renewal of the commission, his obedience, the repentance of the Ninevites, and the hard spirit of Jonah. Some theolgians have considered the book a parable, but its place in the Old Testament Canon, and still more the manner in which Christ refers to it, Matt. 12: 39-41; 16:4; Luke 11: 29-32, seem to give it the character of real history. An interesting feature of the book is the progress it evinces from a narrow Jewish spirit, in which it begins, to a thoroughly general view, in which it ends. It teaches the lesson that God's mercy and the working of his Spirit are not confined to the Jewish people and the visible Church, but extend also to the heathen.

Jon'a-than (whom Jehovah gave). [1] An Israelite of the tribe of Levi, who became a priest of the idol set up by Micah in Mount Ephraim, and which was afterward taken away and set up at Laish by the Danites. Judg. 17: 7-13; 18:30.

[2] One of the sons of Saul, the first king of Israel. He was famous for his peity and valor. 1 Sam. 14: 6-14. Jonathan loved David "as his own soul." 1 Sam. 18:1. Their remarkable friendship is minutely described in 1 Sam. 18: 1-4; chapters 19, 20, etc. Jonathan, two of his brothers, and his father were slain in the battle of Gilboa. 1 Sam. 31:6. David's beautiful and patahetic lamentaion for Jonathan is given in 2 Sam. 1: 17-27. [3] A son of Abiathar, one of the high-priests in the time of David. 2 Sam. l5:27; 1 Kings 1 :42, 43. [4] A son of Shimeah, one of the brothers of David. 2 Sam. 21:21; 1 Chron. 20:7. [5] One of David's valiant men. 2 Sam. 23:32; 1 Chron. 11:34. [6] A descendant of Jerahmeel. 1 Chron. 27:32. [8] A chief man of the Jews, whose son returned with Ezra to Babylon. Ezra 8:6. [9] A Jew who aided Ezra in the investigation of mixed marriages. Ezra10:15. [10] A high-priest for thirty-two years,

Neh. 12:11, called JOHANAN in Neh. 12:22, 23. [11] A priest, the descendant of Melicuh. Neh. 12:14. [12] Another priest, a descendant of Shemaiah, Neh. 12:35, called JEHONATHAN in Neh. 12:18. [13] A scribe in whose house the prophet Jeremiah was imprisoned by the princes of Judah. Jer. 37:15, 20; 38:26. [14] A son of Kareah. Jer. 40:8.

Jop'pa (beauty), an old city of Palestine, in the territory of Dan, and called JAPHO in Josh. 19:46, stands upon a promontory one hundred and sixteen feet high which juts out into the Mediterranean Sea, thirty miles south of Caesarea and thirty-five miles north-west of Jerusalem. It was the seaport into which the cedar from Lebanon was brought for the building of Solomon's Temple, 2 Chron. 2:16, and for the rebuilding of the Temple after the captivity. Ezra 3:7. Jonah sailed from Joppa for Tarshish. Jonah 1:3. Here took place the raising of Tabitha to life by Peter, mentioned in Acts 9:36-43, and Peter's vision. Acts 10:11. The reputed houses of Tabitha and Simon the tanner at Joppa are still pointed out. During the last twenty-five years the city has increased very much and become quite flourishing. It is now called Jaffa, and has about fifteen thousand inhabitants. A railroad from Jaffa to Jerusalem was in progress in 1891.

Jor'dan (the Descender), the principal river of Palestine, has four sources, which are situated among the mountains of Anti-Lebanon--namely: (1) The Hasbany, flowing from a large fountain near Hasbeya, seventeen hundred feet above the sea. (2) The Banias, which rises eleven hundred and forty feet above the sea, near the ruins of Caesaarea-Philippi (now Banias), at the foot of Mount Hermon. (3) The Leddan, which flows from a large fountain on the west side of the site of the city of Dan. (4) The Esh-Shar, a small tributary. After passing through a wide marsh the Jordan flows into Lake el-Huleh, and from this point, in nine miles descends nearly nine hundred feet to the Sea of Galilee. After leaving this sea it flows through a deep valley and over nearly thirty rapids into the DEAD SEA (which see), sixty-six miles distant in a direct line, but about two hundred miles by the course of the river. The distance in a direct line from its sources to its mouth is about one hundred and thirty-five miles; its general course is from north to south; its whole descent is about three thousand feet; its width is from forty-five to one hundred and eighty feet, and its depth from three to twelve feet. The lowest of its four principal fords is opposite Jericho, one is east of Sakut, and two more are near the Sea of Galilee. The Jordan is first mentioned in Gen. 13: 10; it was crossed by Jacob, Gen. 32:10, and passed over by the Israelites when entering the Promised Land. Josh. 3:14; Ps. 114:3. It is mentioned many times in the Old Testament, and wonderful miracles are connected with it, among which is the curing of Naaman. 2 Kings 5:14. The principal events associated with it in the New Testament are the baptism of the multitudes by John the Baptist, Matt. 3:6, and of Jesus. Mark 1:9.

Joseph, jo'zef (he will add). [1] The eleventh son of Jacob, the first whom he had by Rachel. Gen. 30:24. His father's fondness for him excited the envy of his brothers, and they sold him for twenty pieces of silver to the Ishmeelites, who carried him to Egypt, where he became "governor over all the land of Egypt." The wonderful story of his life is contained in Genesis chapters 37, 39-50. He died at the age of one hundred and ten, and his bones were brought out of Egypt and buried in Shechem. Josh. 24:32.

[2] The father of Igal the spy. Num. 13:7. [3] A Jew who married a foreign wife. Ezra 10:42. [4] A priest in the time of Joiakim. Neh. 12:14. [5] A son of Asaph. 1 Chron. 25: 2,9. [6,7 8] Three ancestors of Christ. Luke 3:24, 26, 30. [9] The husband of Mary the mother of Jesus. He was a carpenter by trade, Matt. 13:55, and a "just man." Matt. 1:19. The account of his life is contained in Matt. 1:16-25; 2: 13-23; Luke 1: 27;2: 4-51; 3:23; 4:22; John 1:45; 6:42. Nothing is found in the Bible concerning Joseph after Jesus was twelve years old. He is generally supposed to have died before Christ began his public ministry. [10] Joseph of Arimathaea, a wealthy member of the Sanhedrin and a disciple of Christ. He went to Pilate and begged the body of Jesus, and laid it in his own new tomb. Matt. 27:57-60

[11] A discpline called also BARSABAS, who was a candidate with Matthias to take the place of Judas among the apostles. Acts 1:23.

Joshaphat, josh'a-fat, (whom Jehovah judges), one of David's valiant men. 1 Chron. 11:43.

Josh'u-a. [1] The great leader of the Israelites in the conquest of Canaan; was the son of Nun, of the tribe of Ephraim, and was born in Egypt. His original name was OSHEA, Num. 13:8, or HOSHEA, Deut. 32:44, but it was changed to JEHOSHUA (whose help is Jehovah), Num. 13:16, of which JOSHUA is a contraction, and JESHUA or JESUS, which is the Greek form. He was one of the twelve spies, and he and Caleb were the only ones that told the truth. Num. 14:6-9. After the death of Moses he led the Israelites across the Jordan, defeated and subjugated six nations and thirty-one kings during a war of six years, and then divided the Promised Land among the twelve tribes. After ruling the people for many years he caused them to renew their covenant with Jehovah, and made the vow "as for me and my house, we will serve the Lord." Josh. 24: 15. His influence on his generation was very great. Josh. 24:31. He died one hundred and ten years old, and was buried at Timnath-serah in Ephraim. Josh. 24:30. [2] An Israelite of Beth-shemesh. 1 Sam. 6:14, 18. [3] A govenor of Jerusalem who gave his name to one of the gates. 2 Kings 23:8. [4] A high-priest after the captivity. Hag. 1:1; Zech. 3:1. He is called JESHUA by Ezra and Nehemiah.

Josh'u-a, the Book of, consists of three parts: the first, chapters 1 to 12, narrates the conquest of Canaan; the second, chapters 13 to 22, its partition; and the third, chapters 23, 24, contains the two addresses of Joshua to the people.

Ju'bi-lee, the Year of, was the final consummation of the sabbatical system in use among the Jews, and according to which every seventh day was Sabbath day, every seventh year a Sabbatical year, and every fiftieth year--that is, every year following after the close of seven sabbatical years, each of seven years--a jubilee year, beginning on the Day of Atonement and ushered in by the blast of trumpets. The principal feature of this jubilee, and one not entirely unknown to other people, was the return of all landed estates, except houses built in walled towers, Lev. 25:29-31, to the family whose inheritance it originally had been, irrespective of the manner in which it had been alienated. Minor features were the giving up of all

J

pledges, the setting free of all servants, etc.

Ju'dah (praise). [1] The fourth son of Jacob and Leah, Gen. 29:35, one of the patriarchs. He saved the life of his brother Joseph by advising his sale, Gen. 37:26-28, and was surety for the safety of Benjamin. Gen. 43:3-10. His touching plea for Benjamin's liberty is contained in Gen. 44:14-34. His father's prophetic blessing on him is very remarkable. Gen. 49:8-12. [2] Father of two Levites who were overseers of the rebuilding of the Temple. Ezra. 3:9. [3] A Levite who took a foreign wife. Ezra. 10:23. [4] A Benjamite. New. 11:9.

Ju'dah, King'dom of, embraced the territory of the tribe of Judah and also the greater part of that of Benjamin on the northeast, Dan on the north-west, and Simeon on the south. Edom, which was conquered by David, was faithful to Judah for a time. After the kingdom of Israel was divided, B.C. 975, Judah existed as separate kingdom until B.C. 588. Jerusalem, its capital, was taken at that time by Nebuchadnezzar.

Ju'dah, Ter'ri-to-ry of, occupied by the tribe of Judah in Canaan, is described, with its cities, in Josh. 15. It comprised western Palestine from the Dead Sea to the Mediterranean. Its northern boundary extended from Beth-hogla, a little southeast of Jericho, to Jabneel, about four miles below Joppa, on the Mediterranean. Its southern boundary extended from the south end of the Dead Sea westward to the river of Egypt, now called Wady el Arish. Part of this territory was afterward cut off for Simeon. The north-western part was given to Dan.

Ju'dah, Tribe of, was the largest which came out of Egypt. Num. 1:27. It was composed of descendants of the patriarch JUDAH (which see). King David was of that tribe.

Ju'dah, City of, is mentioned in 2 Chron. 25:28, and is probably the city of David, a name of Mount Zion at Jerusalem.

Ju'das (praise). [1] JUDAH, the patriarch. Matt. 1:2,3. [2] JUDAS, the betrayer of Christ. He was the son of Simon, was one of the apostles, the treasurer of the first Christian community, and was surnamed "Iscariot," which probably means Ish Kerioth, "the man from Kerioth," a town of Judah. Josh. 15:25. After being with the Lord during nearly his whole public ministry he betrayed him, Matt. 26:15, for thirty shekels or

128

pieces of silver, the price of a slave. After being present at the beginning of the last paschal meal (though not at the institution of the Lord's Supper) he led the Temple guard and attendant mob to the garden of Gethsemane, and by a kiss showed them Christ, whom they wanted to seize. Matt. 26:48. But after the deed was done Judas "brought again the thrity pieces of silver to the chief priests and elders, saying, I have sinned in that I have betrayed the innocent blood," and went to the southern hill-side of the valley of Hinnom, to the place now called Aceldama, and hanged himself. Matt. 27:3-10. [3] The one called JUDA in Mark 6:3. See Matt. 13:55. [4] One of the apostles, John 14:22, and a brother of James. Jude 1. He is called LEBBAEUS in Matt. 10:3, THADDAEUS in Mark 3:18, and JUDE in Jude 1. [5] JUDAS OF GALILEE, the leader of an insurrection against the Roman enrolment under Augustus, successful at first, but finally defeated. Acts 5:37. [6] JUDAS in whose house Paul found shelter in Damascus during his blindness. Acts 9:11-17. [7] JUDAS, surnamed Barsabas, who, together with Paul, Barnabas, and Silas, was chosen to carry the decisions of the Council of Jerusalem, A.D. 50, to Antioch. Acts 15:22-33.

Jude, one of the apostles, Jude 1, is called JUDAS in Luke 6:16; John 14:22; Acts 1:13, and surnamed LEBBAEUS in Matt. 10:3, and THADDAEUS in Mark 3:18.

Jude (called a brother of James), **the Epis'tle of,** was written about A.D. 65, and bears in its general aspect a strong resemblance to the Second Epistle of Peter. It was probably addressed to the same persons and for the same reasons. Some of its details, however--the prophecy of Enoch and the dispute between the archangel Michael and Satan--are not mentioned anywhere else.

Ju-de'a or **Ju-dae'a, the Wil'der-ness of,** is wild and desolate, and extends from the hill country near Jerusalem to the Dead Sea. Its average width is about fifteen miles. It is a rough and barren country, having only small places covered with grass, and was the scene of the temptation of Christ. Matt. 4:1; Mark 1:13.

Judg'es. [1] A class of magistrates originally appointed by

Moses, Exod. 18:13-26, as his assistants. [2] Those judges whose history is given in the book of Judges. They were raised up for special emergencies, had extraordinary civil and military powers, and were given to the Israelites about four hundred and fifty years, until Samuel the prophet. Acts 13:20.

Judg'es, the Book of, is so called because it narrates the history of the Israelites from about twenty years after the death of Joshua to the time of Saul, the first king of Israel, during which period they were governed by fifteen judges. The author is not known, nor the time when it was written, but it is evidently compiled from trustworthy materials. The book consists of an introduction, chapter 1 to chapter 3:8; an account of God's successive deliverances of the Israelites, chapter 3:8 to chapter 17; and an account of the invasion of Laish by the Danites, connected with the story of Micah, an idolater in Mount Ephraim, and Jonathan his priest, chapter 17 jand 18; also a narrative of the revenge of the insult to "a certain Levite," chapters 19 to 21.

Judg'ment, Judg'ments are words often mentioned in the Bible. Their meaning is generally determined by the connection in which they are used.

Judg'ment Hall, a room in the palace of the Roman governor, used for the trial of causes and the administration of justice. John 18:28.

Judg'ment Seat, Matt. 27:19, was an elevated place in the judgment hall. Sentence was pronounced from it.

Judg'ment, Day of, the day when Christ shall judge the world in righteousness. Acts 17:31.

Ju'piter, in the mythology of Greek-Roman paganism the highest and mightiest of the Olympian gods, the father and ruler of gods and men, is mentioned twice in the New Testament. Acts 14:12, 13; 19:35.

Jus'ti-fi-ca'tion, Rom. 4:25, an act of free grace by which God pardons the sinner and accepts him as righteous on account of the atonement of Christ. Faith is the only means of justification.

K

Kab or **Cab,** 2 Kings 6:25, a measure for dry things.

Ka'desh (sacred) or **Ka'desh-Bar'ne-a,** on the southern frontier of Cannan, often mentioned in the Old Testament, has been identified with Ain Gadis, about fifty miles south of Beersheba. The Israelites encamped there the second summer after they left Egypt. Num. 33:18. It is the same as MERIBAH-KADESH, Ezek. 47:19, EN-MISH-Pat, Gen. 14:7, and RITH-MAH, Num. 33:18. On account of the rebellion of the Israelites as they were about to enter Canaan they were obliged to remain forty years in the wilderness, and seem to have made Kadesh their principal camp. At this place the rock was smitten for water. Num. 20: 1-21. Here Miriam died.

Ke'dar (dark-skinned), a son of Ishmael. Gen. 25:13; 1 Chron. 1:29. Some of the principal tribes of Arabia descended from him. They and the country in which they lived are called Kedar. Isa. 21:16; Jer. 49: 28.

Ke'desh (sanctuary). [1] A town in the south of Judah. Josh. 15:23. [2] A city of Issachar assigned to the Levites. 1 Chron. 6:72. Called KISHON in Josh. 21:28. [3] A city of Naphtali assigned to the Levites. It became a city of refuge and was the residence of Barak, Judg. 4:6, where it is called KEDISH-NAPHTALI. It was the place where the tribes of Zebulun and Naphtali were assembled by Deborah. Judg. 4:11. Tiglath-pileser captured it. 2 Kings 15:29. The city of the Canaanites mentioned in Josh. 12:22; 19: 37 is probably the same place. Kedesh is now called Kades.

Ke'dron or **Kid'ron** (black brook), a noted brook, dry in the summer, but a torrent in the rainy season. It rises about a mile and a half north-west of Jerusalem, and flows near the east side of the city, between it and Mount Olivet, through the deep valley of Jehoshaphat and the wilderness of Judea, into the north-west part of the Dead Sea. This brook is called CEDRON in John 18:1. David crossed over Kidron when fleeing from Absalom. 2 Sam. 15:23. Christ also crossed it on his way to Gethsemane, John 18:1, the night before his crucifixion. It is mentioned also in 1 Kings 2:37; 15:13; 2 Kings 23:4, 6, 12; 2 Chron. 15:16; 29:16, etc.

Ke-mu'el (helper). [1] A son of Nahor, the brother of Abraham. Gen. 22:21. [2] A prince of Ephraim, one of those who divided Canaan. Num. 34:24. [3] A Levite, the father of Hashabiah. 1 Chron. 27:17.

Ken'ites (smith), one of the tribes which occupied Canaan in the time of Abraham, to whom their land was promised. Gen. 15:19. They were mentioned in Balaam's prophecy. Num. 24:21. Part of the tribe joined Israel. Judg. 1:16.

Kern'els (acrid), seeds of grapes. Num 6:4.

Ket'tle (boiling), a vessel used in cooling and also for sacrifical purposes. 1 Sam. 2:14. The same word in the original is translated "basket" in Jer. 24:2; "caldron" in 2 Chron. 35:13; and "pot" in Job 41:20.

Ke-tu'rah (incense), the wife of Abraham after the death of Sarah. Gen. 25:1; 1 Chron. 1:32.

Kid, a young goat, was one of the luxuries of ancient times. Gen. 38:17; 1 Sam. 16:20. Kids were also used for sacrifices. Num. 7:16, 22, 28.

Kid'ney (longing?), the supposed seat of desire. See marginal note, Job 19:27. The fat upon the kidneys of sacrifices was to be burned. Exod. 29:13. In Deut. 32:14 "kidneys" is used for kernels of wheat because of their richness and shape.

Kin'dred, a word used in the Bible to denote the following: [1] Relatives by birth. Luke 1:61; Acts 7:13. [2] Family in a larger sense. Acts 4:6; 7:19. [3] A tribe. Rev. 5:9; 14:6. [4] Descendants in a direct line. Acts 3:25. "Kinsfolk," "kinsman," and "kinswoman" are used in the same way.

Kine is the old English word for cows.Gen 32:15; 41:2-27.

King. [1] God, "the King eternal." 1 Tim. 1:17. [2] Christ, "the King of kings," 1 Tim. 6:15, and the king of the Jews. Matt. 27:11; Luke 19:38; John 1:49. [3] The title "king" is applied to human rulers without regard to the extent of their dominions. The kings of the Hebrews were considered to be God's representatives. Saul was their first king, and was succeeded by DAVID (which see). The word "king" is also applied to the tetrarch Herod, Matt. 14:9; to the people of God, Rev. 1:6; to the devil, Rev. 9:11; to death, Job 18:14.

King'dom of Christ. Matt. 13:41; Eph. 5:5, etc. **King'dom of God.** Matt. 6:33; Mark 1:14, etc. **King'dom of Heav'en.** Matt. 3:2; 4:17, etc. These terms have nearly the same meaning, and denote the blessedness of the followers of Christ, partially attained in this life, and perfectly in the world to come.

King, First and Second Books of, like the two books of Samuel, were anciently one unbroken narrative. Their Hebrew name was their first words, "Now King David." The Septuagint Version called them the third and fourth books of the Reigns or Kingdoms, the two books of Samuel being the first two.

The First Book of Kings covers the history of one hundred and twenty-six years, from the anointing of Solomon, B.C.

1015, to the death of Jehoshaphat, B.C. 889.

The Second Book of Kings contains the history of about three hundred years, from the death of Jehoshaphat, B.C. 889, to the destruction of Jerusalem by Nebuchadnezzar, B.C. 588. The last three verses of First Kings ought to be the first three of Second Kings. There is added to the second book a brief notice of the setting free of Jehoiachin, king of Judah, from prison by the king of Babylon and of his kind treatment of the captive for the rest of his life. The description of the reign of Solomon, the building of the Temple and the palaces, etc, is very minute and exact. Then follow the separation of the ten and the two tribes, forming the two kingdoms of Israel and Judah, and their respective histories. The style is simple and the narrative is interesting and instructive. The author is not known. A Jewish tradition in the Targum mentions Jeremiah as their author. Some think they were written by Ezra. The books have always had a place in the Old Testament Canon, and the discoveries of modern science in Babylon, Nineveh, Moab, and Egypt bear witness to thier accuracy.

Kish (a bow). [1] Father of King Saul. 1 Sam. 9:1,3; 10:11,21. In Acts 13:21 he is called CIS. [2] A Levite, the grandson of Merari. 1 Chron. 23:21; 24:29. [3] A Benjamite. 1 Chron. 8:30; 9:36. [4] A Levite. 2 Chron. 29:12. [5] A Benjamite who was an ancestor of Mordecai. Esth. 2:5.

Kish'i (bow of Jehovah), a Levite of the family of Merari, 1 Chron. 6:44, called KUSHAIAH in the marginal notes of this verse.

Kiss, a salutation especially common in the East, was used to express reverence as well as affection. It was practised between parents and children, Gen. 27:26; between near male relations and friends, Gen. 33:4; 45:15. King Saul received the kiss of allegiance from the prophet Samuel. 1 Sam. 10:1. In the early days of the Church it was a pledge of Christian brotherhood and love. Rom. 16:16; 1 Cor. 16:20.

Knead'ing-troughs, -trawfs, used in making bread, are mentioned in Exod. 8:3; 12:34. They were either circular pieces of leather made so that they could be drawn up into a kind of bag, or were small woooden bowls. the Arabs now use both kinds. The same word in the original is translated "store" in Deut. 28:5, 17.

Knee and **Kneel'ing.** The word "knee" is often used figuratively. The knees are the seat of strength. Deut. 28:35; Isa. 35:3. Kneeling was a sign of subjection, and became a customary posture in prayer. 2 Kings 1:13; Isa. 45:23; Dan. 6:10, 11; Luke

22:41; Acts 9:40, Rom. 11:4.

Knife, a word used as the translation of several different Hebrew words meaning cutting instruments of various kinds. Knives were not generally used in eating. Gen. 22:6.

Knock, a sign of importunity, Matt. 7, 8, or a summons to open a door. Judg. 19:22. It is the custom in the East to knock or to call out at the outer gate, but not at room-doors. Creditors were obliged to stand outside of the house and call. Deut. 24:10, 11.

Ko'rah (baldness). [1] A son of Esau and Aholibamah, Gen. 36:5; 1 Chron. 1:35, named as son of Eliphaz in Gen. 36:16. [2] A son of Iszhar, the grandson of Levi. He was leader in the rebellion against Moses and Aaron, and was destroyed, with many of his companions, by the Lord. Exod. 6:18, 21, 24; Num. 16: 1-35; 26:9, 10.

K

L

La'a-dah (order), a son of Shelah, the son of Judah. 1 Chron. 4:21.

La'ban (white), the son of Bethuel and brother of Rebekah. He was the father of Leah and Rachel. Rebekah sent her son Jacob to him, Gen. 27:43, so that he might escape from the anger of his brother Esau, whom he had wronged. Jacob served Laban seven years for Rachel. Laban deceived him and gave him Leah as a wife, and afterward Rachel, for whom he served seven years more. Gen. 29:18-28.

Lace (twisted) was the blue cord which bound the high-priest's breastplate to the ephod. Exod. 28:28. Also called "wires" in Exod. 39:3, "thread" in Judg. 16:9, and "line" in Ezek. 40:3.

Lad'der from earth to heaven, seen by Jacob in a vision. The Hebrew word "ladder" means a staircase. Gen. 28: 12-17. Compare John 1:51.

La'dy, in Isa. 47:5, 7, is applied to Babylon as mistress of nations. In Judg. 5:29; Est. 1:18 "ladies" means princesses. In 2 John 1:5 "lady" is used as a title, or possibly as a proper name.

Lake. The Sea of galilee is called "the lake of Gennesaret" in Luke 5:1, and "the lake" in Luke 5:2; 8:22, 23,33.

Lamb, a title given to the Lord Jesus Christ as the atoning sacrifice for the sins of his people. Rev. 5:6, 8, 12, 13. In John 21:15 "lambs" means disciples of Christ.

La'mech, la'mek (strong). [1] The son of Methuselah and father of Noah. Gen. 5:25,31; 1 Chron. 1:3; Luke 3:36. [2] The son of Methusael, a descendant of Cain. He was the father of Jabal, Jubal, and Tubalcain. Gen. 4:18-24.

Lam-en-ta'tions of Jer-e-mi'ah, the book following immediately after Jeremiah's prophecies, contains a series of poems artistically composed, in which the fate of Jerusalem is described. The first, second, and fourth chapters consist of twenty-two verses each, corresponding to the twenty-two letters of the Hebrew alphabet, each verse beginning with the corresponding letter. The third chapter has three verses under each letter, but in the fifth chapter, though it also has twenty-two verses, the alphabetical order is not observed.

Lamp. The lamps used in ancient times are sometimes called candles in the Authorized Version. They were made in various forms, and from clay, terracotta, bronze, etc. They were filled generally with olive-oil, which was abundant in Palestine. Pitch, tallow, was, etc. were also used for the same purpose.

135

The lamps of the Hebrews were probably kept burning all night. A darkened house denoted the extinction of its former occupants, Job 18:5, 6; Prov. 13:9; 20:20, or its desertion, but a constant light in the night was a sign of prosperity. Prov. 31:18. As the streets were not lighted at night in ancient times, lamps were carried by persons passing through them after dark, and it was necessary to fill the lamps frequently from vessels which the travelers carried. See Matt. 25:3, 4, 8, in the parable of the Ten Virgins.

Land'marks. Fences and walls were not common in Judea. Mark 2:23. The boundaries of fields were sometimes indicated by rows of trees, but in many instances by heaps of stones at the corners. In Deut. 27:17 a curse is pronounced upon him "that removeth his neightbor's landmark."

Lan'guage. In Gen. 2:20 it is stated that Adam "gave names to all cattle," etc. In Gen. 11:1 it is mentioned that "the whole earth was of one language, and of one speech." This language was used until about a hundred years after the deluge. When the tower of Babel was commenced the "Lord confounded the language" then used. Gen. 11:6-9.

Laodicea, la-od-i-se'ah, the old city of Diospolis, Asia Minor, which the Syrian king Seleucus II. enlarged and beautified and renamed after his wife Laodice. It became a great commerical centre. A Christian church was established there at an early date, probably from Ephesus. It was wealthy and lukewarm. Rev. 1:11; 3:14 -18. From the Epistle to the Colossians, 4:15, 16, it appears that it was a Christian church at Laodicea to which Paul worte a letter. Some refer this passage to the Epistle to the Ephesians, which was a circular letter. Laodicea is now an insignificant village.

Latch'et, a strap or string used to fasten a sandal to the foot. Mark 1:7.

Lat'in, the language of the Romans, is mentioned in Luke 23:38.

Lat'tice, a kind of latticed window or balcony fronting the street in Eastern houses, 2 Kings 1:2, and used only on public days.

Laud, in Rom. 15:11, means to extol by words of praise or by song.

Laugh, as used in Prov. 1:26; Ps. 2:4; 37:13, with reference to God, denotes that he pays no regard to the person referred to.

La'ver, a vessel containing water for the priests to wash their hands and feet with before they offered sacrifices. It stood without the Tabernacle, near the altar of burnt-offering.

Exod. 30:18, 21. The Temple of Solomon had ten brazen lavers. 1 Kings 7:27-39.

Law, The, a term applied in the New Testament to the Mosaic legislation, and sometimes to the whole old dispensation as distinguished from the dispensation under the Gospel. "The law and the prophets" means the Scriptures of the Old Testament.

Law'yers. The Hebrew lawyers were expounders of the law in the synagogues and schools. They did not plead in courts, and were entirely different from lawyers of the present time. Matt. 22:35.

Laz'a-rus, an abbreviation of **El-e-a'zer** (whom God helps). [1] A man of Bethany, the brother of Martha and Mary. Jesus raised him from the dead. John 11:1 to 12:11. [2] The name given by Christ to a beggar who was the subject of one of his parables. Luke 16:19-31.

Leaf. A fresh leaf of a tree is used to denote prosperity, Ps. 1:3; Ezek. 47:12, and a faded leaf as a symbol of decay. Job. 13:25; Isa. 64:6. the word is figuratively used in other ways.

Leagues (alliances for mutual aid) were made by Joshua with Gibeon, Josh. 9: 15,16; by David with the elders of Israel, 2 Sam. 5:3; by Hiram and Solomon, 1 Kings 5:12; and by others. No league was to be made with the Cannanites, Exod. 23:32, 33; with the Amalekites, Exod. 17:8, 14; or the Moabites. Deut. 2:9-19.

Le'ah (wearied), Laban's elder daughter, whom he substituted instead of Rachel as a wife for Jacob. Gen. 29:16-25.

Leath'er. The Jews used leather for clothing, Job 31:20; Heb. 11:37; for girdles, 2 Kings 1:8; Matt. 3:4; and for covering, Exod. 26:14. Simon the tanner lived at Joppa. Acts 9:43.

Leav'en is sour dough used to raise the new dough with which it is mixed. Exod. 12:15. The Jews were forbidden to use leaven or have it in their houses during the seven days of the Passover. For this reason this festival was sometimes called the "feast of unleavened bread." Luke 22:1. The word leaven is often used figuratively. Matt. 13:33; 16:6.

Leb'a-non and **An'ti-Leb'a-non** (exceeding white), referring to the snow-capped peaks form a double mountain-range which, enclosing the valley of the Orontes, runs through Syria from north to south, and gives that country a configuration of four parallel belts very similar to that of Palestine. The highest peak of Lebanon is Jebel Mukhmel, ten thousand two hundred feet. The highest point of Anti-Lebanon is Mount Hermon, nine thousand feet above the Mediterranean. The country was promised to the Israelites, but was never conquered by them. Josh. 13:2-6; Judg. 3:1-3. The western part, Lebanon, was under Phoenician rule; the eastern, Anti-Lebanon, under the sway of the king of Damascus. In the southern part of Anti-Lebanon the wild tribes remained independent for a long time and occasionally caused much trouble to their neighbors. With the Phoenicians in the eastern part the Israelites maintained very friendly relations in the reigns of David and Solomon, and they became well acquainted with Lebanon, its cedars, Song of Solomon 5:15, its cool breezes, its magnificent springs, etc. When, after the death of Alexander the Great, B.C. 323, a Syrian monarchy was established in Lebanon under the dynasty of the Seleucidae, Palestine became for a time a dependency of that kingdom.

Leek, a vegetable resembling an onion. One kind of leek has been raised in Egypt from very ancient times. Num. 11:5. the original word is often translated "grass," and in one case "herb."

Left hand. In Gen. 14:15; Job 23:9 left hand means "the north." In Judg. 3: 15; 20: 16 "lefthanded" means able to use the left hand as effectively as the right hand. Many of the tribe of Benjamin were left-handed, that is ambidextrous.

Le'gion, a body of roman soldiers, originally composed of about three thousand, and subsequently of between six thousand and seven thousand men. In Matt. 26:53; Mark 5:9, 15 the word refers to a large but indefinte number of angels or of devils.

Lem'u-el (dedicated to God), a king to whom Prov. 31:2-9 was addressed by his mother. Nothing is known conerning Lemuel except that he was a king.

Len'tiles, a plant of the same family as the garden pea, but smaller. 2 Sam. 23:11; Gen. 25:34. Lentiles are still common in Palestine, and are used in making pottage, and, when mixed with barley, beans etc., are made into bread. Ezek. 4:9.

Lep'er, a person afflicted with leprosy, a disgusting disease still common in Egypt, Syria, and other Eastern countries. Its progress and effects are described in Job 2: 7,8,12; 6:2; 7:3-5; 19:14-21. Many cases of leprosy are mentioned in the Bible.

Let, in 2 Thess. 2:7, means hinder; prevent.

Le'vi (joining). [1] The third son of Jacob by Leah. Gen. 29:34; 34:25-31. [2] The tribe descended from Levi, No. 1. Exod. 2:1; Num. 1:49. [3,4] Two ancestors of Joseph, the husband of Mary. Luke 3:24, 29. [5] The original name of

Matthew the publican and apostle. Matt. 9:9; Mark 2:14; Luke 5:27, 29.

Le'vi'a-than, an animal described in Job 41, may be the crocodile, which was once common in the Zerka or Crocodile River in Palestine, which flowed into the Mediterranean Sea. The word "leviathan," in Ps. 74:14; Isa. 27:1, seems to mean crocodile, but in Ps. 104:26 some sea monster is evidently referred to. Perhaps the whale.

Le'vites, in Num. 35:2; Josh. 21:3, 41, etc., means all the descendants of Levi, or the whole tribe of Levi. The term "Levites" is generally used to designate those descendants of Levi who were not priests. 1 Kings 8:4; Ezra 2:70; John 1:19, etc. The Levites were employed in the lower services of the Tabernacle and of the Temple and as special servants of the Lord. Deut. 10:8, 9; 18:1, 2; 33:8-11. Many cities were allotted to the Levites.

Le-vit'i-cus, the third book of the Pentateuch and of the Old Testament. In Hebrew the book is named from the first words, "And he called." The present name refers to its contents as a book of Levitical or ceremonial regulations. The historical extent of Leviticus is very small, being only one month, the first month of B.C. 1490.

Lewd, in Acts 17:5, means bad; and **Lewdness,** in Acts 18:14, means wickedness; crime. These words elsewhere refer to licentiousness.

Lib'er-tines, in Acts 6:9, means those Jews who were taken prisoners in the Syrian wars, carried to Rome, reduced to slavery, and afterward set free. They had a synagogue in Jerusalem.

Libya, lib'i-ah, a name applied, in Ezek. 30:5; 38:5; Acts 2:10, to that part of northern Africa which is west of Egypt. It was peopled by a Hamitic race mentioned in the Old Testament as LEHABIM.

Lice, the third plague of Egypt, were miraculously sent to induce Pharaoh to let the Israelites go out of Egypt. Exod. 8:16, 17; Ps. 105:31. These lice were probably ticks which live in the sand.

Lies of all kinds are condemned in the Bible. Lev. 19:11; John 8:44.

Lil'y. Only one true lily, the scarlet martagon, is now found in Palestine. A white and fragrant kind was probably once found on the coast, and may have been the one referred to in Song of Solomon 2:1. The word "lily" is probably used in the Bible for any beautiful flower resembling a lily. Matt. 6:28; Luke 12:27.

Line, in Amos 7:17; Zech. 1:16, refers to the method of measuring land with a cord. Lines naturally came to mean a piece of land or an inheritance. Ps. 16:6. In Ezek. 40:3 it means a measuring-line about one hundred and forty feet long.

lin'e-age, in Luke 2:4, means family or race.

Lin'en, Exod. 28:42, was well known and much used in ancient times, especially in Egypt, where the finest quality of it was made.

Lin'tel, the top piece of a door-frame, that which rests on the two side-posts. On the Passover night the Hebrews were commanded to strike it with the blood of the sacrificial lamb. Lintel, in Amos 9:1; Zeph. 2:14, means the projecting capital of a column.

Li'on of the tribe of Jud'a, a title given on one occasion to the glorified Saviour. Rev. 5:5.

Li'ons, probably of the Asiatic species, smaller and less formidable than the African lion, were found in Palestine as late as the twelfth century, but have now disappeared in that country. The lion was the emblem of the tribe of Judah.

Liq'uor, in Num. 6:3, means drink made from steeped grapes. In Song of Solomon 7:2 it means highly flavored wine. In Exodus 22:29 "liquors" means the juice of the olive and grapes.

Live'ly, in 1 Pet. 2:5, means living. In Exod. 1:19 it means vigorous; full of life.

Liv'ing Crea'tures. These words were applied by Ezekiel to certain beings which he saw in vision by the river Chebar. Ezek. 1:5, 13-15, 19-22; 10:15, 17, 20.

Loan. The Mosaic law required the rich to relieve the poor by loans as well as by alms. Exod. 22:25; Lev. 25:35-37. No interest was to be taken. Exod. 22:25; Lev. 25:36; Deut. 23:19. These laws had no reference to foreigners. The Jews took interest from them.

Locks of a clumsy kind were used in ancient times. 1 Kings 4:13; Song of Solomon 5:5; Judg. 3:24.

Lo'cust, an insect of the grasshopper kind, remarkable for its voracity and numbers. When mature it can fly to a considerable height. The locusts of Eastern countries are not exactly like those of America. In an immature state they are sometimes called caterpillars. Locusts were often instruments of divine judgment. Exod. 10:4-15; Deut. 28:38-42; Joel 1:4; 2:25.

Log, Lev. 14:10, the smallest measure for liquids that was used among the Israelites, was the seventy-second part of a bath, and contained about two-thirds of a pint.

Loins, the lower part of a man's back and the parts within, represented the seat of strength. Deut. 33:11; Job 40:16. When working or travelling the Hebrews girded up their loose garments about the loins. In 1 Pet. 1:13 this custom is referred to figuratively.

Lo'is, the grandmother of Timothy. She was commended by Paul on account of her faith. 2 Tim. 1:5.

Look'ing-glass. That which is thus translated was a plate of highly polished metal. Exod. 38:8; Job 37:18.

Lord, a title used -- [1] To denote the Godhead generally. Matt. 1:22; Mark 5:19; Luke 1:6, etc. [2] With personal reference to the Lord Jesus Christ. Matt. 7:21; Mark 1:3; Luke 1:43; John 1:23. [3] Applied as a title of respect to men. Matt. 10:24; Mark 12:9; Luke 12:36; John 13:16, etc. "Lord" is the translation of two Hebrew words, "Jehovah" and "Adonai." When it represents the former it is printed in capitals. Gen. 15:4. When it is the translation of Adonai it is printed with a capital initial. Ps. 97:5, etc.

Lord's Day. Since the time of the apostles the first day of the week has been kept sacred by Christians in commemoration of the ressurection of Christ. Rev. 1:10.

Lord's Supper. This was instituted by Christ on the night preceding his crucifixion. It is a memorial of Christ's atoning death and a visible token of Christian fellowship. Matt. 26:19-30; Mark 14:16-26; Luke 22:13-20; 1 Cor. 11:23-26.

Lot (a covering) was the nephew of Abraham and the son of Haran. Gen 11:27. He had many flocks and herds, and dwelt in Sodom, although he abhorred the sinfulness of its inhabitants. When Sodom was destroyed by God on account of sin Lot and his family were saved by means of a special messenger from the Lord; but his "wife looked back from behind him, and she became a pillar of salt." Gen. 19:26. The Ammonites and Moabites descended from Lot.

Love. The perfect exercise of love includes our whole duty to God and our fellow-creatures. Matt. 22:37-40; Rom. 13:8, 10. The love of God to man is manifested in Jesus Christ. Rom. 5:8.

Love-feasts were held in connection with the Lord's Supper. 2 Pet. 2:13; Jude 12. Compare 1 Cor. 11:20-22.

Lov'er, in Scripture, often means an intimate friend. 1 Kings 5:1; Ps. 38:11.

Low'er parts of the earth, in Isa.44:23, means valleys. In Ps. 63:9; Eph. 4:9 it means the abode of disembodied spirits secluded from view. In Ps. 139:15 it means the womb.

Lu'ci-fer (light-giver) is found in the Bible only in Isa. 14:12, where it is applied to the king of Babylon to denote his glory, like a morning star. Some suppose the passage refers to the fall of Satan.

Lu'cre, gain in money or goods; "filthy lucre," in 1 Tim. 3:3, 8' Tit. 1:7,11, means ill-gotten and base gain.

Luke the Evangelist (Greek, Lucas) 2 Tim. 4:11; Philemon 24, was not of Jewish but of Gentile descent, and was by profession a physician. Col. 4:14. Traditon adds that he was also an artist, a painter. The date and place of his birth and death are not known. He was the true and trusted companion of Paul in his later journeys. He joined him at Troas on his second journey, Acts 16:10, and accompanied him to Philippi. Some years later he again met him at Troas, Acts 20:5, and remained with him until the close of his first Roman captivity. Acts 28:30. He was the author of the Gospel which bears his name, and of the Acts of the Apostles, both of which are addressed to one Theophilus, probably a Christian convert of distinguished character and position.

Luke, the Gospel of, was written from the oral tradtions of eye-witnesses and earlier documents (Luke1:1-4), which a liberal education enabled the author to use with discretion and discrimination. It was written for the Gentiles (as Matthew's Gospel was for the Jews), and corresponds to the teaching of Paul. It carries the genealogy of Christ back to Adam. and exhibits Christ as the Healer of all diseases and Saviour of all men. As a narrative it is more complete than any of the other Gospels, and, on account of its chronological notices, more firmly constructed. Chapters 1 and 2 and the whole section from chapter 9:51 to 18:4, including the account of the Nativity, the presentation in the Temple, the sending out of the Seventy, etc., and the parables of the Good Samaritan, the Lost Sheep, the Prodigal Son, etc., are peculiar to it. It was probably written at Caesarea about A.D. 58-60.

Luke'warm, in Rev. 3:16, denotes in different persons who remain entirely unimpressed by the call from the Lord.

Lu'na-tic, in Matt. 4:24; 17:15, seems to mean epileptic.

Lust, in Exod. 15:9; 2 Tim. 4:3, means desire of any kind.

Lycaonia, lik-a-o'ni-ah, a province of Asia Minor, bounded south by Cilicia, north by Galatia, east by Cappadocia, west by Phrygia and Pisidia, was twice visited by Paul. Acts 14:1-23; 16:1-6. Its principal cities were Iconium, Derbe, and Lystra.

M

Ma'a-cah (oppression), 2 Sam. 3:3, or **Maachah,** ma'a-kah, 1 Chron. 3:2, a wife of King David and the mother of Absalom.

Maachah, ma'a-kah. [1] A daughter of Nahor, the brother of Abraham. Gen. 22:24. [2] The father of Achish, king of Gath. 1 Kings 2:39. He is called MAOCH in 1 Sam. 27:2. [3] The mother of King Abijah. 1 Kings 15:2; 2 Chron. 11:20. [4] The concubine of Caleb, the son of Hezron. 1 Chron. 2:48. [5] A Benjamitess who became the wife of Machir. 1 chron. 7:15, 16. [6] The wife of Jehiel, the founder of Gibeon. 1 Chron. 8:29; 9:35. [7] The father of Hanan, who was one of David's warriors. 1 Chron. 11:43. [8] The father of Shephatiah, a ruler of the Simeonites. 1 Chron. 27:16.

Mac'ca-bees, the Family of the, properly called "Asmonae-ans", or Hasmonaeans," from Chasmon, the great-grandfather of Mattathias, of the sons of Jehoiarib. 1 Chron. 24:7. Judas, one of the sons of Mattathias, was surnamed Maccabaeus, and became the leader in a general revolt against the despotism of Antiochus Epiphanes, who was king of Syria B.C. 175-164, plundered the Temple, and persecuted the Jews. Judas Macca-baeus conquered Lysias, the Antiochian general, and the Jews re-entered Jerusalem, B.C. 165. Judas was killed in the battle of Eleasa, and the contest for independence was successfully continued by his brothers Jonathan and Simon until B.C. 135.

Mac-e-do'ni-a (extended land), an ancient kingdom of Europe north of Greece, and bounded east by Thrace, west by Illyr-icum, and north by the Balkan mountains, between it and Moesia, became known in the history of the Jews through Alexander the Great. (See Hebrews.) The great Macedonian empire was named from this small kingdom. In New Testament history it plays quite a conspicuous part, being the first Euro-pean country which was visited by the apostles. Paul was there twice, Acts chapters 16 and 20, and perhaps a third time. Compare 1 Tim. 1:3; Phil. 2:24. Thessalonica and Philippi were two of its principal cities. In both of them Paul founded flourishing Christian churches, as his epistles to the Thessalo-nians and Philippians show.

Mad'men (dunghill), a town of Moab whose destruction was foretold by Jermiah. Jer. 48:2.

Mag-da-le'ne, a female native of Magdala, is a word used to denote a woman named Mary who was relieved of "seven devils" by Christ and became his devoted disciple. Luke 8:2, 3.

Magi, ma'ji, was the Chaldean name of the priests or wise men who in the ancient Eastern empires, Media, Persia, Babylonia, and Assyria, occupied the place next to the king. They were generally his advisers, but sometimes became his judges. In Persia the Magi were, as priests, the only ones allowed to perform the sacred religious rites, and as scholars, were the only persons supposed to be able to explain the past and predict the future. The Jews, who had known them well since the days of the captivity, always spoke of them with respect. Dan. 1:20; 2:24; 5:11. The Magi or Wise Men who came to worship Christ at his birth, Matt. 2:1-14, may have received the first germs of the Messianic idea from Jews in exile. They were the forerunners of the heathen converts and gave rise to the legend of the three kings.

Mag'ic, superstitious ceremonies practised to hurt or to benefit mankind. The Hebrews were forbidden to consult magicians. Lev. 19"31; Deut. 18:9-14. Magicians are often mentioned in the Bible. Notice the case of Pharaoh. Exod. chapters 7, 8, and 9.

Ma-gi'cian, one who practised magic. Gen. 41:8; Exod. 7:11.

Mag'is-trate, a word used to denote civil officers with legal authority, as in Ezra 7:25; Luke 12:11, and to signify Roman colonial officers. Acts 16:20, 22, 35, 36, 38.

Ma'gog (region of Gog). [1] A son of Japheth. Gen. 10:2; 1 Chron. 1:5. [2] The word is used to denote the people descended from him. Ezek. 38:2; 39:6. [3] it is used prophetically to denote one of the parties in the last assault on the camp of the saints and the beloved city. Rev. 20:8.

Mah'lon (sickly), a son of Elimelech and Naomi. Ruth 1:2, 5; 4:9, 10.

Ma'hol (dance), the father of Israelites famous in the time of Solomon for their wisdom. 1 Kings 4:31.

Mail, coat of, in 1 Sam. 17:5, means armor which covered the upper part of the body, that is, the breast and back.

Malachi, mal'a-ki (messenger of Jehovah), the last of the prophets of the Old Testament, lived after the captivity, later than Haggai and Zechariah, and after the completion of the Temple. He was probably a contemporary of Nehemiah, B.C. 433.

Malachi, the Book of, contains a prophecy of the coming of Messiah and the announcement that Elijah will return as his forerunner. It is called the "seal," because it is the last book of the Old Testament.

Malcham, mal'kam (their king). [1] A son of Shaharaim, a Benjamite. 1 Chron. 8:9. [2] An idol of the Ammonites and

Moabites. Zeph. 1:5.

Mam'mon, a word signifying riches, employed by Christ to indicate worldly goods or the desire for them. Matt. 6:24; Luke 16:9, 11, 13.

Man, a word used in the declaration of God's purpose to create a human being. It is also frequently employed as the name of the first man (Adam), and is used to denote mankind in a general sense. Gen. 1:26, 27; 2:5, 7.

Ma-nas'seh (forgetting). [1] Joseph's first-born son. Gen. 41:51; 46:20; Num. 26:28, 29. [2] A king of Judah. 2 Kings 20:21; 1 Chron. 3:13; 2 Chron. 32:33. He was the son and successor of King Hezekiah, and became king B.C. 696, when twelve years old. He was taken captive by an Assyrian king and carried to Babylon, but was allowed to return to Jerusalem. He died B.C. 641. He is called MANASSES in Matt. 1:10. [3] A Levite whose grandson Jonathan became an idolatrous priest of the tribe of Dan. Judg. 18:30. [4] A Jew who married a foreign wife. Ezra 10:30. [5] Another Jew who married a foreign wife. Ezra 10:33.

Man'ger, crib or feeding-trough, Luke 2:7, 12, 16, in which the infant Saviour was laid.

Man'na (what is this?), miraculous food which God game to the Israelites during their wanderings in the wilderness. Its history and nature are fully described in Exodus, chapter 16. It was called bread from heaven, and was furnished daily for forty years. Deut. 29:5, 6. A different substance called "manna' drops from various trees, principally the tamarisk, in the valleys around Sinai. The manna now used as a medicine is the dried juice of the manna ash found in southern Europe.

Man'slay-er, Num. 35:6, 12, one who had killed another; could flee to a city of refuge. See CITIES OF REFUGE.

Man'tle is the translation of four Hebrew words, and means, in Judg. 4:18, a coarse cloth used for making beds in tents; in 1 Sam. 15:27, a garment like the official priestly robe; in Isa. 3:22, a lady's wrapper with sleeves; and in 1 Kings 19:13, 19; 2 Kings 2:8, 13, 14, the principal garment of the prophet Elijah.

Mar-a-nath'a, a Syriac or an Aramaic expression, meaning "the Lord cometh." 1 Cor. 16:22.

Mark, or **John Mark,** as he is also called, Acts 12:12; 15:37, was a Jew, probably a native of Jerusalem, where his mother, Mary, resided. He was a cousin of Barnabas, Col. 4:10, and closely connected with Peter, who calls him his (spiritual) son. 1 Peter 5:13. Mark accompanied Paul and Barnabas on their first missionary journey, but left them at Perga. Acts 13:13. Afterward, however, he was again with Paul in Rome. Col.

4:10; Philemon 24. Ancient writers call him "the interpreter of Peter," and his gospel "the Gospel of Peter." He is called MARCUS in Col 4:10.

Mark, the Gos'pel of, has something in its general character and in its details which seems to show that it in some manner came from the lips of Peter. It describes the power of Christ's ministry and the impression it produced on the people with striking rapidity and energy, and with many pictorial details which have been traced to the preaching of Peter.

Mar'riage was instituted in paradise, Gen. 2:18-25, and was confirmed by Christ. Matt. 19:5, 6; Mark 10:5-10. He was present at the marriage feast in Cana. John 2:1. In the time of Christ weddings were often celebrated with great feasting and rejoicing. When the marriage feast was to take place the bridegroom went to the house of the bride with his friends, called "the children of the bridechamber" in Matt. 9:15. A great procession was formed, which with torches and lamps accompanied the bride to the house of the bridegroom. Matt. 25:1-10. There is no instance of polygamy after the captivity on record in the Old Testament.

Mars' Hill is the city of Athens in Greece. Paul addressed the "men of Athens" from it. Acts 17:22-31.

Mar'tha, the sister of Mary and Lazarus. Luke 10:38, 40, 41; John 11:1, 5. she and her sister Mary were devoted friends and disciples of Christ and were much beloved by him. She was a good housekeeper, and represents the practical life, while Mary was contemplative.

Mar'tyr. This word is found in the Bible only in Acts 22:20, where mention is made of Stephen, and in Rev. 2:13; 17:6.

Ma'ry. This name corresponds to the Old Testament name MIRIAM. [1] MARY, the mother of Jesus, Acts 1:14; Matt. 1:16-25; 2:11-23; Mark 6:3; Luke 1:26-56; 2:4-51. She was, by marriage, connected with Elisabeth, the mother of John the Baptist, and was at the marriage in Cana of Galilee, John 2:3; is mentioned in Matt. 12:46; Mark 3:31-35; Luke 8:19; and was present at the crucifixion of Christ, John 19:25-27, where she was commended to the care of the beloved John. She was one of the praying company in the upper room at Jerusalem, Acts 1:14, after the ascension of Christ. According to tradition, she died in Jerusalem after A.D. 50. As the mother of our Lord, she will always be "blessed among women," as Elisabeth greeted her. Luke 1:42. [2] MARY, the wife of Cleophas. John 19:25. she was present at the crucifixion and the burial of Christ, Matt. 27:56, 61; went with others to anoint him, Mark 16:1-10;

received the news of his ressurection, Luke 24:6, 10; met and worshipped him. Matt. 28:1, 9. [3] MARY, the mother of John Mark, Acts 12:12, and aunt of Barnabas. Col. 4:10. she was a pious woman, and lived in Jerusalem. The disciples met at her house on the night when Peter was miraculously delivered from prison. Acts 12:7-12. [4] MARY, the sister of Lazarus and Martha. Luke 10:39. She was a devoted disciple and friend of Christ, and heard from him the words, "Mary hath chosen that good part, which shall not be taken away from her." Luke 10:42. See also John 11:1; 12:3. [5] MARY MAGDALENE, Matt. 27:56, a woman of Magdala in Galilee. She was relieved of "seven devils" (demons) by Christ, and followed him. Luke 8:2, 3. She was a woman of good character, and was prominent among those who ministered to Christ and his disciples. She was present at the crucifixion of Christ, John 19:25; was at his burial, Mark 15:47; was with those who went to anoint him, Mark 16:1; and was the first to whom Christ appeared after his resurrection. Mark 16:9. See also John 20:11-18. the popular belief that Mary Magdalene was a woman of unchaste character rests merely on tradition, which identifies her with the un-named "woman that was a sinner" and that kissed the Saviour's feet. Luke 7:37. [6] MARY, a disciple at Rome to whom Paul sends salutation. Rom. 16:6.

Mas'ter, a word which often means "teacher," Luke 6:40; John 3:10, and hence is often applied to Christ. Matt. 22:16, 24, etc. The word is used also to denote ownership, as a term of respect to superiors, etc.

Mat-ta-thi'as. [1,2] Two ancestors of Joseph, the husband of Mary. Luke 3:25, 26. [3] The head of the family of the Maccabees.

Mat'thew (gift of God) was a Jew by birth and was the son of Alphaeus. His original name, before he was converted and called to the apostleship, was LEVI, Mark 2:14; Luke 5:27, and he was a publican, or collector of taxes and customs on persons and goods crossing the Sea of Galilee, at Capernaum, on the route between Damascus and the Phoenician seaports. He was present in the upper room at Jerusalem after the ascension of Christ, Acts 1:13, and tradition tells us that he suffered martyr-dom in Ethiopia.

Mat'thew, the Gos'pel of, occupies, very appropriately, the first place in the New Testament Canon. Matthew wrote first a Gospel in Hebrew (Aramaic) for Jewish readers, which con-sisted chiefly of discourses of the Saviour, but which has been lost. The Greek Gospel of Matthew, as we have it, is not a translation, but an original work on a larger scale. It represents Christ as the Messiah and King of Israel, and constantly points to the fulfilment of prophecy. Its arrangement is according to topics, and groups together the discourses, parables, and miracles. It gives us the fullest record of the Sermon on the Mount (chapters 5 to 7), the parables (chapter 13), the prophecies of the destruction of Jerusalem and the end of the world (chapters 24 and 25). The style is simple, dignified, and majestic. It was written while Jerusalem, which is called "the holy city," "the city of the Great King," was still standing, between A.D. 60 and 70. The destruction of Jerusalem is foretold as an impending event, without any hint of the fulfilment of the prophecy.

Matthias, math-thi'as (gift of Jehovah), a disciple who was chosen by lot to take the place of Judas Iscariot among the apostles. Acts 1:23, 26.

Meas'ures. no specimens of the Hebrew system of measures survive, and we cannot hope to reconstruct it. We know, however, that their measures of length were nearly all borrowed from the human body. It should be borne in mind that the following lengths and capacities are only approximately correct:

Measures of Length.

A finger was about three-fourths of an inch.

A hand-breadth (four fingers) was about three inches.

A span (three hand-breadths) was about nine inches.

A cubit (two spans) was about eighteen inches.

A fathom was a little over six feet.

A reed was about one hundred and twenty feet.

A furlong was about six hundred feet.

A mile (Roman), about four thousand eight hundred feet, was over nine-tenths of an English mile. Another Eastern mile was about one-fifth longer than an English mile.

A day's journey was about twenty-five or thirty miles.

A Sabbath day's journey was nearly one mile.

Measure of Quantity.

A log was about two-thirds of a pint.

A cab was about three pints.

An omer (ten ephahs) was a little over a gallon.

A bushel, the Greek modius, was about a peck.

The measure, equal to about a peck and a half, is the translation of the Hebrew seah.

An ephah or bath was about seven gallons.

A firkin was between nine and ten gallons.
A lethech was about four bushels.
A homer or cor was about eight bushels.

Meat, when mentioned in the Bible, never means flesh. The word is used to denote any other kind of food. It is first mentioned in Gen. 1:29. The "meat-offering" was always a vegetable offering, a cake made of flour and oil. Lev. 2:1.

Media, me'di-ah (middle land), Esth. 1:3; Isa. 21:2, was bounded north by the Caspian Sea, east by Parthia, south by Persia, and west by Assyria. For a long time it seems to have been a dependent of Assyria, but in B.C. 633 it became an independent kingdom under Cyaxares, who conquered Assyria and destroyed Nineveh. In B.C. 558 Media was united to Persia under Cyrus--the "Medes and Persian" of Dan. 5:28; 6:8, etc.-and from that time it shared the destinies of that empire. The Medes are mentioned in connection with the Parthians. Acts 2:9.

Me'di-a-tor, one that interposes between persons who are at variance for the purpose of reconciling them. It is a title of Christ, 1 Tim. 2:5; Heb. 12:24, who is the only mediator between God and man.

Med'i-cine. The medical skill of the Egyptians was widely celebrated. Medicine is mentioned in Prov. 17:22; Jer. 30:13; 46:11; Ezek. 47:12. Luke was a physician.

Meek'ness is a Christian grace, and means humble serenity of spirit and submission to the divine will. Eph. 4:2; 1 Tim. 6:11.

Melchizedek, mel-kiz'e-dek, or **Mel-chisedec,** mel-kiz'e-dek, the New Testament form of the name (king of righteousness), is mentioned three times in the Bible: first in Gen. 14:18-20, where, as king of Salem and priest of the Most High God, he meets Abram in the valley of Shaveh, blesses him, and receives tithes from him; next in Ps. 110:4, where Messiah is described as a priest "after the order of Melchizedek;" and finally in Heb. 5:6, 7, where an analogy is drawn between him and Christ.

Melita, mel'i-tah (honey), now MALTA, is an island in the Mediterranean, seventeen miles long and nine miles broad, situated sixty-two miles south of Sicily, and is an English possession. The bay where Paul was shipwrecked on his voyage to Rome, Acts 27:1-44, is still called St. Paul's Bay.

Mel'ons of many kinds are common in the East and grow luxuriantly in Egypt. The Hebrews remembered and longed for them in the desert. Num. 11:5. Melons are abundant in Palestine, especially the watermelon, which grows to a very large size.

Mem'phis, Hos. 9:6, a chief city of ancient Egypt. Its ruins are on the west bank of the river Nile, about ten miles south of Cairo. It was founded by Menes, the first king of Egypt, contained the temples of Apis, Isis, and Serapis, and was the capital of that country for many centuries. It is mentioned under the name of NOPH in Isa. 19:13; Jer. 2:16; 44:1; 46:14, 19; Ezek. 30:13, 16. Its overthrow was predicted by Isaiah and Jeremiah B.C. about 600. Its ruins were used in building Cairo, the capital of modern Egypt, about A.D. 630. for some time the exact location of Memphis was unknown, but modern explorations have uncovered many of its wonderful antiquities.

Me'ne, Me'ne, Te'kel, U-phar'sin, Dan. 5:25, a Chaldee sentence miraculously traced on the wall at the impious feast of Belshazzar, Dan 5 1-5, and signifying his impending doom. Mene means "he is numbered;" Tekel, "he is weighed;" Upharsin, "they are divided."

Me-phib'o-sheth (extermination of idols). [1] A son of King saul. David delivered him into the hands of the Gibeonites, who hanged him. 2 Sam. 21: 8,9. [2] A son of Jonathan and grandson of King Saul. 2 Sam. 4:4; 9:6; 21:7. He is called MERIBBAAL in 1 Chorn. 8:34; 9:40.

Mer'chant man, in Matt. 13:45, etc. means merchant.

Mer'chants, Gen. 23:16; 1 Kings 10: 28, carried on their business in ancient times principally by caravans or traveling companies which had their regular seasons and routes. Joseph was sold to the merchants of an Egyptian caravan. There was also considerable trade by water.

Mer'cy is a distinguishing attribute of God, and signifies the divine goodness exercised toward the guilty and wretched, in harmony with truth and justice. Ps. 85:10.

Mercy-seat, the name given to the lid or covering of the ark of the covenant. On the ends of it were the cherubim. It was of pure gold. On the Day of Atonement the high-priest sprinkled the blood of the sin-offerings before and upon the mercy-seat as a propitiation. Lev. 16: 11-16. God was believed to be present in a peculiar manner at the mercy-seat to make known His holy will and to hear and answer prayer. Exod. 25:22.

Me'rom, Wa'ters of (waters of the high place), a small lake in the course of the river Jordan, about eleven miles north of the sea of Galilee. Josh. 11:5,7.

Mer'ry, in 2 Chron. 7:10; Prov. 17:22; Luke 15:32; James

M

5:13, means joy and happiness, not noisy mirth.

Me-shil'le-moth. [1] An Ephraimite, father of Berechiah. 2 Chron. 28:12. [2] A priest of the family of Immer. Neh. 11:13. Same as MESHILLEMITH in 1 Chron. 9:12.

Mes'o-ba-ite, a name applied to Jasiel, one of David's valiant men. 1 Chron. 11:47.

Mes-o-po-ta'mi-a (between the rivers) was the Greek name of the fertile plain between the Euphrates and the Tigris. Acts 2:9;7:2. The Hebrew name was Aram-naharaim (Aram of the two rivers), Gen. 24:10, or Padan-aram (the plain of Aram). Gen. 25:20. It was inhabited by independent tribes, mostly of Chaldean origin, until conquered by Assyria.

Mes'sen-gers were sent to distant towns and provinces by Jewish kings to proclaim laws and edicts. 1 Sam. 11:7; 2 Chron. 36:22. Messengers were sent by many others besides kings. John the Baptist is called a messenger in Matt. 11:10.

Mes-si'ah, the name by which Daniel indicates the Redeemer. Dan. 9:25,26. Same as MESSIAS. John 1:41; 4:25. The word "Messiah" is often used in the Old Testament in its literal sense, signifying one who has been anointed. 1 Sam. 24:6; Ps. 105:15. It has the same meaning in Hebrew as Christ has in Greek. It generally refers to CHRIST (which see).

Mete, in Matt. 7:2, means measure.

Me-thu'se-lah (man of dart, or he dies and it is sent-- namely, the flood) was the son of Enoch and the grandfather of Noah. Gen. 5:27: 1 Chron. 1:3. He was the longest-lived man, and died at the age of nine hundred and sixty-nine years.

Mi'cah (who is like Jehovah?). [1] An Ephraimite who, having fallen into idolatry, hired a Levite to be his priest. His idols were stolen from him by the Danites. Judg. chapters 17 and 18.

[2] The sixth of the minor prophets, a native of Moresheth-gath, west of Jerusalem, in Gath. He was a contemporary of Isaiah, and prophesied during the reigns of Jotham, Ahaz, and Hezehiah, B.C. 750-698. [3] Micah, a Reubenite.1 Chron. 5:5. [4] The son of Merib-baal. 1 Chron. 8:34, 35. Called MICHA in 2 Sam. 9:12. [5] A Levite of the family of Asaph, 1 Chron. 9:15. He is called MICHA in Neh. 11:17,22, and MICHAIAH in Neh. 12:35. [6] A Levite of the family of Kohath, 1 Chron. 23:20, called MICHAH in 1 Chron. 24:24,25. [7] The father of Abdon, 2 Chron. 34:20, and called MICHAIAH in 2 Kings 22:12.

Mi'cah, the Book of (see MICAH, No 2, above), refers with great definiteness to Samaria and Jerusalem, the complete devastation of the former and the temporary destruction of the latter. His prophecies of Messiah have the same character, and he predicted that Christ should be born at Bethlehem. Mic. 5:2.

Michael, mi'ka-el or mi'kel (who like God?). [1] The father of Sethur the spy, from Asher. Num. 13:13. [2,3] A man of Gad and one of his ancestors. 1 Chron. 5: 13, 14. [4] A Levite of the family of Gershom. 1 Chron. 6:40. [5] A chief man of Issachar. 1 Chron. 7:3. [6] A descendant of Benjamin. 1 Chron. 8:16. [7] A captain of Manasseh who joined David at Ziklag. 1 Chron. 12:20. [8] The father of Omri. 1 Chron. 27:18. [9] A son of King Jehoshaphat. 2 Chron. 21:2. [10] The father of Zehadiah. Ezra 8:8. [11] The angel who is called by Daniel the prince of the people of Judah. Dan. 10:13, 21; 12:1. Also, the archangel mentioned in Jude 9, and the leader of the hosts of the angels. Rev. 12: 7-9.

Michal, mi'kal, a daughter of King Saul and wife of David. 1 Sam. 14:49; 18:20,27.

Mid'dle Wall of Par-ti'tion, in Eph. 2:14, refers to the sacred barrier between the court of the Gentiles and the inner parts of the Temple.

Mid'i-an-ites, the descendants of Midian, were the inhabitants of the region from the Sinaitic peninsula to the banks of the Euphrates. They traded much with Palestine, Lebanon, and Egypt. It was probably the Midianites and the Ishmaelites who bought Joseph. They at first joined Moab against the Israelites, Num. chapters 22,24 25, and afterward attempted hostilites on their own account. Judg. 6: 1-40, but failed in both instances. They were finally incorporated with the Moabites and the Arabs.

Mid'wives. The two midwives Shiphrah and Puah, mentioned in Exod. 1:15 were probably the superintendents or representatives of a class. Midwives are also mentioned in Gen. 35:17; 38:28.

Mig'dol (tower). [1] A place situated near the north end of the Red Sea. Exod. 14:2; Num. 33:7. [2] A city in the northeast part of Egypt near Palestine. It contained a colony of Jews. Jer. 44:1; 46:14.

Might'y, a title which is sometimes given to the true God. Gen. 49:24; Ps. 132:2,5; Isa. 1:24; 49:26; 60:16.

Mil'cah (queen or counsel). [1] A daughter of Haran. She was the wife of Nahor, a brother of Abraham. Gen. 11:29;22:20, 23. [2] A daughter of Zelophehad. Num. 26:33; Josh. 17:3.

Mile. A Roman mile about 4800 feet, is over nine-tenths of an English mile. Another kind of Eastern mile is about one-fifth longer than an English mile. The English mile is the same as the United States mile. Matt. 5:41.

Mi-le'tus, a seaport of Ionia, Asia Minor, on the southwestern side of the Latmian Gulf, directly opposite the mouth of the river Meander, was visited by Paul on his return from his third missionary journey. He met there the elders from Ephesus and made the parting address which is recorded in Acts 20: 15-38.

Milk of cows, camels, sheep and goats was used in Palestine, and is frequently mentioned in the Old Testament. Gen. 18:8; 49:12; Exod. 3:8, 17.

Mill. Exod. 11:5; Numb. 11:8. The mills mentioned in the Bible were not buildings, but pairs of round millstones about two feet in diameter and about six inches thick. The lower or "nether" millstone was slightly convex on the top and was stationary. The upper stone was correspondingly concave on the lower side, and in its centre was a hold through which the grain was poured into the mill. The top of the upper stone had an upright handle by which it was rapidly turned. The meal came out around the outside of the mill and fell upon a cloth or a board on which the mill stood. These mills were operated by women, Matt. 24:41, and were used by each family every morning. No man was allowed to take "the nether or the upper millstone to pledge: for he taketh a man's life to pledge." Deut. 24:6. The stopping of the noise of these mills in the moring was a sign of desolation. Jer. 25:10; Rev. 18:22.

M

Mil-len'ni-um means a period of one thousand years, and is, in its religious use, applied to the era prophetically mentioned in Rev. 20:1-7.

Mil'let, a kind of grain cultivated in Palestine and elsewhere. Ezek. 4:9. The name "millet" is applied to two kinds of grain--namely, the seeds of panic-grass and the durah or Egyptian corn, which somewhat resembles maize.

Min'cing, in Isa. 3:16, means walking with very short steps.

Min'is-ter. This word, when used in the Bible, sometimes means one who is in the voluntary attendance upon another person. Joshua was the minister of Moses. Exod. 24:13. Elisha was the minister of Elijah. 1 Kings 19:21. In Heb. 8:2 Christ is called "A minister of the sanctuary;" that is, as our High-Priest.

Min'strel, a singer or musician. Minstrels were employed at funerals and in time of death, as in the case of Jairus' daughter, Matt. 9:23, and also on other occasions. 2 Kings 3:15.

Mint, a common herb of little value, resembling garden sage. Various species of it are found in Palestine. It was used in ancient times for seasoning and in medicine. The Jews were required to pay tithes on all produce of the earth. Deut. 14:22, but were more careful concerning trifles than about important matters. Matt. 23:23.

Mir'a-cle, an act or event produced by supernatural or divine agency. The New Testament uses three terms to denote miracles--namely, signs wonders, and power or mighty works.

Mir'i-am (rebellion). [1] A daughter of Amram and the sister of Moses and Aaron. 1 Chron. 6:3. She was watching the ark of bulrushes in which the infant Moses was laid, and when the daughter of Pharaoh discovered it Miriam called her mother as a nurse for Moses. Exod. 2: 4-10. She led the women of Israel in a triumphant song after the passage of the Red Sea. Exod. l5:20. She was smitten with leprosy for murmuring against Moses, but was restored to health in answer to Moses' prayer. Num. 12: 1-15. She died at Kadesh and was buried there. Num. 20:1. [2] A descendant of Judah. 1 Chron. 4:17.

Mis'chief, in Ezek. 7:26; Acts 13:10, means serious harm.

Mite, the least valuable Jewish coin, worth about two mills of United States money. Mark 12:42. See MONEY.

Mi'tre, the head-dress of a Jewish priest. It was made of fine linen and in the form of an Eastern turban, and had on its front a gold plate containing the inscription "Holiness to the Lord." Exod. 28:4, 36-39.

Miz'ah and **Miz'peh** (watch-tower). [1] The place on Mount Gilead where Jacob made a covenant with Laban and put up a heap of stones as a witness. Gen. 31:43-49. It is called Mizpeh of Gilead in Judg. 11:29. Jephthah met his daughter there. Judge. 11:34. [2] A city of Moab. 1 Sam. 22:3. [3] The land of MIzpeh, in northern Palestine, occupied by the Hivites. Josh. 11:3. It may be the same as No. 4. [4] The valley of Mizpeh. Josh. 11:3,8. [5] A city of Judah. Josh. 15:38. [6] A city of Benjamin. Josh. 18:26. Saul was elected king there. 1 Sam. 10: 17-21.

Miz'zah (fear), one of the sons of Reuel, the son of Esau. Gen. 36: 13, 17; 1 Chron. 1:37.

Mo'ab (of the father). [1] The son of Lot and his eldest daughter. Gen. 19:37.[2] The same name is also used to denote the descendants of Moab and the land in which they lived. Gen. 36:35; Exod. 15:15. The territory of the Moabites was in three parts, having different names: 1.The Land of Moab, lying east of the Jordan and the Dead Sea and between the rivers Arnon and Jabbok. Deut. 1:5. 2. The Field of Moab, a district east of the Dead Sea and south of the river Arnon. Ruth 1:2. 3. The

Plains of Moab, a district in the Jordan valley east of that river and opposite Jericho. Num. 22:1.

Mo'ab-ites, the descendants of Moab, the son of Lot's eldest daughter. Gen. 19:37; Num. 22:4.

Moabitess, mo'ab-ite-ess, a female inhabitant of Moab. Ruth 1:22; 2 Chron. 24:26.

Mod-er-a'tion, in Phil. 4:5, means conciliatory spirit.

Mon'ey. The first money was not coined, but was in the form of wedges, rings, etc. Money mentioned in the Old Testament before the captivity means a particular weight of some precious metal. After the captivity Persian, Greek, Syrian, Roman and national Jewish coins were used by the Jews. The first Jewish coins were made in the time of Simon Maccabaeus, B.C. about 139. Shekels, half-shekels, etc. of gold, silver, and copper were then produced. No image of any man was allowed on them.

MONEY OF THE BIBLE. --As in many cases the money of the Jews was represented by certain weights not definitely established, the following equivalents in United States money can only be regarded as approximate. The purchasing power of money in Bible times was about ten times as great as it is now:

A mite was worth about two mills.

A farthing: one kind, the kodrantes, was worth about four mills; another kind of farthing, the assarion, was worth about a cent and a half.

A gerah was worth about three cents.

A penny, or the Roman denarius, was worth about fifteen cents.

A bekah was worth about twenty-seven cents.

A silver shekel was worth between fifty and sixty cents.

A daric or dram was a Persian coin worth about five dollars.

A gold shekel was worth nearly ten dollars.

A pound was worth about sixteen dollars.

A talent of silver was worth about one thousand dollars.

A talent of gold was worth about thirty thousand dollars.

Mon'ey-chang'ers are mentioned in Matt. 21:12; Mark 11:15. They exchanged foreign for Jewish money, which was to be used in paying Temple dues. The money changers Jesus drove out of the Temple were guilty of charging a large premium for making this exchange.

Month. The Hebrews usually designated their months by numbers--namely, first month, second month, etc. They also had a special name for each of them. The length of their month was regulated by the changes of the moon, and was reckoned from one new moon to the next one. A thirteenth month, called

M

VE-ADAR, was inserted among the months about once in three years, or seven times in nineteen years, to make up for the difference between the Jewish year and the solar year, the one now used.

HEBREW MONTHS IN ONE YEAR

Months of the Sacred Year	Corresponding Months of the Civil Year.	Beginning with the New Moon.
Abib or Nisan	Seventh	March or April
Zif or Ziv	Eighth	April or May
Sivan	Ninth	May or June
Tammuz	Tenth	June or July
Ab	Eleventh	July or August
Elul	Twelfth	Aug. or Sept.
Ethanim or Tishri	First	Sept. or Oct.
Bul	Second	Oct. or Nov.
Chislieu or Kislieu	Third	Nove. or Dec.
Tebeth	Fourth	Dec. or Jan.
Shebat	Fifth	Jan. or Feb.
Adar	Sixth	Feb. or March

Moon is called "the lesser light" in Gen. 1:16. Many of the feasts and sacred services observed by the Jews were regulated by the new moon, which was always the beginning of the month and was celebrated with special sacrifices. Num. 28: 11-15. The moon was worshipped under various names by the heathen. The idolatrous Jews burned incense to it. 2 Kings 23:5; Jer. 8:2.

Mordecai, mor'de-kay (little man, or worshipper of Mars). [1] A chief man among the Jews who returned from Babylon with Zerubbabel. Ezra 2:2, Neh.7:7. [2] A Jew of the tribe of Benjamin. He was the cousin and guardian of Esther, whose Hebrew name was Hadassah and who became queen of Ahasuerus, king of Persia. Mordecai was despised and abused by Haman, a chief officer of Ahasuerus. Haman devised a plan for the extermination of the Jews in the territory ruled by that king, but Mordecai, aided by Esther, defeated his purpose. Haman was hanged and Mordecai was raised to power and wealth.

Mor'ti-fy, in Rom. 8:13; Col. 3:5, means put to death (figuratively).

Mo'ses (drawn out), the great leader and lawgiver of the Israelites and the moulder of their national character was the youngest child of Amram and Jochebed. Their other children were Miriam and Aaron, Miriam being the oldest. The life of Moses falls naturally into three periods of forty years each. Acts 7:23, 30, 36. Hid by his mother in the "ark of bulrushes," Exod. 2:3, he was found and adopted by the daugher of Pharaoh, and was educated in the splendor of the Egyptian court, trained in all the skill of Egyptian life and civilization, initiated in the secret wisdom of the priesthood, and placed in a prominent and conspicuous position close to the ruler. In his fortieth year he slew a Hebrew. Exod. 2:12, and to escape the wrath of Pharaoh he fled to Midian, where he spent the next forty years in tending the flocks of the Midianite priest Jethro, whose daughter Zipporah he married. Exod. 2:21. The Egyptian court with its associations had afforded Moses a rich field for practical observation, but the rugged life he now led as a sheperd had its own advantages, and the solitude of the desert proved inviting for deep meditations and for maturing great plans. At the age of eighty Moses received the divine commission to deliver his people from their bondage. Exod. 3: 3-10. This task was accomplished in forty years that were full of troubles, but also full of the most extraordinary events. (See the books of Exodus, Leviticus, Numbers, and Deuteronomy for a detailed account of their wanderings in the wilderness.) When finally, the Israelites approached the land of Canaan, ready to enter upon their national life, Moses forbidden by God to accompany them because he had struck the rock at Meribah instead of speaking to it, as God had commanded him, ascended Mount Nebo, and from Pisgah's top the LORD showed him the Promised Land. With his eye not dim nor his natural force abated, he was one hundred and twenty years old when he died in the land of Moab, and "there arose not a prophet since in Israel like unto Moses, whom the LORD knew face to face." Deut. 34:7,10. He was the author of parts of the PENTATEUCH (which see), and of the ninetieth Psalm, which was probably written in the wilderness.

Most High, a name often applied to God. Num. 24:16; Ps. 21:7 etc.

Mote, in Matt. 7:3, means a very small particle of anything.

Moth'er is sometimes used in the Old Testament in place of grandmother. 1 Kings 15:10. In Gen. 3:20 Eve is called "the mother of all living." The name is applied to Deborah as a political leader. Judg. 5:7.

Moun'tains. Among the principal mountains and mounts mentioned in the Bible are those of Ararat, Ebal, Hermon, Hor. Horeb, Lebanon, Moriah, Nebo, Olivet, or Olives, Sinai, Tabor, and Zion. Each of these and many others are mentioned in separate articles.

Mourn, Mourn'ers. The Hebrews made great manifestations of their grief at the death of friends and relations. Gen. 50:10. The usual period of mourning was seven days, but the mourning for Moses and for Aaron continued thirty days. Num. 20:29; Deut. 34:8. Special mourning was made for an only son. Zech. 12:10. Hired mourners were often employed.

Mul'ber-ry trees, in 2 Sam.5: 23, 24, is generally agreed to be a mistranslation. Many different meanings are suggested, among which is aspen or poplar.

Mules, the offspring of the horse and the ass, were ridden by distinguished men among the Jews. 2 Sam. 13:29. In Gen. 36:24 mules means hot springs.

Mur'der. Under the Jewish law one who slays another from enmity, hatred, or by lying in wait is called a murderer.

Mu'sic, 1 Sam. 18:6, formed an important part of the religious services and festivites of the Hebrews. The sons of Asaph, Heman, and Jeduthun were appointed by David for the musical service. Musical instruments were invented by Jubal. Gen. 4:21. Among those used by the Jews were the harp, the sackbut, the psaltery, cymbals, trumpets, organs, etc.

Mus'tard, mentioned in Matt. 13:31, 32; 17:20; Luke 17:6, is the black mustard, which grows to a very large size in Palestine.

Myra, my'rah (flowing, weeping), an ancient city and seaport of Lycia, on the south-west coast of Asia Minor. Acts 27:5.

Myrrh, mer, a precious gum from a low thorny tree found chiefly in Arabia. It was one of the ingredients of the holy ointment, Exod. 30:23, and of the embalming substance. John 19:39. It is also used in medicine and as a perfume.

Myr'tle, a fragrant and beautiful shrub common in northern Palestine. It is used in contrast with the brier to illustrate the glory of the Church. Isa. 41:19; 55:13. The myrtle was used for wreaths for ancient victors.

Mys'te-ry, in the New Testament, means a spiritual truth which cannot be discovered by reason, but is now revealed, although its full comprehension is beyond our finite understanding. The Gospel is called a mystery. Eph. 3:9; Col. 1:26.

N

Na'am (pleasantness), one of the sons of Caleb, the son of Jephunneh. 1 Chron. 4:15.

Na'a-man (pleasantness). [1] The "captain of the host" of the king of Syria. He was highly esteemed by the king for his mighty deed, but he was a leper. He heard of the fame of the prophet Elisha through a captive Jewish girl, went to him, and was miraculously cured of his leprosy after washing seven times in the river Jordan, according to the direction of the prophet. 2 Kings 5:1-19. Naaman promised Elisha that he would "henceforth offer neither burnt-offering nor sacrifice unto other gods, but unto the Lord." [2] One of the sons of Benjamin. Gen.46:21; [3] A son of Bela, the son of Benjamin. Num.26:40; 1 Chron.8:4. [4] The name apparently of a son of Ehud (or Abihud?). 1 Chron. 8:7.

Na'bal (fool), a wealthy inhabitant of Maon whose possessions were in Carmel. He was unfeeling and "evil in his doings," and refused in the most insulting manner to aid David, who had protected him from robbers. David immediately undertook to destroy him and his property, but was prevented from doing so by the discreet intervention of Abigail, the wife of Nabal. See 1 Sam. 25:2-38. Nabal died suddenly soon afterward, and Abigail subsequently became a wife of David.

Na'both (fruits), an inhabitant of Jezreel in Issachar whose vineyard Ahab, the king of Israel, coveted and obtained by the wicked artifice of his wife Jezebel, who had Naboth put to death. 1 Kings 21:1-19.

Nachon, na'kon, the name of the threshing-floor, between Kirjath-jearim and Jerusalem, near which Uzzah was slain for touching the ark of God. 2 Sam. 6:6. It is called CHIDON in 1 Chron. 13:9, and PEREZ-UZZA in 1 Chron. 13:11.

Na'dab (liberal). [1] One of the sons of Aaron. He and his brother Abihu were miraculously destroyed for offering strange fire to the Lord. Lev. 10:1-3. [2] A son of Jeroboam I., whom he succeeded as king of Israel. 1 Kings 14:20; 15:25-31. [3] A son of Shammai. 1 Chron. 2:28. [4] A son of Gibeon. He was the uncle of King Saul. 1 Chron. 8:30.

Na'hath (rest). [1] A grandson of Esau. He was a duke (chief) in Edom. Gen. 36:13; 1 Chron. 1:37. [2] One of the Levites, a descendant of Kohath. 1 Chron. 6:26. [3] A Levite who lived in Hezekiah's reign. 2 Chron. 31:13.

Na'hum (consolation). One of the twelve minor prophets, of whose private life nothing is known except what is stated in

Nah.1:1, where he is called "the Elkoshite." He prophesied B.C. about 713, and probably during the reign of Hezekiah.

Na'hum, the Book of, consists of one poem, of such eloquence, sublimity, and ardor of thought and language that it places its author in the highest rank of Hebrew poets. Its theme is "the burden of Nineveh"-that is, the coming punishment of that city and the Assyrian empire for the cruel treatment of the Jews.

Nails of various kinds are mentioned in the Bible. In Deut. 21:12 finger-nails are mentioned. The nail used by Jael in killing Sisera, Judg. 4:21, 22, was a tent-pin, such as is driven into the ground to hold the cords of a tent. Nails of iron are mentioned in 1 Chron. 22:3, and nails of gold in 2 Chron. 3:9. Nails are mentioned in John 20:25; Col. 2:14, in connection with the crucifixion of Christ.

Na'in (beauty), a city of Galilee where Christ raised to life the only son of a widow. Luke 7:11-16. It is now a small village called Nein.

Na'ked. This word is used in its literal sense in reference to Adam and Eve, Gen. 2:25, and in Job 1:21 in reference to himself. In 1 Sam. 19:24; John 21:7 it signifies that the usual outer garments were not worn. The word "naked" is often used figuratively, meaning spiritual destitution. Rev. 3:17.

Names are first mentioned in Gen. 2:11. In Gen. 2:20 it is mentioned that Adam gave names "to all cattle, and to the fowl of the air, and to every beast of the field." Names of persons and places referred to in the Bible have generally special meanings which have reference to some particular circumstance connected with them. Many highly significant names are applied to Christ.

Na-o'mi (my delight), the wife of Elimelech and the mother-in-law of RUTH (which see). Naomi, with her husband and two sons, moved from Bethlehem to Moab on account of a famine in their native land. Ruth 1:1, 2. Elimelech and his two sons died in Moab. Naomi returned to Bethlehem with her daughter-in-law Ruth, a native of Moab.

Nap'kin, in Luke 19:20; John 11:44; 20:7, means a little cloth. In Acts 19:12 the same word in the original is translated handkerchief. The word napkin had a much wider meaning in ancient times than at present.

Na'than (given). [1] A prophet in the times of David and Solomon. He was highly esteemed by them. David conferred with him concerning the building of a house for the Lord. 2 Sam. 7:1-17. In a fine allegory Nathan rebuked David for his sin against Uriah. 2 Sam. 12:1-10. See Ps. 51, referring to David's repentance for this act. Nathan was one of the biographers of David, 1 Chron. 29:29, and also of Solomon. 2 Chron. 9:29. [2] A son of David by Bathsheba. 1 Chron. 3:5. [3] Father of one of David's valiant men. 2 Sam. 23:36. [4] A chief man who returned to Jerusalem with Ezra. Ezra 8:16. [5] A descendant of Judah, of the family of Jerahmeel. 1 Chron. 2:36. [6] Father of Solomon's principal officer. 1 Kings 4:5. [7] The brother of one of David's valiant men. 1 Chron.11:38. [8] A Jew who took a foreign wife. Ezra 10:39.

Na-than'a-el (gift of God), a native of Cana in Galilee who confessed the Messiahship of Jesus and was with the apostles after the resurrection. John 1:45-49; 21:2. Christ called him "an Israelite indeed, in whom is no guile!" Some suppose Nathanael to be the same as the apostle Bartholomew.

Naught, in 2 Kings 2:19; Prov. 20:14, means bad; worthless; nothing.

Naught'i-ness, in 1 Sam. 17:28; James 1:21, means wickedness.

Naught'y, in Prov. 6:12, means wicked.

Naves, in 1 Kings 7:33, means the centres of wheels which have spokes.

Naz-a-rene', a native of Nazareth. Matt. 2:23; Acts 24:5.

Naz'a-reth (separated?), a city of lower Galilee, about sixty-five miles north of Jerusalem, nearly half-way from the river Jordan to the Mediterranean Sea, and about fourteen miles from the Sea of Galilee. It is not mentioned in the Old Testament (except by an indirect allusion of prophecy, Matt. 2:23), or by any writer before the time of Christ, and had a bad reputation among the Jews, John 1:46, but "Jesus of Nazareth" has made it a household word throughout Christendom. It was the home of Jesus from his childhood until he commenced his public ministry and was rejected by his own townsmen. Luke 4:28-31. The place is now called En-Nasirah, and has about 8000 inhabitants. It is a retired mountain village inhabited by Greeks, Moslems, Maronites, Roman Catholics, and about one hundred Protestants. It has a Protestant (English Episcopal) church, and an orphan asylum founded in 1874. "In Bethlehem we feel the joy of our Saviour's birth; in Jerusalem, the awe and anguish of his crucifixion, but also the glory of his resurrection; in Nazareth we look at the humble abode of his youth and early manhood. Talent and character are matured in quiet seclusion for the great battle of public life."

Naz'a-rite, one who consecrated himself to the Lord for a time, during which he abstained from certain things. Num. 6:2; Judg. 13:5.

Nebuchadnezzar, neb-u-kad-nez'zar, or **Nebuchadrezzar,** neb-u-kad-rez'zar (may Nebo protect the crown!), the greatest of the kings of Babylon, was the son of Nabopolassar, the founder of the Babylonian empire, and he reigned B.C. 605-561. Sent by his father against the Egyptian king Pharaoh-necho, he defeated the latter in a great battle on the Euphrates River, Jer. 46:2, conquered all the countries in Asia which Pharaoh-necho had occupied--namely, Syria, Phoenicia, Palestine, etc.--captured Jerusalem, and carried away as captives a part of its inhabitants, among them Daniel and his companions. Dan. 1:1-4. On the death of Nabopolassar, B.C. 605, Nebuchadnezzar ascended the throne. Jehoiakim, king of Judah, who had been made a vassal of Nebuchadnezzar, revolting in B.C. 602, Nebuchadnezzar made him a prisoner, but afterward released him. His son Jehoiachin also revolted, but this time Nebuchadnezzar inflicted a heavy punishment. Jehoiachin, with a number of the principal inhabitants of Jerusalem and all the treasures of the Temple and palace, were carried to Babylong, 2 Kings 24:12-16, and Jehoiachin's uncle Mattaniah, whose name was changed to Zedekiah, was made king of Judah. Zedekiah also revolting, Nebuchadnezzar broke down the walls of Jerusalem, destroyed the Temple, razed the whole city to the ground, put out the eyes of Zedekiah, and carried him and the inhabitants of Judea captives to Babylon, B.C. 588. See JERUSALEM. The first four chapters of the book of Daniel contain an account of events during the reign of Nebuchadnezzar, including the divine infliction of madness which he for a time suffered. During his reign he rebuilt all the cities of upper Babylonia and constructed vast temples, palaces, etc., including the famous hanging gardens of Babylon.

Nebuchadrezzar, neb-u-kad-rez'zar, in Jer. 21:2, 7, etc., Ezek. 26:7, is the more correct form for the name NEBUCHAD-NEZZAR.

Ne-he-mi'ah (consoled by Jehovah). [1] The son of Hachaliah, Neh. 1:1; was the pious restorer and governor of Jerusalem after the Babylonian exile. He lived in the fifth century B.C., and was cup-bearer, a very high position, to the Persian king Artaxerxes, who afterward appointed him governor of Jerusalem and permitted him to rebuild that city. Neh. 2:1-6. Nehemiah was the model of a Hebrew patriot and statesman. [2] A chief man among the Jews who went up to Jerusalem with Zerubbabel after the captivity. Ezra 2:2; Neh. 7:7. [3] The son of Azbuk who repaired part of the wall of Jerusalem after the captivity. Neh. 3:16.

Ne-he-mi'ah, the Book of, the sixteenth of the Old Testament Canon, is a continuation of the book of Ezra, and narrates how Nehemiah (No. 1, mentioned above) returned to Jerusalem, rebuilt the walls in spite of the insidious opposition of some of his countrymen, and, in conjunction with Ezra, re-established the law and the Sabbath in the country and introduced other necessary reforms.

Ne-hush'tan (a piece of brass), the name which King Hezekiah gave in contempt to the brazen serpent that Moses had formerly set up, Num. 21:8, 9, in the wilderness, and which the Israelites had preserved, worshipped, and offered incense to. It was therefore broken in pieces and destroyed by King Hezekiah. 2 Kings 18:4.

Neigh'bor. Luke 10:29. The Pharisees confined the meaning of this word to people of their own nation or to their own friends. Christ taught them, in the parable of the Good Samaritan, that all men are neighbors. Luke 10:30-37.

Neph'ew. This word, in the Authorized Version, always means either "grandchild" or "descendant" generally, which was its old English meaning. Job 18:19; Isa. 14:22.

Ne-than'e-el (given of God). [1] One of the captains of Issachar in the wilderness. Num. 1:8; 10:15. [2] A son of Jesse. 1 Chron. 2:14. [3] A priest in the time of King David. 1 Chron. 15:24. [4] One of the Levites. 1 Chron. 24:6. [5] A son of Obededom. 1 Chron. 26:4. [6] One of the princes in the reign of Jehoshaphat. 2 Chron. 17:7. [7] A Levite in the time of King Josiah. 2 Chron. 35:9. [8] A Jew who took a foreign wife. Ezra 10:22. [9] A priest in the time of Joiakim. Neh. 12:21. [10] One of the players on musical instruments when the wall of Jerusalem was dedicated. Neh. 12:36

N

Net'tles, in Job 30:7; Prov. 24:31; Zeph. 2:9, probably refers to a shrub resembling the common nettle, but larger. The well-known wild nettle is common in Palestine.

New Moon. Each of the Hebrews months commenced with the new moon. Moses appointed special sacrifices for that time. Num. 28:11-15.

Ni-ca'nor (conqueror) was one of the first seven deacons of the early Church in the time of the apostles. Acts 6:5.

Nic-o-de'mus (victor of the people), a noted Pharisee and Jewish ruler who "came to Jesus by night" and conversed with him concerning his doctrine. John 3:1-20. He defended Christ against the Pharisees, John 7:50, 51, and brought spices to anoint his body. John 19:39.

Ni-cop'o-lis (city of victory). There were several cities of this name in ancient times. The one at which Paul determined to winter, Tit. 3:12, was probably the noted Nicopolis in Epirus.

Niger, ni'jer (black), the surname of Simeon, one of the prophets and teachers who were at Antioch. Acts 13:1.

Night is first mentioned in Gen. 1:5. In John 9:4 it is figuratively used to signify death, and in 1 Thess. 5:5 to denote sin. Its meaning is evident in Rev. 21:25; 22:5.

Night'hawk is mentioned in Lev. 11:16 and Deut. 14:15 as an unclean bird. It is not the bird known in the United States by that name, but is probably a kind of owl common in Egypt and Syria.

Nile (blue, dark), the famous river of Egypt, is formed by the junction of the White Nile and the Blue or Black Nile. The White Nile is the principal stream, and rises in Lake Victoria Nyanza, most of which is south of the equator. The Blue Nile rises in the mountains of Abyssinia. The whole length of the Nile is about four thousand miles. Its course below the junction of the Blue and the White Nile is nearly north, and it flows into the Mediterranean Sea by two principal mouths, forming a delta which commences one hundred miles from the Mediterranean Sea and extends one hundred and sixty miles along its shore. As rain seldom falls in Egypt proper, its fertility depends entirely on the annual overflow of the Nile, which generally commences in June and begins to decrease in October. It leaves a deposit of mud which fertilizes the vallley. The overflow of the Nile is distributed by numerous canals and by the use of buckets with which it is raised above the water-level. The Nile was worshipped as a god by the ancient Egyptians. Its greatest width is about three thousand three hundred feet. The word "Nile" is not found in the Bible, but that river is referred to as SIHOR in Josh. 13:3; Isa.23:3; Jer.2:18; as SHIHOR in 1 Chron. 13:5; as "the river" in Gen. 41:1; Exod. 1:22; 2:3, 5; and as "the flood of Egypt" in Amos 8:8; 9:5.

Nim'rod (strong). [1] One of the sons of Cush, the son of Ham. In Gen. 10:9 he is mentioned as a "mighty hunter before the Lord." He was also noted as a conqueror and as the founder of Babylon. [2] The name is also used to denote the kingdom he founded, "the land of Nimrod." Mic. 5:6.

Nin'e-veh (dwelling of Nin?) stood on the eastern shore of the Tigris, two hundred and fifty miles north of Babylon and five hundred and fifty miles north-west of the Persian Gulf. It was founded by Asshur, Gen. 10:11, or, according to another translation, by Nimrod (who "went out into Assyria"). Nineveh became the capital of Assyria, probably during the reign of Sennacherib, and remained so till its destruction, after a siege of two years, by the combined forces of the Medes and the Babylonians, B.C. 606. Its site is marked by a number of huge mounds. In Scripture it is mentioned principally in the books of Jonah and Nahum. Concerning its extent scholars are not agreed. It was at all events one of the largest cities that ever existed, having within its walls not only gardens and groves, but also vast pastures. Up to the midddle of the nineteenth century very little was known about the city, but since that time excavations have disclosed large portions of the city walls, three temples of various dates, the palace of Shalmaneser, three palaces of Sennacherib, a palace of Tiglath-pileser II., and a temple of Nebo. These architectural monuments, with numerous pieces of sculpture and various specimens of industrial art in metal, glass, alabaster, etc. which have been found in mounds of Nineveh, show that Assyrian civilization exercised a decided influence on Persia and Greece. The most precious discovery, however, is that of vast remnants of the library of Tiglath-pileser, consisting of tablets and cylinders of burnt clay covered with arrow-headed or wedge-shaped characters. These curious inscriptions have been deciphered, and they furnish a complete confirmaton of the truth of the Biblical records.

Nisroch, nis'rok (great eagle?), one of the Assyrian gods, in whose temple at Nineveh the Assyrian king Sennacherrib was murdered by his sons. 2 Kings 19:37; Isa. 37:38.

N

Ni'tre, mentioned in Prov. 25:20 and Jer. 2:22, means an earthy and alkaline salt which resembles, and is used like, soap. It rises from the bottom of Lake Natron in Egypt, and is not in any respect like the nitre used in manufacturing gunpowder.

No'ah (rest), the son of Lamech. He was the ninth after Adam, and was preserved with his family in the ark from the flood which destroyed the rest of the human race. He "found grace in the eyes of the LORD," Gen. 6:8, and was "a preacher of righteousness." 2 Pet. 2:5. He built an altar immediately after leaving the ark and offered sacrifices unto the LORD. Gen. 8:20. His history and that of the flood is given in Genesis, chapters 5 to 9. He died at the age of nine hundred and fifty years. Gen. 9:29. He is mentioned in Heb. 11:7 among the heroes of faith.

No'ah (motion), a daughter of Zelophehad. Num. 26:33; Josh. 17:3.

No'ble-man, John 4:46-54, came to Christ to beseech him to heal his son, lying "at the point of death." This nobleman, according to the marginal notes, John 4:46, may have been a courtier or a ruler connected with the court of Herod.

No'e, Matt. 24:37; Luke 3:36, and elsewhere in the New Testament, the patriarch NOAH (which see).

Nose Jew'els were strung upon a ring of gold or some other metal, which was put through one of the nostrils. Isa. 3:21.

Nov'ice, in Tim. 3:6, means, as in the marginal notes, one newly come to the faith; one recently converted and received into the Christian Church.

Num'bers. Among the Hebrews special significance was given to certain numbers. Seven implies perfection, and is often used in the Bible. There are seven days in the week; the Revelation of John mentions seven churches, seven angels, seven golden vials; also seven heads and seven crowns of the dragon.

Num'bers, the fourth book of the Old Testament and of the Pentateuch, is so named because it gives an account of the numbering of Israel. It also contains sundry laws given to the Israelites and interesting facts connected with their journey through the wilderness, notably the sedition of Miriam and Aaron, the report of spies sent to search out Canaan, the brazen serpent raised by Moses, Balaam and his ass, etc.

Nurse. The nurse of Rebekah went with her to Canaan, and was buried with great mourning. Gen.24:59; 35:8. Nurses were highly esteemed in ancient times.

Nur'ture, in Eph. 6:4, means education; training.

Nuts, in Gen. 43:11, probably means pistachio-nuts. They resemble almonds, but taste like walnuts. In Song of Solomon 6:11 nuts means English walnuts.

O

Oak stands in the English Bible for six Hebrew words (most of which mean strong), and sometimes denotes any strong tree or a grove of trees rather than any particular tree. In many instances, Gen. 35:4; Judges 6:11, it represents the elm tree of Hosea 4:13, and the TEIL TREE (which see) of Isa. 6:13. It often served as a landmark and to designate the locality of great events. Gen. 35:4; Josh. 24:26. the word translated "plains," Gen. 12:6, the word translated "plains," Gen. 12:6, Deut. 11:30, means places noted for groves of the oak. The wood of the oak was used for idols. Isa. 44:14. Botanists find three species of the oak in Palestine. "Abraham's Oak," in the field of Mamre near Hebron, still lives, and is the noblest and most venerable tree of historic interest.

Oath. To take an oath is to call God to witness what we affirm. The custom was observed in the days of the patriarchs. Gen. 21:23. God also bound himself by oaths. Acts 2:30; Gen. 26:3. The taking of an oath was accompanied by the raising of the hand toward heaven, also by putting the hand under the thigh. Gen. 24:2, 3. Our Lord prohibited the use of profane and careless oaths. Matt. 5:34-36.

O-ba-di'ah (servant of Jehovah). [1] The head of a family which apparently descended from David. 1 Chron. 3:21. [2] A descendant of Tola, the son of Issachar. 1 Chron. 7:3. [3] A son of Azel, a Benjamite. 1 Chron. 8:38; 9:44. [4] A Levite, the son of Shemaiah. 1 Chron. 9:16. [5] A Gadite who joined David in Ziglag. 1 Chron. 12:9. [6] The governor of the house of Ahab, king of Israel. He hid and fed many of the Lord's prophets during the persecution of Jezebel. 1 Kings 18:3-16. [7] One of the princes of Judah who taught the people the law in the reign of Jehoshaphat. 2 Chron. 17:7. [8] The father of Ishmaiah. 1 Chron. 27:19. [9] A Levite overseer of repairs of the house of the Lord in the time of Josiah. 2 Chron. 34:12. [10] A son of Jehiel. Ezra 8:9. [11] A priest who sealed the covenant made by Nehemiah. Neh. 10:5. [12] A porter for the sanctuary. Neh. 12:25. [13] OBADIAH, the fourth of the minor prophets, lived after the destruction of Jerusalem, B.C. 588, but nothing more is known about him. Obadiah, verse 1.

O-ba-di'ah, the Book of, begins with the denunciation of the Edomites for their wicked and cruel conduct toward the Jews in the days of their misfortune, and closes with predicting the discomfiture of the Edomites and the restored glory and happiness of the descendants of Jacob. The striking resemblance between the first nine verses of Obadiah and Jeremiah 49:7-16 seems to indicate that one of these prophets had read the other's prophecy.

O'bed (serving). [1] A son of Boas and Ruth and father of Jesse. Ruth 4:17, 21, 22; 1 Chron. 2:12. He was an ancestor of Joseph, the husband of Mary. Matt. 1:5; Luke 3:32. [2] A son of Ephlal, who was a descendant of Judah. 1 Chron. 2:37, 38. [3] One of David's valiant men. 1 Chron. 11:47. [4] A porter for the Tabernacle in the time of David. 1 Chron. 26:7. [5] The father of Azariah, who was one of the captains who aided Jehoiada the priest in making Joash king of Judah. 2 Chron. 23:1.

O-be'di-ence of men to God is their supreme duty. Acts 5:29. It should be from the heart. 1 John 5:2, 3. It is also due from children to parents, Exod. 20:12; from servants to their employers, Eph. 6:5; and from citizens to the government. Rom. 13:1-5.

Ob-la'tion, an offering to god. Lev. 2:4, 7.

Ob-serv'ers of times, in Deut. 18:10, 14, refers to men who had a superstitious regard for days that were supposed to be lucky or unlucky, as decided by astrology. All such men were condemned. Deut. 18:9-14.

O'ded (erecting). [1] The father of Azariah the prophet. 2 Chron. 15:1, 8. [2] A prophet in Samaria. 2 Chron. 28:9-11.

Of'fend and **Of'fence** often mean that which causes one to stumble, or to sin. Thus, in Matt. 5:29 the meaning is, if thy right eye "causeth thee to stumble," as in the Revised Version. In Rom. 9:33 the Saviour is referred to as a "rock of offence," because his life, teachings, and death were so totally different from what the Jews had expected as to actually prove an obstacle to their accepting him as the long-promised Messiah.

Of'fer-ing, Ob-la'tion, that which is presented to the Lord as a confession, consecration, expiation, or thanksgiving, formed a very important part of the religious worship among the Jews. The offerings were from the animal and vegetable kingdoms, and were known as burnt-offerings, meat-offerings, heave-offerings, peace-offerings, sin-offering, trespass-offerings, etc., etc. Each had its own special significance, and minute directions were given for its preparation and observance.

Of'fi-cer, in Exod. 5:14, means a "scribe who keeps registers and tables," and generally has that meaning in the Old Testament. In the New Testament it is applied to bailiffs and those who collect fines. Matt. 5:25; Luke 12:58.

Og (long-necked?), the king of Bashan who fought against the passage of the Israelites through his dominions. Deut. 3:1. He was of gigantic stature, Josh. 13:12, but was defeated and slain, together with his sons. Deut. 1:4; Num. 21:34. His long "bedstead of iron" was preserved as a memorial of his stature. Deut. 3:11.

Oil. Among the nations mentioned in the Bible oil was used for anointing the head and body, especially on festivals and joyous occasions. Hence the use of oil is significant of joy and gladness, Ps. 23:5, and the omission of it denoted sorrow. 2 Sam. 14:2. The oil was made from the olive-berry, and was often perfumed with spices. It was also used by the Jews in the consecration of kings and high-priests, 1 Sam. 10:1; Exod. 29:7; in their meat-offerings, Lev. 2:4-7; for illuminating purposes in lamps, Matt. 25:3; in the preparation of food, taking the place of butter and lard, 1 Kings 17:12; for medicinal purposes, Luke 10:34; and for anointing the dead. Matt. 26:12. In ancient times the methods for extracting the oil from the olive-berry were very simple: Two reserviors, usually eight feet square and four feet deep, were arranged one above the other; the berries were placed in the upper one and were then trodden out with the feet. Another method crushed the berries under stone rollers and then subjected them to a heavy pressure.

Oil tree, in Isa. 41:19, and the olive tree, in 1 Kings 6:23, 31-33, are the same words in the original, but there is some doubt whether the "oil tree" and the olive are the same. Some believe it to be the oleaster, a shrub resembling the olive in leaf and general appearance, and yielding from its berries an inferior oil.

Oint'ments were used by the Hebrews more as a luxury than for medicinal purposes. They were generally made from olive oil perfumed with spices, and those used by the rich were very costly. Matt. 26:7-9.

Ol'ive. From the earliest times in Bible history the olive has been the most common of the fruit-tree of Palestine. In appearance it is not unlike our apple tree, and it thrives best where its roots can find their way into the crevices of a rock. The fruit is plum-shaped and when ripe is nearly black. The chief value of the olive tree is the oil which is expressed from its fruit, which is used for many purposes and forms an important article of commerce. From the extreme old age to which it attains, the beauty of the tree when in fruit, and the value of its products many figurative allusions are made to it in the Bible. Judg. 9:8, 9; Ps. 52:8; Hos. 14:6. The olive-branch is universally regarded as an emblem of peace. Gen. 8:11. The wood of the tree is close-grained, finely veined, and of a dark amber color.

Ol'ives, Mount of, or **Mount Olivet,** overlooking Jerusalem on the east, is memorable for many important and solemn events connected with the life of Christ. On its eastern slope, at Bethany, he performed his last miracle, John 11:44, and from here he made his triumphal entry into Jerusalem. Matt. 21:1-9. In a garden at its foot he was betrayed by Judas, and from it he ascended into heaven after his resurrection. Acts 1:12. Olivet is a ridge about three thousand feet high, two miles long, running north and south, and so near to the walls of Jerusalem that from its summit almost every street in that city can be easily seen. It affords the finest view of the temple area and all the prominent buildings. The mount was formerly covered with olive trees (hence the name), but is now almost bare, except at the foot, in the Garden of Gethsemane. Titus destroyed all the trees at the siege in A.D. 70. On one of its peaks, now known as the "Mount of Offence," Solomon engaged in idolatrous worship. 1 Kings 11:5-7.

Omega, o'me-gah or o-meg'ah, Rev. 1:8, the last letter of the Greek alphabet, is used in connection with ALPHA, which is the first letter of that alphabet, as a title of Christ.

O'mer, a measure used by the Hebrews. It was the tenth part of an ephah, and contained nearly five pints. Exod. 16:16, 36.

Om-nip'o-tent, all-powerful. In Rev. 19:6 the "Lord God omnipotent" is mentioned.

Om-ni-pres'ence, present in all places at the same time; as the omnipresent Jehovah.

Omniscient, om-nish'ent, all-seeing; as the omniscient God.

O'nan (strong), the second son of Judah by the daughter of Shuah the Canaanite. He refused to obey the law concerning raising up children by the wife of his deceased elder brother. Gen. 38:4, 8, 9; 1 Chron. 2:3.

O-nes'i-mus (useful), a native of Colosse. He was a slave of Philemon, and probably fled from him. Philemon 15. He was converted at Rome under the preaching of Paul, who wrote the Epistle to Philemon in his behalf. According to tradition, he became bishop.

On'ion. This well-known garden vegetable grew in great perfection in Egypt, where it attained a large size and exquisite flavor, differing from "the onions of our country as much as a bad turnip differs in palatableness from a good apple." The Israelites longed for them. Num. 11:5.

O'nyx, a precious stone, Exod. 25:7, consisting of different colored bands or layers, and evidently of great value from the uses made of it. Exod. 28:9-12; 39:6, 13. "Onyx stones," 1 Chron. 29:2, were used in the construction of the Temple.

Ophrah, of'rah (female fawn). [1] A town of Benjamin. Josh. 18:23; 1 Sam. 13:17. [2] A town of Manasseh. It is called Ophrah of the Abi-ezrite in Judg. 6:11, 24.

Or'a-cle, in the Old Testament, in all cases (excepting 2 Sam. 16:23, where it means "word") refers to the Holy of Holies in the Temple, where the ark of the covenant was and where God declared his will to the Israelites. 1 Kings 6:5, 19-23; 2 Chron. 3:16. In the New Testament "oracles" is applied to the Scriptures, which contain the will of God.

Or'di-nan-ces generally mean--(1) the laws and commandments of God, Exod. 18:20; (2) of civil rulers. 1 Peter 2:13. It also refers to religious ceremonies, as in Heb. 9:1, 10. In 1 Cor. 11:2 the word "ordinances" is rendered "traditions" in the marginal notes and the Revised Version.

Or'gan, in Gen. 4:21, was probably what the ancient Greeks called the "pipe of Pan." It consisted of a set of reeds of uneven length, closed at one end and blown into with the mouth at the other end. In skilful hands it produced moderately good music.

Orion, o-ri'un, one of the constellations. It contains about eighty stars, and is mentioned in Job 9:9; 38:31; Amos 5:8.

Or'na-ments were worn by the Hebrews and the people of the East, and the first mention of them is made in Gen. 24:22, where bracelets and earrings were presented to Rebekah by the servant of Abraham. Men wore rings and gold chains, Gen.41: 42, and the women rings for the fingers, nose and ears, bracelets, anklets, and hair ornaments. Isa. 3:18-23. In 1 Peter 3:4 the apostle exhorts the women to wear the "ornament of a meek and quiet spirit" rather than gold and jewels.

Or'nan, a Jebusite by whose threshing-floor the angel of the LORD stood. 1 Chron. 21:15-25; 2 Chron. 3:1. He is called ARAUNAH (which see) in 2 Sam. 24:16-24.

Or'pah, a daughter-in-law of Elimelech and Naomi. She was a Moabitess, and appeared inclined to accompany Naomi when she returned to the land of Judah, but turned back to her own people. Ruth 1:4, 14.

Or'phans, by the Mosaic law, were to be treated with special leniency and kindness, and were accorded special privileges. Deut. 24:17, 21. In James 1:27 to visit the orphans is regarded as one of the acts of pure and undefiled religion. "Comfortless," in John 14:18, is translated "orphans" in the marginal notes.

O'see is the Greek form of the name HOSEA (which see).

Rom. 9:25.

Os'trich, so well described in Job 39:13-18, is the largest of birds, often attaining the height of seven feet. It cannot fly, but it runs with an astonishing rapidity that the fleetest horse cannot equal. It is a shy bird, loving solitary and desolate places. The "owl," in Job 30:29; Isa. 13:21; Micah 1:8, means the ostrich.

O-ver-seers', in Acts 20:28, denotes one placed in charge or over a congregation, and bearing the same relation to it as a presbyter or elder, Acts 20:17, where the same persons are meant as in verse 28. In all other passages of the New Testament the corresponding Greek word is translated bishop.

Owl, as used in Deut. 14:16; Ps. 102:6; Isa. 34:11, 15, probably refers to some one or other of several species of owl that are found in Syria and Egypt. The word translated "owl" in Isa. 13:21; 34:13; Jer. 50:39; Micah 1:8, etc., really means OSTRICH (which see). The sacred writers evidently used the word to allude to some bird that loved solitary and desolate places.

Ox was also applied in a general sense like "herd," and is often rendered "kine." It was clean according to the Levitical law, and its strength and patience, as well as its value for food, made it one of the highly prized possessions of the Jews. Besides answering all the uses to which we put the ox tribe, in those days they were also used for threshing (treading out) the grain, Deut. 25:4, and for sacrifices.

Ox'-goad. Judg. 3:31.

O

P

Paarai, pa'a-ra, one of David's valiant men. 2 Chron. 23:35. He is called NAARAI in 1 Chron. 11:37.

Pa'dan (field) is used alone in one passage, Gen. 48:7, to denote the place elsewhere called PADAN-ARAM.

Pa'dan-a'ram (the low highland), the country to which Abraham sent his servant to obtain a wife for Isaac, Gen. 24:10; 25:20, and to which Isaac told Jacob to go for his wife, Gen. 28:2, is one of the Hebrew names for MESOPOTAMIA (which see). By some it is supposed to designate more particularly the plains of Mesopotamia from the mountainous districts in the north.

Pad'dle, Deut. 23:13, a short broad blade, similar to that on an oar.

Pa'don (deliverance), one of the Nethinim whose descendants returned with Zerubbabel from Babylon. Ezra 2:44; Neh. 7:47.

Paint, Painting. Paint was used by the Hebrews to color walls and beams of their houses, Jer. 22:14, and the heathen used it to adorn their temples with representations of their idols. Ezek. 23:14. It was also used in Assyria and Egypt, as their ruins and monuments show. Painting the eye was practised to some extent among the Hebrew women, but the custom was held in contempt. Jer. 4:30.

Pal'ace, in the Old Testament, denotes either the whole group of buildings that form the royal residence, and which are enclosed by the outer wall, Dan. 1:4, or simply one of those buildings. 1 Kings 16:18. In the New Testament the word generally means the residence of a wealthy or prominent person. Matt. 26:3; Luke 11:21. The "palace," in Philip. 1:13, is rendered in the marginal notes "Caesar's Court;" in the Revised Version, "praetorian guard" (Greek "praetorium").

Pal-es-ti'na, Exod. 15:14, from its inhabitants, the Philistines, was the name given to the country lying along the Mediterranean coast, between Joppa and Gaza. The same country is called PHILISTIA in Ps. 60:8; 87:4; 108:9.

Pal'es'tine (land of sojourners), a country on the east shore of the Mediterranean Sea, is sacred not only to Christians, but to Jews and Mohammendans.

Names--PALESTINE, in Joel 3:4; PALESTINA, in Exod. 15:14; Isa. 14:29, 31; and PHILISTIA, in Ps. 60:8; 87:4; 108:9, refer only to the country of the Philistines, who occupied a part of the eastern shore of the Mediterranean Sea south of Joppa.

The original name of Palestine was CANAAN. Gen. 12:5; 16:3; Exod. 15:15; Judg. 3:1. It is also called the PROMISED LAND, LAND OF ISRAEL OR ISRAELITES, LAND OF JUDAH OR JUDEA, and the HOLY LAND. The name Palestine now includes the whole land of the Hebrews on both sides of the Jordan. In this sense the name was first applied by Josephus and by Greek and Roman writers, and it has ever since been so called, although the HOLY LAND is now its more popular name.

Situation and Extent--Palestine, or the Holy Land, extends from latitude 33 16' north to latitude 31 north, comprising an area of about twelve thousand square miles (less than one-third larger than that of the State of New Hampshire), and bounded west by the Mediterranean Sea, south and east by the desert which separates it from Egypt, Arabia, and Mesopotamia, and north by the mountains of Lebanon and Anti-Lebanon, which separate it from Syria. The average length of the country is about one hundred and fifty miles, and the average width is about eighty miles.

The surface of the country--is diversified, and consists of four belts: the coast-land, the western mountains, the Jordan valley, and the eastern mountains. These belts run from north to south, nearly parallel with each other and with the shore of the Mediterranean, gradually converging as they near the north.

The coast-land, comprising in the north the old Phoenicia and in the south the old Philistia, or the land of the Philistines, is lowland, from six to twenty miles broad, and only broken at the point where the Carmel ridge branches off from the hills of Samaria and extends for about twelve miles in a north-western direction across the coast-belt directly to the Mediterranean Sea. This ridge is not very high, its highest peak being only about 1740 feet. When it reaches the Mediterranean it forms a bold promontory over 500 feet high, jutting out into the sea. The sides of this ridge rise abruptly from the plain, and the valleys that cut it are sharply cleft. Along the whole coast-line there is no good harbor and only one bay of importance--that of Acre, formerly ACCHO, just north of Mount Carmel.

The western mountain-belt, "the backbone of Palestine," from twenty-five to thirty miles broad, is an offshoot from Mount Lebanon, and comprises the hills of Galilee, whose highest points are Safed, 2775 feet, and Jebel Jermuh, 4000 feet; the hills of Samaria, whose highest points are Ebal, 3077 feet, Gerizim, 2849 feet, and Tell Asur, 3400 feet; the hills of

Judea, whose highest points are Jerusalem 2593 feet, Olivet, 2683 feet, Hebron, 3040 feet, and Berrsheba, 788 feet, and then falls abruptly off toward the desert. As the coast-belt is broken at one point by the Carmel ridge, so is the western mountain-belt split at one point, between Galilee and Samaria, by the plain of JEZREEL (which see). The western-slope of this belt, that toward the coast-land, though bold and somewhat rugged, is generally gradual and very fertile, while the eastern slope, toward the Jordan Valley, is wild and barren.

The valley of the Jordan is one of the most curious geographical phenomena on the globe. Through it runs the river Jordan, which, after a tortuous course in which it descends three thousand feet, empties into the Dead Sea. This valley is at its greatest width about ten miles broad, but generally only three miles, and at places quite narrow. Its sides rise from 2000 to 4000 feet, generally in abrupt and confused forms. This portion of the valley that is well watered is very fertile, but the sides are for the most part sterile. The view around the Dead Sea is forbidding and in some localities awful, but the Sea of Galilee is very inviting.

The eastern mountain-belt begins at Mount Hermon in the north, runs south for about two hundred miles, and ends in Mount Hor. It forms the high table-lands of Moab and Bashan, which slope on the east very gently, almost imperceptibly, down to the desert.

The climate of Palestine varies with the external form of the country. From November to April in Palestine is generally the wet season, and from April to November the dry. During the dry season it rarely rains, and even during the wet season the sky often remains perfectly clear for weeks. The rainfall varies from 14 to 32 inches a year; 25 inches are considered necessary to insure a good harvest.

P

The coast-land has very mild winters, but the summers are hot.

In the western mountain-belt the winter sometimes brings quite violent storms with penetrating cold winds and even a little snow, but generally there are weeks of delightful weather. During the summer the days are warm, though rarely oppressively so, and the nights are cool.

The Jordan valley has a semi-tropical climate, very trying to foreigners.

The climate of the eastern mountain-belt is somewhat colder than that of the western.

The soil, where it is well watered, is very productive.

Travellers are amazed at the great number of brilliant flowers which cover the whole country during February and March (the wet season), but in July and August (during the dry season) even the grass has gone; and many districts which evidently have once been in a high state of cultivation now lie waste because the art of irrigation, once generaly practised, has been neglected or forgotten. There is plenty of water, however, in this country for irrigation. Besides Lake Huleh (called the Waters of Merom, Josh. 11:7) and the Sea of Galilee, there are numerous perennial streams flowing into the Jordan or running down the western slope to the Mediterranean, and a remarkable number of springs and fountains. The water of the Dead Sea is unavailable, being to such an extent impregnated with salt, pitch, and other minerals that fish cannot live in it and plants cannot grow near it. East of the Jordan there are large forests of pine and oak, but west of that river the forests have disappeared, except on Mount Tabor and Mount Carmel. Even the cedars of Lebanon are steadily becoming less numerous.

Productions--The plains of Bashan and the Jordan valley are regarded as among the finest wheat-lands in the world; cotton and the sugar-cane grow luxuriantly in the coast-land and the Jordan valley; the olives, figs, grapes, and almonds of Palestine are celebrated, and vegetables of every kind and of excellent quality are easily raised. The apple and the potato do not succeed there.

Fisheries of Palestine are principally in the Sea of Galilee (Lake of Gennesaret) and in the Jabbok, Jordan, and Kishon Rivers. Among the fishes caught there are the barbel, blenny, bream, carp, dog-fish, minnow, perch and the sheat-fish.

Though the Palestine of to-day is not a country flowing with milk and honey, it is certainly evident that it once was; and probably it might be made so again.

Animals--Of the wild animals mentioned in the Bible, the lion, the unicorn, (a species of wild ox), the "behemoth" (probably the hippopotamus), Job 40:15, and the crocodile (the 'leviathan' of Job, chapter 41) have disappeared, but the gazelle, jackal, fox, and wild boar are still found in Palestine. The most common domestic animals are the sheep, the goat, the ass, the mule, and the camel.

Birds of prey are vey abundant now, as in olden times; also the turtle-dove, Song of Solomon 2:11, 12 the partridge, etc. The ostrich has disappeared.

The mineral deposits of the country are at present almost wholly unimproved, but are considered to be of great value.

Lead, copper, sulphur, salt, bitumen, etc. are found in great quantites; also iron and coal occur. The region around the Dead Sea is supposed to contain a great accumulation of petroleum.

Mountains--Among the most important are Carmel, Ebal, Gerizim, Gilboa, Gilead, Hermon, Lebanon, Moriah, Nebo, Olivet, or Mount of Olives, Pisgah, Samaria, Tabor, and Zion.

Cities, Towns, and Villages--Among the most important are Accho, Ain, Beer-sheba, Bethany, Beth-el, Bethlehem, Bethsaida, Bezer, Caesarea, Caesaarea Philippi, Capernaum, Chorazin, Dan, Decapolis, Gennesaret, Golan, Hebron, Jericho, Jerusalem, Joppa, Kedesh, Magdala, Mamre, Nazareth, Ramoth, Samaria, Shechem, Shiloh, and Tirzah.

Rivers and Brooks.--Among the most important are Arnon, Cherith, Jabbok, Jordan, Kanah, Kedron (called also Kidron and Cedron), Kishon, and River of Egypt.

Seas and Lakes--The principal are the Dead Sea (called also the Salt Sea, the Sea of the Plain, and Lake Asphaltites), the Sea of Galilee (called also the Sea of Tiberias and the Lake of Gennesaret), and Lake Huleh, or the Waters of Merom.

History--Palestine had no strong government under the JUDGES (which see). During the reigns of David and Solomon it attained its highest prosperity. Visible decay began, B.C. about 975, with the secession of the ten tribes. Assyria crushed the northern kingdom of Israel B.C. about 720, and Babylon the southern kingdom of Judah B.C. about 587. Since that time Palestine has been under foreign rule. Persians, Greeks, and Romans succeeded one another in the mastery.

In the time of Christ, under the Romans, there were four provinces--Galilee, Samaria, and Judea on the west side of Jordan, and Peraea on the east side. Since A.D. 637, when Palestine was conquered by the Saracens, it has, with little interruption, been under Turkish rule. The Turks seized the country in A.D. 1073, and by their barbarous treatment of Christian pilgrims provoked the Crusades. Roman rule was established in 1099, held Jerusalem till 1187, and remained in Acre till 1291. In 1517 the Ottomans came in and made Palestine part of the Turkish empire. It was suddenly taken from the sultan by Mehemet Ali, viceroy of Egypt, in 1832, but European governments intervened and in 1841 it was given back again.

Palm'er-worm, a destructive insect, perhaps a species of locust, is mentioned in Joel 1:4; Amos 4:9 as a figurative illustration of the punishment that would befall the rebellious Jews.

Palm Tree. The date-palm abounds in Arabia, Egypt, in the whole of southern Asia, and in northern Africa, but it is now rare in Palestine, though when the scenes mentioned in the Bible occurred this tree was very common there. It is one of the most beautiful of trees, growing to a height of from sixty to one hundred feet, with no branches, strictly-speaking, except the mass of graceful evergreen shoots which adorn its summit. The fruit of the palm (dates) is an article of food for the people, camels feed on the seed, and the leaves, fibres, and sap are all valuable. The Arabs speak of three hundred and sixty uses to which the different parts of the tree may be applied. A single tree will bear over two hundred pounds of dates. The palm tree lives more than two hundred years, and is most productive from the thirtieth until the eightieth year. The tree was held in great estimation by the Hebrews, and hence the frequent allusions to it in the Bible. Ps. 92:12, 14; Jer. 10:5; John 12:13. In Rev. 7:9 it is used with special force and beauty, as the palm was an emblem of victory and was carried before the conqueror in the triumphal processions.

Pa'per, Pa'per Reeds. PAPER REEDS, Isa. 19:7. or BUL-RUSHES (which see), are found in the Upper-Nile, in Egypt, and upon the northern shores of the Sea of Galilee. PAPER, 2 John verse 12, was first made from this plant. The stalk, by means of a needle, was slit into thin layers or strips that were made as broad as possible, in some instances ten to fifteen inches wide. The strips were then laid side by side on a flat surface and immersed in water, which caused their edges to adhere to each other as though they were glued. After being dried in the sun and covered with a sort of sizing the sheets were beaten with hammers and finally polished. Writing on paper thus made was done by means of a fine hair-pencil (brush).

Par'a-ble, a method of teaching through pictures of human life, was much employed in ancient times, and striking instances occur in the Old Testament, notably Nathan's parable of the ewe-lamb by which David was made his own judge, 2 Sam. 12:1-7; Isaiah's parable of the vineyard. Isa. 5: 1-7 etc. Our Saviour used parables in his discourses to the people ("and without a parable spake he not unto them." Matt. 13:34), and, as recorded in the New Testament, they present forcibly yet briefly the most important spiritual truths concerning the kingdom of God, its growth, value, relation to the world, conflict and ultimate triumph. There is nothing equal to the parables of Christ in all literature; they are inexhaustible, simple enough for a child, and deep enough for the most advanced sage and saint. See epecially Matt., chapter 13, and Luke, chapter 15.

Par'a-dise is a word of Persian origin, and means a garden, orchard, or other enclosed place filled with beauty and delight. Hence, it is used figuratively for any place of peculiar happiness, and particularly for the kingdom of perfect happiness which is the abode of the blessed beyond the grave. Luke 23:43: 2 Cor. 12:4; Rev. 2:7.

Parch'ments, the skins of sheep or goats so dressed and prepared as to render them fit to write on. The skins of beasts were extensively used by the early writers, but they were rudely prepared. About two centuries before Christ a method was discovered for producing a very fine material. This the Latins called pergamena, which is translated in 2 Tim. 4:13, "parchments."

Par'don, as used in the Bible in reference to God's grace excercised toward man, has a very different meaning from the word as used by us in our dealings with one another. There it means covering up, Ps. 85:2, blotting out. Ps. 51:9, or removing our transgressions far from us. Ps. 103:12, and no longer remembering them. Heb. 8:12.

Par-ti'tion, Mid'dle Wall of, Eph.2:14, is supposed to have reference to the wall in the Temple which separated the court of Israel from the court of the Gentiles, and is used here figuratively to denote whatever distinguished the Jews as the favored people of God, from the heathen or Gentiles.

Pas'sion, in Acts 1:3, denotes the last sufferings and death of Christ. "Like passions," in Acts 14:15; James 5:17, means having the same human feelings and propensities.

Pass'o-ver, a Jewish feast, commemorates the exemption or the "passing over" of the families of the Israelites when the destroying angel smote the first-born of Egypt. Exod. 12: 23-29, and also their departure from the land of bondage. On the fourteenth day of the first month (Nisan), at even, the Passover was to be celebrated, and on the fifteenth day commenced the seven days feast of unleavened bread. Lev. 23:5. Strictly speaking the term Passover is applied only to the fourteenth day of the first month (that is, form the evening of the fourteenth to the evening of the fifteenth), but as used in sacred history the word includes the seven days' feast of the unleavened bread. Luke 2:41; John 2:13, 23:6:4;11:55.

Pa'tience, as applied to God, is that manifestation of his love which causes him to bear long with sinners and to repeatedly warn them of judgments to come. Exod. 34:6; Rom. 2:4. In man

179

it denotes a meek and trustful endurance of whatever trials God may send him, and love and forbearance with his fellow-man. Rom. 2:7; 1 Thes. 5:14.

Pat'mos, a rocky and barren island, about twenty miles in circumference, situated in the Aegean Sea, about twenty-four miles west of Asia Minor and north of the east end of the island of Crete, is memorable as the place to which the apostle John was banished. Rev. 1:9.

Paul (small) or **Saul** (asked for), whose character, both as a man and as the great apostle to the Gentiles, stands out in the New Testament with such distinct outlines, was born in the Greek city of Tarsus, Cilicia, and with Roman citizenship, Acts 22:28, 29, but of Jewish parents belonging to the tribe of Benjamin. His original Jewish name was Saul; his Gentile name which he uses in all his epistles, was Paul. He studied Jewish law under Gamaliel in Jerusalem, Acts 5:34, and attracted, while yet a young man, considerable attention on account of his passionate devotion to his faith. Belonging to the sect of the Pharisees, he appeared as one of the foremost among the persecutors of the Christians, Acts 7:58, but on his way from Jerusalem to Damascus he was suddenly converted by a revelation of the exalted Saviour. Acts 9:8, 9. He retired for three years, A.D. 37-40, to Arabia, in quiet preparation for the great work to which he called at his conversion. He lived by the mechanical trade which, after the custom of Jewish rabbis, he had acquired. It was tent-making, which flourished in his native province of Cilicia. He labored a year with Barnabas at Antioch, and built up this mother-church of Gentile Christianity and centre of his missionary labors. From Antioch he made five journeys to Jerusalem, A.D. 40,44 50 54,58. From Antioch he started on his three great missionary journeys, the first A.D. 45-49 (Acts 13 and 14), the second A.D. 51-53 (Acts 15:36 to 18:22), and the third A.D. 54-57 (Acts 18:23 to 21:33). On his last journey to Jerusalem he was made prisoner, sent to Casarea for two years A.D. 58 to 60, appeared before Festus and King Agrippa, appealed to Caesar, went to Rome, and was kept a prisoner there from A.D. 61 to 63, but turned his prison into a pulpit, preaching to his distant congregations in the Epistles to the Ephesians, Colossians, Philippians and Philemon. The account breaks off with the close of his first Roman captivity (Acts 28:31). What then happened is not known with certainty. Ancient tradition is unanimous as to his martyrdom in Rome, and the reputed place on the Via Ostia where he was executed by the sword is still shown (at a place called The Three

Fountains, about two miles from the Basilica of St. Paul). Some Biblical scholars place that event during the Neronian persecution, A.D. 64, while others suppose a later date, A.D. 67 or 68, after an intervening fourth missionary tour to the East, and perhaps to Spain (whither he intended to go. Rom. 15:28). In this case we must assume a second Roman imprisonment. In his last epistle he takes farewell of the world and is ready for martyrdom (2 Tim. 4: 6-8). Paul is perhaps the most remarkable and influential character in history, next to his Lord and Master; he was a unique man for a unique work: he was providentially equipped by his Jewish descent, Greek education, and Roman citizenship for the apostleship of the Gentiles; he labored more in word and deed than all other apostles, and secured the victory of Christianity as the universal religion of the world. He is the model missionary, and an inspiration to all ages. His EPISTLES are a unique body of literature, full of deep and burning thoughts that can never die. They were written between 52 and 63, and touch upon all points of the Christian's faith and duty and the highest topics that can engage our attention. For his Epistles see the separate titles.

Pearl, found principally in the shells of the pearl-oyster, has always been highly prized as a gem, and the ancients regarded it among the most precious substances. Matt. 7:6; 1 Tim. 2:9. The pearl-oysters grow in clusters in deep water, and they are found in the Persian Gulf, on the coasts of Java, Sumatra, etc., etc. The oysters are brought up by divers who are specially trained for this arduous and dangerous work. The pearls are generally small, not as large as a cherry-stone, but some reach the size of a walnut, and one has been valued at $350,000. "Pearls," in Job. 28:18, probably means "crystals."

Pe'let (deliverance). [1] One of the sons of Jahdai. 1 Chron. 2:47. [2] One of the sons of Azmaveth. 1 Chron. 12:3.

Pe'leth (swiftness). [1] A Reubenite whose son On joined the conspiracy against Moses. Num. 16:1. [2] A descendant of Pharez, the son of Judah. 1 Chron. 2:33.

Pen'ny. The word translated "penny" in Matt. 18:28; 22:19, etc. is the Roman denarius, and formed the bulk of the silver coins current in Palestine at that time. Its value was about fifteen cents in our money, and in those days it was the regular pay of a day-laborer.

Pentateuch, pen'ta-tewk (five volumes), is the collective name for the first five books of the Old Testament, the Five Books of Moses, and was introduced by the Septuagint (Greek) translators, as were also the special names of the single books, each referring to the specific contents of each book: GENESIS (origin or beginning), because it gives an account of the origin of the world and the human race and the beginning of history; EXODUS, because it narrates the departure from Egypt and the wanderings through the wilderness; LEVITICUS, because it establishes the service of the Levites and the priesthood of Aaron's descendants, and draws the fundamental lines of the theocratic (that is, as administered by the immediate direction of God) form of government; NUMBERS, because it records the two censuses taken by Moses and some legal enactments connected therewith; and DEUTERONOMY (the second law), because through the repetition of the Decalogue (the Ten Words) and the three addresses of Moses to the Israelites it forms, as it were, a recapitulation or final summing-up of the whold legislation. The Hebrews indicated the single books simply by the first word with which each begins: Bereshith,Shemot, etc. The collective names with which Scripture designates all the five books taken together are: "A book of law of the LORD given by the hand of Moses," 2 Chron. 34:14; "the book of the law of the LORD," 2 Chron. 17:9; "the book of the law ," 2 Kings 22:8; "the book of the covenant," 2 Kings 23:2; "the law of Moses," Ezra 7:6; 'the book of the law of Moses," Neh. 8:1; "the law," Matt. 12:5; Luke 10:26; John 8:5, 17. The composition and authorship of the Pentateuch have been and still are the subject of elaborate critical discussions which do not come within the scope of this popular summary. For the several books, see GENESIS, etc.

Pen'te-cost, from a Greek word meaning fiftieth, is used in the New Testament to denote the second great festival of the Jews, which was celebrated on the fifieth day after the sixteenth of Nisan (the second day of the PASSOVER festival. Lev. 23:15,16. In the Old Testament it is called the "feast of weeks," Exod. 34:22, and the "day of the firstfruits," Num. 28:26, and was originally appointed as a simple thanksgiving for the harvest, which in Palestine was gathered between Passover and Pentecost. On the day of Pentecost the Holy Spirit was poured out on the Christian Church. Acts 2:1-41.

Pe'res, in Dan. 5:28, means "he was divided." In the original language it is the same word as "Upharsin," Dan. 5:25, but in a different case or number.

Pe'rez (a rent). [1] An ancestor of Jashobeam. 1 Chron. 27:3. May be same as Pharez, the son of Judah. [2] A son of Judah, Neh. 11:4, 6, called PHAREZ (which see) in Gen. 38:29.

Per'fect, Per-fec'tion. Complete, entire in all its parts, and

182

without defect or blemish. While being perfect does not elevate a thing above its kind, still it gives to it the highest value it can ever reach. As used in Gen. 6:9; 1 Kings 15:14; 2 Kings 20:3; Job 1:1, the word does not necessarily imply freedom from sin, but blamelessness or uprightness. "Be ye therefore perfect," in Matt. 5:48, is rendered in the Revised Version "Ye therefore shall be perfect."

Per'fume, Prov. 27:9, was much used in the East to give an agreeable odor to the person and apparel. The word as used in Exod. 30:35 means a composition to be used only in the Temple service. The occupation of the apothecary consisted chiefly in making perfumes and ointments.

Per'ga-mos (place of nuptials) was for a century before and a century after the birth of Christ a large and celebrated city situated in southern Mysia, with about 120,000 inhabitants, an impregnable fortress in which enormous public treasures were kept, one of the largest libraries in the world, etc. It was the centre of the worship of Aesculapius, the place in which parchment was greatly improved, etc. It contained one of the seven churches of Asia, and is mentioned, Rev. 1:11; 2:12-17, as the city where, according to the Revised Version, "Satan's throne is." The city is now called Bergama, and has about 30,000 inhabitants.

Per'iz-zites (villagers), a nation which inhabited the hill country south of that afterward occupied by the tribe of Judah. Gen. 13:7; Exod. 3:8.

Per'se-cute, Per-se-cu'tion. The using of force or compulsion in matters of conscience or religious belief, or the infliction of pain or punishment on account of same, is persecution. Matt. 10:23; Acts 8:1.

Per'sia, the last of the four great Asiatic empires, was founded, B.C. about 588, by Cyrus, and destroyed, B.C. 330, by Alexander the Great. Persia proper corresponded nearly to the present Persian province of Shiraz, a high plateau four thousand feet above the level of the sea, extending north-ward from the Persian Gulf, but separated from the Mesopotamian lowland by wild mountain-ranges. It was inhabited by a people entirely alien to the Chaldees, Assyrians, Babylonians, Hebrews, Phoenicians, etc., but remotely related to the Greeks and Romans. The kings of the Persian empire were generally friendly toward the Hebrews. At Babylon Cyrus became acquainted with them, and made a decree allowing them to return to Jerusalem and rebuild the Temple. A later kings, Artaxerxes, cancelled Cyrus's permit, and for some time the work on the

P

Temple ceased, but his successor, Darius Hystaspes, confirmed the decree of Cyrus, and even furthered the work. The Ahasuerus of the book of Esther was probably that Xerxes who failed so ignominiously in his attempt to conquer Greece and penetrate Europe.

Pes'ti-lence, in Exod. 5:3; Deut. 28:21, Jer. 21:6, etc., expresses all kinds of distempers and calamities.

Pes'ti-lent, in Acts. 24:5, means mischievous and disposed to lead others astray.

Pe'ter (stone or rock), Syriac, CEPHAS, was a son of Jonas or John, a brother of Andrew, a native of Bethsaida in Galilee, a fisherman by trade, and resided with his wife and mother-in-law at Capernaum. His original name was Simon or Simeon, but when he was called to the apostleship the Lord gave him the name Peter, John 1:42; Matt. 16:18, with a prophetic reference to what he should do and be for the Church. Among the apostles he stands out with singular vividness and impressiveness, one moment nearest to us, and in the next, it would seem, nearest to God. He had an impulsive temperament and was always in a hurry, the first to confess and the first to deny the Lord; but he sincerely repented and strengthened his brethren.

The earlier apostolic work of Peter is recorded in the first part of Acts, chapters 1-12 and 15. He laid the foundation of the Church among the Jews on the day of Pentecost, Acts 2, and he admitted the first Gentiles, Cornelius and his family, to baptism. Acts 10:47, 48. Of his later activity we have only a few notices. A controversy sprang up between him and Paul at Antioch concerning the treatment of Gentile converts, Gal. 2:11, but it was only temporary, and ended with perfect harmony between the two great men. 2 Pet. 3:15. From 1 Cor. 9:5 we know that at that time, A.D. about 57, Peter and his wife were engaged in missionary work, probably among the dispersed Jews in Asia Minor, to whom his two epistles are addressed. According to a tradition unanimously accepted by the whole Christian Church of antiquity, he suffered martyrdom in Rome, on the Vatican hill (where now St. Peter's church stands), probably during the Neronian persecution in A.D. 64.

Pe'ter, the First E-pis'tle of, is addressed to the Jewish churches in Asia Minor, and dated from Babylon. 1 Pet. 5:13. This may mean the old famous city of Babylon in Asia, which for centuries after its destruction continued the seat of a large Jewish colony and a centre of Jewish learning. But it may also have been used in a figurative and mystic sense for heathen Rome (as in Revelation 17:5).

Pe'ter, the Sec'ond E-pis'tle of, was written shortly before his martyrdom, from the same place and to the same churches as his first epistle, but it was not mentioned or used till long after his death, and was at the time of Eusebius (about A.D. 320) numbered among the disputed books. It is, as it were, his last will and testament; a warning against dangerous errors; refers to the transfiguration; and points to the new heavens and the new earth.

Petra, pe'trah (rock), in the marginal notes, Isa. 16:1, is translated SELA (which see) in the text. Petra is the Greek name of a famous city of Edom.

Pha'ra-oh, the father of Bithiah, who became the wife of Mered, who was a descendant of Judah. 1 Chron. 4:18.

Pha'ra-oh (sun) was the national or official title of the Egyptian kings of the old native dynasties. Besides PHAR-AOH-HOPHRA and PHARAOH_NECHO (which see) there are six kings called Pharaoh mentioned in the Bible: (1) Pharaoh in the time of Abram. Gen. 12:15, etc. (2) Pharaoh in the time of Joesph. Gen. 37:36; chapter 41. (3) Pharaoh in the infancy of Moses, the "new king over Egypt, which knew not Joseph." Exod. 1:8, 11; 2:15. This is the Pharaoh of the oppression, usually identified with Rameses II. of the nineteenth dynasty, the conqueror and master builder, called Sesostris by the Greeks. (4) Pharaoh when Moses was sent to deliver the Israelites from bondage. Exod. 3:10, etc. The Pharaoh of the exodus, who perished with his army in the Red Sea (Meneph-tha, the son of Rameses II., whose reign was inglorious and marked the period of decline). (5) Pharaoh whose daughter Solomon married. 1 Kings 3:1; 2 Chron. 8:11; Song of Solomon 1:9. (6) Pharaoh in the time of Isaiah. Isa. 30:2,3; 36:6.

Phar'i-sees, The, formed in the time of our Lord the most powerful party among the Jews both in politics and religion. In politics they were national and opposed to the Roman rule. They were the leaders of the people in its desperate fight for its political independence, and they employed every means in their power to oppose the intrusion of Greek-Roman civilization, its paganism, and its vices. In religion they adhered strictly to the letter, but departed from the spirit, of the Old Testament. In opposition to the Sadducees they accepted and defended the doctrines of the resurrection of the body, a future reward or punishment, a divine providence, etc., but they also maintained that there existed an oral tradition descended from Moses, and to that tradition, of which they pretended to be the sole possessors, they ascribed an authority equal to the law. By this means they attempted to keep the conscience of the people in abject slavery, and troubled men's minds with questions like this: Whether it was permitted to eat an egg which was laid on a Sabbath day, etc., etc. Hence the scathing denunciations of our Lord. Matt. 23:23-33; Luke 16:14, 15. Among the Pharisees, however, were some of the noblest characters, such as Nicodemus, Joseph of Arimathea, and the wise Gamaliel (Acts 5:34), and from them came the great apostle of the Gentiles, Paul.

Phe'be (shining), a noted member and "servant of the church at Cenchrea" whom Paul commended. Rom. 16:1.

Phenice, fe-ni'see. [1] Another form of the names PHOENICIA or PHENICIA. See the latter. [2] A town and harbor on the south-west side of the island of Crete, in the Mediterranean Sea. The captain of the ship on which Paul was a prisoner undertook to sail into it, but could not. Acts 27:12-14. Phenice, No. 2, is more properly called Phoenix, and has been identified with the modern Lutro.

Phenicia, fe-nish'i-ah, now called PHOENICIA, is the narrow strip of coast-land, between the Mediterranean Sea and Lebanon, which extends from the "Ladder of Tyre:" to Nahr Auly, about thirty miles. Although now only a desert strewn with ruins, Phoenicia was at one time one of the most flourishing places in the world. The name does not occur in the Old Testament, but is found in the New Testament in the form "Phenice," Acts 11:19; 15:3, and "Phenicia," Acts 21:2. The Phoenicians were closely related to the Canaanites, Gen. 10:15, and to the Israelites, Traces of the Phoenician tongue which have come down to us, inscriptions on coins, monuments, etc., can be understood only by means of the Hebrew language. The relations between the two peoples were also generally very cordial. The wheat, honey, oil, balm, etc. of the Israelites were bought and exported by the Phoenicians, and Phoenician mechanics and artists went up to Jerusalem in the service of David and Saul. At the same time the Phoenician and the Hebrew fleets sailed together for Ophir. In religion the difference between the two peoples was very marked. The religion of the Phoenicians was a kind of nature-worship in its most abominable form, and the rites and ceremonies and practices involved in the worship of Baal and Astarte point toward the lowest forms of sensuousness and cruelty. The Phoenicians therefore exercised a degrading influence on the Hebrews, especially after the separation between Israel and Judah. They sided with Israel, whose people they seduced to idolatry, and made wars against Judah in which they even went so far as to sell their prisoners to the Edomites as slaves.

Phil-a-del'phi-a (brotherly love), a city on the borders of Lydia and Phrygia, Asia Minor, was founded in the second century B.C., and continued to flourish until the close of the fourteenth century A.D. It was the seat of one of the seven churches of Asia, and is mentioned in Rev. 1:11; 3:7-13. Its modern name is Alah Shehr, and it has about 10,000 inhabitants.

Phi-le'mon, a Greek to whom Paul addressed an epistle. Philemon 1;1. He had been converted to Christianity through Paul.

Phi-le'mon, the E-pis'tle to, was written by Paul from Rome, A.D. 62 or 63, and is a gem of Christian courtesy and tenderness. It consists of a singularly powerful and skilfully managed appeal to the natural benevolence and Christian sentiment of Philemon in behalf of Onesimus, his fugitive but converted slave. The epistle has always been a noble testimonial of the Christian doctrine of equal freedom to all men.

Phil'ip (lover of horses). [1] The apostle. He was a native of Bethsaida, and is always mentioned as the fifth of the twelve. Matt. 10:3; Mark 3:18; Luke 6:14; John 1:43-46; Acts 1:13. Little is known concerning him. He is said, according to tradition, to have preached in Phrygia and died at Hierapolis.

[2] The evangelist. He was a deacon in the church at Jerusalem, Acts 6;3-5, and preached in Samaria with great success. Acts 8:6-8. While there he was directed by "the angel of the Lord," Acts 8:26, to "go toward the south, unto the way that goeth down from Jerusalem to Gaza." He obeyed, found the Ethiopian traveller, Acts 8:27-38, preached unto him Jesus, and baptized him. Philip was probably afterward settled in Caesarea. Acts 21:8. He was married and had "four daughters, virgins, which did prophesy," verse 9.

[3] The tetrarch or governor of Gaulanitis, Auranitis, etc., was a son of Herod the Great by his fifth wife, Cleopatra, and reigned from his father's death to A.D. 34. He married Salome, the daughter of Herodias, and is referred to once in the New Testament. Luke 3:1. No. 4. [4] The husband of Herodias.

Phi-lip'pi, a city of Macedonia, was in the time of Paul a place of great celebrity, because around its walls was fought, B.C. 42, the battle between Octavius and Antony on one side and Brutus and Cassius on the other, which caused the downfall of the Roman republic and prepared the way for the establishment of the great Roman empire. In memory of his victory

187

Octavius afterward made it a Roman colony--that is, he settled a number of his veteran soldiers there and gave them land to cultivate. Philippi was the first place in Greece that received the gospel. The first convert was Lydia. Acts 16:14, 15. Paul visited the city twice. Acts 16:12-40; 20:6. Paul and Silas, thrown into prison there, were miraculously released, and the jailer and his family were converted. During Pauls's imprisonment in Rome, A.D. 62-64, the Christians of Philippi sent Epaphroditus to him with a present of money, which became the occasion for THE EPISTLE TO THE PHILIPPIANS.

Phil-lip'pi-ans, the disciples in Philippi, Macedonia, to whom Paul addressed an epistle. Phil. 4:15.

Phi-lip'pi-ans, E-pis'tle to the, was written by Paul, then a prisoner at Rome, about A.D. 62, to the Christians at Philippi, who had kindly ministered to his necessities. The second chapter contains a very important passage on the doctrine of the person of Christ, referring to his humiliation and his exaltation.

Philistia, fi-lis'ti-ah (land of sojourners), called also THE LAND OF THE PHILISTINES, included the coast-land of Palestine from Joppa in the north to the valley of Gerar in the south, and from the Mediterranean to the hills of Judea. The origin of the Philistines (the Caphtorim, Deut. 2:23; Jer. 47:4; Amos 9:7) has been much discussed, but most scholars now seem to be agreed that the Caphtorim came from the Nile delta in Egypt. At the time of the exodus the Philistines were a powerful people, far superior to the Israelites. They had fortified cities, cavalry, war-chariots, soldiers with copper helmets, etc. Consequently, although Philistisa belong to the Promised Land and was assigned to Judah and Dan, no attempt was made to conquer it. But as soon as the Israelites were settled the feuds with the Philistines began, and they never really ended. There seems to have been a deadly hatred between the two people, and one of the reasons for it was certainly the peculiarly abominable idolatry of the Philistines. Their chief gods were Dagon, Judg. 16:23; 1 Sam. 5:1-5, whom they worshipped under the form of a fish, and Baalzebub, 2 Kings 1:2, 3, 6,16, the fly-god. After "the captivity" the kingdom of Philistia ceased to exist, and after Alexander the Great nothing more is heard about the Philistines.

Phy-si'cian. The study of medicine was followed with great zeal by the Egyptians, even in the days of Joseph. Gen. 50:2. From passages in the books of Moses it appears that in his time there were not only midwives but regular physicians among the Jews. Exod. 21:19. The priests were expected to have some knowledge of medicine, likewise the prophets, but generally it was followed as a separate profession. The ceremonial defilement caused by touching a corpse, Num. 9:6, prevented the study of anatomy, and the medical art, therefore, never reached a high degree of perfection in Palestine. Luke was a physician. Col. 4:14

Pieces of Gold, Pieces of Silver. 2 Kings 5:5; Judg. 9:4. "Pieces," when thus used in the Old Testament, should be interpreted as "shekels." Before the captivity there was no coined money in Palestine and the shekel was the common weight for money. The "piece of silver" in Luke 15:8, 9 is the translation of "drachma," and was equivalent to about fifteen cents. As used in connection with the price paid Judas for the betrayal of our Saviour, Matt. 26:15; 27:3, 9, "piece" has the meaning of shekel, a weight, equal in our money to between fifty and sixty cents.

Pieces of Mon'ey, in Gen. 33:19; Job 42:11; Matt. 17:27, evidently meant "pieces of silver" or "shekels of silver."

Pi'e-ty is found only once in the Bible, 1 Tim. 5:4, where it means the reverence and affection children owe to their parents. For piety toward God the Scriptures use different terms, such as godliness, worship, service, holiness, etc.

Pi'late, Matt. 27:13, or **Pontius** (pon'-shi-us) **Pi'late,** Acts 4:27, was the Roman governor of Judea that delivered Jesus to the Jews to be crucified. Pilate was his surname, and the name generally used in references to him.

Pil'lar, in Gen. 28:18; 35:20; 2 Sam. 18:18, means a monument. In Exod. 13:21; Judg. 20:40 it refers to the shape the fire, cloud, or smoke assumed. In architecture pillars were used both as ornaments and supports. 1 Kings 7:6; Judg. 16:26.

Pil'low, in Mark 4:38, is translated "cushion" in the Revised Version. Jacob used a stone for his pillow. Gen. 28:18. In Ezek. 13:18, 20 pillows are referred to as appliances of luxury.

Pin'na-cle. The word thus translated in Matt. 4:5; Luke 4:9 means not a summit, but a wing, and probably refers to an elevation over Solomon's porch which overlooked the valley of Kidron at a height of from six hundred to seven hundred feet.

Pipe, the simplest and perhaps the oldest of musical instruments, was the principal wind-instrument among the Jews. It was made of different materials, consisted of a tube with holes, similar to the flute, and was used on all occasions. 1 Kings 1:40.

Pisgah, piz'gah (hill or the height), Deut. 3:27, was a peak in the range of mountains called Abarim, on the east of Jordan, opposite Jericho. It was the top of Mount Nebo, from which

Moses beheld the land of Canaan.

Pit, in the Authorized Version, is the translation of several words of different meanings. The pit into which Joseph was cast, Gen. 37:24, was an empty or dry cistern or reservoir, such as are commonly built in that country to preserve the rain-water for travellers and cattle. The word is also used in reference to Sheol, or the under-world, Num. 16:30; Job 17:16, and in Prov. 22:14; Jer. 18:20, 22, etc. it refers to the traps or deep holes made in the ground and covered lightly with branches, in which beasts of prey were commonly caught.

Pitch. this word, as used in Gen. 6:14; Exod. 2:3, means a sort of bitumen or asphaltum which is found in pits and on the surface of the Dead Sea. In its soft or liquid state it is called SLIME, Gen. 11:3, but on exposure it becomes dry and hard like mortar. It was used for a coating on the outside of ships to make them water-proof, and in place of mortar in masonry.

Pitch'er. The custom of drawing water in pitchers still prevails in the East, an earthen vessel with two handles being used for that purpose. It was carried on the head or left shoulder. Gen. 24:16, 18, 45.

Plague, an eminently contagious and destructive disease accompanied by loathsome eruptions, prevailed in the East from the earliest ages. The word was also employed by the sacred writers to express any desolating disease, calamity, or scourge. Lev. 13:3. The judgments of God on Pharaoh are called plagues. Exod. 9:14.

Plain, referring to a tract of land, is often used alone in the Bible, and the particular plain alluded to must be inferred from the context, as in Deut. 1:1; 2:8. The word translated "plains" in Gen. 12:6; 13:18; 14:13; 18:1; Deut. 11:30; Judg. 4:11; 9:6, 37; 1 Sam. 10:3 means places noted for one or more oaks.

Plait'ing, 1 Pet. 3:3, means braiding. The business of dressing the hair is mentioned by Jewish writers as an art by itself, practised by women.

Pledge. That which is given as security for a loan or for the performance of a contract. The Mosaic law contained wise provisions on this subject to protect the poor from oppression. Deut. 24:6, 17.

Plough, a much simpler instrument than that now used, was employed from the earliest times by the Hebrews. It was sometimes made from a crotched stick or branch of a tree with the wooden share shod with a triangular or heart-shaped piece of iron. 1 Sam. 13:20. The plough was guided by a single upright held by one hand, while the other hand wielded the goad. With such an instrument the soil received no more than a mere scratching. "Earing," in Gen. 45:6; Exod. 34:21, means ploughing.

Po'e-try, Hebrew. Poetry and music were closely connected, and figured prominently in the domestic and social life of the Hebrews as narrated in the Bible. The chief subject of their poetry was religion. Exclusive of the historical books and the book of Daniel, the whole of the Old Testament is poetry in the Hebrew, and it is so distinguished in the Revised Version of the Psalms, the book of Job, and the Proverbs. There are also poetic pieces scattered through the historical books, as the Song of Moses, Exodus, chapter 15, the prophecies of Balaam, Numbers, chapter 24, the farewell and blessing of Moses, Deut. 32:1-43; 33:2-29, and the lament of David over Jonathan. 2 Sam. 1:19-27. The Psalms belong to lyric poetry, Job and the Proverbs to didactic poetry; but Job and the Song of Songs may also be classified with dramatic poetry. A characteristic feature of Hebrew poetry is the parallelism of members so called, that is, a correspondence of thought and diction, as the flapping of two wings. Poetry began, we may say, in Paradise, and pervades the first chapters of Genesis. It was cultivated by Moses, the great lawgiver, and continued till after the return from the captivity. David, the greatest of the kings of the Jews, was also the greatest of their poets. Christian psalmody takes its rise, and more or less its form, from the Psalms of David. In the New Testament the parables of the Saviour are poetic fictions taken from real life and illustrating spiritual truths. The book of Revelation is highly poetic in its imagery and diction. The Benedictus of Zacharias, the Magnificat of the Virgin Mary, and the anthem of the heavenly host in the first and second chapters of Luke strike the keynote of Christian psalmody and hymnody.

Poll, Poll'ed. When used as a noun, as in Num. 1:2, 18, 20, 22; 3:47; 1 Chron. 23:3, 24, "poll" means a head. When used as a verb, Micah 1:16; 2 sam. 14:26; Ezek. 44:20, it means to cut off the hair or shave.

Pomegranate, pum-gran'et, meaning "grained apple," is the name of a tree or large bush and its fruit cultivated from early times in Syria, Persia, Egypt, etc. The fruit is the size of the orange, flattened at the ends like the apple, and the rind is a beautiful brownish-red color. The inside of the pomegranate is of a bright pink, with skinny partitions similar to the orange. It abounds with juice of a grateful flavor, and a multitude of small seeds. The tree is rarely over ten feet high, and there are both sweet and sour varieties. Num. 20:5; Deut. 8:8.

Pontius, pon'shi-us, **Pi'late,** a Roman governor of Judea. Acts 4:27.

Pon'tus, the north-eastern part of Asia Minor, extending along the Black Sea, was an independent kingdom until shortly before the death of Nero, during whose reign it was made a Roman province. Polemo II., who married Bernice, the great-granddaughter of Herod the Great and sister of Herod Agrippa, Acts 25:13, was its last king. There seems to have been many Jews in the country. Jews from Pontus were present in Jerusalem on the day of Pentecost, Acts 2:9; Aquila, the helper of Paul, was native of Pontus, Acts 18:2, and Peter addressed his first epistle "to the strangers scattered throughout Pontus." 1 Pet. 1:1.

Poor. While sometimes used in the New Testament to denote those who are humble of heart, Matt. 5:3, the word generally has the literal meaning in the Bible. The poor were specially provided for in the Mosaic law, Exod. 23:6; Lev. 19:9, 10, etc., which surrounded them with safeguards that prevented pauperism and secured for them just treatment.

Porcius, por'shi-us, **Fes'tus,** the Roman governor of Judea who succeeded Felix. Acts 24:27. He is generally mentioned by his surname FESTUS alone.

Por'ters were employed to open and shut the gates of a city or house, to keep guard, etc., etc. Four thousand of them were employed in the Temple in different capacities. 1 Chron. 23:5.

Por'tion. Neh. 8:10. It was customary in ancient times, among the Greeks, Hebrews, and Egyptians, to set before each guest the portion of food intended for him. To set before a guest a greater portion than usual was to confer upon him a special honor. See the distinction shown Benjamin. Gen. 43:34. A "worthy portion," 1 Sam. 1:5, is rendered in the Revised Version "a double portion."

Posts, runners or messengers bearing special tidings, were employed in the East from very early times. See the allusion in Job 9:25. The Persians made their public announcements by means of sentinels, who, stationed at certain distances apart, cried out the news one to the other, and so passed it along. Later a system of posts was established that travelled night and day. The Romans and Persians impressed men and beasts into this public service, a work greatly disliked by the Jews. Matt. 5:41.

Pot'i-phar (belonging to the sun), the captain of Pharaoh's guard to whom Joseph was sold by the Midianites. Gen. 37:36; 39:1.

Pot'sherds are broken pieces of earthenware. They are very numerous among the ruins of ancient cities, and are used in various ways by the poor. They drink water from them, and coals of fire are carried in them from one place to another. Job. 2:8; Ps. 22:15; Prov. 26:23.

Pot'tage. Gen. 25:29. In the East, lentils are boiled or stewed like beans with oil and garlic, and make a dish that is eaten as pottage. Other ingredients were also used. 2 Kings 4:39.

Pot'ter. The making of earthenware was one of the first manufactures. The method employed by the Israelites seems to have been the same as that followed by the Egyptians. The clay was trodden by the feet, and when it had reached the proper consistency a lump of it was placed upon the potter's wheel, which was made to revolve rapidly while the potter worked the vessel into shape. Jer. 18: 2-4. It was then glazed and baked. Such vessels were used not only for cooking, but also for preserving valuables. Jer. 32:14.

Praise, as used in the Scriptures, denotes an act of worship; also thanksgiving.

Prayer is offering to God petitions for mercies desired and thanksgiving and praise for blessings received. For the duty and conditions of prayer, its object and efficacy, and the time, place, manner, etc., etc.

Preach'ing originally meant to herald or proclaim and in that sense it is mainly used in the Bible. In the Epistles, however, the word has nearly the same meaning it has with us now--a public discourse on the truths of religion.

Pre'des'ti-nate, Rom. 8:29, 30. Eph. 1:5, 11, foreordain or elect in Christ to everlasting life.

Prep-a-ra'tion. The word is also used with "day" and refers to Friday, as on that day meals and other matters were prepared for the Sabbath. Matt. 27:62; Mark 15:42.

P

Pres'by-ter-y, the assembly of elders. The name is translated "elders" in Luke 22:66; Acts 22:5, while in 1 Tim. 4:14 the Greek word "presbytery" is retained.

Press, Press Fats, or **Press Vats,** Joel 3:13; Hag.2:16, were two reservoirs or large troughs arranged one higher than the other, most generally on a hillside. In the upper vat was put the fruit, which was trodden by the bare feet of men, and the expressed juice was collected in the lower vat. Sometimes the vats were made in the ground and lined with masonry. Matt. 21:33.

Press'ed in the spir'it, in Acts 18:5, is rendered "constrained by the word" in the Revised Version.

Pricks. Acts 9:5.

Priest, a contraction of presbyter--"elder." Originally there seems to have been no priests--that is, special ministers of religion--among the Hebrews, though there was always a special ministration of religion, which consisted principally in the preparation and offering of the daily, weekly, and monthly sacrifices. This was simply the duty of the head of the household, and descended from the father to the first-born son. Such was the case in the time of the patriarchs. Gen. 8:20; 12:8. But when the Hebrews developed from a household into a people, from a family into a nation, the Mosaic law instituted a special order of men for this specific service. They were inaugurated with very solemn and imposing ceremonies, minutely prescribed, Exod. 29: 1-37; Lev. chapters 8 and 9, and when duly invested with the priestly office they alone had the right to offer sacrifices, to conduct the public service in the Temple, to officiate at purifications, to take care of the sacred fire and the golden lamp, etc. They were maintained at the expense of the whole people. Thirteen cities with pasture-grounds, in the lands of Judah, Simeon, and Benjamin, were set aside for them. Josh. 21: 13-19, and to this general provision were added one-tenth of the tithes paid to the Levites, Num. 18: 26-28; a special tithe every third year. Deut. 14:28; 26:12; the redemption-money paid for the first-born of man and beast, Num. 18: 14-19, etc. As this priestly order was made up exclusively from the male descendants of Aaron, the number of its members was of course at first very small. Josh. 3:6; 6:4, but in the time of David, 1 Chron. 12:27, three thousand seven hundred priests joined him at Hebron, and under the kings the provision made for the maintenance of the order proved so utterly insufficient that many priests lived in great poverty. 1 Sam. 2:36. The number of priests who accompanied Zerubbabel from the captivity was four thousand two hundred and eighty-nine. Ezra 2:36-39. Besides their strictly priestly duties, it also belonged to the office of the Hebrew priest, to sit in judgment at the trial of jealousy, to superintend the lepers, to expound the law to the people, etc.

Prince. This word, in the Authorized Version, besides its usual meaning, is used to denote local governors or magistrates, as in 1 Kings 20:14; satraps (governors of provinces), in Dan. 6:1; guardian angels, in Dan. 10:13, 21; and "a liberal man," in Prov. 19:6. The latter is so translated in the Revised Version. In Dan. 11:8 "princes" means "molten images."

Prince. [1] A title of honor applied to the Saviour. Acts 3:15;

5:31; Rev. 1:5. [2] A title given to the ruling spirit of evil. Matt. 9:34; Mark 3:22; John 12:31.

Prince of Peace, a title given to Messiah by Isaiah the prophet. Isa. 9:6.

Prin-ci-pal'i-ty, in Eph. 1:21, is rendered "rule and authority" in the Revised Version. "Principalities," in Jer. 13:18, is rendered "headtires" in the Revised Version, and in Tit. 3:1, "rulers" and "authorities."

Pris'on. By the Mosaic law the culprit was at once put on trial, and imprisonment was not used as a punishment. The kings of the Hebrews, however, had a prison connected with the palace. 2 Chron. 16:10. The Romans used a tower in Jerusalem and the praetorium in Caesarea as prisons, and the religious authorities had a prison in Jerusalem. Acts 5:18-23.

Proph'et means, first, one who speaks or interprets; then, one who speaks or interprets a message he has received from God; and finally to reveal something with respect to the future. It is necessary to keep in mind these three acceptations of the word prophet, in order to understand that Aaron is called the prophet of Moses, Exod. 7:1; that Abraham is called a prophet, Gen. 20:7; and that there existed among the Hebrews, as part of their system of priesthood, a regular order of prophets, a fixed institution in which prophets were educated. It was Samuel who created this institution, and he was praised highly for his work. Jer. 15:1; Acts 3:24. Schools were founded at Ramah, 1 Sam. 19:19, Bethel, 2 Kings 2:3, Jericho, 2 Kings 2:5, Gilgal, 2 Kings 4:38, etc., and young men were there instructed in the interpretation of the law, in music, and in poetry by some older prophet, who was called their father and master. But there was of course no connection between the prophetical education and the prophetical gift. No doubt many young men went through the prophetical school without ever receiving a message from God, and Amos was called by God, though he had not gone through any school. Besides the prophetesses, the Jews reckon forty-eight prophets. Two of the greatest prophets, Elijah and Elisha, have left no writings. Among the sixteen prophets whose books are found in the Old Testament Canon, ten lived before the captivity: Jonah, Joel, Amos, Hosea, Isaiah, Micah, Nahum, Zephaniah, Jeremiah, Habakkuk; three under the captivity: Daniel, Obadiah, Ezekiel; and three after the captivity :Haggai, Zechariah, and Malachi. John the Baptist was the last prophet of the old dispensation. Matt. 11:7-9; Luke 7:28.

Proph'et-ess meant the wife of a prophet, Isa. 8:3; also a woman that had the gift of prophecy. The most noted of the prophetesses were MIRIAM, Exod. 15:20, DEBORAH, Judg. 4:4, HULDAH, 2 Kings 22:14, NOADIAH, Neh. 6:14, and ANNA. Luke 2:36. The four daughters of Philip the Evangelist prophesied. Acts 21:9.

Propitiation, pro-pish-i-a'shun, the offering made to appease the wrath and conciliate the favor of an offended person. For "Christ, Our Propitiation,"

Pros'e-lyte, a name given by the Jews to such as were converted from heathenism to the Jewish faith. Matt. 23:15. There were two classes: "proselytes of the gate," who adopted the Jewish monotheism and Messianic hopes, but were not circumcised, and "proselytes of righteousness," who were full Jews and generally most bigoted. To the former belonged Cornelius and Lydia and many of the earliest and best members of the apostolic churches.

Psalms, the Book of, from a Greek word which means "to strike the lyre" and "to sing," is the name introduced in the Septuagint (Greek) translation of the Old Testament for that collection of hymns in the Old Testament Canon which in Hebrew is called "Praises" or "Book of Praises." It consists of five divisions (which are marked in the revised Version as they are in Hebrew).

Part I. contains forty-one psalms, of which thirty-seven are ascribed to David and four are anonymous--namely 1, 2, 10, and 33.

Part II. contains thirty-one psalms, 42-72, of which seven are by the sons of Korah, one by Asaph, nineteen by David, three anonymous, and one by Solomon or for Solomon.

Part III. contains seventeen psalms, 73-89, of which eleven are by Asaph, four by the sons of Korah, one by David--namely 86--and one--namely 89--by Ethan the Ezrahite.

Part IV. contains seventeen psalms, 90-106, of which one is by Moses--namely 90--two by David--namely 101-103--and the rest anonymous.

Part V. contains forty-four psalms, 107-150, of which fifteen are by David, one by Solomon, and the rest anonymous, including the fifteen Songs of Degrees or Pilgrim Psalms--namely 120-134--for journeys up to the festivals in Jerusalem, and the five Hallelujah Psalms. The prophetic or Messianic Psalms are 2, 8, 16, 22, 40, 45, 68, 69, 72, 97, 110, and 118. The whole collection of Psalms is not only in point of time but also in rank the first hymn-book and prayer-book for public and private devotion, and is so used to this day by Jews, and Christians of all denominations.

Q

Quails, the birds miraculously given to the Israelites while in the wilderness. Exod. 16:13; Num. 11:31. At the season when they were gathered quails pass over Arabia in immense numbers but the vast quantities thrown into the camp of the Israelites, sufficient to furnish food for the multitude for more than a month, were certainly supernatural.

Quar'ries, Judg. 3:19, 26, is rendered in the marginal notes "graven images."

Queen. This title was applied to the ruling monarch, if a woman, 1 Kings 10:1, to the wife of a king, Esth. 7:1, and also to the mother of a king. 1 Kings 15:13. As a result of the practice of polygamy, the wife of a king did not enjoy the distinction she does now. The queen-mother, however, generally exercised great influence and power.

Queen of Heav'en, mentioned in Jer. 7:18; 44:17, 18, 19, 25, was the name given to the moon by idolatrous Hebrews.

Quick, in Num. 16:30; Ps. 55:15; 124:3, means "alive," and is so rendered in the Revised Version. In Lev. 13:10, 24 the word means having the life of living flesh. In Heb. 4:12 it is rendered "living" in the Revised Version, and in Acts 10:42; 2 Tim. 4:1; 1 Pet. 4:5 it has the same meaning. (So also in the Apostles' Creed, "to judge the quick and the dead.")

Quick'en does not mean to hasten or accelerate, but to keep, preserve, or give life. Ps. 71:20; John 5:21, etc. The context will suggest which meaning should apply.

Quick'sands, Acts 27:17, refer to two gulfs on the northern coast of Africa, greatly dreaded by sailors on account of the variations and uncertainties of the tides on a flat coast that had many sand-bars.

Quit, in 1 Sam. 4:9; 1 Cor. 16:13, is used in the sense of acquit.

Quiv'er, a case or sheath for arrows. Gen. 27:3. It is often used figuratively in the Bible.

R

Ra'a-mah (trembling). [1] One of the sons of Cush, the son of Ham. [2] A country which appears to have been named after Raamah, the son of Cush, and to have been settled by his descendants. It was probably on the south-west shore of the Persian Gulf. Ezek. 27:22.

Raamses, ra-am'seez, an Egyptian city on the river Nile. Exod. 1:11. It is elsewhere called RAMESES.

Rab'bah (greatness). [1] Josh. 13:25. Called "Rabbath of the children of Ammon," Deut. 3:11, or "Rabbath of the Ammonites," Ezek. 21:20, or by the Greeks and Romans "Philadelphia," because it was rebuilt by Ptolemy Philadelphus. It is the modern Amman, a village among wonderful and extensive ruins. It was the capital of the Ammonites, and was situated twenty-two miles east of the river Jordan, and near the source of the river Jabbok. It is often mentioned in the history of David, and was one of the cities of Decapolis. [2] A town of Judah. Josh. 15:60.

Rab'bi (master or teacher) was the name given by the Jews to the teachers of their law. This title was also given to Christ by his disciples and the people. John 3:2,26.

Rab-bo'ni, John 20:16, has the same meaning as RABBI, teacher, only in a higher degree, and was regarded among the Jews as the highest title of honor.

Rab'sha-keh, which probably means "chief of the cupbearers," was the name or title of one of the chief officers of Sennacherib, king of Assyria. 2 Kings 18:17; Isa. 36:2.

Ra'ca (worthless), Matt. 5:22, is a term of reproach and contempt, and is rendered "vain fellow" in the marginal notes. It is retained in the Revised Version with the note, "An expression of contempt."

Race. 1 Cor. 9:24. This word, in the New Testament, refers to the Grecian contests in running on foot, horseback, or in chariots. The most laborious training and preparation were made for these contests, and to win the prize was considered among the greatest of earthly honors. The contestants took off everything that would impede them, the prize was placed in full view, and the victor was crowned as soon as the result was announced.

Ra'chel (a ewe), the younger daughter of Laban. She became the wife of the patriarch Jacob, and was the mother of Joseph and Benjamin. Her history is given in Genesis, chapters 29 to 36. She died soon after Benjamin's birth. Jacob erected a pillar on her grave, near the road from Jerusalem to Bethlehem. Gen. 35:19, 20. Her reputed tomb is covered by a small Mohammedan mosque (place of worship), and is about half a mile from Bethlehem.

Ra'gau, in Luke 3:35, was the same person as REU, mentioned in Gen. 11:20,21, and was an ancestor of Joseph, the husband of Mary.

Ra'hab, a Canaanitish woman of Jericho who received and concealed the two spies sent by Joshua to explore the land of Canaan. She is called RACHAB in Matt. 1:5. Her history is given in Josh. 2:1-23; 6:17-25. Her faith is mentioned in Heb. 11:31.

Ra'hab (violence), in Ps. 87:4; 89:10; Isa. 51:9, is generally supposed to be a symbolical name for Egypt.

Ram (exalted). [1] An Israelite of the tribe of Judah, descended from Pharez through Hezron. Ruth 4:19; 1 Chron. 2:9. Called ARAM in Matt. 1:3, 4; Luke 3:33. [2] A son of Jerahmeel. 1 Chron. 2:25, 27. [3] The head of a family from which Elihu, a friend of Job, descended. Job 32:2.

Ra'ma, ra'mah, in Matt. 2:18, is the Greek form of RAMAH.

Ra'mah (high place). [1] A city of Benjamin. When Jerusalem was captured by Nebuchadnezzar the captives, among whom was Jeremiah, were guarded at Ramah. Jer. 40:1. Jeremiah's prophecy, Jer. 31:15, was fulfilled there. It has been identified with er-Ram, about five miles north of Jerusalem. [2] A town in Mount Ephraim, also called RAMATHAIM-ZO-PHIM. It was the birthplace, home, and burial-place of the prophet Samuel. 1 Sam. 1:19. [3] A town on the boundary of Asher. Josh. 19:29. [4] A fortified place in Naphtali. Josh. 19:36. [5] Another name for the city of RAMOTH-GILEAD. 2 Kings 8:28, 29. [6] A place to which some Benjamites returned after the captivity. Neh. 11:33.

Ra'math of the South, a place in the southern part of Simeon. Josh. 19:8. It is called SOUTH RAMOTH in 1 Sam. 30:27.

Rameses, ra-me'seez (son of the sun), a city and province of Egypt, probably on the east side of the river Nile. It may have been the capital of Goshen. Gen. 47:11; Exod. 12:37. It is also called RAAMSES in Exod. 1:11.

Ra'moth-gil'e-ad (height of Gilead), one of the principal cities of Gad. 1 Kings 4:13; 2 Kings 8:28. It was a city of refuge. It is called RAMAH in 2 Kings 8:29; 2 Chron. 22:6.

Ran'som, Matt. 20:28; Mark 10:45, the price paid to purchase the freedom of a captive or slave. When the children of

Israel were numbered every one was required to give an offering to the Lord as a "ransom for his soul." Exod. 30:12-16.

Rapha, ra'fah (tall). [1] A son of Benjamin. 1 Chron. 8:2. [2] A Benjamite of the family of Saul. 1 Chron. 8:37.

Ra'ven, a bird of prey, was unclean according to the Levitical law. Lev. 11:15. It feeds principally upon carrion, and is said to seize first upon the eyes; hence the allusion in Prov. 30:17, which implies the exposure of the corpse in the open field, than which nothing was regarded as more disgraceful.

Rav'en-ing, in Luke 11:39, means extortion; in Ps. 22:13; Ezek. 22:25, 27 it means to prey with rapacity.

Rav'in, in Gen. 49:27, means to prey with rapacity; in Nah. 2:12 it means prey; plunder.

Ra'zor. This instrument, from the custom of the Jews, who shaved their heads after completing a vow, must have been used from the earliest times. Num. 6:5; Ezek. 5:1. The word is used figuratively in Isa. 7:20.

Reaia, re-a-i'ah (whom Jehovah cares for), one of the descendants of Reuben. 1 Chron. 5:5. Another form of the name REAIAH.

Re-bec'ca. Rom. 9:10.

Re-bek'ah (a cord with a noose, enchaining), the daughter of Bethuel, the nephew of Abraham. She became the wife of Isaac and the mother of Jacob and Esau. An account of her life is contained in Gen. 24:15 to 49:31.

Rechab, re'kab (horseman). [1] An ancestor of Jehonadab, the founder of the Rechabites. 2 Kings 10:15,23; 1 Chron. 2:55; Jer. 35:6-19. [2] One of Ish-bosheth's captains. 2 Sam. 4:2. [3] The father of Malchiah. Neh. 3:14.

Rechah, re'kah (utmost part), a place in Judah. 1 Chron. 4:12.

Rec-on-cil-i-a'tion, Heb. 2:17, as implying the restoration of man to God's favor, denotes a change on the part of both in their relations to and with each other. "Atonement," in Romans 5:11, is better rendered "reconciliation,".

Rec'ord, in John 1:32, 34, etc., means "witness" or "testimony." "Take you to record," in Acts 20:26, is rendered "I testify unto you" in the Revised Version.

Re-deem'er, one who frees by repaying. By the Mosaic law hereditary property that had been sold could be redeemed by the original owner or any of his descendants. In a similar sense the word is used in reference to God redeeming his people from bondage, Exod. 6:6, from sin and the law. Gal. 3:13; Tit. 2:14, etc.

200

Red Sea, a long arm of the Indian Ocean, with which it is connected by the narrow strait of Bab-el-Mandeb, lies between Egypt and Arabia. It is about fourteen hundred and fifty miles long and two hundred and twenty miles wide in its broadest part. Its northern end is divided into two arms, the Gulf of Suez on the west, and the Gulf of Akabah on the east. Between these lies the peninsula of Sinai. The Gulf of Suez was connected with the river Nile by an ancient canal, and is now united to the Mediterranean by the Suez ship-canal. The Red Sea is famous on account of its passage by the Israelites and the destruction of the Egyptians who pursued them. Exod. chapters 14 and 15. The place at which the passage was made is not known, but it was somewhere on the Gulf of Suez, which anciently extended about fifty miles further north. The Red Sea is also called "the sea" in Exod. 14:2, 9, etc., the "Egyptian Sea," Isa. 11:15.

Reed, a plant of the grass family having a long, slender stalk. From it were made musical instruments, paper, and pens. It was also used as a measuring-rod. The sacred writers often used the word to illustrate weakness and fragility. 2 Kings 18:21.

Reed, a measure of length, equal to about one hundred and twenty feet. Ezek. 40:5.

Re-fin'er. In Mal. 3:3 this word is used with peculiar force from the fact that the refiner of silver sat with his eyes fixed steadily on the furnace, watching the process, which was only complete and perfect when the refiner could see his own image in the melted mass. This, during the process, had been covered with a film of the oxide of lead which grew thinner and thinner as the refining approached completion, and then suddenly disappeared, revealing the brilliant surface of the pure silver. The word is used figuratively. Isa. 48:10; Zech. 13:9.

Re-gen-er-a'tion, the birth of a soul previously dead in sin unto a new spiritual life, through the workings of the Holy Spirit. The word is found only twice in the Bible. In Matt. 19:28 it refers to the restoration of all things at Christ's second advent; and in Tit. 3:5 it denotes the new birth through the Holy Spirit. Other words in the New Testament convey the same meaning. John 3:3; 1 Pet. 1:23.

Re-ho-bo'am (enlarger of the people), the son of Solomon who succeeded him as king of Israel, but from whom the ten tribes revolted under Jeroboam. Rehoboam reigned seventeen years. 1 Kings 11:43; 14:21; 2 Chron. 12:16.

Re-ho'both (wide places). [1] The name which Isaac gave to a well which he dug. Gen. 26:22. [2] "Rehoboth by the river." The river referred to is supposed to be the Euphrates. Gen.

36:37; 1 Chron. 1:48. [3] One of the cities founded by Asshur. Gen. 10:11. It is supposed to have been near the river Euphrates.

Reins, in Ps. 7:9; 16:7, etc., means the kidneys or that part of the body which covers the kidneys, and refers to the inward impulses, the reins at one time being considered to be the seat of the affections and the passions.

Re-pent', Re-pent'ance, Matt. 3:2, 8, in its spiritual sense denotes a sense of guilt, an apprehension of God's mercy, sorrow for sin, and a turning away from it unto God. The Greek word denotes a change of mind, and is equivalent to conversion.

Reph'a-im, Val'ley of, was a landmark of Judah's territory, and was situated south or south-west of Jerusalem. 2 Sam. 5:18; 1 Chron. 11:15.

Reph'i-dim (rest, refreshments), the last station of the Israelites before they reached Sinai. It was at Rephidim that the people "murmured against Moses," Exod. 17:3, and that he smote the rock and water came out of it for them to drink. Exod. 17:6. The Amalekites were defeated there. Exod. 17:8-16.

Rep'ro-bate, Rom. 1:28; 2 Cor. 13:5-7; 2 Tim. 3:8, means not approved; unfit; abandoned.

Rere'ward, or, as in the Revised Version, **Rear'ward,** Josh. 6:13; Isa. 52:12; 58:8, in several instances is explained in the marginal notes. In Isa. 52:12 the word has the same meaning as "rear-guard."

Res-ti-tu'tion for injury done intentionally or by accident was strictly enjoined by the Mosaic law.

Res-ur-rec'tion. A fundamental doctrine of the Christian faith is the resurrection of the dead, both of the just and the unjust. The resurrection of Christ, a fact most forcibly and clearly proved, was the crowning demonstration of the truth and divinity of his mission and character.

Reu'ben (behold a son!). [1] The first-born son of Jacob and Leah. Gen. 29:32. He was one of "the twelve patriarchs," Acts 7:8, who were the ancestors of the Jewish nation. [2] The name Reuben is often applied to the tribe which descended from him. Num. 1:5; Deut. 27:13.

Reu'ben, Ter'ri-to-ry of, was on the east side of the Jordan and the Dead Sea. It was bounded on the east by the desert, on the south by the river Arnon, and on the north by the territory of the tribe of Gad. Its boundaries are described in Josh. 13:15-21.

Rev-e-la'tion or **A-poc'a-lypse** is the only prophetic book in the New Testament, and closes the Canon of the Scriptures. It was written "in the spirit on the Lord's day" by the apostle John during his banishment to the solitary , barren, and rocky island of Patmos, in the Aegean Sea, southwest of Ephesus. The time of its composition is not absolutely certain. According to Irenaeus (who wrote about A.D. 170), it dates from the end of the reign of the emperor Domitian, A.D. 95, but it fits better into the period of the great tribulation after the Neronian persecution and before the destruction of Jerusalem--that is, between 64 and 70. The book contains a series of prophetic visions of the struggles and final victory of the Church over all opposition from without and all difficulties from within. It is full of mysteries which have called forth the greatest variety of expositions. No book has been more misunderstood and abused; none calls for greater modesty and reserve in its interpretation. The most important and most intelligible parts are the introduction and the close, namely, the epistles to the seven churches in Asia Minor, which represent the different conditions of the Church in all ages, with appropriate warnings and encouragements (chapters 2 and 3), and the description of the heavenly Jerusalem (chapters 20 and 21), which has inspired the choicest hymns of hope and aspiration. The Revelation is a book of hope and comfort to struggling Christians, and assures final victory and rest.

Re-venge'. While to check the crime of murder the Mosaic law permitted the family of the victim to revenge his death on the slayer, Num. 35:19, 27, the spirit of the law was opposed to revengeful feelings and actions. Lev.19:17, 18. The teachings of the New Testament condemn the spirit of revenge. Matt. 5:39; Rom. 12:17-21; 1 Pet. 3:9.

Rev'e-nue, Ezra 4:13, is rendered in the marginal notes "strength." In other places in the Bible it means "income" or "increase." Prov. 8:19.

Rhesa, re'sah (head), an ancestor of Joseph, the husband of Mary. Luke 3:27.

Rhoda, ro'dah (rose, rose tree), a young woman in the house of Mary, the mother of John Mark. Acts 12:13.

Rhodes (a rose), an island of the Mediterranean, thirteen miles from the coast of Asia Minor, contains about four hundred and twenty square miles. It has a city of the same name celebrated for a brass statue, one hundred and five feet high (the so-called Colossus of Rhodes, one of the seven wonders of the world), and a beautiful temple of Apollo, built by Herod the Great. Paul visited Rhodes on his return from his third missionary journey. Acts 21:1.

Rid'dle. The solving of a riddle often requires the exercising of considerable ingenuity, and the pastime found great favor among the people in the East. Judg. 14:12-19. The Hebrew word means a "hidden saying."

Right'eous-ness. As an attribute of God, the word denotes holiness, justice, and rightness. Applied to man, righteousness denotes the possession of those Christian virtues, faith, hope, and charity, and a conformity of life with the divine law.

Right Hand. In ancient times, as now, the right hand was the symbol of power and strength. Exod. 15:6; Ps. 77:10. It is said the Jews swore by their right hand, and that this is implied in Isa. 62:8. To give the right hand was a mark of friendship. Gal. 2:9. To be seated on the right hand of one higher in position or authority was a token of great honor, 1 Kings 2:19, and as applied to Christ standing on the right hand of God, Acts 7:55, it implies his unequalled dignity and exaltation. Instead of the right hand denoting the east, as is common with us, among the Jews it usually denoted the south.

Rings. The wearing of rings was a very ancient custom. Besides being used as ornaments, Luke 15:22, and seals, Esth. 8:8, they were employed as tokens of authority, and the giving of a ring was the sign of imparting authority. Gen. 41:42; Esth. 3:10. As ornaments rings were worn on the fingers, in the ears and nose, and around the wrists and ankles. Isa. 3:20, 21.

Ring'straked, in Gen. 30:35, means having circular lines or streaks on the body.

Ri'ot, Ri'ot-ing, Ri'ot-ous, Rom. 13:13; Luke 15:13; etc., means extravagant; squandering; revelling.

Ris'sah (a ruin, a worm), an encampment of the Israelites in the wilderness. Num. 33:21,22.

Riv'er of E'gypt, in Num. 34:5; Josh. 15:4, 47; 1 Kings 8:65; 2 Kings 24:7, refers to a river which flows into the Mediterranean Sea, and was the old boundary between Palestine and Egypt. It must not be confounded with the Nile, which is the proper river of Egypt. The Revised Version renders the word more correctly "the brook of Egypt." It is usually dry, or nearly so, in the summer, and is now called Waddy el-Arish.

Riz'pah, one of King Saul's concubines. 2 Sam. 3:7; 21:10, 11.

Rob'bers. Among the wandering tribes of the East, from the earliest times until even now, might has been right, and in consequence robbery has been their chief pursuit. Job suffered from the raids of the Sabeans and Chaldeans, Job 1:14-17, and the allusions in Luke 10:30; 2 Cor. 11:26 show that life and property were alike insecure in Palestine. "Robbery," in Phil 2:6, means "prize" or "a thing to be grasped."

Rod. In the sense of a branch or shoot of a tree this word is applied figuratively to Christ, Isa. 11:1, and to the tribes of Israel as springing from one root. Ps. 74:2; Jer. 10:16. The word is also used in the sense of a staff, Ps. 23:4; as a symbol of power and authority, Rev. 2:27; and to convey other meanings which are made plain by the context. "Passing under the rod," in Ezek. 20:37, may refer to the custom of having the sheep pass under a rod that had been dipped in red ochre and with which every tenth sheep was touched, and so became "holy unto the Lord." Lev. 27:32.

Rol'ler, in Ezek. 30:21, means a bandage.

Ro'mans, the E-pis'tle to the, was written by Paul from Corinth, A.D. 58, shortly before he left that city for Jerusalem. Rom. 15:25; Acts 20:2. There was at that time a large and flourishing Christian congregation in Rome, whose origin is involved in obscurity. Paul had not yet been there; on the contrary, this epistle was written preparatory to his going to Rome. Jews from Rome were present at the Pentecostal miracle in Jerusalem, Acts 2:10, and they may have been the founders of the congregation. As to Peter, we only know that, according to the general tradition of the ancient Church, he suffered martyrdom in Rome, A.D. 64 or later.

This epistle is the most elaborate and the most systematic exposition, in the New Testament, of the great central truth of Christianity, that the gospel is a power of salvation to all on the sole condition of faith in Christ (1:16,17). It shows (1) that all men, Gentiles and Jews, need salvation (1:18-32); (2) that salvation is provided for all by Jesus Christ, and is applied to the believer, in the successive acts of justification, sanctification, and glorification (3:21 to 8:39); (3) that salvation was offered first to the Jews, then to the Gentiles, and that after the conversion of the Gentiles salvation will return to the Jews (chapters 9-11); (4) that we should show our gratitude for this great salvation by a life of consecration to the service of God, which is perfect freedom (chapters 12-15). It closes with salutations (chapter 16). The Epistles to the Romans and to the Galatians furnished the leading impulse in the reformatory movement of the sixteenth century, and they are the Magna Charta of evangelical Protestantism.

Rose. The flower known to us as the rose is not the one referred to in the Song of Solomon 2:1; Isa. 35:1. The Hebrew

205

word translated "rose" probably refers to the polyanthus narcissus, a beautiful and fragrant flower that grows in the plain of Sharon. True wild roses are seldom found except in the extreme north of Palestine.

Ru'bies. A precious stone of a rose-red color, and next to the diamond in hardness, beauty, and value. The Hebrew word translated "rubies" in Job 28:18; Prov. 3:15; 8:11; etc. means "red coral" or "pearls."

Ru'di-ments. "Elements," Gal. 4:3, 9; 2 Pet. 3:10,12, and "rudiments," Col. 2:8, 20, are translated from the same Greek word, and mean the first and simplest principles of a science or literature.

Ru'fus (red), a disciple who lived at Rome. Paul sent salutation to him. Rom. 16:13. He was probably the same person as Rufus, the son of Simon the Cyrenian, mentioned in Mark 15:21.

Ru'mah, a town which was the home of Pedaiah. 2 Kings 23:36. Its location is not known.

Ruth (a friend? or a beauty?) a Moabitess, one of the daughters-in-law of Elimelech and Naomi, who accompanied Naomi on her return to Bethlehem. She became the wife of Boaz and an ancestor of Joseph, the husband of Mary. Ruth 1:4; Matt. 1:5. The history of her life is found in the book of Ruth.

Ruth, the Book of, named from Ruth the Moabitess, the chief person mentioned in it, is a simple but charming narrative of domestic life, with its virtues and happiness, in the thirteenth century before Christ, and receives a special significance from the fact that Ruth was the great-grandmother of King David, who was an ancestor of Joseph, the husband of Mary. The author of the book is unknown.

R

S

Sab'a-oth or **Sa-ba'oth,** in Rom. 9:29; James 5:4, does not mean Sabbath or rest, as many suppose. The word in the Greek means hosts, and it is applied to God as Ruler over all in the same sense that the expression "LORD of hosts" is used in Isa. 1:9.

Sab'bath was instituted by God in paradise for the benefit of man as a weekly day of rest for the body and worship for the spirit. it is found, in some form or other, also among pagans. The Jewish Sabbath was placed at the end of the week in commemoration of the creation. The word means "rest," but the fourth commandment gives that rest a definite religious character, and subsequent legislation made the Jewish Sabbath a day of religious rites and practices. The Christian Sabbath takes the place of the Jewish, with the difference that it is placed at the beginning of the week in commemoration of the resurrection of Christ. It is therefore called "the Lord's Day." Rev. 1:10. The word Sunday means "the day of the sun," and is of heathen origin, but is now used to denote the Christian Sabbath.

Sab'bath Day's Jour'ney, Acts 1:12, was nearly a mile. it was lawful to walk thus far on the Sabbath.

Sab-bat'i-cal Year was appointed by God, Lev. 25:3-7, who commanded that every seventh year should be set aside as a year of rest and for "a sabbath for the LORD." The land was not to be tilled, and whatever the ground might bring forth during that year was to be left to the poor and the beasts of the field. Exod. 23:11. Every seventh year the poor Jew was to be released from his debts. Deut. 15:1, 2.

Sack'but. This musical instrument, mentioned in Dan.3:5, 7, 10, 15, was not a wind instrument (its present meaning), but a stringed instrument played with the fingers, like the harp. It was triangular in form and had a very penetrating sound.

Sack'cloth was a coarse dark fabric made of goats' hair and other materials, and was worn as a sign of mourning or repentance. Gen. 37:34; Jer. 4:8; Matt. 11:21.

Sac'ri-fice. Gen. 31:54. Among all nations of the world, and from the earliest times, it has been the custom of the people to endeavor to appease by sacrifices the anger of the objects they worship. This natural inclination of mankind was gratified and properly directed by the Mosaic law. For the significance and worth of sacrifices from the Hebrew and the Christian standpoints.

Sac'ri-lege is the crime of violating or profaning sacred

207

things. "Commit sacrilege," in Rom. 2:22, is rendered "rob temples" in the Revised Version, and probably refers to the guilt of the Jews in withholding the tithes and offerings which God required of them. Mal. 3:8-10.

Sadducess, sad'du-seez, Acts 5:17, formed in the time of our Lord a small but influential sect among the Jews. They were wealthy and in high position, but their interest in religion was hardly anything more than a superficial ritualism. In doctrine they were strongly opposed to the PHARISEES (which see). They denied the divinity of the oral Law, accepted only the teachings of Moses, and did not believe in the resurrection, Matt. 22:23, nor in angels or spirits. Acts 23:8. Though they are not spoken of in the New Testament so severely as the Pharisees, they were determined adversaries of our Lord. Annas and Caiaphas were Sadducees.

Saint is one set apart or separated for the service of God. Paul uses the word as applying to all Christians. Rom. 1:7; 15:26; Phil. 1:1, etc. The special application of the word to apostles, evangelists, and prominent Christians dates from the fourth century.

Sa'lem (peace), the place of which Melchizedek was king. Gen. 14:18; Ps. 76:2; Heb. 7:1, 2. It was an ancient name of Jerusalem.

Sal'la-i (basket-maker). [1] The head of a family of Benjamites. Neh. 11:8. [2] One of the priests that returned with Zerubbabel, Neh. 12:20, called SALLU in Neh. 12:7.

Salma, sal'mah (clothed, a garment), one of the sons of Caleb, the son of Hur. 1 Chron. 2:51, 54.

Sal'mon (shady), Ps. 68:14, a high hill near Shechem, in Samaria. Probably same as ZALMON.

Sal-mo'ne (clothed), a promontory at the east end of the island of Crete, in the Mediterranean Sea. It is mentioned in the account of Paul's voyage to Rome. Acts 27:7.

Sa-lo'me. [1] A woman who followed Jesus from Galilee and witnessed his crucifixion "afar off." mark 15:40; 16:1. She was the wife of Zebedee and the mother of the apostles James and John. [2] "The daughter of Herodias." She danced before Herod, and asked for the head of John the Baptist. Matt. 14:6-8; Mark 6:22-25. She is not named in the New Testament, but is mentioned by Josephus, an ancient Jewish historian.

Salt was not only important among the Jews as a seasoning and a preservative, but from its use in the sacrifices that were offered to God. Lev. 2:13. New-born children were rubbed with salt. Ezek. 16:4. A "covenant of salt," Num. 18:19; 2 Chron.

208

13:5, indicated a most sacred obligation and a perpetual covenant. With the Arab the eating of salt with any one is a pledge of mutual friendship, and among the Persians and East Indians to "eat the salt" of a person is to be in his employ. Salt abounds in Palestine, and excellent table-salt is obtained from the waters of the Dead Sea.

Sal-va'tion, Exod. 14:13, or deliverance, supposes evil or danger. In its ordinary use, in the New Testament especially, the word is used to denote the deliverance from sin and death through faith in Christ.

Sa-ma'ri-a. In the Old Testament the kingdom of Samaria and the kingdom of Israel were essentially the same. In the time of our Lord Samaria was the name of the middle province of Palestine, situated between Galilee and Judea. When the "king of Assyria" (2 Kings 17:6) took the city of Samaria, B.C. 722, and carried the ten tribes of Israel away as prisoners, the land was repeopled by Assyrian colonists, and from them descended the Samaritans of the New Testament. Probably the colonists were not of purely foreign blood. At all events, they obtained a Jewish priest to teach them "the manner of the God of the land." 2 Kings 17:25-41. But when the Jews returned from the captivity they would have nothing to do with the Samaritans. An offter to help the Jews in the rebuilding of the Temple at Jerusalem was rejected, and the Samaritans set up a rival temple on Mount Gerizim. It stood for two hundred years, but was destroyed by the Jews under John Hyrcanus. In the time of our Lord the hatred between the Jews and the Samaritans was still so bitter that the Galileans when going up to Jerusalem avoided passing through Samaria. See the parable of the good Samaritan, the healing of the ten lepers, and the account of Christs conversation with the woman of Samaria at Jacob's well. Luke 10:30-37; 17:11-19; and John 4:1-42. The gospel was preached successfully among the Samaritians. Acts 1:8; 8:5-26. There yet remains a small community of them, living at Nablus, the old SHECHEM (which see), and possessing the Pentateuch in the old Hebrew or Samaritan writing.

Sa-ma'ri-a (watch-post), **the City of,** was founded by Omri, B.C. 925, 1 Kings 16:23, 24, and by him made the capital of the kingdom of Israel. Even during the period of the captivity it did not cease to be a place of some importance. But it was completely destroyed by the Jews under John Hyrcanus, B.C. 109. Herod the Great, however, rebuilt it with great splendor, and called it Sebaste. Philip preached the gospel there. Acts 8:5, 9. It is the modern village Sebustieh, whose houses are scattered among magnificent ruins.

Sa-mar'i-tans, inhabitants of Samaria. In the New Testament the name Samaritans was given to the people whom the Assyrian king placed in the cities of Israel when he had carried away the ten tribes captive. 2 Kings 17:29; Matt. 10:5; Luke 9:52; John 4:9.

Sam'son (sun-like), the son of Manoah, was an Israelite of the tribe of Dan. He was for twenty years one of the judges of Israel, had wonderful strength, and partially delivered his people from the power of the Philistines, but was finally captured by them, and killed himself and a very large number of his enemies by pulling down upon them the building in which they were assembled. A full account of his life is found in Judg. 13:24 to 16:31. He is mentioned in Heb. 11:32 among the heroes of the faithful.

Sam'u-el (heard of God), a noted prophet, and one of the noblest men of Old Testament times, was the last of the judges among the Hebrews. He was the son of Elkanah and Hannah, and resided at Ramah, but made each year a circuit through the country, administering justice among the people, until he became very old. For account of his life see 1 Sam., beginning with 1:20. His sons having proved unworthy to succeed him, he, under divine direction, anointed Saul king, and when Saul proved unworthy on account of disobedience, Samuel anointed David king, and shortly after that died. 1 Sam. 25:1. Samuel is called SHEMUEL in 1 Chron. 6:33.

Sam'u-el, First and Sec'ond Books of, formed originally one book in the Old Testament, and are also called the First and Second Books of the Kings. They bear the name of Samuel probably because he is the hero of the first part of the history, though it is also probable that he may have written that part of the First Book that narrates the occurrences during his lifetime.

The books of Samuel constitute a history of the Jews for about one hundred and twenty years, or from B.C. 1135 to B.C. 1016, beginning with the birth of Samuel, in the time of the judgeship of Eli, including the establishment of the Hebrew monarchy, and ending with the story of the numbering of the people by David, and his punishment. The narrative may be divided as follows: In the First Book of Samuel: (1) Chap. 1-4. the history of the judgeship of Eli. (2) Chap. 5-12. The history of the judgeship of Samuel. (3) Chap. 13-31. The history of the inauguration and reign of Saul. In the Second Book of Samuel: (4) Chap. 1-10. The history of the internal proceedings which resulted in placing David upon the throne, and of his victories over the surrounding nations. (5) Chap. 11-20. the story of

S

David's sins and of the domestic and national troubles which were the consequence, down to the death of Absalom, David's return to Jerusalem, and the insurrection of Sheba. (6) Chap. 21-24. The history of the remainder of David's reign.

The books of Samuel are among the most interesting of the whole Old Testament, as containing the romantic story of David, the shepherd, soldier, poet, and king.

Sanc'ti-fy is to prepare or set apart a person or thing to a holy use. Exod. 13:2. When applied to men, sanctification denotes the effect of God's spirit upon the soul which is manifested in the exercise of faith, love, and humility toward God and man. Rom. 15:16; 1 Cor. 1:2; 6:11.

Sanc'tu-a-ry, a holy or sanctified place. Ps. 20:2. The name given to the Temple or Tabernacle, Josh. 24:26; to the apartment that contained the golden candlestick, the altar of incense, etc., 2 Chron. 26:18; and the furniture of the Tabernacle. Num. 10:21. It was more particularly applied to the most secret part of the Temple in which was the "Ark of the Covenant" (which see). there no one could enter except the high-priest, and he only once a year, on the day of solemn expiation. Lev. 4:6.

San'he-drin (council), incorrectly called **San'he-drim,** was the supreme privy council among the Jews, at once a court of final appeal and last resort and an executive and legislative assembly. It consisted of seventy-one members, and met in a room adjoining the Temple where the seats were arranged in a semi-circle. Its origin is obscure. The Jews trace it back to the time of Moses. It was probably the result of a long development, but did not become conspicuous in Jewish history until after the Babylonian captivity. After the destruction of Jerusalem, A.D. 70, it was moved to Tiberias, where it continued till A.D. 425, when it became extinct. Christ was condemned by it for blasphemy. Matt. 26:65, 66. Besides the Great Sanhedrin, the name generally given to the council described above, almost every town had its own provincial Sanhedrin, the number of whose members varied according to the population of the place.

Sapphire, saf'fire, a gem noted for its beauty, hardness, and lustre. It was of a blue color, Exod. 24:10; Ezek. 1:26, and formed one of the stones in the high-priest's breastplate. Exod. 28:18.

Sa'rah (princess). [1] The name which God gave to Sarai, the wife of Abram, when his name was changed to Abraham. Gen. 17:15. She was the mother of Isaac (who was born when his parents were very old), and died at the age of one hundred and

211

twenty-seven. Gen. 23:1. she was a subject of special promises, Gen. 17:16, and her faith is commended in Heb. 11:11; 1 Pet. 3:6. The account of her life is found in Gen. 11:29 to 49:31. [2] A daughter of Asher, Num. 26:46, called SERAH in Gen. 46:17; 1 Chron. 7:30.

Sa'tan (adversary) is the name given to the devil, the adversary of goodness and the author of evil. He is also called "the prince of this world," "the wicked one," "the tempter," "the old serpent," etc.

Sa'tyr, in Isa. 13:21; 34:14, means "hegoat," and is so rendered in the marginal notes in the Revised Version.

Saul (desired). [1] One of the kings of Edom. Gen. 36:37, 38. He is called SHAUL in 1 Chron. 1:48, 49. [2] The first king of Israel. he was the son of Kish (Cis), of the tribe of Benjamin. Saul was anointed king by the prophet Samuel. 1 Sam. 10:1. He began well, but ended badly. He persecuted David, his successor. He reigned forty years, Acts 13:21, and fought a great battle with the Philistines, but was defeated with terrible slaughter and his three sons were killed. Saul took his own life on the field of battle. 1 Sam. chapter 31. His history is found in 1 Sam. 9:2-27, and in the remaining chapters of that book.

Scep'tre, an ornamental rod or staff borne by a king or ruler as a token of his authority. Gen. 49:10; Amos 1:5, 8. It may have had its origin in the shepherd's staff, as the patriarchal chiefs were shepherds as well as princes.

Scourge, skurj, Matt. 27:26, a whip or instrucment of punishment used by the Romans and also by the Jews, though probably by the latter only after the Babylonish captivity. It consisted of three lashes made of leather or small cords, to the ends of which sharp pieces of metal or bone were sometimes attached to increase the sufferings of the victim. A citizen of Rome could not be thus punished, though the Romans scourged slaves and foreigners. Acts 22:25, 26. In earlier times a rod was used, and under the law no more than forty stripes could be given. Deut. 25:1-3.

Scribe, in Old Testament times, was a person that was employed in correspondence and in keeping accounts. Sheva, the scribe of King David, is mentioned in 2 Sam. 20:25. His duty was to record proclamations, etc. In New Testament times the scribe was a copyist of the law, and one who prided himself on his knowledge of it and of the traditions of the elders. Matt. 2:4; Mark 1:22.

Scroll, Isa. 34:4; Rev. 6:14, refers to the roll, or ancient form of book.

Sea. In Gen. 1:10 "seas" refers to the ocean. The term sea is also applied to a great collection of water caused by the overflowing of the river Nile or of the river Euphrates.

Salt Sea, Gen. 14;3; Num. 34:12; Josh. 18:19, means Dead Sea.

Sea of Joppa, Ezra 3:7, means Mediterranean Sea.

Sea of the Philistines, Exod. 23:31, means Mediterranean Sea.

The Sea, Ezek. 47:8, means the Dead Sea; in Isa. 9:1; Matt. 4:13, 15; 17:27, the Sea of Galilee; in Josh. 15:46; 16:3; Acts 10:6, the Mediterranean Sea; in Exod. 14:2, 9; Josh. 24:6, 7, the Red Sea.

Utmost Sea, Joel 2:20; Deut. 34:2, means Mediterranean Sea.

Uttermost Sea, Deut. 11:24, means Mediterranean Sea.

Sea of Chinnereth, kin'ne-reth, Num. 34:11, or **Chinneroth,** kin'ne-roth. Josh. 12;3.

Sea of Gal'i-lee. Matt. 15:29.

Sea of Ti-be'ri-as. John 21:1.

Sea, The Dead.

Sea, The Med-iter-ra'ne-an.

Sea, The Mol'ten or **Bra'zen.**

Sea, The Red. Exod. 10:19.

Sea, The Salt. Gen. 14:3.

Seal. This was used in ancient times for much the same purposes as now—to authenticate public and private papers, and also to so secure any receptacle that any access to its contents can be easily discovered. Frequently a ring with an inscription on it was used as a seal. 1 Kings 21:8 Jer. 32:14.

Sea'sons. Gen. 1:14. In Palestine the year is very nearly divided (as in California) into two seasons, the wet and the dry, each subdivided into three periods of about two months each.

The grain harvest is from April to June. The sky is clear and the weather warm, like early summer with us. During the next two months, the vernal summer of the Arabs, the heat increases and people are compelled to sleep in the open air. Then comes the season of fruits, August to October. The heat is now intense, but towared the end of this season the nights begin to grow cool. during these three periods of the dry season the earth is moistened by the dew. Rain does not fall, with the exception of a few days in October.

This "former rain" prepares the earth for seed-time, October to December. The days are still hot, but grow cooler as the season advances. Winter, December to February, brings snow on the highlands and rain-, hail-, and thunder-storms in the

S

lower lands. Toward the end of January the fields become green, and in early February the trees begin to blossom. Spring follows, and lasts till about the middle of April. The weather grows warm, and toward the close of this period the rains cease. The last rain, called the "latter rain," gives strength to the filling grain, which will soon be ready for the harvest.

Sect. This word signifies, primarily, "choice," "party," and means the religious parties among the Jews, Acts 5:17, Christians, 1 Cor. 11:19, etc. There were five sects among the Jews, who, though of one communion and united as a nation, held distinct opinions and practised them. They were known as the PHARISEES, the SADDUCEES, the ESSENES, the HERODIANS, and the ZEALOTS (each of which see). The first three were religious, the last two were political parties. The Pharisees and Sadducees are frequently mentioned in the Gospels; the Essenes (a mystical and ascetic sect) lived retired on the shores of the Dead Sea, and are not mentioned in the New Testament. The early Christians were regarded as a new sect of Judaism, and were called "the sect of the Nazarenes." Acts 24:5. See HERESY.

Se-di'tions, Gal. 5:20, means "divisions."

Seed. Matt. 22:24. In this and many other passages in the Bible the word means progeny; descendants; offspring.

Seer, 1 Sam.9:9, one who forsees events.

Se'ir (hairy). [1] A mountainous district extending from the Dead Sea to the eastern gulf of the Red Sea. It was occupied by the Horites, and afterward by the descendants of Esau. Gen. 14:6; 36:8. Seir sometimes means Edom. [2] Mount Seir, a landmark of Judah. Josh. 15:10.

Sela, se'lah, Isa. 16:1, and **Se'lah** (rock), 2 Kings 14:7, a famous city of Edom. Its Greek name is PETRA, and it is so called in the marginal notes, Isa. 16:1. It was captured by Amariah, who called it JOKTHEEL. 2 Kings 14:7.

Se'lah. Nothing definite is known about this word. It occurs seventy-one times in thirty-nine Psalms, and three times in the book of Habakkuk. It is most probably a direction for the orchestra to fall in with or accompany the other music. It occurs where very warm emotions have been expressed. Ps. 32:7.

Seleucia, se-leu'shi-ah, a city of Syria situated on the Mediterranean Sea, about five miles north of the river Orontes and fifteen miles west of Antioch, of which it is the seaport. Paul and Barnabas embarked from Seleucia on their first missionary journey. Acts 13:4.

Sen'ate, Acts 5:21, refers to the "elders of Israel," who

214

formed one of the three classes that made up the Sanhedrin. The scribes and priests formed the other two classes.

Sennacherib, sen-nak'e-rib or sen-na-ke'rib, the son of Sargon, was king of Assyria, to which at that time the kingdom of Judah was tributary. But Hezekiah, the king of Judah, refused to pay the tribute, and Sennacherib invaded Judea and forced him to submit. Hezekiah revolted a second time, but the army Sennacherib sent against him was smitten by a plague, and 185,000 are said to have died in one night. 2 Kings 19:35. Sennacherib reigned for many years, but was killed by his sons and succeeded by Esarhaddon. 2 Kings 19:37.

Septuagint, sep'tu-a-jint (Seventy), the Greek version of the Old Testament, was made by seventy or seventy-two interpreters, at Alexandria, Egypt, in the third century before Christ, for the Jews of the dispersion (called Hellenists). It is of unequal merit, and often differs from our (Massoretic) Hebrew text. It was used in the synagogues at the time of Christ, and is usually quoted from in the Greek Testament. The oldest manuscripts of the Septuagint are in the Vatican and Sinaitic codices, both of the fourth century; while our oldest Hebrew manuscripts date from the ninth century; hence the Septuagint may in part represent an older Hebrew text. See Bible.

Sep'ul-chre, a place or house for the dead. Mark 15:46. Among the Jews it was not unusual for a single family to have near their dwelling-house a small building of stone or other durable material, without window or door, in which they deposited their dead. Some of the sepulchres were very expensively built, and were whitened, Matt. 23:27, frequently to make them conspicuous and easy to be avoided, as contact with them rendered one ceremonially unclean. Num. 19:16.

Ser'a-phim (princes), an order of angelic beings mentioned in Isa. 6:2, 6.

Ser'gi-us Pau'lus, the Roman deputy or governor (proconsul) of the island of Cyprus, in the Mediterranean Sea. He was converted under the ministry of Paul. A statue with his name has been discovered recently by Cesnola. Acts 13:7, 12.

Ser'jeants or **Ser'geants,** Acts 16:35, 38, were Roman lictors or officers who attended the chief magistrates when they appeared in public, and inflicted the punishment that had been pronounced.

Ser'pent, Gen. 3:1, or snake is a creature noted for its subtilty, its wisdom in avoiding danger, and for the dread it instinctively inspires in man and beast. Serpents abound in Syria, and many of them are poisonous. They were worshipped by the Egyptians and other nations in the East. Frequent allusions are made by the sacred writers to the serpent as an emblem of wickedness, Matt. 23:33, cruelty, Prov. 23:32, treachery. Gen. 49:17. The devil is called "the old serpent," Rev. 12:9, with reference to our first parents. 2 Cor. 11:3. The FIERY SERPENTS mentioned in Num. 21:6; Deut. 8:15 were probably so called from the burning sensation that followed their deadly bite. The FIERY FLYING SERPENTS, Isa. 14:29; 30:6, probably refers to the quick darting movements of the serpents in Eastern deserts.

Ser'pent, Bra'zen. Num. 21:6-9.

Serv'ant. Gen. 49:15. This word, as used in the Bible, does not necessarily imply a domestic or slave, for it was applied to any one under the authority of another. Thus, in Matt. 26:58; Mark 14:54, 65; John 18:36 it means "officers."

Seth (substitution), a son of Adam and Eve. He was nine hundred and twelve years old when he died. Gen. 4:25; 5:8. Called also SHETH in 1 Chron. 1:1.

Sev'en. From the beginning this was the number of days in the week, and hence it has a special emphasis attached to it, and is used in Scripture as a round number, or, as some would say, a perfect number, and in much the same way we use "ten" or "a dozen." Gen. 7:2; Matt. 12:45. In like manner, "seven times" or "seven-fold" means "often," "abundantly," while "seventy times seven" denotes a still higher degree. Gen. 4:15; Matt. 18:21, 22.

Sev'en Stars, The, Amos 5:8, refers to the PLEIADES.

Shadrach, sha'drak (royal?), the name given to HANANIAH by the chief of Nebuchadnezzar's eunuchs. He was thrown into a fiery furnace with Meshach and Abednego, and was unhurt. Dan. 1:7; 3:20-27.

Shallecheth, shal'le-keth (a casting down), one of the gates of the Temple. 1 Chron. 26:16.

Shalmai, (may thanks), one of the Nethinim whose decendants returned with Zerubbabel. Ezra 2:46; Neh.7:48.

Shalmaneser, shal-ma-ne'zer (Salman is gracious), an Assyrian king who invaded Israel, 2 Kings 17:3; 18:9, made Hoshea tributary to him, and prosecuted a vigorous siege against Samaria whichled to its capture and the ten tribes into captivity.

Sheep. This animal was probably the first that was domesticated by the Hebrews, Gen. 4:4, and it often constitued the chief wealth of a family in patriarchal times. It was especially an animal of sacrifice, and there were very few offerings in which it was not permitted. The ancient Israelites probably kept the

216

broad-tailed variety, the tail or "rump" of which is a mass of delicate fat weighing from ten to fifteen pounds, and considered the choicest part of the animal. Exod. 29:22. The sheperd held a position of trust and responsibility. He tended the flock constantly, day and night, Luke 2:8, and was responsible for any that were missing. Luke 15: 4-6. The care he exercised over the sheep gave him great control over them. They recognized his voice and promptlly obeyed his call. John 10: 3-5. The sheep were kept in an enclosure called a sheepfold or sheepcote. John 10:1; 2 Sam. 7:8. In a figurative sense, believers are called sheep on account of their obedience and gentleness. Matt. 25:33; John 10:16. Christ himself is called "the lamb of God." John 1:29.

Sheep Gate, a gate of Jerusalem. Neh. 3:1; 12:39.

Sheep Market, John 5:2, should read SHEEP GATE (which see).

Shek'el denotes a weight, and refers to a certain weight of uncoined metal. the silver shekel was worth between fifty and sixty cents, and the gold shekel about ten dollars. Lev. 5:15.

She'lah (petition), the youngest son of Judah by the daughter of Shua. Gen. 38:5; Num. 26:20.

She'lah (sprout), the son of Arphaxad. 1 Chron. 1:18, 24. He is called SALAH in Gen. 10:24; 11:12.

Shel'o-mith Pacific). [1] A woman of the tribe of Dan. Lev. 24:11. [2] One of the daughters of Zerubbabel. 1 chron. 3:19. [3] A descendant of Gershon, the son of Levi. 1 Chron. 23:9. [4] One of he Kohathite Levites. 1 Chron. 23:18. Called SHELO-MOTH. [5] One who had charge of dedicated things. 1 Chron. 26:25, 26. [6] One of the sons of Rehoboam. 2 Chron. 11: 20. [7] A New whose sons returned with Ezra. Ezra 8:10.

Shem (name), a son of Noah. Gen. 5:32; 9:20-27. The Jews descended from him; also the Aramaeans, Persians, Arabians, and Assyrians. The various languages of the descendants of Shem are called Shemitic languages.7:37.

Shimea, shim'e-ah, and **Shim'e-ah** (the hearing—that is, answering—prayer). [1] A brother of David, 2 Sam. 21:21, called also SHAMMAH and SHIMMA. [2] A son of David and Bathsheba, 1 Chron. 3:5, called also SHAMMUA and SHAM-MUAH. [3] A descendant of Merari, the son of Levi. 1 Chron. 6:30. [4] A son of Gershon, the son of Levi. 1 Chron. 6:39. [5] A man of Benjamin. 1 Chron. 8:32.

Shim'e-am (the hearing—that is, answering—prayer). 1 Chron. 9:38. Same as SHIMEAH, No. 5.

Shim'e-ath (the hearing), an Ammonitess, the mother of

Jozachar. 2 Kings 12:21; 2 Chron. 24:26.

Shim'e-ath-ites, a family of scribes. 1 Chron. 2:55.

Shim'e-i (renowned). [1] A son of Gershon, the son of Levi, Num. 3:18; 1 Chron. 6:17, called also SHIMI. [2] A Benjamite, of the family of Saul, who cursed David when he fled from Absalom. 2 Sam. 16:5-13; 19:23. [3] An officer of David who remained faithful when Adonijah rebelled. 1 Kings 1:8. [4] One of the provision-officers of Solomon. 1 Kings 4:18. [5] A grandson of Jeconiah. 1 Chron. 3:19. [6] A descendant of Simeon. 1 Chron. 4:26, 27. [7] A descendant of Reuben. 1 Chron. 5:4. [8] A descendant of Merari, the son of Levi. 1 Chron. 6:29, 42. [9] The head of the tenth course in the service of song. 1 Chron. 25:17. [10] An overseer of David's vineyards. 1 Chron. 27:27. [11] A descendant of Heman. 2 Chron. 29:14. [12] A Levite in charge of offerings. 2 Chron. 31:12, 13. [13] A Levite who took a foreign wife. Ezra 10:23. [14,15] Two Jews who took foreign wives. Ezra 10:33, 38. [16] An ancestor of Mordecai. Esth. 2:5.

Shi'mi. Exod. 6:17.

Shim'ri (watchful). [1] Head of a family of Simeonites. 1 Chron. 4:37. [2] Father of one of David's valiant men. 1 Chron. 11:45. [3] A Levite in the time of Hezekiah. 2 Chron. 29:13.

Shim'rith (watchful), a Moabitess whose son jehozabad was one of the conspirators against King Joash. 2 Chron. 24:26. She is called SHOMER in 2 Kings 12:21.

Shim'ron (watch-post), one of the ancient cities of Canaan, Josh. 11:1; 19:15, is probably the same as SHIMRON-MERON in Josh. 12:20.

Ship. This word, when applied to vessels on the Sea of Galilee, means a fishing-boat impelled by oars, and sometimes having a mast and sail. Mark 6:48; Luke 8:23. The Jews were not sailors, and the shipping trade on the Mediterranean and Red Seas was held by their heathen neighbors, who had ships of considerable size. These ships were steered by two large paddles, and though they usually had a mast with a huge sail, they were also propelled by oars in the hands of rowers. When one of these vessels was subjected to any great strain likely to make it leak, chains or ropes called "helps" were passed around (underneath) the vessel to tighten the planks. Acts 27:17. Their anchors were like ours, only they had no flukes. The account of Paul's voyage and shipwreck in the twenty-seventh chapter of Acts gives us more information about ancient navigation than all ancient classics. This is the testimony of an expert sea-captain (James Smith of Scotland), who verified the account and found it strictly accurate.

Shi'phi (abundant), a chief among the descendants of Simeon. 1 Chron. 4:37.

shiphmite, shif'mite, 1 Chron. 27:27, a native of SHEPHAM.

Shisha, shi'shah (Jehovah contends), the father of the two scribes of Solomon. 1 Kings 4:3.

Shi'shak, a king of Egypt to whom Jeroboam fled when Solomon sought to kill him. 1 Kings 11:40; 2 Chron. 12:2.

Shit'tim (acacias) was the last encampment of the Israelites before they entered Canaan. It was in the plains of Moab and near Mount Peor. Num. 25:1; 33:49; Josh. 2:1; 3:1. It is also called ABEL-SHITTIM.

Shit'tim, Val'ley of, mentioned in Joel 3:18, may be same as SHITTIM.

Shit'tim Wood was used extensively in the construction and furnishing of the Tabernacle. Exod. 25:10-16. It was the wood of the shittah tree, Isa. 41:19, probably a species of the acacia tree, once abundant and still found in the peninsula of Sinai. The wood is well adapted for cabinet-work, having a close grain. It is hard, tough, and of a brownish color.

Sho'bab (apostate). [1] A son of David and Bathsheba. 2 Sam. 5:14; 1 Chron. 3:5. [2] A son of Caleb, the son of Hezron. 1 Chron. 2:18.

Shobach, sho'bak (pouring), the captain of the host of Hadarezer. 2 Sam. 10:16, 18. He is called SHOPHACH in 1 Chron. 19:16.

Sho'ba-i (taking captive), a Tabernacle porter whose descendants returned with Zerubbabel. Ezra 2:42; Neh. 7:45.

Sho'bal (flowing). [1] A son of Seir. Gen. 36:20: 1 Chron. 1:38. [2] A son of Caleb, the son of Hur. 1 Chron. 2:50, 52. [3] Shobal, in 1 Chron. 4:1,2, is probably same as SHOBAL, No. 2.

Sho'bi (taking captive), a chief of the Ammonites. He provisioned David when he fled from Absalom. 2 Sam. 17:27.

Shoes, Exod. 3:5, **Shoe Latch'et,** Mark 1:7.

Sho'mer (a keeper). [1] A great-grand-son of Asher. 1 Chron. 7:34. [2] Shomer. 2 Kings 12:21.

Sho-shan'nim (lily), in titles of Psalms 45 and 69, and **Shoshan'nim-E'duth** (lily, a testimony), in title of Ps. 80, probably denote the melody that was used for those Psalms.

Shoul'der. To "bow the shoulder," Gen. 49:15, indicates servitude, and to "withdraw" it, Neh. 9:29, denoted rebellion. To "put upon" one's shoulders, Isa. 9:6; 22:22, means to entrust to his keeping or charge.

Shrines, mentioned in Acts 19:24, refer to small models of the temple of Diana, containing a little image of the goddess. Pilgrims to Ephesus bought them to set up in their homes as objects of worship.

Shroud, Ezek. 31:3, means cover, shelter.

Shu'al , the Land of, was probably near Bethel. 1 Sam.13:17.

Shu'al (a fox), an Israelite of Asher. 1 Chron. 7:36.

Shu'ba-el (captive of God). [1] A name in 1 Chron. 24:20. No. 1. [2] A name in 1 Chron. 25:20.

Shu'lam-ite, Song of Solomon 6:13, a woman from Shulem, probably same as SHUNEM.

Shu'nam-ite, a female inhabitant of Shunem. 1 Kings 1:3, 15; 2:17.

Shur (fort-wall), a place situated in the wilderness on the south-west of Palestine. Gen. 16:7; Exod. 15:22.

Shu'shan (a lily), a chief city of Susiana in Persia. It was the winter palace of the kings, and was known to the Greeks as Susa. Neh. 1:1; Esth. 1:2; Dan.8:2.

Shu'shan-e'duth is found in the title of Ps. 60, and is the same as SHOSHANNIM (which see).

Shu'the-lah (noise of breaking). [1] One of the sons of Ephraim. Num. 26:35,36; 1 Chron. 7:20. [2] A descendant of Ephriam. 1 Chron. 7:21.

Sibbecai, sib'be-kay, 1 Chron. 11:29; 27:11, **Sibbechai,** sib;be-kay, 2 Sam. 21:18; 1 Chron. 20:4 (thicket of Jehovah), a descendant of Judah. He slew a champion of the Philistines. He is called MEBUNNAI in 2 Sam. 23:27.

Sib'mah (coolness or fragrance), a town east of the Jordan, Josh. 13:19; Isa. 16:8, called also SHEBAM and SHIBMAH.

Sib'ra-im (twofold hope), a city of Syria, between Damascus and Hamath. Exek. 47:16.

Sick'le. Joel 3:13. From representations on Egyptian monuments the ancient sickle was very much like our implement. The scythe was unknown in Bible times.

Sid'dim, Vale of, Gen. 14:3, is supposed to have been the site of Sodom and Gomorrah. Its exact location is not established. See SODOM. It was the scene of the battle between Chedorlaomer and his allies and the kings of Sodom,Gomorrah, etc.

Si'don or **Zi'don,** one of the oldest cities of the world named after the "first born" of Canaan, the grandson of Noah. Gen. 10:15; 1 Chron. 1:13, stands on the Mediterranean shore, twenty-five miles south of the modern Beirut and one hundrred and twenty-three miles north of Jerusalem, and was in ancient times the principal city of Phoenicia until her own colony, Tyre, situated twenty miles to the south, became the more important. Sidon was celebrated both among the Jews and Greeks for its ship-building industry, its purple-dyed fabrics, its silverware, etc. and though it was often rebuked by the prophets on account of its idolatry and moral laxity, it was generally spoken of with less severity than Tyre. Isa. 23:2; 4, 12; Jer. 25:22; 27:3; 47:4; Exek. 27:8; 28:21; etc. It was once visited by Jesus, Matt. 15:21; Mark 7:24; Luke 4:26, and some of its people went to hear his preaching. Mark 3:8; Luke 6:17. Toward the close of the thirteenth century it came under Turkish rule and gradually sank into insignificance, but is again prospering. It is now called Saida, with a population of about 10,000 (Mohammedans, Greeks, Maronites, and Protestants) and a flourishing fruit-culture (especially of oranges).

Sieve. Isa. 30:28; Amos 9:9. This necessary article for separating the fine meal from the coarse was in very early times made of rushes or papyrus. Sieves were of different degrees of fineness, as ancient writers mention four kinds of meal.

Si'las, one of the chief of the brethren of the early Church, was probably a native of Antioch. Acts 15:37-41. He accompanied Paul on several of his missionary tours, and was imprisoned with him at Philippi. Acts 16: 19-40. He is called a prophet, Acts 15:32, and is supposed to be the SILVANUS mentioned in 2 Cor. 1:19.

Silk. In Prov. 31:22, Revised Version, the word is rendered "fine linen," and it may be that it has the same meaning in Ezek. 16:10,13, as it is a question whether the Hebrews knew anything about silk at that time. It was used however, in New Testament times. Rev. 18:12.

Si-lo'am or **Sil'o-am.** [1] A tower in Siloam, on Olivet, near Jerusalem. This tower fell and killed eighteen men. See Luke 13:4,5. [2] SILOAM, SHILOAH, or SILOAH, a pool near Jerusalem. It is referred to in Isa. 8:6 as "the waters of Shiloah that go softly," in Neh. 3:15 as "the pool of Siloah by the king's garden," and as "the pool of Siloam" in John 9:7,11. It is doubtless the same as a pool now at the mouth of the Tyropoean valley at Jerusalem.

Sil-va'nus (woody). [1] A disciple who accompanied Paul in several of his journeys. 2 Cor. 1:19; 1 Thess. 1:1; 2 Thess. 1:1. Supposed to be same as SILAS (which see). [2] A disciple by whom Peter sent his first epistle, addrressed to the churches in Asia. 1 Pet. 5:12. He may be same as SILVANUS, No. l.

Sil'ver. This precious metal was known very early in human history, Gen. 13:2, formed a common medium of trade, and was then not coined, but used by weight. Gen. 23:16. It was used in the construction of the Tabernacle, Exod. 26:19, for the furniture of the Temple, 1 Chron. 28:14-17, for musical instruments, Num. 10:2, and for adorning idols. Isa. 40:19. In the Hebrew the word was used the apply to money in general. Silver was abundant in Palestine in the time of Solomon, 1 Kings 10:27, who had it brought from Tharshish (probably Spain), 1 Kings 10:22, and from other places. 2 Chron. 9:14. For the beauty and force of the allusion in Mal. 3:3

Sim'e-on (a hearing). [1] The second son of Jacob and Leah. Gen. 29:33; Exod. 1:2. He was one of "the twelve patriarchs," and was the ancestor of the tribe of Simeon. [2] A just and devout man of Jerusalem, who waited for the consolation of Israel and was permitted to see the infant Saviour. Luke 2:25, 34. [3] A disciple and prophet who was at Antioch when Barnabas and Saul returned from Jerusalem. Acts 13:1. [4] Simeon, in Acts 15:14, is applied to the apostle Peter, who was more frequently called SIMON. [5] An ancestor of Joseph, the husband of Mary. Luke 3:30.

Sim'e-on. One of the tribes of Israel is often so called. Num. 1:6; Deut. 27:12; Ezek. 48:24.

Sim'e-on, Ter'ri-tory of, was in the south-west part of Canaan, and within the inheritance of Judah. Josh. 19:1-9.

Si'mon (a hearing). [1] A sorcerer who practised his arts and deceived the people of Samaria. Acts 8:9, 13, 18, 24. [2] A name often applied to the apostle Peter. Matt. 4:18; Mark 1:16; Luke 4:38; John 1:40; Acts 10:5; 2 Pet. 1:1, and elsewhere. [3] Simon the Canaanite, Matt. 10:4; Mark 3: 18; Luke 6:15, called Simon Zelotes in Acts 1:13, one of the twelve apostles. [4] One of the brethren of our Lord. Matt. 13:55; Mark 6:3. [5] A Pharisee in whose house Jesus' feet were washed with tears and anointed with ointment. Luke 7: 36-40. [6] A leper in Bethany. Matt. 26:6; Mark 14:3. [7] The father of Judas Iscariot. John 6:71; 12:4. [8] Simon the Cyrenian, who was compelled to bear the cross of Jesus on the way to Golgotha. Matt. 27:32; Mark 15:21; Luke 23:26. [9] Simon the tanner at Joppa, with whom Peter lodged. Acts 9:43; 10:6.

Sim'ri (watchful), one of the Merarite Levites. 1 Chron. 26:10.

Sin is the transgression of the law of God, 1 John 3:4, and "all unrighteousness is sin." 1 John 5:17. The word is sometimes used for a sin-offering, as in Hosea 4:8; Rom. 8:3; 2 Cor. 5:21.

Sin (mire), a city of northern Egypt, Ezek. 30:15, 16, called by the Greeks Pelusium. It was near the eastern mouth of Nile.

Sin, Wil'der-ness of, is on the east shore of the Gulf of Suez and between Elim and Sinai. Exod. 16:1; Num. 33:11.

Sinai, pronounced si'nay, si'ny or si'na-i (burning bush?). [1] The peninsula of Sinai is a triangular-shaped district lying between the two arms (gulfs) of the Red Sea. Its westerly boundary-line, along the Gulf of Suez, is about one hundred and ninety miles long, its easterly boundary, along the Gulf of Akabah, is about one hundred and thirty miles long, and its northern boundary-line, which stretches from the head of the Gulf of Suez across to the head of the Gulf of Akabah, is one hundred and fifty miles long. The peninsula contains about 11,500 square miles. The narrow strips of low coast-land along the two gulfs are backed by mountain-masses of granite with summits rising to the height of over 8500 feet. These mountains, sharply cleft by deep valleys, enclose on the south, east, and west the wedge-shaped plateau known as the "Wilderness of Wandering." The ancient Egyptians called this peninsula the "land of the gods." and its solitary grandeur impresses all travellers alike.

[2] Mount Sinai, from which the Law was given to the Israelites, is in the southern part of the peninsula of the same name. In the Old Testament the name is used interchangeably with Mount HOREB (which see). It is difficult to locate exactly the Mount Sinai of the Bible, but most scholars now agree that it must have been one of the peaks of Jebel Musa, a gigantic mass two miles long, one mile broad, and running north-east and south-west. Ras Sufsafeh, the northern peak of Jebel Musa, over 7300 feet high, and overlooking a plain that could have easily afforded standing-room for over two million Israelites, meets all the requirements of the text, Exod. 19:11-20; 20:18, and is regarded as the place from which the Law was given. The impression made upon the traveller by standing on that peak can never be effaced. It is the most appropriate pulpit for the proclamation of the law of Jehovah to his people for all generations. The sound of it could be heard in every spot of the surrounding valley Er Rahah, which is two miles long and half a mile wide, and embraces four hundred acres of available standing-ground. All the surroundings are terribly sublime.

Sin'-Mon'ey. Money sent by persons at a distance, with which to buy the required offerings. 2 Kings 12:16. As there was usually some surplus, it was the perquisite of the priest, and was called sin-money or sin-offering money. Num. 18:9.

Sin-Of'er-ing. Lev. 4:21.

Sis'ter. In Scripture this word has a wide application, being applied not only to a full sister, but to a step-sister, or half-sister, 2 Sam. 13:2, and to any near female relative. Matt. 13:56. It also denotes one of the same spiritual family. Rom. 16:1. "Sister's son," Col. 4:10, means "cousin."

Skins of animals were used for clothing, Gen. 3:21, for a covering for the Tabernacle, Exod. 26:14, for BOTTLES (which see), and other domestic purposes. Num. 31:20. They were also used as coverings for shields.

Slav'er-y. Among the Jews there were Hebrew and Non-Hebrew slaves, and both were carefully protected by the law. The former became such through poverty or debt, through theft and inability to repay, or, in the case of females, because they had been sold by their parents as maid-servants. Theirs was the mildest form of bond-service. The Non-Hebrew slaves were captives taken in war or purchased, and they constituted a majority of the slaves among the Hebrews. At the time of Christ slavery was established throughout the world and interwoven with domestic and social life. It was regarded even by the wisest men as a normal state of society. But Christianity, by teaching the common creation and redemption of men, the fatherhood of God and the brotherhood of men, and enjoining the law of kindness and love to all, first moderated the evils of slavery then encouraged emancipation, and the ultimate extinction of the whole institution.

Slime. Gen. 11:3.

Sling, 1 Sam. 17:40; Judg. 20:16, an early weapon of war, with which stones were thrown with great force and accuracy of aim. The slingers formed a regular branch of the army, ranking next to the archers in efficiency.

Slow Bel'lies, Tit. 1:12, is rendered in the Revised Version "idle gluttons."

Smyrna, smir'nah (myrrh), a city of Asia Minor, on the Aegean Sea, forty miles north of Ephesus and opposite the island of Mytilene, is mentioned in Rev. 1:11 and 2: 8-11 as one of the seven churches of Asia. It seems to have been founded by Greek colonists B.C. about 1500, and became an important commercial place in the days of Alexander the Great, B.C. 323. Polycarp, a pupil of the apostle John, was martyred there A.D. 155. It is still a flourishing city with about 180,000 inhabitants.

Snow. Isa. 55:10. The fall of snow in Palestine varies with the face of the countries. It sometimes fallls to the depth of a foot in Jerusalem, but soon disappears. In the ravines of the highest ridges of Hermon and on the peaks of Mount Lebanon snow is found during the whole year.

Snuff'dish-es, Snuffers, Exod. 25:38; 37:23, were articles of furniture belonging to the GOLDEN CANDLESTICK (which see). The snuffers were tongs for removing the snuff from the wicks of the lamps, and the snuffdishes received the snuff thus removed.

Soap was made from oil or other fatty substances and potash obtained from the ashes of alkaline shrubs that grew along the Dead Sea and the Mediterranean. It was a soft soap that was thus made, and it was used from very early times not only for washing purposes, but in the refining of metals. Jer. 2:22; Mal. 3:2.

Sod, Sod'den, Gen. 25:29; Exod. 12:9, means boiled.

Sod'om (burning?), one of the cities in the vale of Siddim which were destroyed on account of the wickedness of their inhabitants. Gen. 10:19; 13:3, 10-13; 19:1-29; Matt. 10:15; 11:23,24. Its exact location is not known. Some place it at the southern, others at the northern end of the Dead Sea.

Sod'om-ite. Deut. 23:17. The word does not imply an inhabitant of Sodom, but rather one guilty of the crime to which the inhabitants of that city were addicted.

Sod'om, Vine of, Deut. 32:32, may refer to one of several plants, growing near the Dead Sea, which bear a beautiful fruit that is not fit to eat.

Sol'o-mon (peaceful), the son of David and Bathsheba, succeeded his father as king of Israel, and reigned forty years. He was noted for his wisdom, and was the chief author of the book of Proverbs. The principal event in his reign was the building of the TEMPLE (which see) in Jerusalem. Solomon was also famous for his riches. 1 Kings, chapter 10. His character in early life was noted for its excellence, but in his latter days he was led into idolatry and other sins by his numerous foreign wives and concubines. 1 Kings, chapter 11. ECCLESIASTES (which see) contains the lesson of his life.

Sol'o-mon's Pools are three large reservoirs, in a narrow valley south-west of Bethlehem, which supplied Jerusalem with water. They are built on different levels, one slightly above the other, and connected by underground passages, so that the water collected in the highest pool can be emptied in the lower pools. The ruins remain to this day. Eccles. 2:6.

Sol'o-mon's Porch, a cloister or colonnade on the east side of the Temple. A double row of white marble Corinthian columns supported the ceiling, which was finished with cedar and forty feet above the floor. John 10:23; Acts 3:11; 5:12.

Son. This word is used in the Scriptures to imply almost any kind of descent or relationship. In Gen. 29:5 it is used for grandson; in Matt. 22:42 for a remoter descendant; in 1 Pet. 5:13 for disciple. "Sons of God" or "children of God" are those that are born of God or regenerated by the Holy Spirit. Adam is called "the son of God," as his creature made in his image. Luke 3:38. In one passage the term is applied to an inanimate object, the threshed-out grain, which is called in Hebrew the "son" of the threshing-floor—Isa. 21:10, marginal notes.

Song of Sol'o-mon, The, SOLOMON'S SONG, or the SONG OF SONGS, or, after the Latin, CANTICLES, is a poem in dramatic form with dialogues and monologues. it is interpreted literally as a picture of pure bridal love, and allegorically as a typical representation of the relation between the Lord and Israel, or Christ and the Church. Each of these interpretations has its charm, and there is no reason why both should not be true. It has always formed part of the Canon.

Sooth'say-er. Dan. 2:27, etc. One who pretended to foretell future events.

Sop means morsel. Among the Hebrews and other nations of the East our modern table utensils were unknown or little used. Food was conveyed to the mouth by the fingers, and in eating liquid food a small piece of bread was dipped into it. John 13:26, 27, 30.

Sor'cer-y was one of the arts of the magicians, by which they pretended to foretell events with the supposed assistance of evil spirits. Exod. 7:11; Acts 8:9.

Soul. The Scriptures evidently distinguish between the spirit and the soul. 1 Thess. 5:23; Heb. 4:12. The word we call soul is used to denote mere animal life— the seat of feeling, appetite, and passion. The spirit is the higher portion of our nature--the seat of intelect and the loftier affections; "the holy of holies in that temple which God has constructed for himself within us." But the word soul is often used in the Bible and in all languages in a wider sense for the internal spiritual side of the constitution of man, as consisting of a mortal body and an immortal soul. Gen. 2:7; Matt. 10:28. In many passages it means person. Rom. 13:1.

Spain, the extreme south-west part of Europe, in ancient times included Portugal, and was known to the Hebrews. Paul desired to preach the gospel there. Rom. 15:24-28. Many scholars identify TARSHISH with the southern part of Spain and with Tartessus.

Sparrows, Matt. 10: 29, 31; Luke 12:6, 7 were little birds of the sparrow-like species that were very plentiful in Palestine. They were sold for food at a very low price and generally in pairs.

Spear. This weapon of warfare was a long wooden staff with a heavy metal point on one end. 1 Sam. 13: 19, 22. The dart and javelin were similar to the spear, only lighter, and were probably used to be thrown with the hand. 2 Chron. 32:5: Num. 25:7.

Speck'led Bird, in Jer. 12:9, probably refers to the HYAENA

Spider. This well-known insect of very singular structure and habits was abundant in Palestine. The hopes and schemes of wicked men are compared with the frailty of the spider's web. Job 8:14; Isa.59:5.

Spir'it is a word used to denote—(1) the Spirit of God, Gen. 6:3; Num. 11:17; Neh. 9:20; Ps. 51:11; Prov. 1:23; Isa. 32:15; Zech. 4:6, etc., or the HOLY GHOST. Matt. 3:11; Mark 1:8; Luke 1:15; John 1:33; (2) An evil, lying, or unclean spirit. 1 Sam. 16:14, 15; 18: 10; 2 Chron. 18:21; Zech. 13:2; etc. (3) A familiar spirit. Lev. 19:31; 1 Sam. 28: 3, 7; Isa. 8:19 etc. (4) The actuating spirit or power in man, 2 Cor. 7:1; Eph. 4:23; James 4:5, as contrasted with the SOUL (which see). The same word in Hebrew and Greek which means spirit, means also wind; hence the comparison in John 3:8.

Sprink'ling, Blood of, Heb. 12:24, refers to the custom of the high-priest, who once a year entered the holy of holies and sprinkled blood on the mercy-seat, to "make an atonement for the holy place because of the uncleanness of the children of Israel." Lev. 16: 15, 16.

Star'-gaz-ers, in Isa. 47:13, implies raving or dreaming about the stars.

Star of the Wise Men. Matt. 2: 1-21. Concerning the appearance of this star there are two theories: (1) A miraculous star, seen only by the wise men, and serving as their guide until it led them to "where the young child was." Matt. 2:9. (2) A remarkable conjunction of Jupiter, Saturn, Mars, and a star of extraordinary brillancy, which took place about the time of Christ's birth (according to astronomical calculations), and which would naturally attract the Magi, with their ideas of astrology and their expectations of the coming Messiah.

Stars. The Hebrews included under the name of stars, the planets and all other heavenly-bodies except mentioned in the Bible, and are very frequently referred to figuratively, as in Ps. 147: 4; Gen. 15:5; 22:17; 26:4; Exod. 32:13; Ps. 8:3,4. In Rev. 22: 16 Christ is called the "morning star," because the light of

S

the gospel day was introduced by him.

Stephen, ste'vn (crown), one of the seven disciples who were appointed to superintend the distributions to the poor. He was "full of faith and of the Holy Ghost," Acts 6:5, and "did great wonders and miracles among the people." Acts 6:8. He was stoned to death, Acts 7:59, and is usually called the first martyr. Saul (Paul) was present, "consenting unto his death." Acts 8:1.

Stew'ard, one to whose care is committed the management of the household, Gen. 43:19; Luke 16:1, etc., and so naturally applied to ministers, 1 Cor. 4:1, and Christians. 1 Peter 4:10. "Steward, " in Gen. 15:2, has a different meaning, and is rendered in the Revised Version "he that shall be possessor."

Sto'ics, a sect of Greek philosophers, among whom contempt of external circumstances and an absolute self-constraint were considered to be chief virtues. Acts 17:18.

Stones, Pre'cious. Though about twenty names of precious stones are mentioned in the Bible, it is impossible to identify them positively with the gems we now know by the same names. The same term was often used for different substances that possessed common properties. For example, "crystal" (kerach) denotes either ice or rock crystal (transparent quartz). Gems, however, were highly prized by the ancients. They were used in the high-priest's breast-plate, Exod. 28: 15-21, and were mentioned by the sacred writers to denote value, beauty, and durability. Isa. 54:11, 12; Rev. 4:3; 21:11, 18-20. For the different precious stones see the separate titles.

Ston'ing was the most general way of inflicting capital punishment. Lev. 20:2. 27: 24:14,16, 23.

Stork. Jer. 8:7. A bird like the crane, only much larger. It feeds on insects and frogs, and seeks its food in marshes and watery places. It was classed among unclean birds. Lev. 11:19. In flying it presents a noble sight with its long red legs extending far beyond its tail. It is fond of the society of men, and in the East it is superstitiously protected. It is noted for its tenderness to its young. Ps. 104: 17; Zech. 5:9.

Strain at, Matt. 23:24, means "strain out."

Strait, Matt. 7:13, is rendered "narrow" in the Revised Version.

Strang'er. The Jews applied this name to any person of foreign birth or who was not a Jew, even though that person lived among them. Exod. 20:10; 2 Chron. 2:17; Isa. 14:1. It was also applied to one not a priest, Num. 3:10, or of a different family. Matt. 17:25.

Strange Gods, a name often applied in the Bible to the false gods of the various nations. Deut. 32:12; Ps. 81:9.

Straw of wheat and barley was used as fodder. Gen. 24:25, 32. It was also very necessary for making brick. Exod. 5: 7-18. As a verb, "straw" means to spread or scatter. Matt. 21:8; 25:24.

Street. 2 Sam. 22:43. In the East the streets are generally made very narrow, in order to secure shade from the hot sun. Mats are sometimes stretched across the streets from roof to roof for the same purpose. Streets were not lighted at night, and the houses rarely having any windows on the street side, travellers were obliged to carry a lantern. Men used to spread their rugs and sit at prominent places on the street, Job. 29:7, and they also performed their devotions there. Matt. 6:5. To "make streets," 1 Kings 20:34, probably means to obtain commercial advantages.

Suc'coth-be'noth (tents of daughters), an idol of the Babylonians for which they built a temple in Samaria when they settled there. 2 Kings 17:30.

Sun. This centre of the planetary system and the great source of light and heat was the object of idolatrous worship from the earliest times. Sun-worship existed among all the nations around Palestine, and the Jews themselves burned incense to the sun. 2 Kings 23:5, 11; Exek. 8:16.

Sun of Righteousness, a title of the Messiah. Mal. 4:2.

Superstitious, su-per-stish'us, in Acts 17:22, is more correctly rendered in the Revised Version "somewhat superstitious" in the text, and "religious" in the marginal notes. The American Revisers prefer "very religious" in the text, which best corresponds to the Greek. Paul was too courteous and prudent to insult and alienate his Athenian hearers by charging them with superstition; he meant rather to compliment them for their overreligiousness that led them to build an altar even to the "unknown God," whom they "unknowingly" (not "ignorantly") worshiped, and whom he came to preach to them.

Sure'ty, one who is bound with and for another. The danger of this situation is plainly shown in Prov. 6:1; 11:15. To strike or join hands with another, Job. 17:3, was a sign of suretyship.

S

Swallows still make their nests in the buildings on the site of Solomon's Temple. Ps. 84:3; Prov. 26:2.

Swan is mentioned in the Bible only in Lev. 11:18; Deut. 14:16, where it is said to be unclean. It is very rare in Palestine and neighboring countries.

Swear. Gen. 21:24. **Swear'ing.** Hos. 4:2.

Swine or **Hog,** an unclean animal according to the law, Deut. 14:8, is despised both by the Jews and the Mohammedans, and is rarely found in Palestine. The occupation of the prodigal son, Luke 15:15, was extremely degrading. Eating swine's flesh is mentioned among sinful practices in Isa. 65:4; 66:17. The herd of swine miraculously destroyed, Matt. 8:32, if it belonged to Jews, was kept contrary to their law.

Sword. The sword in ancient times was short, two-edged, and resembled a dagger. It was carried in a scabbard and suspended from the belt or girdle. Gen. 27:40; Jer. 47:6; Judg. 3:16.

Syc'a-more (fig-mulberry), SYCOMORE in the Authorized Version, a large tree common in Egypt, and once a very abundant in the Jordan valley, but not often found now in Palestine, except near the coast. It closely resembles the common fig tree in its fruit, but has an aromatic leaf shaped like that of the mulberry tree. It bears fruit during over half the year, and its wood is exceedingly durable. Mummy-cases were made from it. It is entirely different from trees of the same name in the United States and in England. 1 Kings 10:27; 2 Chron. 1:15; 9:27; Luke 19:4.

Synagogue, sin'a-gog (an assemblage) a meeting of the Jews for prayer and instruction in the law on the Sabbath and at other appointed times. Such meetings were probably not held before the Babylonish captivity, and took place at first in the open air or in private houses. The buildings subsequently erected for these meetings were also called synagogues. In Rev. 2:9; 3:9 assemblies of those who profess to be God's people while their hearts are not right with Him are called "synagogues of Satan." The GREAT SYNAGOGUE was a council composed of one hundred and twenty men, who, according to Hebrew tradition, formed the Hebrew Canon and established worship in synagogues.

S

T

Taanach, ta'a-nak Josh. 12:21, and **Tanach,** ta'nak, Josh. 21:25 (sandy soil), a royal city of the Canaanites, was west of the Jordan, and was taken by Joshua. It was in Issachar, but was assigned to Manasseh and became a Levitical city.

Tab'bath (celebrated), a place in Issachar or in Ephraim, mentioned in the account of the flight of the host of the Midanites. Judg. 7:22.

Tab'er-na-cle meant originally simply a tent, Num. 24:5; Job 11:14; etc., but received later a specific meaning as the name of that tent which Moses constructed under divine direction for the worship of the Jews. It is described in Exod. 26, and 36: 8-38.

The Tabernacle stood in a court or enclosure, one hundred and fifty feet by seventy-five feet, made of canvas screens hung by hooks and fillets of silver from brazen pillars eight feet apart. This enclosure was broken only on the eastern side, where there was an entrance thirty feet wide hung with curtains of fine twined linen embroidered with figures of cherubim. At the upper end of the enclosure, and facing the entrance, stood the Tabernacle. The latter was forty-five feet long, fifteen feet wide, and fifteen feet high. Its two sides and rear were enclosed with boards, each of which had at its lower end two tenons which fitted into silver sockets placed on the ground, and at the top were fastened by bars of acacia wood run through rings of gold. The entrance was hung with costly curtains. The top of the Tabernacle was covered with fine linen embroidered with colored figures of cherubim; over this was goats'-hair cloth, above which was a covering of rams' skins dyed red, and outside of all was another covering which was composed of "badgers' skins." The Tabernacle was divided into two apartments by a veil or richly-wrought curtain extending entirely across it and from top to bottom. This veil is called the "second veil" in Heb. 9:3, because the outside entrance was also curtained. The outer apartment was called the "sanctuary" or "holy place," also the "first tabernacle," and the inner was the "second tabernacle," or the "most holy place," or the "Holiest of all." Heb. 9:2,3.

Within the court, and oposite the entrance, stood the ALTAR OF BURNT-OFFERING and between that altar and the Tabernacle was the BRAZEN LAVER, Exod. 30:18, in the form of an urn, and containing water for washing the hands and the feet of the priests before they entered the sanctuary.

In the sanctuary, at the left of a person entering it, stood the golden candlestick, opposite to which, on the right, was the table of shew bread. Beyond the golden candlestick and the table of shew bread, and in front of the ark of the covenant, but separated from it by the "second veil," was the altar of incense.

About nine months' labor was required to complete the Tabernacle, which, with its furniture, was so constructed that it could be conveniently taken down and set up again. It was consecrated to the service of Jehovah with solemn ceremonies, Exod. 30:23-33; 40: 9-11; Heb. 9:21, and "a cloud covered the tent of the congregation, and the glory of the Lord filled the tabernacle." Exod. 40:34.

This Tabernacle was built by the Israelites near the close of their encampment at the foot of Mount Sinai, and carried with them in their wanderings in the wilderness, in which they were directed by a cloud. Exod. 40: 36-38. The Tabernacle was always placed in the middle of the camp, surrounded by the tents of the priests and the Levites in appointed order, at some distance from which were the tents of the other tribes, in four large divisions. On the arrival at Canaan the Tabernacle was first placed at Gilgal, Josh. 4:19; then at Shiloh, 1 Sam. 1:3; then at Nob, 1 Sam. 21: 1-9; and finally, in the reign of David, at Gibeon, 1 Chron. 21:29, where it was when the reign of Solomon began. 2 Chron. 1: 1-13.

Two Tabernacle are mentioned in the Old Testament. One was made in the wilderness, and in the other the ark was put by David, where it remained till the Temple was completed. 2 Sam. 6:17; 1 Kings 8: 1; 1 Chron. 16:1. the old Testament was meanwhile at Gibeon.

Tab'er-na-cles, Feast of, lasting eight days, Num. 29: 12-40, was one of the three great feasts of the Jews, and commemorated the long tent-life of the Israelites while journeying through the wilderness. During its celebration the people all lived in booths. Neh. 8: 14-18. The feast was held at Jerusalem, and began on the fifteenth day of the seventh month (Ethanim), about the time when the fruits were gathered, and hence it was also called the feat of ingathering. Exod. 23:16.

Ta'ble. This, in ancient times, was simply a piece of skin or leather spread on the floor, and served both as a table and a cloth. Later a very low table, not much more than a span high, was used, and in the time of Christ the Jews had adopted the Persian custom of reclining at meals. "Table," in Exod. 24:12; Prov. 3:3; Luke 1: 63; etc. means a tablet for writing.

Te'man (south desert). [1] One of the sons of Eliphaz, the son of Esau. Gen. 36: 11, 15. 1 Chron. 1:36. [2] An Edomite chief, apparently of a later period. Gen. 36:42; 1 Chron. 1:53. [3] A district east of Edom. Jer. 49:7, 20; Amos 1:12.

Tem'per-ance, Tem'per-ate, Acts 24:25; Gal. 5:23; etc., mean self-restraint, moderation, self-control in all things, eating as well as drinking. In Titus 2:2 "temperate" means prudent or discreet.

Tem'ple, The, stood on Mount Moriah, Jerusalem and resembled in its general form the Tabernacle. There were three successive temples, built respectively by Solomon, Zerubbabel, and Herod the Great. The last mentioned was the Temple of the time of Christ.

I. SOL'O-MON'S TEM'PLE, B.C. 1005-588. The design, plan, and location of this building were furnished by David, under divine direction. 1 Chron. chaps. 21:22; 28: 11-19. He collected an immense amount of gold, silver, and brass (bronze or copper) for its erection, besides great quantities of iron, stone, timber, etc. although he was forbidden by God from beginning the work, 2 Sam. 7: 5-13. The building was commenced by Solomon in the fourth year of his reign. For seven and a half years 183,600 men were working on the Temple—namely 30,000 Jews in three divisions, 10,000 in each and 153,600 Canaanites, of whom 70,000 were bearers of burdens, 80,000 hewers of wood and stone, and 3600 overseers. Its parts were all prepared at a distance from it, and when brought together the Temple was built; nor was the sound of "hammer, nor axe, nor any tool of iron, heard in the house while it was in building." 1 Kings 6:7. The front of the Temple was toward the east, and the dimensions of the Temple proper were ninetly feet long, thirty feet wide, and thirty feet high—exactly double those of the Tabernacle, after the fashion of which it was made. There were additions to the building for the priests, etc. The Temple was completed B.C. 1005. The brazen laver, which in the Tabernacle was a simple urn, was represented in the Temple by a great basin resting on twelve brazen bulls. The Holy of Holies was a small square dark chamber. There the ark stood on a rough protuberance of the natural rock on which the Temple was built. On each side stood a golden cherub, and the wings of these figures met above the ark. The connection between this chamber and the sanctuary was through folding-doors of olive-wood hung with costly embroidered linen fabrics.

This Temple was destroyed by Nebuchadnezzar, B.C. 588, after having stood more than four hundred years, but it had been plundered during the reign of Rehoboam, 1 Kings 14: 25, 26, by the Egyptian king Shishak, and often afterward. For fifty years after their destruction Jerusalem and Solomon's Temple laid in ruins.

II. ZE-RUB'BA-BEL'S TEM'PLE,B.C. 515-64. In B.C. 536 permisson was given by Cyrus, the Persian conqueror of Babylon, for the captive Jews to return to Jerusalem. Many of them did return with Zerubbabel, governor of Judea, and Joshua (Jeshua), the high-priest. In the second year after their return the foundation of the Temple was laid. Ezra 3:8. The work of rebuilding was superintended by Zerubbabel and Joshua (Jeshua), but was not finished until twenty-years later, B.C. 515, on account of the intrigues of the Samaritans and other parties, as recorded by Ezra. It was in nearly all its dimensions one-third larger than Solomon's Temple, but not so magnificent, Ezra 3:12, 13, and, besides, it had no ark of the covenant and no sacred fire. The principal differences between this and the old building with respect to construction, were the arrangement of the court of worshippers, which was divided into two parts, an outer court for the Gentiles and an inner court for Israel, and the fortress-tower at the north-western corner, which was the residence of the Persian, and afterward of the Roman, governor. This Temple was the scene of more glorious illustrations of the divine attributes than were ever seen in Solomon's Temple,Hag.2:6-9 ; Mal.3;1, and it stood for nearly five hundred years, when it was rebuilt by Herod the Great.

III. HER'OD'S TEM'PLE, B.C. 20-A.D.70. This is the Temple in which Christ worshipped and the apostles until they were expelled, and the destruction of which was predicted by our Lord. It was not strictly a new building, but rather the second Temple completely repaired. The work was done by Herod the Great to secure the favor of the Jews and to make a great name for himself. It was begun B.C. 20, and the main building was in one year and a half , but the whole work was not ended till A.D. 64, under Herod Agrippa II. Solomon's Porch was on the east side. The Temple enclosure had five gates, the gate Shushan being opposite the Temple proper,which was surrounded by several courts of different elevations. The outer court was the court of the Gentiles; next, the court of women; then the court of Israel; then the court of the priests, next to the Gentles and the court of the women was the "middle wall of partition" (Eph. 2:14), which had thirteen openings. The Temple was two stories high. Its front was gilded. Before the entrance to the Holy of Holies hung two veils a cubit apart, and consequently no glimpse of what was behind the veil could be obtained by any one but the high-priest. Among the adjoining buildings was the assembly-hall of the Sanhedrin. This Temple was destroyed by Titus A.D. 70, in literal fulfilment of the prophecy of Christ. Matt. 24:2.

Tempt, Temp-ta'tion. Matt. 22:18; Luke 4:13. These words ordinarily imply enticement to sin. They also denote a trial or a proving. Thus "temptation" in the Lord's prayer, Matt. 6:13, means a trial of our moral nature; for God, being holy, does not tempt men to sin. James 1:13.

Ten Com-mand'ments, Exod. 20:3-17, called by the Jews. "The Ten Words," was the name applied to the writing on the two tables of stone given on Mount Sinai. Five of the commandments enjoin the duties to God, and five the duties to our neighbor. Taken together they form a complete and comprehensive summary of the moral law. Christ summed them up in the two great commandments, "Thou shalt love the Lord thy God with all thy heart, and with all thy soul, and with all thy mind;" and "Thou shalt love thy neighbour as thyself." Matt. 22: 37-40.

Tents, Gen. 13:5, were among the earliest dwellings of man, and they were used by the Hebrews until they entered the Promised Land. The ease with which they could be carried from one place to another specially adapted them to the needs of the people of the East, who had to move frequently to find fresh pasturage for their flocks. Tent-making was the trade of Paul by which he supported himself while preaching the gospel.

Tes'ta-ment, Heb. 9:15, etc., when applied to the Scriptures is used in the same sense as COVENANT (which see). The old covenant (which was a type of the new), is spoken of in Exod. 24:8, and was ratified by the blood of the sacrifices. The new covenant, mentioned in Matt. 26:28, was ratified by the blood of Christ. In the Revised Version the word is always rendered "covenant," except in Heb. 9:16, 17, where it evidently refers to the legal instrument called a "will."

Tes'ti-mon-ny, a solemn affirmation made for the purpsoe of establishing or proving a fact. John 8:17. The word is also used to denote the whole revelation of God's will, Ps. 119: 88; the two tables of stone on which the Law was written, Exod. 25:16; the ark of the covenant in which those stones were deposited, Exod. 25:22; and the Gospel. 1 Cor. 1:6.

Thes-sa-lo'ni-ans, E-pis'tles to. The FIRST EPISTLE was written by Paul from Corinth. A.D. 52, 53, principally for the purpose of correcting certain mistakes which prevailed in

Thessalonica with respect to what the apostle had taught there concerning the second advent. As this epistle did not succeed in setting the matter right immediately, it was soon followed by THE SECOND EPISTLE, from the same place. These two epistles are the earliest among the Pauline writings, and form the oldest portion of the New Testament Canon.

Thes-sa-lo-ni'ca was the most populous city of Macedonia, a great commercial centre, and the seat of a large colony of Jews, who had their synagogue outside the city. Paul visited it, Acts 17: 1-14, on his second missionary journey, A.D. 51, coming from Philippi, but after a short stay was compelled to leave the place by the fanaticism of the Jews. The young church, which had been founded, was left in charge of Timothy, and it was his report of the state of affairs, not unfavorable it would seem, which called forth from Paul two epistles to the Thessalonians. An arch at Thessalonica, considerably older than the first century of our era, has an inscription containing the names of seven of the Thessalonian magistrates, whom it calls "politarch," thus confirming the accuracy of the writer of Acts in using this rare word (in the original) to describe the "rulers," 17: 6, 8, of this city. Thessalonica is now called Salonika, and has a mixed population of about 80,000 (Turks, Jews, and Greeks), and a large commerce by land and sea.

This'tles and **Thorns.** Gen. 3:18. These plants are abundant in Palestine, and prove very troublesome to the husbandman. Thorns were much used for fuel, Ps.58:9, and formed durabale and impenetrable hedges. Hos. 2:6.

Thom'as (twin), one of the twelve apostles. He was also called "Didymus," which means "the twin." Little is known of his history. He would not believe in the resurrection of Christ until he had positvie evidence of it, when he exclaimed, "My Lord and my God."He died a martyr. Matt. 10:3; Mark 3:18; Luke 6:15; John 11:16; 14:5; 20:20-29; Acts 1:13.

Thou'sand Years. Rev. 20:1-7.

Thresh, Thresh'ing-floor. Threshing in the East was performed by means of the flail, Ruth 2:17, by oxen who trod out the grain, Deut. 25:4, and with a threshing-machine or sledge. Isa. 28: 27,28. The latter was a rude affair, having a heavy frame in which were fitted three or four rollers. The machine was drawn by oxen and the rollers passing over the grain crushed it out. Another form of thresing-machine consisted of several planks fastened together, through the under side of which projected pieces of flint or sharpened iron. Isa. 41:15. These served as teeth, and tore the husk of the grain in pieces as they passed over it. When the grain had been well loosened it was winnowed and for this purpose the threshing-floors were situated on a hill-top open on all sides to the wind. The threshing-floor was simply a piece of ground that had been levelled and beaten down hard. 1 Chron. 21: 15:28. Often a whole village would have but one threshing-floor, each husbandman, in a fixed order, taking his turn in using it.

Ti-be'ri-as, a city of Palestine, on the western shore of the Sea of Galilee, was founded by Herod Antipas, A.D. 16-22, and named in honor of the emperor Tiberias. It was for many years after the destruction of Jerusalem the seat of the Jewish Sanhedrin and of Jewish learning. The older Talmud (called the Jerusalem Talmud) was prepared there. Its present name is Tubariyeh, and though it is rather an insignificant place especiallysince itsdestruction in 1837 by an earthquake.

Ti-be'ri-us Cae'sar (TIBERIUS CLAUDIUS NERO) the step-son of Augustus, Luke 2:1, whom he succeeded as second emperor of Rome. Luke 3:1. He was a cruel despot, reigned twenty-three years, commencing A.D. 14, and was murdered.

Ti-mo'the-us (honoring God), Acts 16:1; Rom. 16:21, and elsewhere the name generally applied to TIMOTHY.

Tim'o-thy (honoring God), a favorite disciple of Paul, was born either at Derbe or at Lystra, both in Lycaonia, Asia Minor. His father was a Greek and a heathen, but both his mother and grandmother were Jewesses, and by them he was instructed in the Old Testament Scriptures. 2 Tim. 3:15. He was converted by Paul, and afterward became his companion. While still a young man he took charge of the church at Ephesus. 1 Tim. 4:12. Tradtion makes him bishop of Ephesus. Two of the epistles of Paul are addressed to him. His is also called TIMOTHEUS in the Authorized, but not in the Revised Version, which introduces uniform spelling of proper names.

Tim'o-thy, the First E-pis'tle to, was written by Paul about A.D. 64 (between the first and second Roman captivity). The epistles of Paul to Titus and Timothy are called the "Pastoral Epistles" on account of their contents—instructions concerning pastoral care and church government.

Tim'othy, the Second E-pis'tle to, is the last letter of Paul, written when he was confidently expecting martyrdom, 2 Tim. 4: 6-8. and contains his dying counsel to his spiritual son.

Tire, 2 Kings 9:30, to dress or adorn.

Tish'bite, a name applied to the prophet Elijah in 1 Kings 17:1; 21: 17,28; 2 Kings 1:3, 8; 9:36. He is called the Tishbite from his birthplace, probably Tishbeh, according to the mar-

T

ginal notes of 1 Kings 17:1 in the Revised Version. Tisbeh is twenty-two miles south of the Sea of Galilee and ten miles east of the Jordan, but is not mentioned in the Authorized Version.

Tithes means tenths, and refers to a form of taxation, which under the Levitical law required the Hebrews to render a certain proportion (one-tenth) of the produce of the earth, herds, etc. to the service of God. Lev. 27:30. This one-tenth went to the Levites, who had no part in the soil and were dependent on their brethren for means of subsistence. The Levites, in turn, gave one-tenth of what they received to the priests.

Tit'tle, Matt. 5:18; Luke 16:17, means a very small particle, and refers to the fine stroke or minute turn which often distinguishes one letter of the Hebrew alphabet from another.

Ti'tus was of Gentile descent and converted under the preaching of Paul. Tit. 1:4. He then became the companion of the apostle, and had charge of the church in Crete, when Paul wrote his epistle to him.

Ti'tus, the E-pis'tle to, is one of the pastoral epistles of Paul, and was probably written from Asia Minor in A.D. 64. This and the two epistles to Timothy are called the "Pastoral Epistles" on account of their contents—instructions concerning pastoral care and church government.

To-bi'ah (goodness of Jehovah). [1] A person whose posterity were unable to show their descent. Ezra 2:60; Neh. 7:62. [2] An Ammonite who was a leader in the opposition to Nehemiah. Neh. 2:10, 19; 6:1.

To-gar'mah, descendants of Gomer, the son of Japheth, supposed to have settled in the northern part of Armenia. Gen. 10:3; 1 Chron. 1:6; Ezek. 27:14.

Tola, to'lah (worm). [1] A son of Issachar. Gen. 46:13; Num. 26:23. [2] One of the judges of Israel. Judg. 10: 1,2.

To'lad (birth), a town of Judah, and afterward of Simeon. 1 Chron. 4:29. It is called ELTOLAD in Josh. 15:30; 19:4.

Tongues, Acts 10:46, means languages, especially those foreign to, or unknown by, the speaker.

To'paz, a precious stone in the high-priest's breastplate, is regarded by many to be the modern chrysolite, a rather soft stone of a greenish tinge. Exod. 28:17; Job 28:19; Rev. 21:20.

Tor-ment'ors, Matt. 18:34, were probably keepers of the prison who endeavored, by torturing the prisoner, to find out if he had any money hidden away.

Tortoise, tor'tis, Lev. 11:29, is rendered "great lizard" in the Revised Version, and probably refers to the dhabb, or Arabian lizard, a slow-moving reptile sometimes found two feet long.

The Arabs eat it, but according to the Mosaic law it was unclean.

Touch'ing, Lev. 5:13; Ps. 45:1; Matt. 18:19, means concerning.

Tow'er, a high building erected in vineyards, which served as a shelter and refuge for the watchmen and afford an extenseve view of the surrounding country. Isa. 5:2; Matt. 21:33. Shepherds erected towers for similar purposes. Towers were also built on forts, and near the gates of a city for refuge and defense in time of war. Judg. 9:51.

Tow'er of Shechem, she'kem, a castle or fort in the town of Shechem, to which the people fled when Abimelech besieged the town. Judg. 9:46-49.

Town-clerk. Acts 19:35. This official held a position of great importance in Ephesus. He kept the public records, presided over public gatherings, and performed the duties of the chief magistrate when the latter was away.

Trachonitis, trak-o-ni'tis (a rugged region), a Roman province, in New Testament times, north-east of the river Jordan. Luke 3:1.

Tra-di'tions, Matt. 15:2; Gal. 1:14, certain rules which the Jews claimed were given by God to Moses, and which, though not contained in the written law, were handed down by word of mouth form generation to generation.

Trans-fig-u-ra'tion, The, was a supernatural manifestation of the Saviour's inherent glory in which his divinity and mission were most solemnly attested. It took place, most probably, on Mount Hermon. The events connected with the transfiguration are particularyly described in Matt. 17: 1-9; Mark 9: 2-10; Luke 9: 28-36.

Trav'ail, Job 15:20; Isa. 53:11, means labor' pain; trouble generally.

Tres'pass-of'fering, Lev. 5:6, an individual sacrifice made for some specific sin or offense. Restitution was first to be made, and then this offering presented to God for an atonement.

Trib'ute. The tax paid for the support of the government, or levied on a people by their conquerors. Every Hebrew over twenty years of age was obliged to pay a tribute of a half-shekel (about twenty-five cents) for the maintenance of the Temple-service. Exod. 30:13, 14.

Tro'as a city of Mysia, Asia Minor, on the sea-coast, six miles south of the entrance to the Hellespont, was founded by Alexander the Great, but is now only a heap of ruins. It was visited twice by Paul. Acts 16: 8-11; 20: 5-10.It is now called

T

Eski Stamboul, or "Old Constantinople."

Trum'pet. The difference between this instrument and the HORN (which see), as they were used by the ancient Hebrews, is not known. Silver trumpets were used by the priests alone, to announce the approach

Trum'pets, Feast of, was celebrated on the first day or new moon of the seventh month (Tishri) of the sacred year, which was the New Year's Day of the Jewish civil year. The feast was begun with the sound of trumpets, and, besides the usual sacrifices that took place on the first of each month, there was a total cessation from labor and a special burnt-offering of a young bullock, a ram, and seven lambs. Num. 29: 1-6.

Tu'bal, one of the sons of Japheth. Gen. 10:2; 1 Chron. 1:5. The name Tubal is also applied to his descendants, who apparently settled on the south side of the Black Sea. Ezek. 27: 13; 38:2.

Tu'bal-cain (hammer-blows of the smith?), a son of Lamech (of the family of Cain) by his wife Zillah, Gen. 4:22, was an instructor of every artificer in brass (copper) and iron.

Tur'tle-dove, Ps. 74:19, a species of dove found in great numbers in Palestine. It is smaller than the pigeon, differently marked, and has a soft, plaintive note. The Jewish law permitted the poor, who could not afford a more costly sacrifice, to offer two pigeons or turtle-doves, Lev. 12:8, and their use by Joseph and Mary. Luke 2:24, is an evidence of the outward circumstances of Christ's parents.

Tyre or **Ty'rus** (rock), an ancient and wealthy city of Phoenicia, on the Mediterranean coast, twenty miles south of Sidon, form which it was founded as a colony about two thousand years before Christ. In Josh. 19:29 it is spoken of as a strong city, and the relations between its king, Hiram, and David and Solomon were very friendly. Afterward Tyre became very hostile to the Israelites, and partly on that account and partly because of its idolatry it is spoken of by the prophets with great severity. Isa. 23: 1, 5, 8, 15-17; Jer. 25:22; 27:3; etc. These prophecies were wonderfully fulfilled. It was besieged, but not taken, be Shalmaneser, B.C. 721, and by Nebuchadnez-zar B.C. 592. After a siege of seven months Alexander the Great took the city, B.C. 332, pillaged and burnt it, and sold the inhabitants into slavery. Nevertheless, it was again a flourishing place in New Testament times; Paul visited it and spent seven days there. Acts 21: 3, 4. It is now an insignificant town under Turkish rule.

U

U'cal (I am strong) is found only in Prov. 30:1. Nothing is known of him except that he was one of those to whom Agur spake. See Prov. 30:1.

U'lam (vestibule). [1] One of the descendants of Manasseh. 1 Chron. 7:16,17. [2] One of the descendants of the family of Saul. 1 Chron. 8:39,40.

Un-cir-cum-cis'ion, as in Rom. 4:9; refers to the Gentiles, in contrast with the Jews, who were circumcised. The word was also used to denote impurity or wickedness. Ezek. 44:7.

Un-clean'. Lev. 5:2

Un-cov'er. To uncover the head was a sign of grief or mourning, and also a token of captivity. Lev. 10:6; Isa. 47:2.

Unction, unk'shun, 1 John 2:20, means "anointing," and is so rendered in the Revised Version.

Un-der-gird'ing the ship, Acts 27:17, was to strengthen the vessel by means of ropes or cables called "helps."

Un-leav'ened Bread, Exod. 12:15, 17, was made very thin and from unfermented dough, and was broken, not cut. For the PASSOVER (which see) unleavened bread was prescribed, and hence that festival was often called the 'Feast of Unleavened Bread." Luke 22:1.

Up'per Coasts, Acts 19:1, means the countries of Galatia and Phrygia, in Asia Minor, which Paul passed through on his third missionary journey.

Up'per-most Rooms, Mark 12:39, is rendered in the Revised Version "chief places."

Ur (light), the father of Eliphal, one of David's valiant men, 1 Chron. 11:35, called AHASBAI in 2 Sam. 23:34.

Ur of the chaldees, kal'dees (light?), the place where Abram lived before he was called to go into Canaan. Gen. 11:28, 31; 15:7. Stephen spoke of it, Acts 7:2, as being in Mesopotamia. It was probably in the extreme north of that country, near the source of the river Tigris.

U-ri'ah. [1] 2 Sam. 11:3, 6 and elsewhere. A Hittite, one of David's valiant men, who was the husband of Bathsheba. He is also called URIAS. David caused his death, that his own guilt concerning Bathsheba might be concealed and that she might become his wife. 2 Sam. 11:14-17. [2] A priest whom Isaiah took as a witness. Isa. 8:2.

U-ri'jah (flame of Jehovah). [1] A priest in Jerusalem in the

U

time of King Ahaz. 2 Kings 16:10, 11. No. 2. [2] The son of Shemaiah. Jer. 26:20-23. [3] A priest, the father of Meremoth. Neh. 3:4, 21. May be same as the person mentioned in Neh. 8:4.

U'su-ry, in the Scriptures, means simply interest, and has not the significance that is now attached to the word. Exod. 22:25; Lev. 25:36. The Mosaic law forbad the Jews receiving any interest from each other for the loan of money or anything else, though they might require interest of strangers.

Uz (fruitful in trees). [1] One of the sons of Aram, the son of Shem. Gen. 10:23; 1 Chron. 1:17. [2] One of the sons of Dishan, of the family of Seir. Gen. 36:28; 1 Chron. 1:42.

Uz, The Land of (fertile land), the country of Job, was probably that part of Arabia which is east of Edom and south of Trachonitis. Job 1:1; Jer. 25:20; Lam. 4:21.

Uzza, uz'zah (strength). [1] One of the inhabitants of Jerusalem, who owned the garden in which Manasseh, king of Judah, and his son Amon were buried. 2 Kings 21:18, 26. [2] An Israelite of the tribe of Benjamin. 1 Chron. 8:7. [3] The founder of a family of Nethinim that returned with Zerubbabel. Ezra 2:49; Neh. 7:51. [4] A descendant of Merari, the son of Levi. 1 Chron. 6:29. [5] A son of Abinadab. 1 Chron. 13:7-11.

Uz'za, Gar'den of. 2 Kings 21:26.

Uz'zah (strength), one of the sons of Abinadab. He was miraculously killed for touching the ark of God (see Num. 4:15) while it was being carried back from the country of the Philistines. 2 Sam. 6:3-8. Called UZZA. 1 Chron. 13:7-11.

Uz'zen-She'rah (ear of Sherah), one of the cities of Sherah. 1 Chron. 7:24.

Uzzia, uz-zi'ah (strength of Jehovah), one of David's valiant men. 1 Chron. 11:44.

Uz-z-'ah (might of Jehovah). [1] A son and successor of Amaziah, king of Judah, 2 Kings 15:13; 2 Chron. 26:1, 3, and elsewhere, is also called AZARIAH. He reigned fifty-two years, but was smitten with leprosy by the LORD. 2 Kings 15:2-5. See AZARIAH, No. 3. [2] A descendant of Kohath the son of Levi. 1 Chron. 6:24. [3] The father of Jehonathan, one of David's officers. 1 Chron. 27:25. [4] A priest who took a foreign wife. Ezra 10:21. [5] A man of Judah whose son lived in Jerusalem after the captivity. Neh. 11:4.

U

V

Vag'a-bond means simply a wanderer, fugitive, and in Acts 19:13 the Revised Version renders it "strolling."

Vajezatha, va-hez'a-thah (strong as the wind), a son of Haman, the enemy of the Jews. Esth. 9:9.

Vail or **Veil,** in early times, was worn only on special occasions, Gen. 24:65; 38:14; the Hebrew women generally appearing in public without veils. Gen. 12:14; 1 Sam. 1:12. The veil is now, however, an indispensable portion of a woman's dress in the East (especially among the Mohammedans), where custom forbids her face being seen by any man except her husband.

Val'ley gate, one of the gates of Jerusalem. 2 chron. 26:9.

Va-ni'ah (weak), a Jew of the family Bani. He took a foreign wife. Ezra 10:36.

Van'i-ty, Job 7:3; Eccl. 1:2, means emptiness; giving no satisfaction.

Vash'ni means "second," and by a curious error is applied in 1 Chron. 6:28 to JOEL, the oldest son of the prophet Samuel. It refers to ABIAH, his second son.

Vash'ti (a beautiful woman), the queen whom Ahasuerus, king of Persia, repudated, and who was succeeded by Esther. Esth. 1:9.

Ven'geance does not necessarily imply a revengeful state of mind. The word rather denotes retribution or punishment inflicted as an act of justice. Gen. 4:15; Deut. 32:35; Rom. 12:19, and elsewhere.

Ven'i-son, Gen. 25:28, means the flesh of beasts taken in hunting.

Ver-mil'ion, a bright red coloring substance much prized in the East for ornamenting dwellings and painting images. Jer. 22:14; Ezek. 23:14.

Vi'al, 1 Sam. 10:1, probably was a vessel similar to the CENSER.

Vile, Jer. 15:19; James 2:2, means beggarly; valueless; worthless.

Vine, Vineyard, vin'yerd. The vine was among the first plants cultivated, and a vineyard is mentioned among the possessions of Noah. Gen. 9:20. Vines were usually planted in rows, generally on the southern slope of a hill, and were supported by strong stakes, by trellises or arbors, and sometimes by heaps of stones over which the vines crept, and which offered a dry and warm exposure for ripening the fruit. The vineyards were enclosed with a hedge or wall to protect the vines from the ravages of wild beasts, Ps. 80:8-13, and towers were erected in them for the watchmen. Matt. 21:33.

Vin'e-gar was the name applied to a kind of sour wine used as a beverage. Num. 6:3; Matt. 27:48; etc. In Prov. 10:26; 25:20 it probably refers to the common sharp vinegar.

Vi'per, Job 20:16, is used in the Old Testament probably to designate a certain hissing and venomous serpent. In the New Testament it is used in reference to any poisonous snake. Acts 28:3.

Vis'ion, Dan. 2:19; 7:2, was the means God often employed in early times to reveal himself and his will to men.

Vow, Gen. 28:20-22, a solemn promise or covenant with God, binding one to do certain things by his help.

Vul'gate, the Latin Version of the Bible made by Jerome about A.D. 400. It is "the Authorized Version" in the Church of Rome.

V

W

Wa'fer, a thin cake made of fine flour and used in various offerings, anointed with oil. Exod. 29:2; Num. 6:15, 19.

Wag'on. The Egyptian wagon was a very simple affair resembling our cart, and the wagons mentioned in Num. 7:3, 8 for carrying the Tabernacle were no doubt similarly constructed. Two solid wooden wheels were connected by an axle on which rested the body. Vehicles of any kind are but little used in the East, where travellers and merchandise are carried on the backs of mules, horses, and camels.

Wall of Par-ti'tion, Eph. 2:14.

War. Gen. 14:2. Among the ancients every citizen was a soldier. Their wars were virtually hand to hand combats, carried on with great vigor and ferocity. Mercy was seldom shown the vanquished, unless to make him a slave, and the number of the slain was often appalling. The sword, battle-ax, dart, spear, javelin, bow and arrow, and the sling were the weapons in the hands of the combatants, while shields and targets were used to protect their bodies. Machines for hurling heavy stones in a measure took the place of artillery, and the BATTERING-RAM (which see) was employed to make breaches in the walls of a city through which the besiegers could enter. The CHARIOT (which see), however, was the most dreaded of all the equipments of war. The army was divided into companies, each having its commander or captain. Among the Hebrews these divisions had some reference to the several families or tribes, and the heads of the families were their officers. The armies were led by their kings or commanders-in-chief who were attended by ARMOR-BEARERS (which see). The end of wars is prophesied. Isa. 2:4; Micah 4:3.

Wash, Wash'ing. Mark 7:3,4. The Jews laid great stress on frequent ablutions. The water was not first poured into a basin as is common with us, but the servant poured the water from a pitcher on his master's hands, and the basin was used simply to receive the falling water. 2 Kings 3:11.

Watch'es of the Night. Originally the Hebrews divided the night (from sunset to sunrise) into three watches: "the middle watch," and "the morning watch," but after the captivity they adpoted the custom of the Romans and Greeks and divided the night (twelve hourts from 6 P.M. to 6 A.M.) into four watches of three hours each, called respectively "even," "midnight," "cockcrowing," and "morning." Judg. 7:19; 1 Sam. 11:11; Matt. 14:25; Luke 12:38.

Watch'man. Besides protecting the city and its inhabitants from violence the watchmen were required to call out, as they patrolled the streets, the hours of the night. Watchmen were also stationed at the gates of the city and in the towers on its walls. 2 Sam. 18:24-27; Song of Solomon 5:7; Isa. 21:11, 12.

Wa'ter. During the long seasons of drouth, which periodically occurred in Palestine and other countries of the East, man and beast were likely to suffer great distress, to guard against which great care was taken to collect the rain- and spring water in cisterns or reservoirs. Eccles. 2:6; Isa. 22:9-11. When used figuratively, water is the symbol of purification and regeneration, as in the case of baptism. John 1:26; 3:5; etc. WELLS were also provided, especially where the flocks were pastured, and as they were generally very deep and required great labor to dig and maintain them, they were regarded as very valuable and their possession was often coveted. Gen. 21:25; 26:14-21. The water was usually drawn from wells by means of a pitcher fastened to a rope.

Wa'ter of Jeal'ous-y was a mixture prescribed as a test in cases where a woman was accused by her husband of adultery. See Num. 5:11-31.

Wa'ter of Pu-ri-fu-ca'tion or **Sep-a-ra'tion,** Num. 19:2-10, 17-22, was sprinkled upon a person defiled by contact with the dead.

Wa'ter-pots, John 2:6, were vessels for holding water which was used by the family and guests for washing the hands and feet.

Wa'ters of Me'rom, a lake or marsh situated near the foot of Mount Lebanon, and through which the river Jordan flows. Josh. 11:5,7.

Wa'ters of Strife, the name given by the prophet Ezekiel to a place in the wilderness through which the Israelites wandered. Ezek. 47:19; 48:28.

Wave-of'fer-ing, Exod. 29:24-28, was a peculiar feature in the service of the peace-offering. The right shoulder of the animal sacrificed was "heaved" upward, and the breast "waved," from side to side, before the Lord. Lev. 10:14, 15.

Wax, Ps. 22:14; 68:2; 97:5; Micah 1:4, refers to the well-known substance made from the combs of bees. The word elsewhere in the Scriptures is used as a verb, and means to grow or become. Luke 2:40.

Wed'ding Gar'ment. Matt. 22:11. The host provided the wedding garments and required all those who attended the feast to wear them.

W

Weights. The subject of Hebrew weights is very obscure. The principal weight was the shekel, which varied with the value of the metal weighed by it See SHEKEL in the following list. The weights mentioned in the Bible are as follows:

A gerah was the twentieth part of the shekel of the sanctuary, which was of silver.

A bekah was equal to half a shekel of the sanctuary.

A shekel of gold weighed 132 grains; a shekel of silver, 220 grains; a shekel of copper, 528 grains.

A maneh was equal to one hundred shekels, about three pounds.

A talent was about 3000 shekels.

A mina, in marginal notes, Luke 19:13, is translated pound in the text, and was twelve ounces and a half.

Pound, in the Old Testament, is used as the translation of the Hebrew MANEH (which see). It has the same meaning in John 12:3; 19:39.

Whales, Gen. 1:21, evidently refers to great sea-monsters, without designating any particular species. The white shark in the Mediterranean Sea reaches an enormous size, and is very likely the "great fish" (correct translation) mentioned in Jonah 1:17; Matt. 12:40.

Wheat, Matt. 13:25, was the most important of all grains cultivated in Palestine, and vast quantities of it were produced. It was sown late in the fall and harvested in May. The many-eared variety, or mummy-wheat, was cultivated in Egypt, and is the kind referred to in Pharaoh's dream. Gen. 41:22. In the Authorized Version wheat is mentioned under the general name CORN (which see). The "meat-offerings," rendered in the Revised Version "meal-offerings," were all made of wheat flour. Lev. 2:1.

Wid'ow. The Mosaic law carefully guarded the rights of widows and orphans, and the Scriptures show their claims for care and protection.

Wife. Though the Mosaic law discouraged polygamy, it prevailed among the Hebrews up to the time of captivity. A distinction, however, was always made between the chief wife and the secondary wives, and to that extent, at least, the principle of monogamy was observed. The New Testament goes back to the primitive monogamy; for God gave to Adam only one wife. Hence polygamy is forbidden in all Christian countries.

Wil'der-ness, Exod. 14:3, sometimes means an extensive uncultivated region affording excellent pasturage. The wildernesses of Beer-sheba, Beth-aven, En-gedi, etc. were of this king. Wilderness is also called DESERT. The WILDERNESS in which the Israelites wandered forty years on their way from Egypt to Canaan is included in the peninsula of SINAI. Deut. 1:1; 8:2; Josh. 5:6.

Wil'der-ness-es. The following are the principal ones mentioned in the Bible:

Be'er-she'ba, south of the city of Beersheba and in Simeon. Gen. 21:14.

Beth-a'ven. in the north of Benjamin and a little east of Bethel. Josh. 18:12.

Da-mas'cus, near the city of Damascus, Syria. 1 Kings 19:15,

E'dom, south and east of the Dead Sea. 2 Kings 3:8.

En-ge'di, on the west side of the Dead Sea, in Judah. 1 Sam. 24:1.

E'tham, Num. 33:8, on the east side of the western gulf (Suez) of the Red Sea.

Gib'e-on. apparently on the west of Gibeon, and in Benjamin. 2 Sam. 2:24.

Jer'u-el. 2 Chron. 20:16.

Ju'dah, in the south of Judah. Judg. 1:16; Ps. 63, title.

Ka'desh, near Kadesh-barnea. Ps. 29:8.

Ked'e-moth, east side of the Dead Sea and north of the river Arnon. Deut. 2:26.

Ma'on, west side of the Dead Sea toward its south end. 1 Sam. 23:24, 25.

Mo'ab, part of the land of Moab nearly east of the Dead Sea. Deut. 2:8.

Pa'ran. Gen. 21:21; Num. 10:12; 12:16; 13:3, 26; 1 Sam. 25:1.

Red Sea, Exod. 13:18, same as ETHAM.

Shur, near western gulf (Suez) of Red Sea, on its east side. Exod. 15:22.

Sin. Exod. 16:1; 17:1; Num. 33:11,12.

Sinai, si'nay, si'ny or si'na-i, in vicinity of Mount Sinai, apparently mostly on north side. Exod. 19:1; Num. 1:1,19; etc..

Zin. Num. 13:21; Deut. 32:51; etc.

Ziph, zif. 1 Sam. 23:14, 15; 26:2.

Wine was a common beverage of the ancient Hebrews, as well as Greeks and Romans and other nations. It was kept in every household and offered on occasions of hospitality and festivity. Gen. 14:18. Its misuse, however, is strongly con-

W

demned in the Scriptures. Prov. 20:1; 23:29-32; Isa. 28:1-7. Mixed wine, Ps. 75:8; Prov. 23:30, was wine made stronger by adding spices, herbs, and drugs. In the articles GRAPES and VINE mention is made of the cultivation of the fruit from which wine was principally made, and the method commonly adopted for expressing the juice is treated in the article PRESS, PRESS-FATS . The new wine was preserved in large earthen vessels or jars, and also in bottles made from goats' skins that were fresh and pliable, the better to withstand the strain caused by fermentation.

Wine'bib-ber, Matt. 11:19, means an immoderate drinker of wine.

Wise. "Shalt in any wise rebuke," Lev. 19:17, is translated "shalt surely rebuke" in the Revised Version.

Wise Men. Matt. 2:1.

Witch'craft, 2 Chron. 33:6, was the pretended communication with demons and the spirits of the dead, by means of which the pretender professed to reveal future events, cure diseases, drive away evil spirits, etc. Wizard was a name given to the man, and witch to the woman, who practised witchcraft. Witchcraft is most severely denounced in the Scriptures. Lev. 20:6; Deut. 18:10-12; Gal. 5:19-21.

Wit'ness. By the Mosaic law the evidence of at least two witnesses was required to convict the prisoner, Deut. 17:6, and if the latter was condemned to be stoned, the witnesses were obliged to cast the first stones. Deut. 17:7. A false witness was to receive the punishment which he had endeavored to bring upon the prisoner by his testimony. Deut. 19:19.

Wolf. This animal is still found in Palestine, and is of a pale fawn color. It is a terrible enemy of the sheep and the dread of the shepherds. Isa. 65:25; Matt. 7:15; etc.

Wo'man. The social position of the Hebrew woman in ancient times contrasted very favorably with that enjoyed at the present day by women in the East among the Mohammedans. The book of Proverbs, 31:10-31, gives a beautiful account of the model hebrew woman in her domestic and social relations. She had the care of the household, did the spinning, and made the clothes. She mingled freely in social festivities, and even held public positions. The term "woman," when used in addressing one, implied no disrespect, but rather tenderness and courtesy. Compare John 2:4 with John 19:26,27; 20:13-15.

Won'der-ful, a title of the Messiah. Isa. 9:6.

Wool was the chief material used in the manufacture of clothing, and was highly prized by the Hebrews. Lev. 13:47;

W

Job 31:20; Prov. 31:13; etc. From the allusion in Ezek. 27:18 the wool of Damascus was greatly esteemed in the markets of Tyre.

Word (in Greek Logos, which means both reason and word) is used by John five times as a name or title of the eternal Son of God. John 1:1, 14.

Word of God, a name for the gospel generally. Mark 7:13; Luke 5:1; John 10:35; Acts 4:31, and elsewhere in the New Testament.

Word of Life, a name applied to the gospel generally. 1 John 1:1.

Word of the Lord, applied to the gospel in general. Acts 8:25; 1 Thess. 1:8, and elsewhere in the New Testament.

World. This word is used by the sacred writers in a number of senses, each of which can generally be distinguished by its connection. Thus, in Ps. 33:8 it means the habitable earth; in Isa. 45:17 it refers to time; in Luke 2:1 it means the nations subject to Rome at that time; in John 3:16 it means all mankind. In the widest sense it means the universe or all things visible and invisible, which is expressed in the Bible by the term "heaven and earth," Gen 1:1, or "all things." John 1:3.

Worm'wood, a plant found in Palestine, noted for its extreme bitterness. The word is often used in the same sense as "gall," to denote whatever is offensive and destructive. Jer. 23:15; Lam. 3:15, 19.

Wor'ship. This word is often employed in the Bible to denote simply an act of respect, without implying any religious emotion. Josh. 5:14; Matt. 9:18; Acts 10:25. Worship, as the act of religious reverence and homage paid to God, is commanded in the Scriptures.

Wreath'en, Exod. 28:14, means twisted: twined.

Wrought means "worked," Gen. 34:7; Exod. 36:1; Matt. 20:12, and "did," 1 Kings 16:25; 2 Chron. 21:6; the context generally showing which meaning is intended.

W

Z

Zabbai, zab'ba (pure). [1] A Jew who took a foreign wife. Ezra 10:28. [2] Father of Baruch. Neh. 3:20.

Zab'bud (given), a Jew who returned with Ezra. Ezra 8:14.

Zacchaeus, zak-ka-i (pure), a rich man among the publicans, whom Jesus called while passing through Jericho. The account of his conversion is given in Luke 19: 2-10.

Zachariah, zak-a-ri'ah (remembered by Jehovah), is the same name in Hebrew, as ZECHARIAH (which see). [1] The son and successor of King Jeroboam II. 2 Kings 14:29; 15: 8-11. [2] Father of Abi or Abijah, the mother of King Hezekiah, 2 Kings 18:2, called ZEHCARIAH in 2 Chron. 29:1.

Za'dok (just). [1] One of the two high-priests in David's time He joined David at Hebron. 1 Chron. 12:28; 2 Sam. 20:25. He anointed Solomon king, 1 Kings 1:39, and was afterward made sole high-priest. [2] A priest in King Ahaziah's time. 1 Chron. 6:12. [3] Father of Jerusah, King Uzziah's wife. 2 Kings 15:33; 2 Chron. 27:1. [4] One of the Jews who repaired the wall of Jerusalem. Neh. 3:4. [5] A priest. Neh. 3:29. [6] A Jew who sealed the covenant. Neh. 10:21. [7] A scribe in charge of the treauries. Neh. 13:13.

Zal'mon (shady), **Mount,** a high hill near Shechem. Judg. 9:48, probably same as SALMON. Ps. 68:14.

Zal-mo'nah (shady), the thirty-fourth encampment of the Israelites after they left Egypt. Num. 33:41, 42.

Za-no'ah. In 1 Chron. 4:18 Jekuthiel is called "the father of Zanoah," that is, he was the founder of a village of that name.

Za-no'ah (marsh). [1] A town in the lowlands of Judah. Josh. 15:34; Neh. 3:13, 11:30. [2] A town in the hill country of Judah. Jush. 15:56.

Za'rah (rising of light), a son of Judah and Tamar, Gen. 38:30; 46:12, called ZERAH, Num. 26:20; Josh. 7:1, 18; etc. and ZARA in Matt. 1:3.

Za'red (exuberant growth). Num. 21:12.

Zarephath, zar'e-fath (smelting-house), a town of Phoenicia, on the Mediterranean Sea between Tyre and Sidon. The prophet Elijah found shelter there. 1 Kings 17:8-24; Obadiah, verse 20. It is called SAREPTA in Luke 4:26.

Zar'than (cooling), one of the towns in the Jordan valley. 1 Kings 7:46. It may be same as ZARETAN, ZARTANAH, and ZEREDA.

Zat'tu (sprout), an Israelite whose descendants returned with Zerubbabel. Some of them took foreign wives. Ezra 2:8; 10:27; Neh. 7:13.

Zeal'ots, the name of a party among the Jews who, under the leadership of Judas of Galilee, claimed that God was the only king of Israel, refused to pay tribute to, and at length openly rebelled against, the Romans. They were soon routed, but for some time afterward kept up a sort of guerilla warfare. See Acts 5:37.

Zeb-a-di'ah (gift of Jehovah). [1,2,3] Descendants of Benjamin. 1 Chron. 8:15, 17: 12:7. [4] One of the sons of Meshelemiah. 1 Chron. 26:2. [5] One of the Levites sent by Jehoshaphat to teach the law. 2 Chron. 17:8. [6] A son of Ashahel. 1 Chron. 27:7. [7] Son of Ishmael. 2 Chron. 19:11. [8] A Jew who returned with Ezra. Ezra 8:8. [9] A priest who took a foreign wife. Ezra 10:20.

Ze-bo'im (valley of hyaenas), **Val'ley of,** a ravine apparently east of Michmash in Benjamin. 1 Sam. 13:18.

Ze-bu'dah (bestowed), the wife of Josiah and mother of Jehoiakim. 2 Kings 23:36.

Ze'bul (habitation), an officer of Abimelech, and a governor of Shechem. Judg. 9:28-41.

Zeb'u-lon-ite, Judg. 12:11, 12, or **Zeb'u-lun-ites,** Num. 26:27, the descendants of Zebulun.

Zeb'u-lun (habitation), a son of Jacob and Leah, and the founder of the tribe of Zebulun. Gen. 30:20; Exod. 1:3.

Zeb'u-lun, the name of the tribe descended from Zebulun, a son of Jacob. Num 1:9; Deut. 27:13.

Zeb'u-lun, a place mentioned in Josh. 19:27 in describing the southern boundary of Asher.

Zechariah, zek-a-ri'ah (Jehovah remembers). Besides the prophet Zechariah, the following persons of the same name are mentioned in the Bible. Seven Levites. [1] 1 Chron. 9:21; 26:2, 14. [2] 1 Chron. 15:18, 20; 16:5. [3] 1 Chron. 24:25. [4] 1 Chron. 26:11. [5] 2 Chron. 20:14. [6] 2 Chron. 29:13. [7] 2 Chron. 34:12. Four priest. [8] 2 Chron. 35:8. [9] Neh. 11:12. [10] Neh. 12:16. [11] Neh. 12:35, 41. [12] The son of Jehoiada the high -priest. He was stoned to death at the command of King Joash. 2 Chron. 24:20, 21. [13,14] Two chief men who returned from Babylon with Ezra. Ezra 8:3; 8;11, 16. [15] The father of Iddo. 1 Chron. 27:21. [16] The son of Jeberechiah. Isa. 8:2. [17] A chief of Reuben. 1 Chron. 5:7. [18] A Benjamite. 1 Chron. 9:37, called ZACHER in 1 Chron. 8:31. [19] A priest. 1 Chron. 15:24. [20] A prince of Judah. 2 Chron. 17:7. [21] A son of Jehoshaphat. 2 Chron. 21:2. [22] A man who lived in the time of Uzziah. 2 Chron. 26:5. [23] One who took a foreign wife. Ezra 10:26. [24] A prince who stood beside Ezra while he read the

Z

law. Neh. 8:4. [25,26] Two descendants of Pharez. Neh. 11:4; 11:5. [27] Father of Abi. [28] ZECHARIAH, the eleventh of the twelve minor prophets and a priest, was born in Babylon of priestly descent, and returned to Jerusalem with Zerubbabel and the high-priest Joshua. Ezra 5:1; 6:14; Zech. 1:1, 7; 7:1, 8. He prophesied B.C. 520-518.

Zech-a-ri'ah, the Book of. Of all the prophetic writings this is the most difficult to understand, owing to its concise form of expression and the figurative language employed. The book contains several specific references to the Messiah, 3:8; 6:12; 9:9; 11:12; 12:10; 13:7, in which he is represented as a lowly servant, the priest that should build the Temple of the Lord, the king that should come riding upon an ass, the shepherd betrayed for thirty pieces of silver and crucified, and having his sheep scattered.

Ze'lah (a rib), a city in Benjamin where Saul and his sons were buried. Josh. 18:28; 2 Sam. 21:14.

Ze'lek (fissure), an Ammonite, one of David's valiant men. 2 Sam. 23:37; 1 Chron. 11:39.

Zelophehad, ze-lo'fe-had (first-born), a descendant of Manasseh, died in the wilderness, leaving five daughters but no sons. A law was then established that under such circumstances females should succeed to the inheritance, but they must not marry out of their tribe. Num. 26:33; 27:1, 7; 36:2-11; Josh. 17:3; 1 Chron. 7:15.

Ze'nan (place of flocks), a city of Judah. Josh. 15:37. It may be same as ZAANAN. Mic. 1:11.

Ze'nas, a believer who was skilled in the law of Moses, and whom Paul wished Titus to bring along with him. Tit. 3:13.

Zeph-a-ni'ah (Jehovah hides). [1] The priest whom the captain of the kings of Babylon took to Riblah. 2 Kings 25:18; Jer. 21:1. [2] An ancestor of the prophet Samuel. 1 Chron. 6:36. [3] a priest, the father of Josiah and Hen. Zech. 6:10, 14. [4] ZEPHANIAH, the ninth of the minor prophets, lived in the days of Josiah, a contemporary of Jeremiah, and uttered his prophecies between B.C. 620 and 609.

Zeph-a-ni'ah, the Book of, contains, 1:14, 15, that description of the final judgment from which Thomas da Celano, in the middle of the thirteenth century, took the key-note for his judgment-hymn, Dies irae, dies illa, the most sublime hymn of the middle ages.

Z